The Story of Stories

Also by Kevin Ashton

How to Fly a Horse: The Secret History of Creation, Invention, and Discovery

The Story of Stories

The Million-Year History of a
Uniquely Human Art

Kevin Ashton

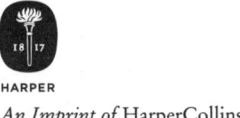

HARPER
An Imprint of HarperCollins*Publishers*

Without limiting the exclusive rights of any author, contributor or the publisher of this publication, any unauthorized use of this publication to train generative artificial intelligence (AI) technologies is expressly prohibited. HarperCollins also exercise their rights under Article 4(3) of the Digital Single Market Directive 2019/790 and expressly reserve this publication from the text and data mining exception.

THE STORY OF STORIES. Copyright © 2026 by Most Like Himself LLC. All rights reserved. Printed in the United States of America. No part of this book may be used or reproduced in any manner whatsoever without written permission except in the case of brief quotations embodied in critical articles and reviews. For information, address HarperCollins Publishers, 195 Broadway, New York, NY 10007. In Europe, HarperCollins Publishers, Macken House, 39/40 Mayor Street Upper, Dublin 1, D01 C9W8, Ireland.

HarperCollins books may be purchased for educational, business, or sales promotional use. For information, please email the Special Markets Department at SPsales@harpercollins.com.

hc.com

FIRST EDITION

Designed by Bonni Leon-Berman

Library of Congress Cataloging-in-Publication Data has been applied for.

ISBN 978-0-06-343869-9

25 26 27 28 29 LBC 5 4 3 2 1

For independent booksellers
and public librarians,
our courageous freedom fighters
in the war of stories

You have to change your mind before you change the way you live.

—Gil Scott-Heron

Contents

Preface: The Untold Story	xiii
Chapter 1 A Million Years of Stories	1
Chapter 2 The Eye of Your Mind	34
Chapter 3 Pictures of Sounds	59
Chapter 4 The War of Stories	92
Chapter 5 The All-Seeing Eye of Providence	136
Chapter 6 One One Zero	169
Chapter 7 Death by a Thousand Stories	210
Chapter 8 The Hyperreal Thing	250
Author's Note: Thank You	293
Acknowledgments	295
Notes	299
Bibliography	341
Index	371

Preface

The Untold Story

The story of stories follows a simple pattern: Every major new storytelling tool increases the number of people who can tell stories and the number of people to whom stories can be told. Nightfires brought people together to become the earliest audiences for spoken stories; the development of rhyme, song, and other aids to memory allowed those spoken stories to be preserved, sometimes for centuries; pictures drawn on the walls of caves turned preservation into permanence and told stories we can still experience thousands of years later; writing enabled storytellers to spread stories to faraway places; printing mass-produced drawing and writing and increased the number of storytellers and the size of their audiences by many orders of magnitude; and so on.

The smartphone, storytelling's *technologie du jour* at the time of writing, is the culmination of this pattern. After a hundred thousand years, the power of sharing stories is no longer exclusive to kings, queens, priests, tribal leaders, and other elites, and is less restricted by status and wealth than ever before. For the first time, we live in a world where everyone can tell stories to everyone.

This is a change both good and bad. The story of stories makes it clear what happens whenever more storytellers can spread stories to larger audiences. New storytelling tools cause revolutions. Some people speak truth to power, while others tell lies to the impotent. Much of our present turmoil is the inevitable result of technology increasing the seismicity of stories.

In this book I want to describe how stories and new tools for telling them change us. The story of stories—which, ironically, is largely untold—offers a map for navigating our strange new world and hope in a difficult, turbulent time.

The plan of the book is roughly this: The first chapters describe the eight great revolutions in the story of storytelling, from the earliest fires to the latest smartphones. We will see how each of these storytelling tools developed, how they ignited social revolutions as great as the number of storytellers and audience members they empowered, and, to illustrate, tell the stories of how they affected the lives of one or more real people. In the last and most speculative chapter of the book we will imagine storytelling's future, from artificial intelligence to artificial sentience and beyond, explore possible storytelling revolutions yet to come, and conclude with some thoughts on how to live well in a world of warring stories.

I have been working on this book for over twenty-five years. In 1998 I saw important, ambient stories going to waste everywhere I looked: stories told by heartbeats, inventories, machines and moving vehicles, stresses on bridges and roofs, the temperatures of bodies and rooms, and countless other physical phenomena. I wondered if giving the then-new internet its own senses could get the world to tell me its stories.

I called my idea the Internet of Things and cofounded and led a research center at the Massachusetts Institute of Technology to make it real. The work was a success. Our research center grew to include over a hundred companies and government entities and opened research labs at five other universities around the world. The technology we developed was licensed to industry, generating revenue for MIT and building a framework that now connects hundreds of billions of devices. We made the Internet of Things into a global reality that changes every life every day.

For example, the Internet of Things is a large part of the system in your smartphone—for better and worse, it helps determine what stories you are told; most major technology companies have Internet of Things divisions; and historians regard the Internet of Things as a milestone in the development of computing and the cornerstone of a new industrial revolution. The Internet of Things has also become famous—the term appears in *The Oxford English Dictionary*, *The Merriam-Webster Dictionary*, and has been the answer to a question on *Jeopardy!*, for example.

While I can take some credit for the Internet of Things, I cannot take much credit for the smartphone; I am not sure anyone can. The smartphone is the sum of the inventions and ingenuity of tens of thousands of people and counting.

But I can take some of the blame.

As someone who helped introduce this new technology to the world, I am curious about, and, I believe, responsible for, understanding more than just how it works functionally; I also want to understand how it works contextually—that is, historically, neurologically, sociologically, and so on; follow its consequences; and assess its benefits and detriments to humanity. This book is, in part, a result of that curiosity.

The story of stories has a happy ending, or at least a hopeful one: It shows that, in the long run, more storytelling inspires more progress, even when it seems otherwise, and that this new age in which everyone can tell stories to everyone may eventually inspire the greatest progress of all.

The Story of Stories

Chapter 1

A Million Years of Stories

1. Fire

One million years ago, in the foothills of East Africa, humans learned to create and control fire and extend their days into the dark. The magic and sanctuary of fire drew tribes together each evening and caused a radical redirection of human evolution. The wavering flames were too dim for gestures, grooming, or play, so these early people socialized using sounds.

There are many ways for living creatures to make deliberate noise. Some fish vibrate their swim bladders; crickets and katydids rub body parts together; and rattlesnakes rattle their tails. For humans and other mammals, the most common noisemaking method is the controlled modulation and vibration of exhalation called *vocalization*.

Vocalization first evolved to send fertility signals and warnings. When our distant ancestors started communicating beside their nightfires, they repurposed the calls and cries they made for foraging, hunting, and mating. But what they wanted to communicate at night differed from what they wanted to communicate by day. Day talk uses imperatives, commands, and warnings to convey information about immediate practical matters. It communicates things like *go there*, *stop*, *mate with me*, or *look out! a hyena!*—the human equivalent of birds cawing and wolves barking. There are few immediate practical matters around a nightly fire, so humans did something no creature had done before: In the warmth and security of their flames, they communicated about events remembered and imagined, from places and times near and far. Or, they started telling stories.

Storytelling requires more nuance than the pointing and hollering of hunting and gathering, and so, over hundreds of thousands of years, beside hundreds of millions of fires, human vocalization evolved, and the grunts and yelps turned into a complex series of sounds about subjects, normally human, acting on objects—the infinitely expressive system of communication we now call *language*. Language did not give us stories; stories gave us language.

The evidence of this is so obvious that we do not see it. It is in all the stories we tell and understand without words: the vestigial stories of dance, mime, music, and painting; the stories told by photographs and long silent scenes on screen and stage; the stories we imagine when we watch quiet strangers through windows or from sidewalk tables at coffee shops, or glance into an adjacent car, or look toward the other end of a bar or across a shelf in a bookstore or library; and the stories we glean from fashion design, interior design, and logo design, and from front yards and facades. These stories transmitted to us without language whisper ancestral truths: that we told and understood stories before we had words; that stories are as intrinsically human as language and mind; that we are all born to tell stories and have stories told to us; and that the first purpose of language is story.

We can still see language's storytelling roots today. Each of our seven thousand languages has a standard sentence made of a subject, a verb, and an object, and describes someone or something doing something to someone or something, or an *event*. Standard conversations consist of putting these sentences together to narrate a sequence of connected events, usually in chronological order, or *storytelling*.

Prehistoric fireside storytelling built social bonds far more efficiently than primate grooming and play. Besides being practical in the dim light of fires, stories could be used to maintain relationships with many people at once, through storytelling to an audience (a word that originally meant "those who hear"); to create distrust of or trust in people not present through the sharing of reputations; and to instill common values and beliefs through the repetition of group history and lore.

Being able to tell and comprehend stories conferred survival advantages and set in motion the evolutionary wheel that eventually led to us. Individuals in groups made more cooperative by stories were more likely to survive than individuals in less cooperative, storyless groups. Good storytellers gained higher social status and were more likely to attract mates and have children. And so, even before our ancestors evolved into modern humans, they evolved into storytellers, a legacy we inherited when we first became *Homo sapiens*. We are all storytellers. We have always been storytellers. Storytelling is not a product of culture or nurture; it is innate. We are the species with story-shaped brains, and none of us can spend a waking day without seeking and sharing stories.

2. The Human Revolution

We are the biggest revolution stories will ever cause. The evolution of storytelling drove the evolution of the human race entire, starting with our ancestor species, *Homo erectus*, which evolved to tell stories and eventually became us: modern *Homo sapiens*, creatures adapted anatomically, behaviorally, intellectually, socially, and psychologically to be storytellers. There is an easy way to know that *Homo erectus* told stories: our cousins the Neanderthals, who also descended from *Homo erectus*, told stories too.

Even in the age of smartphones, oral storytelling is our primary and most fundamental storytelling form. Oral storytelling is not of the past but the present; we still tell most of our stories by speaking face-to-face as our ancestors did beside their fires. Today's major oral storytelling forms include book readings, court hearings, monologues, one-person shows, presentations, sales pitches, sermons, slam poems, speeches, stand-up comedy, and the most common storytelling form of all: conversation.

Newspaper columnists and others often complain that "the art of conversation is dead." They have been telling this story for more than a hundred years, changing only the source of the blame, from "isolated couples" in 1887 to playing cards in 1920, cocktails in 1949, television in 1969, "morning chaos" in 1999, and smartphones in 2018, among many other causes.

The claim has never been true despite being repeated so often. One reason we know this is that every year the US government conducts a survey to measure how much time its citizens spend in face-to-face conversation. In 2022 Americans spent an average of thirty-four minutes a day telling stories to each other, which was twelve minutes less than in 2006, the year before smartphones—one of the more recent things to have supposedly killed conversation—first became available. So, far from being dead and buried, the worst anyone could say is that conversations are 25 percent shorter.

And they would still be mistaken. The decline in face-to-face communication has nothing to do with communications technology (or cocktails, morning chaos, or any of those other blameless suspects): it is a result of a deep and positive social trend nearly a hundred years old.

Since the end of World War II, ever more people have lived alone. Less than one in ten households had a single occupant in 1940; in 2023, the latest year for which data is available, one in four households had a single occupant. The biggest force driving this change is women, who now have more opportunities to become financially independent and have a home of their own. The second biggest force is that people are living longer lives. In short, more people are living alone because of liberation and longevity.

The inverse correlation between more one-person households and fewer people having daily face-to-face conversations has what statisticians call a Pearson correlation coefficient of minus 0.9, where minus 1 would be a perfect match. And fewer face-to-face conversations is not the same as fewer—or shorter—conversations overall. Among people who *do* have daily face-to-face conversations the time spent conversing *increased*, from an hour and fifty-two minutes in 2006 to an hour and fifty-seven minutes in 2022, while people living alone replaced a large proportion of their face-to-face conversations with remote conversations enabled by technologies such as personal computers and phones. New technology is not killing conversation nor merely keeping conversation alive: It is enabling more conversations than ever before.

Almost all conversation is storytelling, and almost all storytelling is conversation. When we talk with people we know, we spend as much as two-thirds of our time sharing stories. When we talk with people we *want to* know, this proportion becomes even higher. A first date is typically a sharing of stories, with prompts such as "Where are you from?" "What kind of music do you listen to?" or "How do you spend your weekends?" The level of mutual interest in these stories is a basic measure of how the date is going, just as successful friendships, romances, marriages, and parent-child relationships depend on continued mutual interest in stories about simple, intimate subjects like "How was your day?"

Bars, cafés, coffee shops, diners, hookah lounges, pubs, restaurants, and tea shops exist largely to provide a safe and neutral space for sharing these small, private stories. It is not a coincidence that we tend to tell such stories in places that serve food and psychoactive substances like alcohol, caffeine, cannabis, and tobacco. We started eating together beside our nightfires as soon as we discovered we could use the flames for cooking as well as talking, and supplemented our meals with psychoactive plant compounds that included caffeine, morphine, and nicotine, and psychoactive beverages made from fermented fruit, honey, and millet. Both eating meals socially and ingesting psychoactive substances change our nervous system to make us better at sharing stories which makes us better at building relationships. Darkness amplifies these effects, which is why we tell more stories at night. The art of conversation has not died, is not dying, and will never die, because we are the same people who told stories around fires a hundred thousand years ago, with the same brains and behaviors.

3. The Universal Story

Our storytelling brains, unchanged since they first evolved, seek and tell stories that follow a simple pattern. This pattern is universal to all cultures, genres, periods, storytellers, storytelling technologies, and styles, and comprises three equally essential parts, like the legs of a stool.

First, all stories feature humanlike characters as the agents of action. This is still true when the characters are supposed to be nonhuman. Stories that star aliens, Anglepoise lamps, animals, ants, trains, trees, and toasters are really about humans, which is why in stories these creatures tend to walk on two feet, talk, have expressive faces and eyes, feel human emotions, and set human goals. They are all rabbits in waistcoats—people pretending not to be people. Even Dr. Seuss, creator of fabulous, apparently nonhuman characters including the Cat in the Hat, the Grinch, and Horton the Elephant, said, "None of my animals are animals; they're all people." These humanlike characters are the story's actors; they take the actions that cause the story to happen. They live at or near the story's center. They are literally the people the story is about: it embraces, revolves around, and surrounds them.

Second, all stories relate a chronology, a sequence of events. The chronology does not have to be told in chronological order—it can have flashbacks, flash-forwards, and meanwhiles—but it has to relate connected events that happened at different moments. We would not call a description of a dozen things that all occurred in the same second a story. A story is always a journey through time.

Third, all stories must reach, or at least be heading for, a resolution. The sequence of events must have a consequence, and that consequence must arise from the actions of its human or humanlike agents. We are compelled to give sequences of events consequences, to seek justice for our characters, and to resolve unresolved stories. An unfinished story is like an unscratched itch: if a story we care about is not explicitly resolved, or if we have to wait to see how it ends because of a "to be continued" cliffhanger climax, we will often try to finish the story ourselves by imagining possible resolutions.

There is nothing new about any of these statements. Aristotle said similar things twenty-four hundred years ago in his treatise *Poetics*, the oldest known theory of stories:

> A story is an imitation of a whole and complete action. The objects of imitation are men. This event should follow that by necessary or probable sequence. A whole is that which has a beginning, a middle, and an end. Stories must not begin or end haphazardly, but must follow the pattern.

And in 1966 French literary theorist Roland Barthes agreed:

> It may safely be assumed that there is not a single narrative in the world without characters. The goal is to give a structural description to the chronological. A sequence is essentially a whole within which nothing is repeated.

The least controversial, most universal thing we can say about stories is that all stories feature character, chronology, and consequence.

4. Why We Tell Stories

The universal pattern of character, chronology, and consequence arises from the reason we tell stories, which we can show with a kind of cognitive illusion.

In 1944 psychologists Fritz Heider and Marianne Simmel asked 114 people to watch and then describe a short film. All but one responded with a story. Here is a typical example:

> A man has planned to meet a girl, and the girl comes along with another man. The first man tells the second to go, then the two men have a fight, and the girl starts to go into the room to get out of the way. The first man follows her into the room after having left the second in a weakened condition, leaning on the wall outside the room. The girl gets worried and races from one corner to the other in the far part of the room. Man number one makes several approaches to her, but she gets out of the room in a sudden dash just as man number two gets the door open. The two chase around the outside of the room together, followed by man number one. But they finally elude him and get away.

All the stories were like this: everyone described a romantic conflict between three people. But Heider and Simmel's film was not about a romantic dispute. It did not even feature people. It was a crude animation showing two triangles and a circle moving randomly around a rectangle.

There was no optical illusion. The test subjects knew they were looking at shapes, not people, but their brains, forged in a million years of fire, interpreted the shapes as representations of human characters and the shapes' random movement as human behavior.

Imagining nonhuman objects as human and giving them personalities to tell stories that explain their activity may seem like a ridiculous way to think, but study after study shows we all do this, even if we do not notice it. Humans instinctively think humanlike behavior causes everything.

In truth, humanlike behavior causes almost nothing. Your story-shaped brain may object to this statement, but its definition of *event* is too narrow, and its understanding of *cause* is too broad. As you read this sentence, somewhere far beyond you a beaver is beginning to dam, a bird is completing its nest, a flower is coming into bud, a star is being born, and an infinite number of other events, astronomical, biological, and geological, are taking place too, and none of them are a result of human behavior.

Even if we restrict our definition of *events* to the relatively infinitesimal number of occurrences that affect human beings, we will still find, if we look past the mere presence of people, that things that happen to humans are more often the consequences of chaos, complexity, evolution, geography, geology, indeterminacy, physics, or probability than of humanlike agency. No pantheon of colorful gods commands the weather. Nature is not a mother. There is no man in the moon.

But understanding does not have to be true to be useful. The human mind did not evolve to determine what is true; it evolved to help us reproduce. Humans are a profoundly social species—we form groups that biologist E. O. Wilson said are as cooperative as ant colonies and beehives—and our individual success depends on our social success. But while other social species interact using instinct, humans interact using intellect. Anticipating, influencing, and understanding other people's behavior is essential for human survival and reproduction—perhaps uniquely so. It is also extraordinarily hard; human behavior is complex, human motivations are often obscure, and humans can be skilled deceivers, among other difficulties.

Storytelling is nature's solution to the problem of being a highly social, highly intelligent species. About half our brain is devoted to storytelling and almost all of it evolved after humans started lighting fires.

Our storytelling brains process social interactions in a very specific, story-centric way. When we meet someone new, for example, we get sensory inputs from seeing and hearing them. But our brains store this raw information only briefly; it decays in a matter of seconds. During that time our brain first processes the information for basic comprehension—understanding what the person says and interpreting basic visual cues such as body language and clothing, for example—then starts comparing it to the vast library of stories, both true and imagined, in our memories as well as to our goals in order to create a new story about what the interaction means: whether the person is likely to be a potential friend, helper, mate, or threat; whether we are interested in what they are saying; and so on. This process has two outputs: It adds a new, developing story to the library in our memory; and it determines how we behave during the interaction.

We can see this process in another experiment.

In the 1980s two psychologists named Nancy Pennington and Reid Hastie simulated a murder trial repeatedly and observed mock juries reaching a verdict.

The simulated trial, which was based on an actual trial, was called *The Commonwealth of Massachusetts v. Johnson*. The defendant, Frank Johnson, is charged with murdering a man named Alan Caldwell outside a bar on the night of May 6, 1976. Earlier in the day, Johnson and Caldwell argued and Caldwell threatened Johnson with a straight razor. The men met again that evening at the bar and had an altercation outside during which Johnson's knife mortally wounded Caldwell.

The prosecution claims Caldwell was unarmed and that Johnson stabbed Caldwell in an act of premeditated murder. The defense claims Caldwell attacked Johnson with a straight razor, that Johnson took out a fishing knife to protect himself, and that Caldwell ran onto it.

If the mock jurors agree with the prosecution, Johnson will spend the rest of his life in prison. If they agree with the defense, Johnson will leave court a free man.

To ensure every jury saw the same thing, Pennington and Hastie filmed a reenactment of the trial. After viewing the film, the jurors retired to a jury room, watched only by a camera placed out of sight, to decide what happened. After the jury reached its verdict, the researchers interviewed each juror and asked how they made up their mind.

The experiment showed the storytelling brain in action: All the jurors aggregated the evidence into a story, then assessed how well that story matched the library of stories in their minds.

We all think this way, even if we do not notice it. A new story is more plausible and preferable if it resembles stories we already believe—not only stories that include direct, personal, actual experiences, but every story we have ever been told. The stories we come to believe throughout our lives form a feedback loop until what we hear most often is what feels most true. Belief grows exponentially.

The process the jurors used is probably taking place in your mind right now. You have likely been imagining Johnson and Caldwell's encounter as a story. The story's basic plot is the agreed-upon facts, but everything else is inferred from and inspired by the library of stories in your mind.

For example, what do your imaginary Johnson and Caldwell look like? Based on their names you might be imagining European Americans. You are probably not imagining, say, Chinese Americans, which you might do if their names were Zhang and Liu. What kind of men are they? Are they wealthy professionals or members of the working class? You have no information about this; whatever you are imagining is inference.

If you examine your story closely, you will probably discover that many of the details are inferences, and that you did not choose these inferences consciously—your story-shaped brain filled in the gaps unprompted, using elements from the stories in your mind's library.

This is what the mock jurors did too. And once their new story fit with their preexisting preferred stories it became the basis of their verdict.

For example, jurors who concluded Johnson was guilty of premeditated murder told stories like this:

These people obviously think in terms of violence. I would have avoided that bar. He went home and got the knife. That's a very big knife. Johnson took that knife before passion occurred. He prepared the situation. He meant to kill him.

Jurors who thought Johnson was not guilty told a different story:

He was showing he was not chicken. To live in that neighborhood, you can't stay out of that bar. It's a different breed of people that stay in bars six or seven days a week. There was a sudden conflict. He was provoked, with the thought that the guy had a razor. Johnson had a fear of bodily harm. So he pulled out his equalizer and got there first.

The average juror's story was 55 percent fact and 45 percent inference. The differences between the different jurors' verdicts were the differences between the libraries of stories in their minds. Every juror authored a different work of fiction based on the same true story.

5. Heroes Are Us

Heider and Simmel's animated shapes and Pennington and Hastie's simulated trial both reveal the same thing: that a fundamental purpose of stories is to distribute glory and shame, which are the currency of community and the social equivalents of wealth and poverty. This is why most stories feature not neutral characters but heroes and villains.

Heider used the lessons from his and Simmel's experiments to create a new field of psychological study, *attribution*, which investigates how we attribute responsibility for events.

When we attribute credit or blame we have three choices: ourselves, somebody else, or nonhuman externalities—for example, geography, physics, or probability. As we have already discussed, these externalities cause almost all events. But our story-shaped brains reduce the problem of attribution to a different and simpler if-then statement: If an event's outcome is good, then we, or people like us, or people with whom we identify, caused it, and if an event's outcome is bad, then others—specifically, people *unlike* us—caused it. Externalities get little to no attribution and when they do we typically humanize them as the will of the gods, or the hand of fate, or something similar. Our story-shaped brain simplifies the world into a product of humanlike agents who can only be heroes or villains and always puts us on the side of the heroes.

This is why the main character in almost every story we like is us, someone who resembles us, someone with whom we empathize, or someone we wish we were, and why the consequences of that character's actions are eventually and invariably good. A happy ending only needs to be happy for the character we see as ourselves; it can be unhappy for all or any of the other characters: the guy who doesn't get the girl, the villain who is killed along with his many anonymous henchmen, the sidekick who makes an inspiring sacrifice, or the billions of people who die in an apocalypse the hero survives.

In group settings our passion for stories in which people like us are the heroes increases by orders of magnitude. Every people's histories, legends, and myths feature a virtuous in-group to which they belong struggling against and ultimately triumphing over a villainous out-group to which they do not belong. The in-group's triumph is never attributed to externalities like chance, geography, or privilege, but to some purportedly unique attribute of the in-group that proves its superiority—its greater courage, godliness, or resourcefulness, for example—and highlights the out-group's inferiority. Stories that unite groups—from families, teams, and tribes to churches, nations, and races—are all fables with the same moral: We win because we are better.

The stories that unite us may not be true—we are probably the villains in our villains' stories, for example—but for our story-shaped brains, truth is beside the point. The information in a story is a conduit for something more important: making and keeping social bonds. Social bonds change our body's chemistry. The hormone oxytocin, which affects our brains and other parts of our nervous system, is released when we are social and inhibited when we are lonely, often with adverse consequences for our health. Sharing stories is one of the most common ways in which humans create and maintain companionship and community. Whether we are applauding or sitting in rapt attention, being part of a group receiving a story bonds us not only to the storyteller but to the other people in the audience too: when we all laugh at the same joke we know we have something in common.

There is a more powerful—and often darker—version of everyone laughing at the same joke: everyone accepting the same assumptions.

A story can only forge bonds between people who accept its judgments, norms, and standards, a few of which may be explicit but most of which are assumed, implied, or subliminal, and established through subtle commission and omission. When the cowboys are always the heroes and the Indians are always the villains, the audience gets a message that need not be stated: Cowboys are good and Indians are bad. This common understanding can take a group beyond fellow feeling and inspire it to take collective action. Sharing stories builds alliances, armies, congregations, communities, corporations, groups, nations, teams, and every other kind of coalition.

And, just as we tell other people stories about ourselves, so we also tell *ourselves* stories about ourselves. Stories provide individual cohesion as well as group cohesion. We get some understanding of who we are from the stories we hear about our race, religion, nation, tribe, and every other group we claim or that claims us, but we also create a personal, private story that, rather than uniting us with disparate others, unites our disparate selves.

Our identity may seem real, but it is not what it appears to be. We experience ourselves as constant, continuous, coherent beings—in essence, the same people throughout our lives. But our identity as we experience it has no basis in physics, chemistry, or biology. Most of the cells that make up our bodies are replaced every few days or years, depending on what type of cell they are. Intestinal epithelial cells—the cells that line our digestive system—have an average lifespan of five days; our skeleton is completely replaced every ten years; our brain's occipital lobe regenerates every fifteen years. Only a few small parts of our body, such as our cerebellum—at the back of our brain—and the lenses in our eyes have the same cells as the day we were born; almost everything else we are made of has been replaced many times over.

Our ever-changing cells are not our identity, then. Our identity is not the backs of our brains, nor the lenses of our eyes, nor even our DNA, which changes too. When we were children, we understood this intuitively. We knew in infancy that identity is not the same as form. We listened to stories of princes turning into beasts or frogs then back into princes; of snakes transforming into young women; of vampires becoming bats; of puppets becoming boys; of donkeys becoming rocks; and hundreds of other tales about shape-shifting and never once doubted the identity of the characters as they changed back and forth. We were not confused. The donkey was the donkey even when he was the rock.

Some people solve the mystery of identity with a different mystery: a nonphysical essence, or "soul." But there is another solution, which does not preclude souls: Identity is story. Our identity is the story about ourselves we tell ourselves. We are our own authors. Or, as poet Toi Derricotte wrote: "I am not the 'I' in my poems. 'I' is the net I try to pull me in with."

And so the social survival advantages of storytelling form a continuum from individual to familial to tribal and beyond. Our ancestors were good at telling stories and, as a result, were more likely to have good physical, mental, and emotional health, find friends and partners, form groups, and therefore have descendants than their peers who were not good at telling stories. Eventually only the storytellers survived, and they became us.

Our mind is made of stories, and we think in stories most of the time. In particular, we think of our life as a story, one in which we are, or hope to become, the hero.

6. Wang

In 1992, an accountant quit his job at a factory in Beijing and walked to his office to collect his belongings. His name was D. S. Wang. He believed it would be his last day at the factory, and he was wrong.

Wang had tried to save the factory, but its leaders had rejected his proposals by declaring them impossible to implement. They thought Wang was too young, his dialect too southern, and his ideas, some of which were inspired by the *Harvard Business Review*, too American.

As Wang neared his office, he could see the shapes of friends and colleagues waiting for him behind its pebble-glass door. He knew they would be disappointed that he had quit. He braced himself to face their sadness.

But when he entered the room they laughed and cheered and pumped his hand and slapped his shoulders. He was the eye of a storm of flashing grins and thundering words.

"*Gōngxǐ nǐ! Gōngxǐ nǐ! Gōngxǐ nǐ, Wáng!*"

"Congratulations! Congratulations! Congratulations to you, Wang!"

The celebration faded when Wang's friends saw his confusion. Soon Wang understood. The factory's leaders had not announced Wang's resignation but the opposite. They told everyone they had promoted Wang and that he was going to be the factory's new director.

This was bad.

Wang did not want to be the factory's new director. He had accepted a new job as a senior executive at the China International Trust Investment Corporation, a multinational conglomerate with a billion dollars to spend on making China better. And, most important, he believed the factory was now beyond saving.

His friends and colleagues begged him to reconsider, to become the director, to stay and lead the factory back to life.

He replied to their pleas by asking a question.

"Can any of you give me a good reason I should stay?" he said. "Because I cannot think of one."

There was a long silence, after which Wang began collecting his things, preparing to leave the factory forever. He was not surprised. It was a rhetorical question, more respectful than telling his friends "no." He did not expect an answer. Wang knew there was no good reason for him to stay. He had searched for one before he quit.

Then one of Wang's friends broke the silence and started telling him a story.

There was, the friend said, a street market a quarter of a mile from the factory where farmers sold, among other things, bok choy, eggplant, longan, and lychee. Each morning the market came alive with the sounds of barter, the colors of ripening, and the smells of fruit crushed underfoot. Each night it fell silent.

And as soon as the market grew dark, shadowy figures started appearing where the market had been, people without faces, their features hidden beneath hats and behind sunglasses and flu masks. They moved in silence, shuffling and stooped. They picked through the forgotten and rotten food, the discarded vegetables, and the downtrodden fruit, and collected anything they might be able to eat, putting it into old string bags, or bundling it up in their coats, or, if they had neither, putting it in their pockets or scooping it into their arms.

When everything that might yet be edible had been picked over and was gone, the figures left as quickly as possible, fading away into the night, hoping no one had recognized them. These were Beijing's forgotten elderly, the city's grandparents and ancestors, starving and poor, trapped in the cracks left by China's transition to a market economy, scavenging to survive.

Wang understood that one of the factory's biggest problems was its retirees; he had said as much in his plans to save it. In those days, China did not have a state-backed system for taking care of the elderly: instead, employers provided their former employees with lifelong pensions. The factory had accumulated over six thousand retired workers, and was adding more all the time. Each one needed at least 10,000 Chinese yuan a year to survive. But the factory could not afford to pay 60 million yuan a year—the equivalent of about $12 million in 1992—to support its retirees and had fallen behind on its pension payments.

When Wang arrived at the factory ten years earlier, he was new to Beijing—a twenty-five-year-old from a small southern rural community, speaking a strange dialect, with no friends or family nearby, and a lot to learn. Some of the factory's master workers had taken care of him, not only by teaching him about the factory's business of electronics manufacturing but also by helping him understand Beijing and the world of work and bringing him home-cooked food. These people became his second family.

And here was the twist in the tale. Those desperate, hungry, shadowy figures shuffling through the street market a quarter of a mile away every day after dark, hiding their shame beneath hats and behind masks, were not strangers. They were retirees from the factory and they included some of the master workers who had taught, fed, and mentored Wang when he first arrived in Beijing.

Wang had long known the factory was not meeting its obligations to its retirees but the problem had always seemed like an accounting difficulty, another business puzzle to solve, as cold and remote as the numbers on his balance sheets.

Hearing the story of the street market transformed Wang's understanding. For the first time, the young accountant experienced the cost of the factory's difficulties not in yuan, jiao, and fen—China's equivalents of dollars, dimes, and pennies—but in fear, shame, and suffering, in pain felt not by strangers but by people who had taken care of him, loved him, and helped him achieve his success, people he had loved in return.

For months Wang had looked at the factory's profits and losses, the value of its assets, its product mix, its market share, its organizational chart, its compound annual growth rate, its strategic plans, its financial projections, and every other number or datum that sensible businesspeople and especially accountants are supposed to care about, and had found no reason to stay.

But after the story ended, Wang drew a long breath, reflected for a few moments, then told his friends he would not be leaving the factory after all. He had asked for a good reason to stay and they had given him one.

A story that took only a few minutes to tell, that gave Wang no new financial data or other business information, that described events he had not witnessed and could not corroborate, told as he was about to walk out the door forever, had changed his mind completely.

7. How We Change Our Minds

There are many hypotheses about how we change our minds—philosophers, economists, psychologists, and others have been debating the topic for centuries—and most make a broadly similar claim: A changed mind is the fruit of reason and the result of an evaluation of facts.

For example, some psychologists believe we change our minds by continually weighing probabilities, using methods proposed by an eighteenth-century mathematician named Thomas Bayes. According to this hypothesis we assess information based on probability, make revisions as new information appears, and change our minds as probabilities change. This is an excellent method for making decisions, and often used by computers, but it is not how humans think. If people changed their minds based on accurate assessments of probability, every casino in the world would be empty.

Most other hypotheses about how we change our minds are similar. They presume a process much like the one D. S. Wang used to decide to leave the factory—analyzing numbers, evaluating data, making projections, and so on—and nothing at all like the one that led him to stay. What actually changed Wang's mind was what changes our minds most of the time: a story.

Wang was an accountant with a background in engineering, and therefore an extremely logical, methodical, and numerical thinker. He had spent months considering whether he should quit the factory in Beijing. At the end of this long process, he had not only decided to quit; he *had* quit, and even accepted a new job. So what was it about the story of the street market that led Wang to change his mind?

The story showed Wang that his choice was between something *rewarding*—a well-paying job at China International Trust Investment Corporation—and something *meaningful*—saving his mentors from poverty and starvation.

Reward and meaning are not the same; they are opposites. "Getting paid" or "becoming rich" may be rewarding reasons to do something, but they are not meaningful reasons. At best, reward is incidental to meaning; at worst, reward is an alternative to meaning: compensation for doing something meaningless.

Researchers at the Massachusetts Institute of Technology showed this distinction. They paid people to build Lego toys at a rate of $2.00 for one toy, $1.89 for a second, $1.78 for a third, and so on, decreasing the payment by 11 cents until it reached 2 cents for the nineteenth toy and remained there. Participants could stop making toys at any time.

There were two groups. Both groups received the same payments, but they achieved different results: the people in the first group made seven toys on average and quit when the pay was $1.34 and the people in the second group made eleven toys on average and quit when the pay was $0.90 One person in this second group made twenty toys, and another made twenty-one.

The difference was simple: People in the first group saw their toy disassembled in front of them immediately after they made it, and people in the second group saw each toy placed on a desk. The accumulation of toys on the desk motivated more work for less pay because it seemed more meaningful. Many other studies show the same thing: that, as long as our basic needs are met, meaning is more motivating than money.

The reason lies in our story-shaped brains. Stories distribute glory to heroes. Glory is social, and reward is individual. If we want to be the hero of our story, and we always do, reward is irrelevant: We must achieve something we believe benefits others, even if it is as modest as making toys and hoping someone might play with them.

Once we understand the power of story, Wang's choice becomes unsurprising, perhaps even inevitable. One of Wang's choices offered reward; the other offered meaning. When Wang listened to the story about the street market, he heard a call to serve, a summoning of meaning, an opportunity to be consequential. The story was incomplete, its starving characters stuck in a loop, cursed to emerge from the gloom every evening forever unless someone intervened. It was a story awaiting the entrance of its hero. Of course Wang changed his mind.

What he did next made history. We will return to his story later.

8. Don't Forget

The original limitation of oral stories was transience: They were said and then gone. Our distant ancestors wanted to repeat the best and most important stories, and so they started looking for ways to make them more memorable.

Remembering stories is difficult. We are bad at remembering things we have been told. When given new information, we forget about half of what we remember every twenty-four hours, until, within a week, there is almost nothing left. Our forgetting gets worse when information is passed from one person to another: Stories are shortened and transformed by each retelling until, around the sixth or seventh iteration, they have been abbreviated to one or two sentences that bear little or no resemblance to the original. We do not realize we are so forgetful. We can express great confidence in memories that are wrong or, in some cases, in memories of things that never happened. We forget, then forget we forgot.

It took great ingenuity to overcome these cognitive limitations, but over tens of thousands of years we developed ways to recall spoken stories with high fidelity.

The basic problem is that memory is finite. A human brain can store somewhere between 90 million and 9 billion gigabytes of information, the equivalent of 30 million to 9 billion high-definition movies. This is a huge amount, but only a fraction is available for remembering spoken information, because so much is used for storing other things, like languages, locations, names and faces, and important moments. The brain's solution to the problem of limited memory is efficiency: It discards detail, and only keeps information that is absolutely necessary.

To solve the same problem of limited memory, computers compress information by looking for repeating patterns and replacing them with a short description, such as a message that says, for example, "25 alternating red and white squares go here," or a mathematical formula that reproduces the patterns, such as "draw a circle with a radius of 20." These methods do not necessarily make things as small as they could possibly be, though, because there is another need to consider: The information must also be quickly and easily retrieved.

Our ancestors developed ways to remember stories by doing much the same thing: embedding patterns in stories so there was less to memorize, without forcing storytellers to pause to remember what comes next.

We still use these patterns today: They include, among other things, alliteration, assonance, melody, meter, repetition, rhythm, and rhyme, which, not by coincidence, are the principal tools of lyricists and poets everywhere.

Here is an example, almost four hundred years old, the first two verses of a folk ballad called "Barbara Allen":

> In Scarlet Town, where I was bound,
> There was a fair maid dwelling,
> Whom I had chosen to be my own,
> And her name it was Barbara Allen.
>
> All in the merry month of May,
> When green leaves they was springing,
> This young man on his death-bed lay,
> For the love of Barbara Allen.

The meter—that is, the pattern of stressed and unstressed syllables—is the same in every first and third line and in every second and fourth line, making it easier to remember how many words go in each and what words they are; the last word of every first line rhymes or half-rhymes with the last word of every third line; there is alliteration in the first line of the second verse ("merry month of May"); and there are internal rhymes and half-rhymes in phrases like "Scarlet Town, where I was bound," "fair maid," "chosen to be my own," and "green leaves"; and both verses, like most of the others—there are about fourteen in all, depending on the version—end the same way: with the ballad's name, "Barbara Allen." All these different compression techniques are embedded in just fifty-four words.

The patterns are not only aids to memory. Our brains respond positively to patterns in signals because, among other things, patterns make perception easier. This is why we tend to find symmetry, geometry, and other artistic patterns aesthetically pleasing. What makes something beautiful also makes it memorable, and that creates a mighty feedback loop, because using patterns to make a story easier to remember is often the same as making a story better.

This is especially true of the most powerful spoken storytelling technique of them all.

9. Singing

For a long time, music was one of the great mysteries of human evolution. It even perplexed Darwin; in 1871 he wrote in *Descent of Man* that

> as neither the enjoyment nor the capacity of producing musical notes are faculties of the least direct use to us in reference to our ordinary habits of life, they must be ranked amongst the most mysterious with which we are endowed.

Some of this confusion, especially in Darwin's Victorian era, has less to do with the difficulty of the question than with the difficulty of accepting the answer. Music has long been venerated as one of our highest, purest art forms, and suggesting it has a practical, biological purpose is sometimes seen as failing to appreciate—and perhaps even *spoiling*—it.

But music does have a practical, biological purpose, or at least a practical, biological *origin*: Music exists today because it was a crucial component in the evolution of storytelling.

Our first music, made long before we had drums or pipes or strings, was singing. All forms of instrumental music are singing's children.

And singing was—and still is—our most effective way of remembering stories.

Singing developed as an incidental effect of the evolution of the human voice. Humans are primates, and all primates make sounds using vocalization, mainly for warning cries and mating calls—signals that, not coincidentally, convey information using, among other things, pitch, rhythm, and tone. About two million years ago, one species of primates developed a simpler larynx—or voice box—than all other primates, which, ironically, enabled more complex and controlled vocalizations. That species was the first human species. A million years later, its descendants used those more complex vocalizations to communicate beside their first fires, where the sounds evolved into stories and language.

Pitch, tone, and rhythm, all of which we associate with singing, are also aspects of speaking. We use tone to change the meaning of a sound—Chinese, for example, is a tone language where different tones signal different words; and even English, which is not a tone language, uses a rising tone at the end of a phrase to indicate a question—and changes in the pitch, tone, and rhythm of speech often convey unspoken information about our emotional state—whether we are feeling happy, sad, or anxious, for example.

There is therefore a spectrum, not a separation, between speaking and singing, from least to most musical. Points along this spectrum, roughly in order, include everyday speech; the Jamaican style of talking over music called "toasting"; rapping; the heavy metal technique of death growl; the speak-singing method known as *sprechgesang*; incanting and chanting, whether in soccer stadiums or temples; the crooning made famous by Frank Sinatra and Tony Bennett; the singing of hymns; the speechlike contemporary style of singing in musical theater, followed by its more traditional style known as "belting"; choral singing; and classical opera, where the voice is used much like a musical instrument. Singing and speaking are not different; they are variants of the same thing.

We can confirm this sameness by looking at the human brain. For example, Broca's area and Wernicke's area, the two regions of the cerebral cortex that process speech, also process music; some of the brain's most important electrical responses to speech and music are indistinguishable from one another; and the process of remembering speech and music uses the same areas of the brain.

Singing is memorable for the same reason related techniques like alliteration and rhyme are memorable: it introduces patterns that make the words in a story more predictable.

Singing's patterns consist of pitch, tone, and rhythm. Pitch, which is how we perceive and distinguish sounds based on how high or low they are, provides an excellent example of how singing helps us remember.

Pitch is exceptionally memorable: almost everyone can remember the pitch of a familiar song to within a semitone—the smallest meaningful difference in any kind of music—even if they have no musical training. We remember pitch well because it is a kind of sensory shorthand. Pitch is not "real" in any external, physical sense; it is how our brains perceive what is called the *fundamental frequency* of a sound.

There is an easy way to imagine this. Picture a tree with a trunk that splits into two boughs. Now picture two branches growing upward out of each of those boughs, and two branches growing upward out of each of *those* branches, and so on. The trunk of the tree is like the fundamental frequency of a voice, and the branches, increasing in number as they increase in height, are the other tones a voice contains, increasing in number of waves per second (more waves per second means higher notes) as exact multiples of the fundamental frequency: one trunk, then two boughs, then four branches, then eight branches, continuing ever higher. These boughs and branches are called *harmonics*. If our brain detects some of these branches, it is extraordinarily good at calculating where the trunk of the tree is, even if the trunk is hidden. This process of identifying the "trunk of the tree" is called *pitch perception*.

Our exceptional pitch perception almost certainly evolved for reasons related to sexual reproduction: male human voices have an average fundamental frequency of 112 waves per second, and female human voices have an average fundamental frequency of 169 waves per second. The pitch of our voices and our pitch preferences fluctuate with fertility, and both male and female voice pitch influence mate choice and reproductive success. Because of this, early humans with better pitch perception had more reproductive success than early humans with worse pitch perception, which led to us becoming a species that is extraordinarily good at perceiving pitch.

But even though we excel at identifying and remembering the fundamental frequency of voices, the trunk of the tree of every human voice has other, higher branches too—the tones we call *harmonic frequencies*—that are exact multiples of the fundamental frequency. We do not notice these harmonic frequencies: A human voice seems like a single sound to us.

Our perception is so focused on the fundamental frequency that we can perceive it even when it is not there. Telephones, for example, cannot transmit frequencies below 300 waves per second, and so cannot transmit the fundamental frequency of a human voice. They only show us those higher-frequency harmonic tones—the higher branches of the tree in our analogy—but it does not matter: We "hear" the fundamental frequency of a voice on a telephone anyway, because our brain does the mathematics of the harmonics to locate the fundamental frequency (or the "trunk of the tree").

For example, if someone's voice has a fundamental frequency of 100 waves per second, the harmonic tones would be at 200, 300, 400 waves per second and so on. If our brain only hears tones that are at 300 and 400 waves per second, it automatically fills in the blank, and we "hear" a voice with a fundamental frequency of 100 waves per second even though the fundamental frequency isn't actually there. (And we do *not* hear a tone of 50 waves per second as well: our brains know when they have found the lowest frequency tone in a voice.)

This "mathematics of the harmonics" is what makes singing stories memorable. Music, whether sung or played on an instrument, is in essence a series of mathematically precise variations on a fundamental frequency. For example, a middle C in western music has a fundamental frequency of about 262 waves per second. That's the trunk of a tree. Notes that sound musical when played with a middle C (also known as C4) are exact multiples of higher branches, including one with double the frequency, or about 524 waves per second (which is called C5 and is from the next octave, or set of eight notes) and another with triple the frequency, or about *786* waves per second (which is called G5 and is from two octaves—or two sets of eight notes—higher).

These precise mathematical patterns enable our brains to predict much of a melody from its pitch, without having to store additional information. The process is so efficient that we can repeat the lyrics of unfamiliar songs after listening to them four or five times, recall the lyrics of familiar songs forty or fifty years after last hearing them, and remember lyrics and melodies even when the rest of our memories are rendered irretrievable by disease.

And melody brings more than memorability: singing is the only storytelling form that can transform audiences into storytellers by enabling many people to tell the same story at the same time. We do this when we sing formal group songs, like hymns and national anthems, and also when we sing informally and spontaneously with ad hoc groups of friends and strangers. For example, a study of more than a thousand nights at pubs and clubs in north England in 2012 found that, on average, three out of every four people in an audience will sing along with a song about Tommy, who used to work on the docks but is down on his luck, and his girlfriend Gina, who works in the diner all day, brings home her pay, and says, "We've got to hold on to what we've got."

This song is called "Livin' on a Prayer," and, if you are familiar with it, the next few lines of its lyrics are probably playing in your mind right now, all because of the memorability of melody.

"Livin' on a Prayer" was written in 1986 by Jon Bon Jovi, Richie Sambora, and Desmond Child in Sambora's parents' basement in Sayreville, New Jersey. Its story was inspired by Child's experience of struggling to make ends meet while living with his girlfriend, who worked in a restaurant and was nicknamed Gina. Bon Jovi had been listening to songs in which "storytellers were doing their best storytelling," and "wanted to relate those stories to people I had gone to high school with. I wanted to tell their stories, because they could have been me if I hadn't learned to play guitar."

As we discussed earlier, group storytelling helps build social bonds in part because it prompts the brain to release oxytocin, which has effects that help us socialize, such as increasing generosity, social behavior, and trust, and synchronizing a group's brain activity.

When we *sing* stories in a group, these effects are amplified. Singing in a group bonds strangers quickly and strengthens connections between friends by releasing not only oxytocin but also endorphins, which relieve stress, reduce pain intensity, and increase pain thresholds.

This is true of all group singing, and it is especially true of *bad* group singing like the singing of "Livin' on a Prayer" in the pubs of north England, where few if any of the singers are trained or professional. The worst group singing is the best group singing, because the benefits of group singing are maximized when we stop worrying about how we sound and just do what people have done for tens of thousands of years: sing for the joy of community and fellowship.

The story the song tells matters too, of course. Groups of people do not spontaneously sing *any* song, no matter how memorable the melody: As with any story, they also need to see themselves in its heroes. "Livin' on a Prayer," written in New Jersey in 1986, is being sung decades later in north England because those ad hoc groups of friends and strangers know that Tommy and Gina's story is their story too.

10. The Problem of Choosing

For tens of thousands of years after language evolved, stories were spoken then forgotten. But after we learned to memorize stories, after story begat poetry and story begat songs, something essential changed. Our new ability to preserve stories meant there were more stories to tell than there was time to tell them. For the first time, we had to choose which stories to tell and hear.

As soon as stories could be remembered, a struggle commenced between the leader and the led, the parent and the child, the authority and the individual, over which stories would be chosen and who would choose them. This problem of choosing continues today, and with good reason: We cannot choose whether stories change our minds, but we can choose which stories they are.

We have already discussed why storytelling is adaptive—i.e., why it evolved: because stories bring us unity, a sense of identity, and a sense of purpose. But those evolutionary benefits of storytelling do not tell us why we prefer some stories over others, any more than the evolutionary benefits of carbohydrates tell us why we prefer candy over carrots.

The obvious answer, *entertainment*, is an empty word, the equivalent of "Here be dragons" written on a medieval map, a hand waving at something unexamined and unexplored.

What exactly *is* entertainment?

The word comes from *entretenir*, a thousand-year-old Anglo-Norman word that originally meant "to keep together" and then "to keep someone in a certain frame of mind." We still use this ancient sense of the word today when we tell ourselves or someone else to "keep it together" or "get it together." Over time, the meaning of *enter-*

tain became broader than just keeping someone in their current state of mind, and "entertaining" became a way "to nurture emotion in others" and *change* their state of mind. To *entertain* is, literally, to evoke feeling. A story is only entertaining if it makes someone feel something.

And what does it mean to "feel something"?

Scientists have been studying—and arguing about—that since at least 1872, when Charles Darwin published his third major work, *The Expression of the Emotions in Man and Animals*, one of the first books ever to be illustrated with photographs, which Darwin used to show human facial expressions. Darwin's greatest contribution to our understanding of emotions was to point out something that should be obvious, but somehow still remains obscure 150 years later: that emotions are not exclusive to us. The cliché "Emotions are what make us human" is obvious nonsense. In Darwin's words:

> As long as humans and all other animals are viewed as independent creations, a stop is put to our natural desire to investigate the causes of emotion. This doctrine has proved as pernicious with respect to emotion as to every other branch of natural history. Some emotions, such as the bristling of hair under the influence of extreme terror, can hardly be understood, except on the belief that humans once existed in an animal-like condition. The community of certain emotions in allied species, as in the movements of the same muscles during laughter by humans and monkeys, is more intelligible if we believe in their descent from a common progenitor.

Or, anyone who thinks "emotions are what make us human" has never been welcomed home by a dog. Emotions do not "make us human"; they make us one of the nine million different species living on this planet. As Darwin put it, "Even insects express anger, terror, jealousy, and love by their stridulation."

Understanding that all creatures feel emotion matters because it shows that emotion started evolving four billion years ago with the first single-celled organisms, that emotion pre-dates cognition, that emotion is the progenitor of communication, and that emotion is the seed of the tree of life. Emotions are physiological reactions to survival-related stimuli such as threats, the approach of potential mates, or the presence or absence of food.

In the earliest creatures, emotion was a purely internal response to things sensed directly. Then, half a billion years ago, emotion began manifesting in ways that could be detected externally, and some living things started gathering information by observing the emotions of others. Noticing fear in a neighbor might indicate a nearby threat, for example. Eventually this sharing of sensory data led to deliberate signaling, then to responding to one signal with another—or, *communicating*—and then, in humans, to storytelling and language.

It should not be surprising or controversial that story is a primary vehicle for emotion, or that we feel emotion when we are told stories. First, emotion has an intimate evolutionary connection to communication; and second, emotion is motivation, and motivation is how stories connect character to consequence.

Emotion is why stories change our mind far more often than information, statistics, or any other form of communication. If anything, Darwin underestimated emotion's ubiquity: emotion is found in all living things from bacteria to trees, and is billions of years older than cognition. Life could feel long before it could think.

An emotion is a biochemical message triggered by threats and opportunities. The most common response to that message is to move, which is where the word *emotion* comes from: the noun is derived from a now obsolete verb, *emove*, which meant "to make something move." Emotion moves us literally as well as figuratively.

Evolution does not invent; it extends. We *interpret* signals from others using recently evolved areas of our brains, but our *reactions* to those signals are produced by the ancient mechanisms of the very earliest parts of our nervous systems. As a consequence, our responses to signals from others are largely indistinguishable from our responses to things we sense for ourselves: we feel much the same emotion, with much the same intensity, no matter whether we are experiencing something or being told about it. Our minds are a million years of thinking built on a billion years of feeling.

And so there is no chasm or dichotomy between information and imagination, no story so true or important that it cannot or should not be told to entertain. Cognition is nothing without emotion. If you want to tell anyone anything, tell them a story. There is no truth we do not feel.

The arc of the story of stories is that every improvement and reinvention of our storytelling tools increase the number of storytellers, the number of stories they can tell, and the number of people to whom they can tell them, which makes the problem of choosing harder, and the power of choosing greater.

You have that power now.

Will you continue with this story, or set it down and never return?

Chapter 2

The Eye of Your Mind

1. Drawing

In the beginning, there were *marks*—scat and spoor, scratches and scents, prints of hooves and paws—that at first incidentally or instinctively and then sometimes deliberately denoted territory, communicated identity, and signaled for mates.

As we evolved, we learned to read the marks of our predators, our prey, and each other, and came to see the utility of marking. When we developed the faculties of story and language, the way we made marks became more conscious, skillful, and technological, until, about seventy-five thousand years ago, we started using a reddish, iron-rich soil called ochre to sketch patterns on rocks and stencil our hands on the walls of caves.

About twenty-five thousand years after that, on what is now the Indonesian island of Sulawesi, someone used a piece of ochre to draw four pigs on a cave wall in so much detail that even today we can identify their exact species. These pigs are, for now, the oldest figurative drawing we have found, but this was certainly not the first time our ancestors drew realistic-looking pictures.

The Sulawesian pigs serve a clear purpose: they are not static or isolated but interacting to help tell a story, playing roles like Varaha in Hinduism's Vedas; the Erymanthian boar of Greek mythology; the pigs in the parable of the prodigal son; Straparola's King Pig; Zhu Bajie in *Journey to the West*; this little piggy who went to market; the many pigs of *Animal Farm*; Wilbur in *Charlotte's Web*; Babe the sheep-pig; *The Lion King*'s Pumbaa; Peppa Pig; and the pigs and piglins of *Minecraft*, among many others.

The first drawings and paintings were not exclusive to caves. People likely drew on bark, rocks, skins, stones, wood, themselves, and each other too, and probably did all of those things far more frequently than and long before they drew in caves. But none of those surfaces could wait unspoiled for tens of thousands of years for us to discover them. Only caves endure so long.

The great mystery of why our ancestors went to the trouble of painting in caves, which are cramped, dangerous, dark, difficult to reach, and do not have flat, smooth surfaces on which to paint, is easily solved once we realize art is storytelling, not decoration.

When illuminated by flames, as they were tens of thousands of years ago, many of the images on the walls of the world's caves change and move as if by magic. Our cave painting ancestors were animators and moviemakers. Caves were their theaters; cave walls were their screens; fat-burning lamps were the bulbs in their projectors; and complex, overlapping drawings and paintings, mainly of animals, skillfully and deliberately rendered to exploit dynamic and uneven surfaces, and almost certainly accompanied by a dramatic oral story, were their movies.

It is easy to imagine the people led to these secret places to witness these marvelous motion pictures feeling the feelings we feel when we enter a movie theater. We will see this throughout the story of stories: All the stories and storytelling tools of different generations are fundamentally similar and only superficially different, because the brains telling and being told the stories are always functionally and structurally the same. We are never as different from one another as we think we are.

Drawings and paintings were not exclusive to any continent, culture, or moment, even though the first discovery of a cave painting in Europe at the turn of the twentieth century, amplified by colonial chauvinism, briefly made it seem that way. When our ancestors spread beyond East Africa to Asia, Europe, Australia, and the rest of the African continent, they created pictures as they went, taking drawing and painting, the first tools of storytelling, with them all over the world.

2. The Screen in the Brain

The pigs on the wall of the cave in Sulawesi are not pigs. They are *pictures* of pigs, which means, as with all pictures of pigs, that they resemble pigs in very few ways: they are not alive; they do not feel like pigs if you touch them; they do not move; they do not oink; they are not pig-sized; they are not three-dimensional; and so on. The very many ways the pictures of pigs are not like pigs raises questions: What exactly *is* piglike about them? Why does everyone who sees those marks in that cave in Sulawesi instantly think "pigs"?

We learned the answer to these questions in 2014, when scientists at the University of Minnesota made a startling discovery: Our brain's visual cortex acts almost exactly the same way whether we are looking at pictures or remembering them. Our brains process thought much like they process light.

The activations are so similar that you can tell which picture someone is remembering by watching their brain activity. This finding leads to a clear and incontrovertible conclusion: We have screens in our brains that display not only what we look at but also what we think, dream, and remember. We experience what we imagine and what we see in much the same way.

But the screen in our brain does not display thoughts with the same fidelity as sights: Our memories appear with only low-level visual features, such as edges and blobs, and our brains imagine the rest. This is how storytellers and storytelling technologies evoke real things with simplified images: Cave paintings like the pigs in Sulawesi—as well as, for example, cartoons, sketches, and even brief oral or written descriptions such as "one stationary eye in the mahogany face, and one revolving one"—provide low-level visual features that inspire glorious pictures on the screen in our brain. Storytellers supply a few well-chosen details, and our brains complete the image.

This new understanding of how visualization works also solves an ages-old mystery: why all our storytelling technologies are so similar. Everything from the first cave painting to the last smartphone tends to take up the space of one of two shapes: a rectangle about 1.5 times wider than it is high, or a rectangle about 1.2 times higher than it is wide.

And now we know why: All our storytelling technologies are the shape of the screen in our brain. Our visual cortex has a field of view about 1.5 times wider than it is high, and, at its center, a field of focus about 1.2 times higher than it is wide. We tell stories with tools shaped like our field of view or our field of focus. Cave art, landscape paintings and photographs, movies, stage plays, storefronts, and video games are shaped like our field of view. Mirrors, portraiture, printing, statuary, windows, and writing—this page, for example—are shaped like our field of focus. Images on smartphones, of course, can be either.

Even the scenes we visualize when we recall memories or listen to music and spoken stories take the shape of the screen in our brain. Regardless of art, medium, or technology, the result of all storytelling is visual. Storytelling's purpose is to put something on the screen in somebody's brain.

3. Signals We Can See

Visual storytelling evolved from visual signaling in the same way oral storytelling evolved from oral signaling like cries and calls. But, unlike cries and calls, intentional visual signals are rare among other species. Only a few animals, including black bears, desert ants, wildcats, and wolves, send signals by deliberately making visible marks, and those visible marks are all very simple compared to the audible and olfactory signals made by these and other animals. Information-rich visual signaling is uniquely human, even before we consider the complex signals of the visual arts.

Visible marking emerged in humans as a byproduct of tool use. The stone tools we used to butcher animals and sharpen bones and rocks into points made marks incidentally that, over time, we also started making intentionally. These early marks were likely for decoration, not explicit communication, but because this conscious, intentional marking started hundreds of thousands of years ago in our ancestor species *Homo erectus*, it coevolved with storytelling and eventually became a way of signaling.

Marking is one of two uniquely human visual signals that evolved before language. The other is *pointing*, which is used only occasionally by wild primates and a few other species such as ravens, but is an essential element of human communication, and a signal infants understand and use even before they can speak. Pointing has many meanings, but they are all variations of "look over there," and used to direct someone else's visual attention to something specific.

Once we learned to combine these two uniquely human visual signals—pointing and marking—to show things not present by directing attention to figurative drawings, our natural faculties for storytelling were fully developed. We could tell stories using words or pictures or both. Every subsequent change in storytelling comes from technique or technology.

Our brains are very good at distinguishing between a signal, which is something someone is trying to tell us, and our other method of perception, a *stimulus*, which is something we discover for ourselves. Unless we are experiencing psychosis, our brains never confuse signal and stimulus. We always know the difference between a pig and a picture of a pig.

But *memory* is different: seeing a picture of a pig and remembering a picture of a pig use the same parts of the brain as seeing and remembering an actual pig, and this can sometimes lead us to think we remember seeing a stimulus—an actual pig—when in fact we saw a signal—a picture of a pig.

This effect is easy to show. How many actual pigs have you seen during your life? Your answer may surprise you. The many thousands of pictures of pigs you have seen during your life have given you a tacit sense of familiarity with pigs, an understanding that pigs are common, and perhaps, in consequence, a vague feeling that you encounter real pigs fairly frequently. But unless you own or work with pigs, you have probably seen few real pigs. What you *have* seen is many *pictures* of pigs, which may cause a minor, and easily corrected, error in your memory of your life.

4. Two Hundred Billion Drawings

We have made two hundred billion pictures since someone ochred pigs on a wall in Sulawesi.

If we could lay them all side by side in chronological order, we would see that most of our pictures are of people, animals, or landscapes, and that these three subjects are spread evenly across the years, always equally popular.

The anatomical and geological accuracy of the pictures would not vary much, and that may come as a surprise. One of the great myths of European history is that the Greeks and Romans created beautiful, realistic art using techniques that, when lost, sent Europe (and presumably, by extension, the rest of the world) into centuries of backward "dark ages" until a magical rebirth, or "renaissance," occurred in Florence, Italy, in the 1400s, and artists such as Leonardo da Vinci and Michelangelo rediscovered the wisdom of the ancients and created unparalleled masterpieces.

This is, of course, nonsense. Leonardo, Michelangelo, and others created great works of art in and around Florence during the late 1400s and early 1500s, but art was not stuck in centuries of doldrums prior to that, and the Florentine Quattrocento did not mark a new beginning. Human creative behavior is innate and therefore constant. But describing history is *storytelling*, so histories conform to the structure of character, chronology, and consequence. Reality tells bad stories—it is too collaborative, continuous, and convoluted—so historians often give arbitrary periods catchy brand names, clear beginnings, and a handful of heroes whose spectacular consequences bring those arbitrary periods to convenient, if imaginary, ends.

The myth of the Renaissance is one such story. It was first told in 1860 by a Swiss historian named Jacob Burckhardt, in a book called *The Civilization of the Renaissance in Italy*, which introduced all the sweeping ahistorical claims about the period's art, humanity, and modernity we still hear from schoolteachers and tour guides today.

But our two hundred billion pictures show anatomical and geological accuracy coming and going across their entire range, not just in periods placed on pedestals by white European patriarchs. If we cast our gaze leftward from the present, far past *David* and the *Mona Lisa*, we will see anatomically accurate polar bears and seals made by the Paleo-Inuit peoples over two thousand years ago; realistic, oversize heads created by the Olmecs of Mesoamerica over three thousand years ago; and lifelike gods and goddesses drawn in Mesopotamia over four thousand years ago, among many hundreds of millions of other accurate images. Art's apparent realness ebbs and flows for reasons of economics, taste, or technology, but never for want of skill.

5. René

During the exceptionally cold winter of 1929, in the Parisian suburb of Le Perreux-sur-Marne, a Belgian émigré painted a picture on five square feet of canvas.

The picture was unremarkable: It showed a briarwood tobacco pipe of a type mass-produced by the Chacom pipe company, which sold throughout France for about a hundred francs, the rough equivalent of four dollars: approximately the same price as a magnifying glass, razor, or towel.

Seven years later a gallery in New York displayed the picture. No one bought it, and the *New York Times* gave it a scathing review: "A painter's technical skill is almost entirely wanting in the work. The canvas is for the most part arid with respect to those qualities we call esthetic."

The painter was René Magritte and the picture was titled *La Trahison des images*, which means *The Treason of Images*. Magritte's *catalogue raisonné* mistranslated the title as *The Treachery of Images*, and that is what the painting has been called in English ever since.

In 1954 *La Trahison des images* started a surprising journey toward fame, not because of its pipe, but because of a sentence painted beneath the pipe: *Ceci n'est pas une pipe*—"This is not a pipe." Another gallery in New York displayed it, and this time the *New York Times* review was tepid rather than scalding: "Visitors are likely to be divided into groups that hate or respond to this work. A painting of a pipe is called 'The Treachery of Images' and bears the inscription 'This is not a pipe.' So—."

So . . . what? We will never know. The critic from the *Times* ended his comment there, biting his tongue instead of completing his criticism.

We can be sure the end of the sentence would not have been kind, though: he also described the exhibition as "mystigoguery."

But *La Trahison des images* was no longer being ignored. In fact, it was attracting what may be the best attention avant-garde art can get: column inches of ire from a sexagenarian art critic at a stuffy newspaper of record.

The art world struck back immediately. *ART Digest*, a periodical read by artists, art buyers, and auctioneers all over America, published what may be the first picture of *La Trahison des images* to appear in a magazine and beneath it wrote,

> Magritte achieves startling results. With a method and logic distressing in its conclusions, he has challenged our casual acceptance of the identity of a word with the image for which it stands. His lucidity enforces the disarming simplicity of his attack on basic principles of common sense. Magritte's lesson is so potent that we will never take this familiar world quite so for granted again.

La Trahison des images was unstoppable after that: it became a shibboleth separating the avant-garde from the establishment; a litmus test of whether a mind was old or young; a line drawn between modernism—art about the world outside—and postmodernism—art about the world within.

The history of art is a series of reactions and counterreactions, of fists and placards waved between generations, of movements classical and neo-, high and low, pre- and post-, old and nouveau.

The argument about *La Trahison des images* centered on the relationship between words, images, and the things they represent. Some saw "Ceci n'est pas une pipe" as a pedantic statement of the obvious, trying and failing to be profound. Others were certain it was burning with meaning: Michel Foucault, a French philosopher, wrote an entire book called *Ceci n'est pas une pipe*, claiming exactly that, for example.

But the argument had no notion of evolution, neurology, and the half-a-billion-year history of communication.

Humans are uniquely adapted to perceive the world through one another's senses. When we look at *La Trahison des images*, we understand that the painting and the sentence are both signals, and that someone, in this case René Magritte, is therefore trying to tell us something.

Even infants pointing at pictures from the laps of their caregivers know a picture of a cat is a signal, not a stimulus, and a real animal resembling the one in the picture is a cat too, even though it is a stimulus, not a signal. Our story-shaped brains give us an innate understanding of how signals and stimuli are different and how they are the same. Our problem is not deciding whether the pipe that is not a pipe is a pipe; it is deciphering the signal Magritte is sending us.

That signal is deliberately ambiguous. Magritte could have written "*Ceci est une peinture d'une pipe*"—"This is a painting of a pipe"—or even nothing at all, but chose not to.

Our most popular ambiguous signals are puns, which put words with more than one meaning in a context where more than one meaning makes sense: "Corduroy pillow makes headlines," "This vacuum cleaner sucks," "Whiteboards are remarkable," and so on.

Which brings us to an obvious, if seldom asked, question: Is Magritte's ambiguous signal a pun?

Probably.

The word *pipe* has two meanings in French: It can be either a device for smoking or a common sex act. This second meaning is so frequent that translation software often translates *une pipe* as the sex act, not the smoking device, and the same is true of *ceci est une pipe*. Only *ceci n'est pas une pipe* is sure to lead to *une pipe* being translated as a smoking device, and that is because of Magritte's painting. The treasonous image is betraying the sentence by showing the wrong pipe.

There is a lot of extraordinary evidence to support this extraordinary claim.

Toward the end of his career, Magritte seems to have been jumping up and down and waving his arms trying to draw our attention to the true meaning of *La Trahison des images*. He painted many variations of his famous pipe. In one of his latest and least known versions, an erect penis replaces the stem of the pipe. We only have to imagine someone smoking such a pipe to see Magritte's unambiguous double entendre.

There are other clues too.

For example, Magritte copied the pipe in *La Trahison des images* from an image in a comic strip called *Les facéties du sapeur Camember* (The Antics of Sapper Camember), by a pioneering author named Georges Colomb. Colomb's illustration shows a pipe with wings flying away; Magritte removed the wings and reappropriated the pipe for *La Trahison des images*. Colomb's flying pipe ends a story in which Camember visits his sweetheart, gives her some bonbons and a peck on the cheek, and asks for *une pipe* in return. She leads him on a little, but does not give him *une pipe*, and he leaves disappointed. It is not clear whether *une pipe* had its second meaning as a sex act when Colomb wrote the story in the 1890s, and *Sapeur Camember* was ostensibly for children, so Colomb's *une pipe* may have been a pipe, even though its other meaning makes the story make more sense. But Magritte left no doubt about how *he* interpreted Colomb's flying pipe: one of his many erotic drawings is of the same flying pipe, except the pipe is an erect penis and gonads.

There is far more evidence than this, but we will rest the case here.

Many intellectuals are incredulous that the solution to Magritte's riddle may be nothing more than a smutty pun. How dare anyone suggest that this iconic work, which Michel Foucault believed to be about "the intersection of representation by resemblance and of representation by sign" is actually a dick joke.

But you cannot celebrate *La Trahison des images* for the ambiguity of what it is *not*, then argue it is unambiguously *not* something you wish it wasn't.

And this is the point—and perhaps Magritte's too. Signals can be misunderstood.

Ambiguous signals were less likely when all stories were oral. If someone tells you a story you do not understand—or, for that matter, agree with—you can talk to them about it because they are present. But that is not true of painting or most other methods of telling stories. In a world of ever improving storytelling technologies, we receive ever more signals from people not present because of time, space, or, as with René Magritte and *La Trahison des images*, both.

6. Reality Is an Interface

Is Magritte's painting really a dirty joke?

To answer that, we must understand what *really* really means.

What we call *reality*, for all creatures, including us, is the neurological equivalent of a graphic user interface; a way to navigate the challenges of surviving and reproducing; a reductive London Underground–like map of our environment created by evolution. Any resemblance between our perceptions and truth is incidental.

Reality solves a specific problem. Almost everything living has more than one way of sensing its environment. When those senses disagree, their brains must resolve the disagreement. What we perceive as "reality" is nothing more or less than that resolution: our brain's best guess at what is happening around us; our mind placing a bet on which senses are right and wrong; our nervous system's final adjudication of our environment.

We experience the power of failing to solve this problem when we take to the sea: All humans, even experienced sailors, suffer seasickness, which results from disagreement between our different motion sensing systems. We detect motion with our eyes and with five sensors—three semicircular canals and two otolith organs—in each of our ears. When those sensors sense movement that our eyes do not see, as often happens aboard ships, our brains cannot resolve the competing inputs and we vomit, possibly because the sensory conflict triggers the response we evolved to expel neurotoxins. Astronauts experience the opposite problem, space sickness, when they vomit because their eyes sense movement but their ears, floating weightlessly, do not.

In almost all other cases of sensory conflict, our brains do not induce vomiting but determine which inputs to accept and which to reject by deciding what is "real."

Resolving conflicting inputs is not free. Attention is the price of perception, and we—and all other sentient organisms—have a limited amount of attention to spend. Brains eke out their attention budget by trying to buy the most reality for the least attention: they use assumptions, hierarchies, rules of thumb, shortcuts, and other tricks to make good enough guesses about the things they need to know. What they *don't* do, ever, is waste attention trying to determine what is objectively real to any degree that philosophers, who have been playing jargon ping-pong over reality for thousands of years, might endorse. Brains hide the incomprehensible and infinite complexity of the physical world behind icons and illusions made of species-specific sensations, offering us only simplified glimpses of the universe on a need-to-know basis. These simplified glimpses are the reality of reality. There is no such thing as a rainbow, for example: the physics of light is that it is a bunch of waves/particles oscillating within a certain frequency range. Our brains perceive those waves/particles as light and subsets of that frequency range as colors because it is helpful to us when we are doing things like foraging and hunting.

Perception is evolution's ultimate reality hack, but it can get things wrong, especially when confronted by technologies that were invented long after it evolved; this is why boats and spacecraft make us barf, why airplanes cause jet lag, why walking does not, and why it is essential to understand the story of stories to live well in our present age.

Signals add complication to the problem of perception. Not all signals are correct—a signaler may mistake a shadow for a predator, for example—and not all signals are honest—a signaler may try to scare you away from your food, a common ploy among birds. When deciding what is real, every member of every species that communicates must assess and resolve conflicting inputs not only from their own senses but also from the senses of others. If you are an antbird in the rainforest of Peru, and another bird in your flock signals "Hawk!" while you are chasing an especially nutritious spider, and you haven't seen or heard a hawk yourself, which reality do you choose? Do you abandon your food and flee, or do you assume your neighbor is mistaken or trying to mislead you and continue the chase? Both choices carry risk; if you are wrong, you might either miss lunch or *be* lunch.

Being a member of the species of stories increases this complication of signaling by several orders of magnitude. There was a time, many tens of thousands of years ago, when every individual discovered a great deal of what they knew, perhaps even *most* of what they knew, directly, using their own senses. But as we evolved into the species of stories, the proportion of knowledge we gained by being *told*, that came via the hearsay of the senses and perceptions of others, increased and kept increasing with every new storytelling technology, so that today almost everything we know comes indirectly from other people's stories, and almost nothing we know comes directly from our senses.

The self-evident fact that most of what we know is hearsay is something we have tried to deny since at least the age of Plato, when Europe first started to write. In his dialogue *Theaetetus*, written around 369 BCE, Plato uses the example of a court case to assert that stories—which philosophers call *testimony*—are not knowledge at all: "When the jurors are rightly persuaded of something one could not actually know except by being present—when they judge it, that is, on hearsay, and yet with a true opinion, they judge it without knowledge."

After Plato, most philosophers discussing the subject of how we know things, which they call *epistemology*, have been strangely silent about the dominant, vital role of storytelling. C. A. J. Coady, one of the few philosophers who specializes in testimony, says:

> Thinking about knowledge, at both the casual and the philosophical level, has for the most part either ignored testimony altogether or it has been cursory and dismissive. Modern epistemologists tirelessly pursue the nature and role of memory, perception, inductive and deductive reasoning but devote no analysis and argument to testimony. This tradition of neglect is a bad one. Our reliance upon testimony is too important and too fundamental.

Most of us think about knowledge at what Coady calls the casual level. For example, in July 2020, during the first year of the COVID-19 pandemic, many people saw, shared, and replied to an internet post that asked the following leading question: "If the media never told us about the virus, would you know it existed? Answer honestly . . ." This question, which implies "the virus" is not common or real if you have only heard about it from "the media," makes Coady's point: Few of us realize how little we would know if "the media never told us" about it. We each have more personal experience of COVID-19 than of almost anything else we unquestioningly believe in, from Audrey Hepburn and the aurora borealis to Western Australia and whale song. In our world of constant mass communication, we depend almost entirely on stories to decide what is real.

The thing to wonder about when you wonder about comic books, movies, narrative nonfiction paperbacks, smartphones, television, TikTok, video games, or any other storytelling technology, is not addiction, eye damage, government spying, health risks, maladapted kids, rising crime, social isolation, violence, or any of the other baseless fears that are recycled as if fresh with remarkable fidelity from technology to technology and generation to generation. The great and invisible danger of smartphones, televisions, video games, and all other storytelling technologies arises from the fact that your reality is made of stories, and so is everyone else's.

7. Family from Another Species

The claim that reality is an interface, not the truth, and that almost all of our knowledge comes from signals, not stimuli, may be difficult to accept or even comprehend, especially when hearing it for the first time. One way to understand what I mean when I say reality is a fabrication—you do not, of course, have to agree with me—is by comparing our reality to the reality of a different species that has access to the same sensory inputs as us: our dogs.

Half of all homes have a dog. A dog is a family member from another species. Dogs receive the same stimuli as us, but interpret them with a different nervous system, and as a result have a different experience of reality.

A dog's dominant sense organ is its nose: smelling is to dogs as seeing is to us. Depending on its breed, a dog gets up to 100 million times more information from scent than we do. We cannot easily conceive of all the things a dog learns about us through its nose. By smell alone, a dog can tell, among many other things, that we have malignant melanoma, bladder, breast, ovarian, prostate, or lung cancer, long before any medical tests. Our scent goes with us everywhere: we are constantly shedding microscopic, cornflake-shaped particles of dead skin that weigh 200 millionths of an ounce. Each particle carries a unique scent—from our skin, from the four bacteria each one of us typically hosts, from our bodily secretions, and from vapors that surround us.

These scent-carrying particles do not fall to the ground. They fly up, carried by air currents surrounding our bodies at 125 feet a second—even faster in hot weather or if we are wearing certain clothes. They change direction depending on how we move, and eventually disperse eighteen inches above our head. They broadcast our unique smell for many hours. Once emitted, they decay, signaling time like a ticking clock.

Dogs can smell things that are far away and, because of their wet nose, detect the direction it is coming from. They can smell what has happened in the recent past. Most importantly, because of the chemical changes emotions cause, and the way air flows around our bodies when we move, they can smell how we feel. Your dog can smell your depression, fear, happiness, nervousness, sadness, and stress.

A dog's vision is almost as different as its sense of smell. Dogs can identify moving objects two-thirds of a mile away, but anything twelve inches or closer is a blur. Dogs have up to 270 degrees of peripheral vision; they can see us from over their shoulders without turning their heads. Dogs see in two colors, while we see in three. A dog's world is blue, yellow, and white: what looks blue to us also looks blue to dogs, but red looks yellow, and green looks white. This two-color vision is one reason dogs can see much better in the dark than we can, because it enables them to differentiate between shades of gray that are indistinguishable to us; another reason is that their eyes contain a reflector called a *tapetum lucidum*, which works like an amplifier of light—this reflector is also why dogs' eyes look strange in flash photographs.

Sound is far less important to dogs than scent and sight, but their hearing is different from ours too: most of us can hear sounds with frequencies up to five kilohertz; dogs can hear sounds with frequencies up to fifty kilohertz, a range that includes sounds made by prey animals that are inaudible to us. Rats, for example, emit short fifty-kilohertz sounds when they are happy—say, when they are playing, or when a familiar human tickles them—and long twenty-two-kilohertz sounds when they are afraid or in pain. Many rodents, including mice, voles, and lemmings, have similar behaviors. If you ever have wild mice or rats in or near your home, your dog will know—and probably try to tell you about it—long before you realize.

Your dogs will also know where the rodents are. A dog's outer ears, or *pinnae*, contain a dozen muscles that can move them up and down and rotate them in and out, enabling dogs to locate precisely where sound is coming from—and also make cute baroos. We have nine similar muscles attached to our outer ears, but these are vestigial.

And so our dogs live in our homes while also living in another world: They access the operating system of the universe using a yellow-and-blue interface where scent is sight, night is not dark, and the distant giggles of rats and mice are easy to hear and find. We meet dogs at the intersection of their reality and ours, and neither is any more real than the other.

More important to the story of stories, only a tiny fraction of what a dog knows about its world comes from intentional marks, even though dogs are domesticated wolves, and wolves have some of the most complex marking behaviors among nonhuman mammals.

Most dog owners understand that a brief raised-leg urination, nearly always by males, is a way to mark territory, and that dogs on neighborhood walks may spend as much time as they can on smelling—and sometimes marking over—marks made by others.

But dogs mark in two other ways as well.

One is scat, which, particularly when deposited in a visually prominent place, is sometimes a mark, not an elimination.

The other is a surprise to almost every dog owner: When your dog looks like it is doing a terrible job of trying to cover its scat by scratching at the ground with its back legs while standing in the wrong place and facing the wrong way, it is not trying to cover its scat at all; it is leaving a visible, territorial signal, just like a wolf—the signal that, a million or more years ago, starting evolving in primates, continued evolving in hominids, and eventually became the art of René Magritte, and the visual signaling of all of the rest of us too.

8. The First Symbol

Scratches led to our oldest, most successful marking system, and people used it every day, all over the world, for at least 42,000 years. Writing, which was invented around 3000 BCE, must remain popular until 39,000 CE—the three hundred and ninety-first century—to prove equally useful.

The marking system was *tallying*, which was a way of notching bones, branches, and sometimes bodies to record financial transactions.

The British Empire reached its peak by documenting its debts with tallies and only tallies, using branches of hazel harvested from the banks of the River Thames, sawn into sticks about eight inches long, then incised with marks of varying widths to record the amount of money being borrowed. An incision as thick as the palm of a hand represented £1,000, an incision as thick as an earlobe, £20, and so on, down to pennies if necessary. Once incised, clerks working for royal officials called chamberlains split the stick along its length into two halves, each bearing the same incisions. The lender kept one half, called the stock, and the borrower kept the other, called the foil. Only one stock and foil could match, because of the incisions and also the grain of the wood, which made the system tamperproof.

For reasons that are not entirely clear, people used tallying in almost exactly the same way all over the world; either merchants and traders spread the technology, or people in many places invented it independently, or both. In 1271 the use of tallies in Yunnan, China, amazed Marco Polo, from Venice, Italy, because the Yunnanese used them "exactly as it is done with our tallies."

The British government used tally sticks until 1826, not long before the ascent of Queen Victoria, and accumulated so many that their eventual disposal by burning caused a fire that destroyed the Palace of Westminster, the home of the British Parliament.

Despite being so important so recently—depending on how old you are, your four or five times great-grandparents and all your ancestors before them probably used tally sticks—we have largely forgotten tallying, but its legacy surrounds us. We have stockholders and stock exchanges because the lender's half of the tally was called a stock, and the lender could sell it to another investor before the debtor repaid the debt it documented, for example.

Most importantly, tallies play a central and ongoing role in the story of stories. Tallying gave us the word *symbol*, which comes from the Ancient Greek for tally, *symbolon*. Aristotle introduced its current meaning in his text *De Interpretatione*, written around 330 BCE, by using the split tally as a metaphor for what we now call symbolism. In Aristotle's metaphor, one half of the tally represents an actual object; the other half represents the word or sign for it, and we cannot think of one without also thinking of the other.

9. Writing Without Language

Tallying evolved into signs: branding on livestock and slaves; hallmarks on jewelry; inscriptions on clay counters, seals, and tablets; and maker's marks on ceramics and jars. These were signs, not marks or pictures, because they pointed directly at unambiguous meanings. Such signs are sometimes called proto-writing, but the name is misleading: writing, unimaginable and far in the future, was never their purpose. Signs like these are languageless writing: *languageless* because they refer directly to things themselves without words as an intermediary, and *writing* because they conform to conventions that make them less ambiguous than marking, and more functional than drawing or painting.

Technologies of story, once established, never disappear. We still use languageless writing today: examples include the buttons on automobile dashboards, video game controllers, and other electronic devices; emoticons and emoji; the icons of computer interfaces, smartphones, and websites; insignia of rank and function; laundry instruction labels; logos; maps; mathematical notation; road and restroom signs; sheet music; and the tags of graffitists, among many others. This is another reason the term *proto-writing* is wrong. It cannot be *proto*-writing if it exists *after* writing too.

Writing language was never an intention or destination. Every improvement, every inching toward it, came from improvisation, from trying to fix something or make something incrementally better. Marking became writing by becoming one useful thing after another again and again.

Technology is evolutionary. Every step in a technology's development must be an end in itself, because every new tool must be useful to endure. Just as biological evolution has no use for half an organ, so technological evolution has no use for half a tool. Utility drives innovation: the more we use a thing, the more we improve it. Growing societies used languageless writing for administration, allocating rations, counting and accounting, identifying property, and making lists of assets, expenses, and people. Languageless writing became ever more useful—and therefore ever more used—as hunting and gathering became farming and agriculture, settlements became cities, tribes became civilizations, and our need for administration increased.

The progress of technology is a spectrum, not a staircase: a dynamic and endless metamorphosis, a fluid shifting of function and form with few sharp edges and no sudden changes, which is why the terms *proto-writing* and *writing* lose their definition if we look at them too closely: they are concepts, convenient but not concrete.

Use streamlines technology. The streamlining of languageless writing included the development of more efficient writing tools, simpler signs, and more signs to represent more things—some languageless writing systems had over fifteen hundred signs, for example. But languageless writing eventually met a barrier: We cannot represent quantities with pictures. There are many ways to draw a picture of a sheep or an ear of barley, but no obvious way to draw a picture of the number 102.

10. How to Draw Pictures of Numbers

In the shadow of an icy volcano called Mount Ararat, between the Black and Caspian Seas, a river of melting snow and rain flows first in tiny veins then widens, and splits, and merges, again and again while meandering west for more than four hundred miles. This river is called the Murat Su, and it is the largest of the five tributaries of the mighty Euphrates. A few hundred miles to the east, another mighty river, the Tigris, runs alongside the Euphrates like a mirror image, and they both course south into the Persian Gulf at the edge of the Arabian Sea.

Between the Euphrates and the Tigris there is a vast, lush plain, unique in an otherwise dry place. The plain drains water from a third of a million square miles of its surrounding land, and its shape and nature never stay the same. Sediments of silt, clay, and sand deposited on the plain by rivers and winds constantly reshape it; the ocean floods in and out over thousands of years, a tide but in geological time, changing the depth and salinity of the water; the occasional rumble of tectonic plates makes some of the land subside; and the rivers rise and fall and sometimes flood, varying with the rain and snow on Ararat and all peaks west.

The plain has had many names. Today it is part of what we call Iraq. In Syriac, a variant of Aramaic once spoken in the region, it was called Beth Nahrain, or "between rivers," the Greek translation of which became the plain's English name: Mesopotamia. The people who first lived there called it Kengir, the Country of the Noble Lords, and themselves the *Saĝ-gíg*, the Black Headed Ones. We call them Sumerians, and their land Sumer.

Until 4000 BCE much of the plain was beneath the sea, and the few people who lived on the rest were rainfall farmers—farmers who did not use irrigation to supplement occasional rain—and nomadic fishers, gatherers, hunters, and herders of sheep and goats.

Then the sea receded to reveal hundreds of square miles of fertile soil. Irrigation farmers settled in this new land, built large farms, and traded surplus food with each other and with the rainfall farmers, fishers, gatherers, herders, and hunters to create a busy local economy. Most of the irrigation farmers grew barley, taking advantage of recent mutations that strengthened stalks, made hulls easier to remove, and tripled the number of ears. Their other crops included apples, beans, cucumber, dates, emmer, figs, garlic, grapes, lentils, lettuce, onions, peas, pistachios, and wheat. Meat came from deer, ducks, gazelle, geese, and domesticated pigs; milk from goats and sheep, which also produced abundant wool; seafood from crab, fish, and turtles; and honey from hives watched by beekeepers. The plain thrived, and its settlements expanded.

By 3500 BCE, humanity's first cities had appeared beside the Euphrates and the Tigris: the cities of Eridu, Kish, Jemdet Nasr, Ur, and the greatest city among them, Uruk, which over the centuries grew to cover almost five hundred hectares—nearly two square miles. Thousands of years later, Jerusalem would only be one-fifth of Uruk's size, and Classical Athens would only be half as big. Uruk's population rose to forty thousand, with tens of thousands more living in its suburbs.

When Sumer was less populated, trade was simple. Transacting parties trusted each other, and they memorized their transactions or recorded them on tally sticks. But once Sumer's population grew beyond the boundaries of good faith and memory, its traders sought the security of documentation, regulation, and surveillance, and the shared benefits of public works such as flood prevention and large-scale irrigation. Sumer's cities arose to meet these needs, and their bureaucrats used languageless writing to document all the transactions.

The Sumerians wrote on one of the plain's most abundant materials: clay, which washed down from the mountains and into the tributaries as sediment. They mixed it with other materials, like straw and ground shards of broken pots, to harden it and make it waterproof, then molded it into a rectangular tablet around seven inches high and three and a half inches wide, barely bigger than a smartphone.

Sumer's scribes wrote on the clay while it was damp, using another locally abundant material, reeds. Initially, the Sumerians sharpened the reeds to a point and made strokes with sweeping curves, but around 3000 BCE they started cutting the reeds at an oblique angle, which created a stroke with a distinctive wedge shape. Then they adapted their signs to be made of connected wedges pressed into the clay. The shape made by these reeds eventually gave the writing its English name: *cuneiform*, from the Latin for "wedge shaped," or "wedge-writing."

When the writing was complete, the Sumerians left the tablets to dry in the sun or, for important documents, wrote "*a-na pi ša-ṭar ṣar-pa la-bi-ri-im*"—"according to the kiln-fired writing"—on them, then baked them so no one could alter them.

This languageless writing system could express many things, but it could not record quantities, and so could not replace tally sticks. The Sumerians set out to solve this problem so they could write everything in clay.

First, they used clay's plasticity to reinvent counting tokens, which people had used for thousands of years and were usually pebbles. The Sumerians' counting tokens had three-dimensional shapes. Some were geometric, like discs, spheres, rhombuses, and tetrahedra, that stood for different quantities and could combine to record large numbers; others were three-dimensional equivalents of written signs and represented actual things, such as animals.

Once the Sumerians could record a number using tokens, their next problem was keeping those tokens together. The Sumerians' first solution was to put the tokens in bags made of cloth or leather, but later they invented a more secure container: a hollow clay ball called a bulla in English, after the Latin for "bubble." A scribe would put the tokens in the bulla, then seal it by rolling an inch-long hardstone cylinder all over its surface. The cylinder was embossed with an image, often of people, which left an impression on the clay and made the ball tamper-proof.

After some time—we do not know how long—the Sumerians also started writing symbols on the outside of the balls to show how many tokens were inside. At least some of these symbols reflected the shapes of the three-dimensional tokens.

Then the Sumerians had a realization that was both a step and a leap: They could eliminate the ball and the tokens by simply writing the symbols representing quantity on a clay tablet. This was a step because the Sumerians' first signs for numbers were often pictures of the corresponding tokens, which were physical things; it was a leap because the tokens and therefore the signs represented numbers, which are abstractions. The Sumerians had found the solution to the problem of how to draw pictures of numbers, and it was simple: don't.

Discovering how to draw numbers by not drawing numbers carried the Sumerians across a cognitive boundary. If numbers did not have to be pictures of things, then *no* written signs had to be pictures of things; they could be mere shapes instead of illustrations.

Once the Sumerians started using writing for one system of abstractions, numbers, it was only a matter of time before they started using writing for another even more powerful system of abstractions: the sounds of their language.

Chapter 3

Pictures of Sounds

1. Writing

When a particle of chert, a type of sedimentary quartz formed from the skeletons of ancient sea creatures, breaks away from its parent rock beneath the surface of a river, a process of shape-shifting begins: the chert bounces and rolls downstream in a motion called saltation, abrading until, hundreds of miles later, it has transformed from a sharp, irregular stone into a smooth, spheroidal pebble that alters the river's bed, banks, composition, course, depth, direction, fauna, flora, flow, trajectory, and turbulence until it washes through an estuary into an ocean where it reshapes the floor of a sea and then a beach and therefore a coast. A pebble changes the world entire.

All change is the same: all things that change erode and compound with the currents of time and the saltation of use, undergoing gradual morphogeneses like globs in a lava lamp. There are laws of change just as there are laws of physics: all change has cascading consequences, many of which are unforeseen; all change is connected and therefore holistic; all change is continuous—there is no moment when one thing becomes another, no grain whose abrasion means a pebble is born, because a pebble is a concept we use to organize the world, distinguished only in our perception, a thought not a thing; all change is unending, at least on any timescale we can contemplate; and, most important and perhaps least obvious, all change is reciprocal. The river changes the pebble and the pebble changes the river.

The laws of change apply to technology as much as geology. We change our technology and our technology changes us.

Our story-shaped brains may crave neat beginnings—a call to adventure, a flash of inspiration, a moment of truth—but change does not work that way.

Languageless writing gradually led to something else: writing where symbols signaled sounds, not things, in order to record languages.

The difference was subtle at first. For example, the Sumerians excavated their clay from quarries, which was an activity important enough to warrant its own written sign:

When we rotate this character ninety degrees clockwise, we find a stylized image of a person breaking ground with a shovel, and can easily see how this was once a picture in a system of languageless writing, and is now in transition to something more abstract: a visual signal not of an idea but of a spoken word.

All four of the world's independently invented writing systems—Sumerian cuneiform, Egyptian hieroglyphs, Chinese characters (or Hanzi), and Maya script—started this way. The symbols of languageless writing became ever more abstract, simplifying over time, worn smooth by constant use, until they barely resembled the things they signaled, and became signs for words instead.

After that, it became natural to think of the symbols as signaling not only words but also the *sounds* of those words.

A typical language has tens of thousands of words, but only thirty or so sounds, which is why every language reuses the same sounds to make different words, as with Magritte's pipe.

In Sumerian, the sound "shar" signals the noun *garden* and the verbs *write*, *run*, and *chase away*. The written symbol for *garden* is, of course, a picture of a garden, rotated ninety degrees, like all Sumerian writing:

When this symbol came to mean not only the spoken word for *garden* but also the sound of that word, it could signal *write*, *run*, and *chase away* too.

Most sounds in Sumerian are also words: For example, the sound "si" is the word for "horn," and the sound "in" is the word for "straw." Many Sumerian words use more than one sound, of course. The Sumerian word for "toward" is *sin*, pronounced "si in." It was easy for the Sumerians to figure out how to write *sin*: they just wrote the symbols for "horn" (*si*) and "straw" (*in*) next to each other.

Broadly speaking, the four independently invented written languages—Sumerian (written in cuneiform), Old Egyptian (written in hieroglyphs), Old Chinese (written in Hanzi), and Classic Ch'olti' (written in Maya script)—all had many single-sound words that could be combined like this. This was no coincidence: There is an evolutionary pathway from languageless writing to writing a language in which every sound is also a word, just as there is an evolutionary pathway from a piece of chert to a pebble.

2. Enheduanna

Writing was not a storytelling tool at first. For many centuries, it was used for little more than the ancient equivalent of receipts: recording how many slaves, head of livestock, and other assorted property people owned or owed.

And then, in 2285 BCE, in a three-hundred-year-old temple in the city of Ur on the coast of the Persian Gulf, a woman named Enheduanna changed the world by using writing to tell a story. Here is part of it:

> You drew me toward my holy quarters,
> I, the High Priestess,
> I, Enheduanna.
> There I raised the ritual basket,
> There I sang the shout of joy,
> But that man cast me among the dead.
> I am not allowed in my rooms.
> Gloom falls on the day, light turns leaden, shadows close in,
> The dreaded southern storm cloaks the sun.

Writing was six hundred years old—as old as the printing press is today—when Enheduanna wrote these words. Enheduanna is humanity's first author, and therefore the source of every story ever written, including this one.

Few storytelling technologies were invented to tell stories—motion pictures, for example, were developed to analyze how animals and humans move; televisions were derived from "indicator tubes" for measuring and understanding the behavior of electrons; and the first computers broke secret codes, calculated missile trajectories, and tabulated census data—but in every case, storytelling eventually became their principal application.

We do not know why Enheduanna, high priestess of the moon god Nanna, wrote her story instead of speaking it, but we do know the consequences. The most obvious is that Enheduanna made her story permanent: Writing is how we know who she is and what she did, forty-five hundred years later.

But another consequence was far more important during Enheduanna's lifetime: Writing increased Enheduanna's audience by several orders of magnitude. A spoken story can typically reach no more than ten people at a time, but because writing was centuries old and essential for commerce, many of Ur's twenty thousand residents could read. Enheduanna reached an audience of thousands rather than tens by writing instead of speaking.

While many people in Ur could read, few could write, so Enheduanna had a near monopoly on written stories. When a relatively small number of storytellers can reach a relatively large audience, their stories can be told unchallenged, and unchallengeable stories are almost always self-serving.

For example, Enheduanna's story may seem like a spiritual, lyrical poem, but it is, in fact, far more than that. Enheduanna is describing actual events. As part of a regional power struggle, Lugal-Ane, the King of Ur—"that man"—banished Enheduanna from the temple and exiled her to the steppes west of the city, where lepers—"the dead"—were also sent. By recounting these events in writing, Enheduanna ensured that thousands of literate citizens in Ur and its neighboring cities saw the struggle from her perspective—a point of view that cast Enheduanna as a hero and Lugal-Ane as a villain.

Was Lugal-Ane a villain? We do not know, and more importantly, neither did most of Ur's population. Lugal-Ane spoke his version of the story rather than writing it, and so had a much smaller audience than Enheduanna. What we *do* know is that Lugal-Ane was deposed and Enheduanna was reinstated. There is no way to determine how much Enheduanna's writing influenced this outcome, but one thing is certain: The first written story was not only poetry; it was also propaganda.

This should not be a surprise: When we rise above the timescales of generations or centuries and examine the whole pattern of our existence, we see that the oscillation between the concentration and distribution of the power of storytelling has been shaping humanity for its entirety. Our history comprises periods of relative stability when a new storytelling technology concentrates the power of story and enables an elite few to create the appearance of homogenous thinking, followed by spasms of upheaval when that same storytelling technology becomes cheap enough to distribute dissent.

No story is neutral. No story is objective. Every story is a machine to change your mind.

3. Deep in the Turquoise Mine

Picture a man named Professor Flinders Petrie, a British archaeologist in his mid-fifties, striding through Egypt in 1905, looking for buried treasure. The man you are imagining is likely the man himself: self-serious; severe; a wearer of frock coats and other formal attire even in the desert; and, by then, white-bearded—the archetypical gentleman explorer who inspired a main character in perhaps every mummy movie ever made.

The professor's wife is about to make a confusing discovery: Deep in a turquoise mine on the Sinai Peninsula, fifty miles northwest of Mount Sinai, Hilda Petrie, a geologist, turns over a broken rock and finds an inscription, thousands of years old, that looks nothing like cuneiform or hieroglyphs.

Flinders turns over a fallen block and finds more of the strange characters. He sees four larger blocks that are too heavy for one person to lift and calls for some of his workers to come and help him.

The discovery exemplifies a dilemma European intellectuals faced throughout the nineteenth and twentieth centuries. Flinders Petrie is a racist, convinced of the genetic superiority of white people like himself. This may seem like a contradiction, given his interest in Egypt, which has one foot in Africa and another in Asia, but it is not; many of Petrie's European archaeologist peers are also white supremacists. Their passion for these places is patronizing: the story they tell themselves—and the world—is that, yes, there were fascinating ancient civilizations outside of Europe long ago, but they were primitive, prototypical, and prone to superstition, which is why they collapsed and disappeared. The civilizations that endured were the *European* civilizations of Greece and Rome, which gave the world art, logic, philosophy, poetry, prose, reason, straight roads, and viaducts, among many other wonders. The name Europeans gave to these two cultures exemplifies this hierarchical thinking: They are called *classical*, from the Latin for "belonging to a class," a term that was introduced in the late 1700s and became ever more common during the nineteenth and twentieth centuries.

But in the early 1900s, Europe is having an identity crisis. European intellectuals have long assumed that Europeans are a superior people who created and invented the modern world. Discoveries made during the last hundred years now threaten the foundations of that assumption. For example, Napoleon's army invaded Egypt in 1798 and discovered the Rosetta Stone, which enabled hieroglyphs to be deciphered, proving they were writing; and then, in the 1850s, archaeologists discovered a previously unknown Asian people called the Sumerians who invented writing long before the Egyptians.

Both these writing systems challenge Europe's presumed cultural superiority, but there is an easy response: to claim that only the Europeans' alphabet is *real* writing, because it is simple, elegant, and far superior to these predecessors, which are clumsy, complicated, and heavy with characters and signs.

In the lamplit turquoise mine, Petrie's workers turn the blocks over one by one, like cards in a hand, revealing new inscriptions each time. Flinders and Hilda exchange a long look. They have already guessed what they are looking at: an alphabet far older than the Greeks'.

The Petries have discovered that Asians, not Europeans, invented the alphabet, and that Europe is therefore not merely the last continent to get a writing system; the Europeans were also the only people not to invent one.

4. Water in the Air

Our story-shaped brains, which assume almost everything important results from human behavior, often lead us to think that successes in one part of the world—especially if it is *our* part of the world—and failures in another—especially if it is *not* our part of the world—must be because of some self-serving but vague tribal attribute, such as culture, genes, or work ethic.

This assumption made European intellectuals defensive about the Asian invention of the alphabet. And they were *very* defensive: Until at least the 1980s, European scholars were making a last stand by claiming that the Greek alphabet was the only "true" alphabet because the Greeks had added seven extra letters for vowels.

But Europe's failure to invent writing has nothing to do with human behavior. Culture is a weak explanation for anything, because human nature is universal. When people do something in one place and not another, the place is far more likely to be the cause than the people. The invention of writing exemplifies this. In each of the places where pictures became writing, the process was entirely a consequence of geography.

The Sumerians did not develop writing first because of some innate superiority, just as the Europeans did not *fail* to develop writing because of some innate *inferiority*. Sumer in 3000 BCE was the place and time of a unique coincidence of technology and geography; at the dawn of agriculture, after tens of thousands of years of increasingly sophisticated human marking, a fertile wetland bordered by two large rivers emerged from an ocean.

The fertility of the wetland led to mass agricultural settlement, which led to surplus food, which led to complex trading arrangements, which led to a need for complex accounting systems, which led to the saltation of use, which led to the continuous improvement of preexisting marking systems. The Sumerians could continuously improve their marking systems only because their two rivers, fed by tributaries that originated in the mountains hundreds of miles to the north, brought them clay that was plastic enough to be used as a writing surface, and reeds they could use as styluses. The need for writing was driven by economics, and Sumerians could meet the need for writing *because of* economics. Writing was cheap and plentiful in Sumer, which meant it could be constant, voluminous, and, when necessary, experimental.

We know writing was cheap because we have found thousands of ancient Sumerian tablets, and few of the oldest ones are from temples, tombs, or other sacred places. Most of the tablets modern scholars use to decipher cuneiform were found in layers of trash piled up to support the floors of new buildings. These first artifacts of writing, so precious today, are the Sumerian equivalent of wastepaper. Sumerians considered documents to be consumable, disposable, and practically cost-free. Writing emerged first in Sumer because of the abundance of food and clay.

But the heart of the matter is how the Sumerian language *sounds*.

Written language evolved from pictures of things to pictures of words to pictures of syllables. But pictures of syllables are only possible in languages where most syllables are also a word, and those languages tend to be ones where most syllables are a consonant followed by a vowel.

In Chinese, for example, syllables are almost always a consonant followed by a vowel, or sometimes a vowel finished with a nasal consonant, a sound like the "ng" in *Beijing*. Chinese seldom uses consonant clusters—a series of consonants one after the other. Sounds like the "br" in *bread*, the "lf" in *gulf*, or the "lm" in *film* rarely appear in Chinese.

The same is broadly true of the Mayan language Classic Ch'olti', where no words start with a vowel and most are a consonant followed by a vowel, and Sumerian, where some words start with a vowel, but there are no clustered consonants. Old Egyptian is a slight exception; it typically alternates vowels and consonants, but sometimes allows two—but only two—consonants together.

Languages that follow this pattern have a problem to solve: After infancy, humans can only make and distinguish between a few vocal sounds. English, for example, has about twenty-four consonants—sounds that involve closing the airway with the tongue or jaw—and about twenty vowels—sounds made with an open mouth. English could make fewer than five hundred single-syllable words if it only used syllables comprising one of those consonants followed by one of those vowels. But it can make over three hundred thousand single-syllable words because it also uses clusters of many consonants and consonants after vowels.

Chinese does not need consonant clusters because it adds one of four tones to each vowel instead. For example, in Chinese, the consonant "m" and the vowel "a" can make four words: *mā* with a level tone means "mom," *má* with a rising tone means "hemp," *mǎ* with a dipping tone means "horse," and *mà* with a departing tone, where the pitch falls, means "scold."

All four of the first written languages use tones somewhat similarly. But even with modifications like tones, there are only so many syllables you can make with consonant plus a vowel, and so, in languages that manipulate vowels instead of using consonant clusters, almost every syllable is likely to also be a word. This incidental feature of tone languages has an unexpected consequence: As soon as all the one-syllable words can be written, all the multisyllable words can be written too, by grouping one-syllable words together.

Why do each of these languages use tones?

Because Sumer, Egypt, China, and Mesoamerica are all at subtropical latitudes, which means they all are, or were, places with high humidity.

And with very few exceptions, indigenous tone languages are only spoken in humid places: mainly the great swath of tropical and subtropical land that stretches from southern Asia, through central Africa, to Mesoamerica and South America.

Humidity is essential when speaking a tone language. Inhaling dry air reduces the amount of mucus on our vocal cords, which alters the way they vibrate and makes our vowels *jitter* (wobble in pitch), *shimmer* (wobble in amplitude), and become noisier and less harmonic. These effects can be heard and measured almost immediately after we breathe dry air. As a result, it is easier to control vowels in humid climates than it is in dry climates.

Europe has a dry climate. It is harder to make vowel sounds using tones in Europe, which is why European languages rely on consonant clusters that cannot easily be used as standalone words. For example, in English, the word *string* starts with a consonant cluster signified by *s*, *t*, and *r*. Changing those initial consonants makes new and completely unrelated words—*bring, fling, ring, sing, thing, wing*, and so on—but breaking out those consonant clusters into, for example, the sounds "str," "br," and "fl" makes no words at all.

And because "str," "br," and "fl" are sounds but not words, there is no way to draw pictures of them, which means there is no way to get from pictures of things to pictures of syllables, which means there is no way to get from languageless writing to writing a language.

In short, Europe's failure to invent writing had nothing to do with culture, and everything to do with climate. The air was too dry.

5. The Ox and House

We do not have to wonder whether Europeans could have found a way to get from pictures of things to pictures of syllables: They tried. In 1400 BCE the Greeks adapted picture-based writing from another language, Minoan, and used it almost entirely for accounting. Few Greeks could read it, and even fewer could write it. Then around 1100 BCE, for reasons that are still not well understood, Greek civilization collapsed, and the Greeks did not write again for hundreds of years.

But while Greece slumbered in its dark ages, the Canaanites, a seafaring people living in independent city-states in what is now Lebanon and parts of Israel, Palestine, and Syria, solved the problem of how to write languages laden with clusters of consonants.

We can guess how it happened. Canaanites traded with, worked for, and were sometimes enslaved by Egyptians. Some Canaanites learned to read and write Hieratic, a simplified form of Egyptian hieroglyphics developed for writing on papyrus, a writing surface made from a plant that grows in the shallows of the Nile, with reeds dipped in ink. Hieratic was a flowing script that could be written quickly by joining some characters together—a style now known as *cursive*, after the Latin *currĕre*, "to run." Sometime around 1800 BCE, or possibly a few centuries earlier, one or more of these Canaanites adapted Hieratic so that they could use it to write their own language too.

The adaptation was ingenious. The Canaanites selected hieroglyphs of things whose names start with the sounds of the Canaanite language and used the hieroglyphs to represent those sounds. For example, the Canaanites' word for ox was *aleph*, so they used the hieroglyph for *ox*, which looked like an ox's head, to represent an "a" sound. Their word for house was *beth*, so they used the hieroglyph for *house*, which looked like the plan of a house, for the sound "b," and so on. If you were Canaanite, and could identify what thing a character represented, you would also know what sound that character represented, and could read.

Using characters to represent sounds instead of syllables made the writing system very efficient, especially for consonant-laden languages where most syllables are not also words. For example, every native English speaker knows around twenty to thirty-five thousand words, created from around three thousand syllables. A writing system for English that used one character for each syllable would therefore need about three thousand distinct characters. But those three thousand syllables are composed of only thirty-five to forty-four distinct sounds, depending on what definition of *sound* you use. And so, if you write sounds, not syllables, you can represent an entire language in very few characters. This is what the Canaanites did, and it gave them a complete writing system using just thirty-two characters.

The first two of those characters, *aleph* and *beth*, the signs for "ox" and "house," gave the Canaanites' writing system its English name, *alphabet*.

Some pictures the Canaanites chose are still discernible today, thirty-five hundred years later, in the Latin alphabet used by 143 nations. For example, if you turn a capital *A* upside down, you can see the head of the ox, horns and all; a capital *B* is the plan of a two-room house; the letter *c* is a boomerang, *gimel*; *l* is from *lāmed*, a shepherd's crook; *m* comes from *mēm*, water, and is the shape of two waves; and *o* is an eye, *'ayin*, now without the pupil of its original Egyptian hieroglyph. These vestigial pictures exemplify how our tools improve by evolution more than invention.

Alphabets were easy to understand, easy to learn, and easy to adapt. Even the letters were simple: the Hieratic script had been developing for seventeen hundred years—meaning it was as old as the official Roman Catholic Church is today—and the saltation of use had made its characters clean and clear. In addition, writing surfaces and tools were now light, portable, and widely available. The Egyptians had been manufacturing papyrus from plants for two thousand years, and pens from reeds and ink from iron for one thousand years, and Egyptian merchants were delighted to export those products to Egypt's neighbors. Alphabetic writing was cheap, mobile, and flexible, moving from place to place and language to language without obstacles or friction.

The alphabet spread like ink spilled on a map east from Egypt, along the Mediterranean coast, becoming the Phoenician alphabet, the Old Hebrew alphabet, the Samaritan alphabet, the Aramaic alphabet, and the South Arabian alphabet. Then, perhaps around 600 BCE, it traveled north and west across the Mediterranean to Cyprus, Crete, Kos, Rhodes, Ionia, and eventually Athens, five centuries after the Greeks abandoned writing and twelve centuries after the alphabet was invented.

The effect of the alphabet's gradual diffusion into Greece was, more or less, a unique alphabet for every island, dialect, and region, all somewhat the same but not quite, some using different characters for the same sound, some using the same characters for different sounds, some writing the same characters differently, and all with their own spellings. There was an Arcadian alphabet, a Boeotian alphabet, a Corinthian alphabet, an Ithacan alphabet, a Laconian alphabet, and enough others to make twenty-three alphabets in all. There were almost as many alphabets in Greece as there were characters in Greece's alphabets.

This was both good and bad. It was good because Greece was finally writing—the plasticity of alphabets providing at last a writing system suitable for the consonant clusters of European languages—and bad because there was little agreement between the alphabets, and the lack of agreement could only get worse over time, as local changes accumulated. Written Greek was in danger of fragmenting into many mutually incomprehensible forms.

And so in 403 BCE, Eucleides, the ruler of Athens, issued a proclamation. Eucleides decreed that the Ionian alphabet, from the city-states and islands of Ionia to the south and southeast of Athens, would from that moment on replace the Athenians' own alphabet and become the official alphabet of Athens. The decree was an act of standardization much like—and at least as important as—the color television standards of 1953 or the internet becoming publicly available in 1995.

Successful standardization is both a beginning and the end of a beginning. The beginning standardization ends is the inevitable period of disarray when a new technology is a novelty, and used so little and so unseriously that consistency, compatibility, and interoperability matter little. It is a miracle that the technology works at all, and no one cares each producer has their own recipe. Early cars had a variety of driver controls, for example, including boat-like tillers to steer and train-like levers to accelerate. The universal control layout we use today, with a wheel for steering and foot pedals for accelerating, braking, and operating the clutch, only became standard after many years of driving in other ways.

What standardization *begins* is a new era of widespread use, and rapid saltation that improves the technology.

The development of writing in Greece followed this pattern. For the first few centuries after the alphabet arrived, few people could read or write, and there was little to read, so the differences in alphabets did not matter much. Writing was local or personal and often pretend. Four out of every five Greek vases from the 400s BCE that depict writing show nonsense, not actual words. Writing was aspirational, intriguing, and mysterious, but almost no one in Greece could actually do it.

Around 450 BCE, a hundred and fifty years after writing arrived on their islands, the Greeks started writing stories. Their first written stories were transcriptions of the old oral epics *Iliad* and *Odyssey*, both attributed to Homer—who may or may not have been a real person and, if he or she was, almost certainly did not author both works—and perhaps the plays of Sophocles, Aeschylus, and, later, Aristophanes. This transition from short-form writing to long-form writing was the tipping point that made the standardization of Greek writing essential.

The decree of Eucleides marked the end of this beginning. Writing had arrived in Europe at last.

6. George

William Gladstone, the Prime Minister of the United Kingdom, the First Lord of the Treasury, the Chancellor of the Exchequer, and the son of Britain's wealthiest slave owner, concludes a four-hour cabinet meeting, hurries to his private carriage, and travels west as fast as two horses and London's traffic will allow, through the gaslit black of the December evening, up Whitehall, around Trafalgar Square and Piccadilly Circus, and northwest along Regent Street to the headquarters of the Society of Biblical Archaeology in Mayfair.

William is rushing to an unlikely lecture being given by an unlikely lecturer. George Smith was born and raised in the squalor of the tenements and terraces of nineteenth-century Chelsea, and left school at fourteen to become a printer's apprentice. In the great hierarchy of Great Britain, George's parents are of such low status that even now there is no record of their names or occupations.

Socially, George cannot be much farther from William, who has worldwide influence, wealth, and a weekly meeting with Queen Victoria.

But this evening—December 3, 1872—George cannot be much *nearer* to William: the Prime Minister has a reserved seat in the center of the front bench, and George, alone but for his notes, will stand about three feet away, with only a lectern between them. Peer-level proximity between two men of such distant classes was unthinkable a few years ago, but the British mind is changing, and George is about to become a principal agent of that change.

In 1872 British aristocrats, along with much of the rest of the world, believe that the Bible is historically accurate and so have inferred that the earth is about five thousand years old, and that God created the different abilities and tendencies they associate with different classes, races, and genders. God made men superior to women, white people superior to people of color, and aristocrats superior to the working mass. The hierarchy that puts rich white English men above everyone else is not self-serving; it is the natural order of things.

George has discovered something from the ruins of a library in a palace in a city on the eastern bank of the Tigris River named Nineveh. In the seventh century BCE, Nineveh was the largest city in the world and ruled by Ashurbanipal, a genocidist and the last true king of the

Assyrian Empire. Despite his brutality, he loved writing, and because he loved writing, he wrote what may be the first autobiography, which is how we know about his atrocities. Here, for example, is Ashurbanipal's own description of his destruction of a country named Elam, which was about the size of Massachusetts:

> With the support of the gods, I entered the land of Elam, and brought about the Elamites' defeat. I conquered fourteen fortified cities, twenty villages, and an untold number of royal residences and smaller settlements. I annihilated the people living in them, and devastated an area of sixty leagues.

Sixty Assyrian leagues is approximately 120 miles, and Elam was approximately 360 miles wide, so in this passage alone, Ashurbanipal is describing "devastating" a third of a nation and "annihilating" tens of thousands of its people.

Ashurbanipal's love of writing was also a love of reading: he built the world's first great library by collecting and curating over a hundred thousand cuneiform tablets, many of which he took forcibly from Nineveh's neighbors.

After Ashurbanipal died in 631 BCE, the Assyrian Empire collapsed. Nineveh was sacked twice: first in 614 BCE by the Medes, a people from Iran, then again in 612 BCE by the Babylonians. Because of these attacks, Ashurbanipal's library was destroyed, forgotten, and lost.

Which brings us back to George awaiting William a hundred generations later.

In 1851 an Iraqi archaeologist named Hormuzd Rassam and his British colleague Henry Layard found Ashurbanipal's lost library while excavating in Iraq. Some of the library's tablets were intact, but most had shattered into fragments. Rassam and Layard shipped everything they could to the British Museum in London: around a hundred thousand items in all.

The discovery fascinated George. In 1860 he started spending his lunch hours looking at the tablets, and a few years later gave up his promising printing career to become a menial employee of the British Museum, hired to sort through a jumble of undeciphered cuneiform fragments from Ashurbanipal's library.

The job was incredibly difficult; George was too junior to be allowed a gas lamp, and had to work by natural light, which was impossible on London's many foggy and rainy days; the tens of thousands of fragments were often so dirty that only a few characters were legible, but so delicate only one specialist contractor could clean them; and they were, of course, all written in Assyrian and Sumerian cuneiform. A new form of amusement called the jigsaw puzzle was becoming popular in Britain at that time, and behind the scenes at the British Museum, George was trying to solve the hardest jigsaw puzzle imaginable: thousands of pieces, some missing, many illegible, from thousands of unknown texts, written in a strange and ancient language, which he could only examine in whatever quality of daylight was coming through the window, and he could only get cleaned when the sole authorized restorer was available.

Yet George did it. In the words of a colleague, "He acquired gradually, by long practice, a very remarkable skill in the execution of the task."

And while solving the puzzle, George discovered something amazing, which is why William, along with many other distinguished members of London's great and good, are assembling before him this evening. They are all expecting George to present powerful new evidence that the Bible is historically accurate and literally true.

But that is not what is about to happen.

7. Songs of God

It is no coincidence that Bible scholars once believed the world was about as old as writing. The world's great religions are all rooted in the times and places where long-form writing first became possible. The Torah was written around 600 BCE, when people from the Kingdom of Judah were held captive in Mesopotamia. Cuneiform had evolved into several more efficient scripts by then, and one of these scripts, probably Imperial Aramaic, was used to write the first Torah. The Bible was first written in Greek around 350 CE using uncial, a new, all-caps writing style invented for a new writing surface called parchment, which was made from animal skin. And the Qur'an was first written around 634 CE, at almost exactly the moment Arabic writing became an alphabetic script.

The impact of writing on the Indian religions of Hinduism and Buddhism is especially instructive. Writing first appeared in India around 350 BCE, and became practical for long-form documents at the turn of the first millennium. The most authoritative Hindu texts were more than a thousand years old when writing them down first became possible. Until then, Hindus preserved them from generation to generation by a strict tradition of oral transmission that kept not just the words but also the sounds of the words, like an ancient system of high-fidelity human audio recording. Buddhist texts were about four hundred years old, and Buddhism, likely inspired by Hinduism, also used a formal system of oral transmission to preserve religious teachings.

Both religions had therefore made centuries-long investments in detailed oral transmission at the time writing became an option. In Hinduism, one result of that investment was a large and privileged class of specialists called Brahmins who devoted their lives to remembering and teaching others to remember their religion's scared lessons. Writing was a threat to the Brahmins and their way of lives: a competitive force, a disruptive technology, a new way of doing things that imperiled their importance and sense of identity, and they resisted it by forbidding writing, more or less. The Brahmins said Hinduism's most sacred texts could never be written. They allowed the writing of some newer texts, such as the *Bhagavad Gītā* , or the "Song of God," from the Sanskrit epic *Mahabharata*, but made it clear that these texts were of secondary importance. The written texts were called *smriti*—"things that are remembered"—and were attributed to human authors and given less authority. The older, orally transmitted texts were called *shruti*—"things that are heard"—and were the words of the gods, given preeminent authority in Hindu teachings. This act of protectionism and prohibition lasted for a thousand years, and the *shruti* were not written down until around 1000 CE.

Buddhism, in contrast, adopted writing immediately, despite centuries of oral transmission. Buddhism has two main branches: Theravada Buddhism and Mahāyāna Buddhism. Theravada's fundamental text is a collection of teachings known as the Pāli Canon; Mahāyāna Buddhism has additional texts, called the Mahāyāna sutras. All these texts were written down almost as soon as writing them down became possible, probably sometime between 100 BCE and 100 CE.

This thousand-year difference in writing sacred texts had significant consequences: Buddhism, with its portable written texts, spread out of India toward China, mainly along the Silk Road trade routes, and became an international religion; Hinduism, restricted to oral transmission via its Brahmins, did not.

To corroborate the role of writing in religion, we need only look at the three other written religions. Judaism spread when Jews dispersed around the world, taking their written teachings with them, and Judaism influenced Christianity and Islam, both of which spread internationally too: Christianity around the Mediterranean, into the Roman Empire, and then Northern Europe; Islam in North Africa, Western Asia, and Southern Europe. Only Hinduism, the one unwritten major religion, stayed home in India.

This distribution of religions, established by new writing technology in the first few centuries of the first millennium, persists two thousand years later. Christianity is the dominant religion in Europe and its former colonies; Islam is the dominant religion in North Africa and

Western Asia; Buddhism is the dominant religion in Sri Lanka, Mongolia, Thailand, Myanmar, and Laos; and Hinduism is the dominant religion only in India and neighboring Nepal. India is a vast nation, of course, and 1.2 billion people practice Hinduism today, but Hinduism's late adoption of writing prevented it from spreading internationally when other religions were traveling far beyond their original borders.

The evidence of the importance of writing to the world's major religions hides in plain sight: religious writing venerates writing. Among many other examples, the Hebrew Bible says, "Write all the words that I have spoken to you in a book," "The writing was God's writing," and "Oh that my words were written! Oh that they were inscribed in a book!"; the Christian Bible contains all these and also "Write in a book what you see"; the Qur'an says, "By the pen and that which they write" and "We shall roll up the skies as written scrolls are rolled up"; and the Buddhist sutras say, "This perfection of wisdom has been written down in a book" and "The spot of earth where this discourse is written down is like a shrine for the world together with its gods."

Religions may appear to change minds with *spoken* words—gurus, imams, lamas, ministers, monks, pastors, priests, rabbis, and other teachers speaking directly to small groups—but religion's oral teaching is entirely informed by, centered on, and a consequence of *written* stories—stories from, for example, the Bible, whose name means "book"; the Ketuvim, from the classical Hebrew for "writings"; the Pentateuch, in Greek, "five scrolls"; the Qur'an, named from the Arabic verb *qar'a*, "to read"; or scripture, a word that means "writings."

This celebration of long-form writing when long-form writing was new should not surprise us. The power of writing in a world that had never seen writing before was part of the power that diffused written religions. For hundreds of years the Torah, the Bible, the sutras, or the Qur'an would have been the first and only long-form writing most people who saw it had ever seen.

When we look with wonder at the latest new storytelling technology, we are likely experiencing the same emotions our first-millennium ancestors felt when they saw their first book: All those smooth, supple surfaces, covered in a flowing script written in liquid ink that, by some mystery, encoded a hundred thousand spoken words or more, would have seemed like a miracle, a thing of unimaginable magic. Writing makes words immortal. Of course it seemed like something that could only be delivered by God.

8. The Deluge

George, so nervous he is sweating in December, drinks a little water, clears his throat, and, as soon as William is seated, makes ready to begin.

It is a time of great conflict among British intellectuals. Traditional thinkers believe the Bible is so literal and historically accurate that the date of the earth's creation can be calculated by analyzing the book of Genesis. One such analysis claims that God made the world at noon on October 23, 4004 BCE, for example, while others calculate that the world began in 3992 or 2761 BCE.

But there is a new idea sowing doubts about the historicity of the Bible and therefore the God-granted superiority of the British aristocracy. Two of its proponents are Charles Lyell, who argues that the earth developed slowly and continuously, and Charles Darwin, who extends Lyell's work to include all living things. According to Lyell and Darwin, the world is many millions of years old; it was shaped by natural processes, not humans or humanish agents; and its human inhabitants are incidental, not central.

The British Museum has been advertising George's lecture as the announcement of a new discovery about one of the most consequential examples of divine, human-centered action: God's destruction of the world entire in a flood, and His salvation of a six-hundred-year-old man named Noah, who, at God's command, built a ship for himself, his family, and mating pairs of every kind of animal. The story, which appears in the holy books of Judaism, Christianity, and Islam, is told early in the book of Genesis, the first book of the Bible, and is the foundation for all that follows it. If George can prove that the story of Noah is literally true, then Lyell and Darwin's demons, so indifferent to the centrality of humanity and so insufficient for sustaining the British Empire's hierarchy of class, gender, and race, can be slain once and for all.

George starts by telling his audience how he discovered a broken tablet describing "a ship that rested on a mountain, the sending forth of a dove, and its finding no resting place and returning"; details his search through thousands of tablet fragments for the rest of the text; then says he has assembled nearly all of the story, which he will now "publish to the world."

This is the story George found:

In the time before humans, the gods were as man. The mother goddess Mami created humans out of clay, and for almost twelve hundred years, all was well with the world. But then the humans multiplied so much that the land was bellowing like a bull. The noise disturbed the god Enlil, so he created a great deluge to wash the humans away. Another god, Enki, warned a man named Utnapishtim about the coming flood, and told him to build a great boat, with walls each ten times twelve cubits in height. Utnapishtim loaded the boat with all the beasts and animals, and he and his wife launched it as soon as the storm started, while the land shattered like a pot. The storm lasted for six days and seven nights, and on the seventh day, all became calm. The boat came to rest on a mountain named Mount Nisir, and Utnapishtim sent a dove to find land. When Enlil discovered what Utnapishtim had done, he allowed humanity to survive, and made Utnapishtim and his wife immortal.

The members of the Society of Biblical Archaeology are bewildered. This both is and is not the story of Noah. Their applause is more stoic than enthusiastic, and soon fades away. Then the Prime Minister rises to speak. How will William respond to George's shocking news?

By changing the subject. He says:

Every effort to examine the questions raised here today must begin with Homer, the friend of my youth, middle age, and old age, from whom I hope never to be parted as long as I have any breath in my body. The Homeric Poems are, in my opinion, a natural point of connection with all prior studies, and the agency of the people known to us as the Phoenicians connects Greece itself with the Assyrian plain that yielded the record under discussion. All the slowly accumulating knowledge of the East, instead of tending to unsettle my faith in the sacred documents, tends greatly to confirm it.

Or, George's discovery is only interesting because it might help illuminate events that took place in Europe one thousand miles and several thousand years away, and it poses no threat to the idea that the Bible is a literal, historic document.

Other attendees disagree. One says George's discovery "establishes the existence of historic germs in the Bible, but also shows the traditions of the Hebrews are on a par with the traditions of other races of the same regions, not different from them; in other words, these new traditions take up a decidedly threatening, not confirmatory, attitude towards the orthodox theory of verbal inspiration"; and another concludes that Ashurbanipal's library must be "the place where Noah's story, and that of the Creation, and the building of Babel, and all the other great legends of the Bible, find their fountain text."

The world pivots. William's "faith in sacred documents" becomes the past, and "the great legends of the Bible" becomes the future. Before George's lecture, the *Encyclopaedia Britannica*, a great bellwether of British consensus, then a hundred years old, described Noah's ship, or "Ark," as a historical certainty, and in extraordinary detail:

> The dimensions of the Ark, as given by Moses, are 200 cubits in length, 50 in breadth, and 30 in height, which some have thought too scanty, considering the number of things it was to contain, but Buteo and Kircher have proved geometrically the ark was abundantly sufficient for all the animals supposed to be lodged in it. The number of species of animals is much less than is generally imagined, not amounting to a hundred species of quadrupeds, nor to two hundred of birds. Bishop Wilkins computes all the carnivorous animals equivalent to twenty-seven wolves, and all the rest to two hundred and eighty cows. To feed the former he allows 1,825 sheep, and for the latter, 109,500 cubits of hay, all which is easily contained with a great deal of room to spare.

After George's lecture, the *Encyclopaedia*'s view changes completely. The ninth edition, published in 1875, says:

> It is best to regard the story of the deluge as a subdivision of primitive man's explanations of creation. The deluge is practically a second creation. We, in the adult age of the world, have renounced those mythical forms of expression. The various deluge stories must be viewed in combination, and explained on a common principle. Seniority belongs to the Babylonian deluge discovered by Mr. George Smith. It came from the library of King Ashurbanipal, and dates from about 660 BCE, but may well have been composed between 1000 and 2000 BCE, while the myth itself will of course be much older.

In a single evening, George has undone the geometry of Buteo and Kircher, the computations of Bishop Wilkins, and the work of the hundreds of other pastors and scholars who have collectively calculated the reality of the Ark down to its last bale of hay.

But consensus is not conclusion. The proportion of people who believe in the literal truth of Noah, and therefore the historicity of the Bible, is reduced, but not to zero, and the debate about Noah continues to this day. Some believe the story is a myth, passed down through generations and around among cultures. Others are convinced that so many similar stories are undeniable proof of veracity—that the tale of the flood is a collective memory carried by the many cultures of our species—and that its divine nature is merely underlined whenever its problems can only be solved by miracles.

The argument will never end, in part because of a concern about writing almost as old as the tablet George discovered.

9. Aristocles

It is 403 BCE, the year Athens standardized its alphabet. Aristocles, a broad-bodied wrestler in his mid-twenties, walks across the city on a bright blue morning, between the fifty-foot-high columns of the Temple of Olympian Zeus, still under construction after centuries of building, goes through a minor gate in the city's wall onto a dirt path dappled with a calico of sun and dust, passes the Cynosarges gymnasium, alive with the sounds of philosophers teaching, and heads toward a short wooden bridge over the River Ilisos, which, despite being called a river, is little more than a cold, gentle stream that flows past the southern boundary of Athens to the Bay of Phalerum on the Aegean Sea.

Aristocles sees a friend on the bridge: a sixty-something philosopher named Socrates, also taking a walk beyond the city wall. Aristocles catches up to Socrates, and together they walk barefoot through the cooling shallows of the Ilisos to a grove of plane trees, where they sit and rest in the shade of the noonday sun.

"Shall we discuss the rules of writing and speech?" says Socrates.

"Very good," says Aristocles.

And with these words, Socrates, a member of the last generation of Greek orators, and Aristocles, a member of the first generation of Greek writers, begin a conversation about the differences between oral and written stories.

Socrates, fully aware that younger generations—including, perhaps, *us*—may make fun of him, describes two problems.

One is a problem of authority. Socrates says: "The men of old deemed that if they heard the truth even from oak or rock, it was enough for them; whereas you seem to consider not whether a thing is or is not true, but who the speaker is and from what country the tale comes."

The other is a problem of immutability:

Writing is like painting; the creations of the painter have the attitude of life, and yet if you ask them a question they preserve a solemn silence. And the same may be said of written speeches. You would imagine that they had intelligence, but if you want to know anything and put a question to one of them, the speaker always gives one unvarying answer. And when they have been once written down they are tumbled about anywhere among those who may or may not understand them, and if they are maltreated or abused, they cannot protect or defend themselves.

These two problems are really one problem, as Socrates well knew. The first problem—that storytellers may get more credibility from their biographies than from their stories—applies to oral storytelling as well as written storytelling. But the second problem—the inability to challenge, clarify, or get answers to questions—was only true of writing, especially in 403 BCE, when oral stories could only be told to a few people at a time, and it makes the first problem worse.

Writing's immutability reminds us that, just as a painting of a pipe is not in fact a pipe, so writing is not in fact language. It is important to know the difference between a sound and its echo. Writing is an *illusion* of language, language's shadow, not a rabbit but merely a cloud that looks like one; at most, a *record* of language, rendered imperfectly and approximately in a wholly different form. Writing is to language as maps are to streets.

Writing has limitations and powers that language does not have. One limitation *and* power is that writing cannot be argued with. Writing derives strength from unchangingness, from the fact that it is the unalterable voice of its creator. This is especially dangerous when combined with a presumption that writing and writers have *authority*, a word blended from the Latin *augeō*, "originate," and the Greek *authentikós*, "genuine."

We are taught from infancy to venerate writing. But is writing really better than any other technology of story, or is it just older? Nothing is true because it is written, or untrue because it is unwritten. Reading is not believing: the truth may not be in writing, but somewhere else.

This prejudice about the authority of written stories soon extended to cultures that could write them. Humanity's story of itself was rent in two at the moment of writing's invention. Time was divided into "history," *after* writing, and "prehistory," *before* writing. Places were divided into "civilized," *with* writing, and "uncivilized," *without* writing. The word *illiterate* became a pejorative, and people who could write wrote to aggrandize the importance of writing. Writing became a form of supremacy. We know a lot about the achievements of written cultures because they were written, and little about the achievements of oral cultures because they were not. History may or may not be written by victors, but it is certainly written by those who can write.

Writing's immutability and unaccountability can make it a tool of dictators and dogmatists and turn authors into statues, stood on pedestals, deaf and mute, their work either an uninterrogable plane of confusion or a screen onto which readers project their own imaginings, interpretations, and fancies.

Or: Writing is monologue, but reading is dialogue. If you want to argue with me on this point, you are out of luck. I wrote it long ago and far away. I cannot hear your challenge, no matter how astute, articulate, and correct it is, and I will not answer. Your dialogue is not with me, but the void.

The story of Socrates's problem with writing is itself an example of Socrates's problem with writing. We cannot argue with Socrates, or ask him what he meant, or whether he said any of these things. We only know—or *think* we know—what Socrates said because Aristocles wrote about it, using the pseudonym Plátōn. Today, Plátōn is better known by the anglicized version of his pseudonym: Plato.

Socrates raised these objections only about writing, because writing was the only new technology of story in his lifetime. And what he predicted came true: Written stories soon seemed more legitimate than oral stories, even though the first stories written in Greek were oral stories transcribed.

Early written stories were exclusive. Knowledge of writing and access to writing tools were reserved for social elites. This created a powerful feedback loop: Only written stories had authority, and only authority had written stories.

This feedback loop applies to storytelling technologies invented *after* writing too. Socrates was describing a general problem of what we now call *mass communication*.

10. The Secret Life of Stories

Writing separates story and storyteller, and leaves readers to determine a story's meaning by themselves. One of the most important consequences of this separation—and one that applies to all other forms of mass communication too—is that every reader is likely to imagine and interpret the same story differently. What the writer writes is not what the reader reads.

And that raises a question: Is a story what is written or what is read?

This is not a new concern. Literary theorist Roland Barthes, among many others, wondered about it. Barthes concluded a story is not what is written but what is read; so much so that he proclaimed the "death of the author," saying: "The reader is the space on which all the quotations that make up a writing are inscribed; a text's unity lies not in its origin but in its destination. The reader holds together the written text. To give writing its future, the birth of the reader must be at the cost of the death of the author."

Barthes argued that there are two kinds of story: the *readerly* story, which requires little interpretation by the reader—the story is readerly because the reader mainly reads—and the *writerly* story, which requires a lot of interpretation by the reader—the story is writerly because the reader does so much interpretation that they almost write the story themselves.

Or, some stories are so straightforward that they lead every reader to imagine a similar story, and others are so ambiguous that they lead every reader to imagine a different story. A stop sign is an example of something extremely straightforward and readerly: Everyone who reads it understands it the same way. A Rorschach test—a psychological test in which someone is shown an image comprising nothing but inkblots and asked "What might this be?"—is an example of something extremely ambiguous and writerly: Everyone who "reads" it understands it differently. Neither of these two things are stories, and no stories are as extreme as these two things, but every story lies somewhere between.

Consider, for example:

> In the light
> of the moon
> a little egg
> lay on a leaf

This is the opening sentence of *The Very Hungry Caterpillar* by Eric Carle, written in 1969 for children between one and three years old. Even though this story is at the obvious readerly end of the spectrum, and the sentence is accompanied by a glorious picture of a moonlit egg on a leaf on a tree, there is still a lot to imagine and interpret: When is this? Where is this? What is the weather like? And so on. Every child who reads or is told this story will answer these questions in their own way.

At the other end of the spectrum, there is:

> riverrun, past Eve and Adam's, from swerve of shore to bend of bay, brings us by a commodious vicus of recirculation back to Howth Castle and Environs.

This is the opening sentence of *Finnegans Wake* by James Joyce, written in 1939, and known by a consensus of readers and critics alike to be a particularly difficult book to read. But even *Finnegans Wake* is not a Rorschach test. Its opening sentence bounds our imagination, leading us to think of a bending river near a place named Howth Castle. We cannot reasonably interpret it any other way.

There are many opinions about what the river might *represent*. It could be a metaphor for a stream of urine; a slurred allusion to the word *reverend*; or simply the River Liffey, which runs through the "commodious vicus," or spacious village, of Dublin, Ireland, before flowing into Dublin Bay to the southwest of Howth Castle. It could represent all of these things, or some of them, or none of them and something else entirely, but it is reasonable to assume that everyone reading the first sentence of *Finnegans Wake*, especially for the first time, will imagine a river, and that no one will imagine an egg on a leaf.

The possibility that one thing might represent another exists in all stories, not just ambiguous, writerly ones. We can also opine about what Eric Carle's "little egg" might stand for. A caterpillar hatches out of it—a *very hungry* caterpillar, naturally—which, through the course of the story, prepares to become, then *does* become, a butterfly. Potential metaphors abound, not least because *The Very Hungry Caterpillar* is a story for children going through the transition from infant to toddler.

No story is completely obvious. No story is completely ambiguous. No story requires no interpretation. If we accept these things, we are led to a strange conclusion: No story is complete until it is told, because all stories are finished in the mind of the reader.

This is true of spoken stories too, but there is a vital difference: Writing removes readers from the community of audience. When a book is read to a group, that group is an audience, because reading a book aloud to a group is a form of oral storytelling. But if that same group of people each read the same book to themselves privately and silently, something is lost. They are no longer an audience, but a plurality of readers barely connected if at all by their common text, even if are all reading the same text in the same room at the same time. Walter J. Ong, a professor of English literature who specialized in studying the transition from oral to written storytelling, put it this way:

> It is misleading to think of writers as dealing with an "audience." Writers address readers—only, they do not quite "address" them: they write to or for them. Orators have before them a true audience, a collectivity. "Audience" is a collective noun. There is no such collective noun for readers. "Readers" is a plural. Readers do not form a collectivity, acting here and now on one another and on the speaker as members of an audience do.

Writing not only separates us from the author, it separates us from each other too; it isolates us from the nightfire and individualizes our interpretation, creating for every story a multiverse of universes in which some things are somewhat different and some things are somewhat the same. Writing tells its stories one at a time, to each of us alone, by whispering in the privacy of our minds.

And our story-shaped brains prefer it this way. If every possible question about an event in a story were answered by that story, and if every conceivable detail was included, would that make the story better? No. Storytelling is the art of ambiguity, a collaboration between the storyteller and the person to whom the story is being told. Good storytelling inspires us to write our own story in our own mind. Reading a story and writing a story are less different than we realize: we coauthor every story we are told, giving each one a secret life, and nothing else would be as satisfying.

Chapter 4

The War of Stories

1. Printing

In the middle of the first millennium, Chinese Buddhists became convinced an apocalypse was imminent. This apocalypse was not part of Indian Buddhism; it was uniquely Chinese, a remixing of young ideas and old beliefs that recurs throughout the history of storytelling.

According to Chinese Buddhist prophecy, the process that led to the end of the world would begin between 50 CE and 993 CE. A great flood, accompanied by raging winds and mighty thunder, would cover the earth in water thirteen miles deep, plagues would kill anyone who survived the flood, and apocalyptic riders on dragon-horses would kill anyone who survived the plagues. Only eighty-four thousand chosen people would survive all the cataclysms. A dragon king would rescue these especially pious Buddhists and transport them to a magic city on an island in the ocean, where they would live in peace forever, while Buddhism collapsed everywhere else, to be born again later.

The impending apocalypse gave Chinese Buddhists two problems: how to ensure their personal survival by becoming one of the chosen people, and how to preserve Buddha's scriptures so Buddhism could be reborn in the postapocalyptic world.

Buddhism traveled to China slowly via the Silk Road. Six hundred years earlier, after the Buddha died and was cremated, Buddhist *bhikkhus*, or monks, had divided his ashes and distributed them around India and Nepal, where they were relics as revered as the Buddha himself. When there were no more ashes to meet the needs of the growing faithful, Buddhists declared that the Buddha's words were also relics. This led them to place copies of his scriptures in mounds called *stupas* in India, and later in tiered towers called *pagodas* in China, Japan, Korea, and other parts of East Asia.

One of these scriptures had an especially large impact on the story of stories. In the Dhāraṇī Sutra of the Seal on the Casket, the Buddha says,

> Those who copy this sutra will in effect copy all the sutras ninety-nine billion times. All the buddhas will support, protect, and remember that person. Ninety-nine billion buddhas, as numerous as the sands of the Ganges, will come to support them day and night, packed sideways like sesame seeds in a pile.

These words inspired Chinese Buddhists to copy sutras, and therefore writing, as much as possible, because repeating and reproducing scriptures was a virtuous act that made *merit*, a powerful cosmic force that could improve their next life and perhaps even bring them enlightenment.

This drive to accumulate merit through reproduction led to extraordinary efforts, as monasteries across China sought ways to preserve the sutras for eternity. None were more ambitious than the monks of the Cloud Dwelling Monastery, founded in 600 CE in the southwestern corner of Beijing, whose mission was to carve all of Buddhism's holy scriptures into stone. After five hundred years, twenty generations of monks had carved ten million characters into five thousand slabs of black limestone, and they were still only a third of the way through: There were ten thousand more slabs left to carve—a thousand more years of work if they kept the same pace.

So, in this sacred place where limestone dust sometimes made it hard to breathe and the chisels echoed all day anyway, a monk whose birth name was Wang and whose Buddhist name was Tongli studied the system, watching every movement, counting the minutes spent on every task, and noticing every squandered moment. Where others saw piety, Tongli saw process.

According to Tongli's observations, four monks worked in sequence to carve every slab: two to carry, one to prepare the surface, one to chisel in the characters. As a result, when one monk was working, at least two others were waiting. He had identified a problem that, a thousand years later, would be called *queuing theory*. Tongli calculated that if they kept up their current pace, even the latest dates prophesied for the apocalypse would arrive long before the work was finished.

Tongli standardized the size of the slabs so that two people could carry one slab easily; started the practice of carving on both sides of the tablet; divided the monastery's labor into dedicated masons, curators, calligraphers, and carvers; and took advantage of new technologies for storytelling.

The Chinese had been reproducing pictures by stamping them onto bronze, ceramic, and silk for thousands of years. The stamps eventually became wooden squares for creating repeating decorations, and while they were never used to duplicate writing, are an early example of what we now call movable type.

China's first tool for reproducing writing appeared around 100 BCE: seals, which Buddhists pressed into clay to duplicate mantras, sacred sounds incanted repeatedly for meditation and other purposes, usually comprising only a few syllables. Six centuries after inventing seals, the Chinese invented another tool for reproducing writing, called *bēitiē* in Chinese and *rubbing* in English; *bēitiē* artists pressed their writing surface over words carved into stone, then gently dabbed ink onto it to duplicate the impression. The Chinese used rubbings to copy and learn the artistic handwriting of calligraphy and for reproducing classic Chinese literature including *The Art of War*, the *I Ching*, and books by and about Confucius.

For most Buddhist temples, these techniques were enough. But in the Cloud Dwelling Monastery, where the very end of the world was at stake, Tongli knew they needed something more. The monks could not simply replace carving with rubbing—the monastery's mission was to make permanent, apocalypse-proof copies of Buddha's sacred teachings by chiseling them in stone and storing them in deep, purpose-built caves in the nearby Taihang Mountains. Tongli had the monks carve wooden printing blocks first, make a rubbing print from each block, and copy it into stone.

The mere fact of having a flat rubbing to copy, rather than another stone tablet, or a silk scroll in a different shape with a different layout, made the carving easier. But there was another benefit too: Carving the wooden blocks also created the means to make unlimited paper copies of the scriptures.

Because of Tongli's innovations, the speed at which the Cloud Dwelling Monastery carved its tablets changed. The monks produced over four thousand stones in two and a half years, almost the same number they had created in the previous five centuries. Tongli had realized that standardization was the secret of scaling up storytelling.

The monks eventually completed their stone library. Those black limestone sutras still exist, hidden in sealed caves behind stone doors that do not open, visible only if you shine a flashlight through the grid on the door into the dark chambers beyond: a silent and immortal testament to the monks' fear of Buddhism's destruction and their determination to prevent it.

But carving into limestone, no matter how standardized, was not a practical, everyday solution to the problem of reproducing writing, any more than seals, which could reproduce phrases quickly, and rubbing, which could reproduce pages slowly. China's Buddhists still needed a better, faster way to duplicate writing.

This put China in a unique position. The East Asian cultural sphere already had the most advanced duplication technology in the world, and because of the Dhāraṇī Sutra of the Seal on the Casket, the value of writing in these countries was wholly unconstrained by whether anyone could read. Merit came from reproducing the sutras, and was not diminished if nobody read them. The total available market for copies of sutras was karmic, not material, and therefore infinite. But in China, Japan, and Korea, more copies meant more merit, regardless of levels of literacy.

And so, in the middle of the first millennium, Chinese Buddhists wanted to survive the apocalypse, and make sure Buddha's words were available to the postapocalyptic world.

By chance, both these problems had the same solution: Copy as many sutras as possible, as quickly as possible. The Chinese had a uniquely urgent need to invent printing.

A thousand years later, Europe had a similar decoupling of printing from reading, but it had nothing to do with religion and everything to do with our other big motivation for telling stories: entertainment.

2. The Mysterious Master of the Playing Cards

On Sunday, April 9, 1424, at dawn, Saint Bernardino lit an enormous bonfire in the Piazza of Saint Croce in Florence, Italy. In the months that followed, he did the same thing in Perugia, Casale, Viterbo, Orvieto, and Siena.

One enthusiastic attendee described the Florentine conflagration in writing:

> You never saw such a beautiful fire. The flames leaped high into the air to the utter confusion of the devil, and to the glory and honor of our Lord Jesus Christ. I will not speak of the cries which

seemed like thunder, or of the tender weeping which manifested great devotions.

Bernardino's fires came to be called bonfires of the vanities, because their fuel comprised sinful objects. The fire in Florence included "several baskets of dice," "false hair," "four hundred gaming tables," high-heeled shoes, makeup, mirrors, perfume, "other abominations," and "over four thousand sets of playing cards old and new."

Those thousands of playing cards are especially noteworthy because in 1424 playing cards were newly arrived in Europe.

Playing cards first appeared in China around 760 CE—almost as soon as block printing on paper became common there—with a game called *yèzi xì*, or the Game of Leaves. The Chinese quickly adopted cards as an alternative to dice in games of chance. Other games using printed paper cards followed, many of which were drinking games. For example, *jiàbīn xīnlíng*, the Mind Instruction for Fine Guests, had the following rules:

> A party with wine will make things harmonious, and if there are drinking rules, the wine will flow. If the rules are simple, they will be respected. Respected, the wine goblet rules will not be disturbed. The responsibility to rectify the players' mistakes is given to the Game Warden. Those who speak too much will be punished. The Game Mistress is in charge of this. Those who spill a drop will be punished. The Mistress of the Endgame is in charge of this. This is called the Mind Instructions, but the mind actually does not have to labor.

Just as Buddhism had traveled east along the Silk Road, so playing cards traveled west, shape-shifting as they went. China's leaf games became India and Persia's *ganjifeh*, Egypt's *mamluk*, and, finally, Europe's playing cards. When playing cards reached Europe in the late 1300s, they had evolved considerably from their Chinese ancestors. While Chinese cards were long and narrow, printed with intricate patterns in black ink, European cards were shorter, wider, and were stamped with bold colors using wooden blocks. The suits evolved too—what were coins and strings in China were cups and batons when playing cards arrived in Europe, the ancestors of today's diamonds and clubs.

While Chinese Buddhists had developed printing to multiply merit, European card makers used it to multiply profit. In both cases, the saltation of innovation was the fact that printing did not require reading. Wherever playing cards went, paper—which the Chinese had invented around fifteen hundred years earlier—and printing followed.

Europe initially imported paper from Egypt and Turkey. As card games became ever more popular, demand increased until it made economic sense to manufacture paper in Spain, then France, and then Italy.

Germany's first paper mill opened in Nuremberg in 1390, and, soon after, Europe's first block printing appeared there and in other nearby cities. Although prayers, scriptures, and other religious material are more often associated with early printing, playing cards were the first things printed on paper in Europe, just as they were among the first things printed on paper in China.

That an observer could plausibly claim there were four thousand decks of playing cards in a bonfire in 1424, and that there were enough to help build great public fires in other cities too, is a testament to how quickly paper and printing became cheap and commonplace in Europe.

Playing cards drove the development of European papermaking and printing just as sutras had done in China, and for much the same reason: playing cards had value for people who could not read, which was almost everyone.

The popularity of block-printed playing cards created an entirely new market for European artists, who could carve an image in wood, or engrave one in copper, then reproduce and sell it many times over.

The first master of the new medium worked anonymously in Alsace, most likely in Strasbourg. This artist became known as the Master of the Playing Cards because of their most popular product, and they influenced many engravers who followed: artists who then became known by other, similar names, including the Master of the Banderoles, the Master of the Gardens of Love, and the Master of the Year.

While the identity of the Master of the Playing Cards is still unknown, we know the name of another artisan working nearby who the master's work inspired, a maker not of playing cards but of mirrors. He was the great-grandson of the founder of the Mainz city mint, who had inherited his great-grandfather's talent for metallurgy. He had been tinkering with coins, lead, and tin since childhood, and in 1434 started making mirrors in a secret workshop somewhere among the farms and waterways of the border between France and Germany.

His name was Johann Gensfleisch, and his story begins with a pilgrimage that did not happen.

3. Margery

It is the twentieth day of July in 1433, which is both a Saturday and the feast day of Saint Margaret, and a sixty-year-old woman dressed all in white is standing fast in the crowd in the great octagonal chapel at the center of Aachen Cathedral, weeping. Most of the men present, some of whom are clergy, are looking at her with hostility, not sympathy: they know a hysterical and probably heretical woman when they see one.

But none of them dare challenge her.

A strange power emanates from this woman in white, although the men glaring at her cannot explain its nature. Each of them knows only what their intuition tells them: that asking her to leave, or even to stop weeping, will end badly for them.

They are right to keep their distance. The woman's name is Margery Kempe, and what they are sensing is the almighty power of an independent woman who knows that men are not her superiors, not even if they are members of the clergy, whom she often challenges on scripture interpretation and wins, even though men expect women to have no opinions on such matters, and, if they do, to never speak them aloud.

Margery has endured more than any man could. This is an age when giving birth is the most dangerous thing a woman can do, with risks including death by exhaustion, hemorrhaging, infection, and obstructed labor, which kills both infant and mother, as doctors and midwives rarely conduct caesarean sections, and even then only if the mother is dying or dead. The risks are the same with every birth; they do not diminish if a woman has given birth previously. Yet Margery Kempe has faced this great pain and danger fourteen times and given birth to fourteen children, most of whom still live. She has also successfully defended herself in a trial for heresy, the penalty for which was usually death, sometimes by being burned alive. She has traveled on three ships and a wagon from her home in Bishop's Lynn, Norfolk, England, on her pilgrimage to Aachen, a dangerous, three-month journey of over seventeen hundred miles that included being infested by lice, and she has an important role to play in the story of stories. This is a woman you do not fuck with. If all the angry men in Aachen Cathedral united, they still could not intimidate her.

People fill the chapel because today is the one day in every seven years when Aachen Cathedral displays its four great relics: the nightgown the Virgin Mary wore while giving birth to Jesus; the swaddling clothes of the infant Jesus; the cloth used to wrap John the Baptist's decapitated head; and, most sacred of all, the loincloth worn by Jesus during his crucifixion.

The nature of these relics is one reason for printing's late arrival in Europe. The westward spread of printing faced a seemingly impossible obstacle: There was little value in reproducing writing when almost no one could read, and little value in learning to read when there was almost nothing to be read.

This self-perpetuating cycle, an ouroboros of an obstacle, meant that literacy levels in the Middle Ages were determined mainly by religion: Buddhism, Judaism, and Islam encouraged reading and writing among the laity so the faithful could study scripture; Hinduism less so; and Christianity not at all.

These differences made the westward diffusion of paper and printing from China uneven. India, for example, was slower to adopt paper and printing than many Muslim nations to its west, and Europe had little use for either technology. Handwritten manuscripts on parchment or vellum served Europe's literate ruling classes adequately, and unlike Buddhists, Christians did not assign miraculous properties to copies and reproductions: they reserved their reliquaries for real things.

Medieval Christianity faced a crisis of scarcity: with Christ's body ascended to heaven, the faithful had too few sacred remains to satisfy growing demand. Just as the first Buddhist relics were the ashes of the Buddha, so the first Christian relics were the remains of Christ—the word *relic* comes from *reliquiae*, the Latin for "remains." But, unlike the Buddha, Christ left very little of his body on earth, because according to the faith of most Christian denominations, he ascended to heaven sometime after the resurrection, taking his body with him. The few corporeal relics of Christ are pre-resurrection remains, such as bloodstains on the cloth that wrapped his head after he died; his foreskin, which was removed when he was circumcised as an infant; parts of his umbilical cord; and the sweat on a towel used to mop his brow while he carried the cross.

Medieval Christians therefore faced a shortage of relics, just as Buddhists had centuries earlier. Their first solution was to expand the definition of *relic* to incorporate other people's remains: the bones of the apostle James; the heads of the apostles Paul and Peter; the bodies of the saints Bernadette and Francis Xavier; and the tongues of the saints Anthony of Padua and John of Nepomuk, for example. Just like the Buddhists hundreds of years earlier, the clergy tried to divide the relics so that they could display them in more than one place, but even with apostles and saints included, there were not enough body parts to endow an ever-increasing number of churches. So the ecclesiastics redefined *relic* again, this time to include any items that Jesus, his family, the apostles, or the saints had *touched*.

Aachen Cathedral's relics fall into this category of "contact relics." They do not contain corporeal remains, but they have been in contact with the bodies of Christianity's most sacred people: John the Baptist, the Virgin Mary, and Jesus Christ himself.

The cathedral has displayed these items every seven years since 1349, and Aachen has become the destination of a great septennial pilgrimage.

The number of pilgrims, to Aachen and elsewhere, soon grew so large it created an additional problem: how to give everyone access to the holy powers of the relics when the cathedral is so crowded few people can get close to them.

The solution came not from heaven but from new technology: small, affordable mirrors made of glass "silvered" with a mixture of lead and other metals. These mirrors were convex, and nothing like as clear as the mirrors made of polished marble or steel that aristocrats hung in their stately homes, but they were portable and, most importantly, they were so cheap that ordinary people could buy them. Affordable, ubiquitous mirrors were one of the most significant inventions of the Middle Ages, and at least as important as the flat high-definition displays that appeared at the start of the twenty-first century. When the clergy saw this new technology, they saw an opportunity to serve more pilgrims, and declared that the mirrors could reflect and even store the miraculous rays emanating from relics.

Aachen Cathedral immediately started selling commemorative badges with built-in mirrors to visiting pilgrims, and the mirrors became so popular that metallurgists of Aachen's guilds could not keep up with demand. The cathedral gave up its monopoly and announced that anyone anywhere could supply mirrors to its pilgrims, inspiring many Germans to try their hand at mirror making.

In 1564 Leonardo Fioravanti, an Italian alchemist, described the process most German mirror-makers used:

> The Germans make little mirrors out of glass. They create a hollow glass sphere; put a mixture of lead, tin, silver pyrite, and residue from wine barrels inside it; rotate the sphere so that the mixture sticks to the glass; throw away any excess; then cut the sphere into round pieces, which are the little mirrors mentioned above.

Among the many Germans who see opportunity in these holy mirrors is Johann Gensfleisch. Johann has a simple, if ambitious business plan: to make thirty-two thousand mirrors and sell them for a profit of one gulden each at the Aachen pilgrimage of 1439. A gulden is a lot of money: a week's wages for a skilled artisan, enough to buy about twenty-five pounds of meat, thirty-two pounds of cheese, or a night in a guesthouse.

The two men who help with the work will get one-eighth of the profits each, the investor who provides the startup capital will get a quarter, and Johann will get half: a windfall roughly equivalent to $5 million in 2024. Johann spends much of 1438 imagining how he might spend his new wealth.

Margery Kempe has come to Aachen a few years too early to purchase one of Johann's mirrors, but Margery and Johann will soon become connected, and together they will transform storytelling.

4. Johann

Andreas Dritzehn and Andreas Heilmann, often known as "the two Andreases," turn the great wooden screw to lower the platen and apply pressure to the bed of Johann Gensfleisch's strangely modified press. On every other screw press the Andreases have heard of, there are high squeaks and low moans as the screw descends, as if it were complaining about its labor. But in Johann's press, the turning screw is silent.

They arrived at Johann's secret workshop, hidden somewhere among the waterways of Strasbourg, for the first time several months ago, one early morning at the end of January 1438. When they discovered the screw press, which was spotlit by a slant of sunshine coming through the skylight, they exchanged looks of concern. Screw presses were an ancient technology used to make wine in Europe since the eleventh century, and derived from the lever and weight presses that had been crushing grapes in Cyprus and Syria for three thousand years. The Andreases had joined the business to make mirrors, not wine.

When Johann showed them how to pour a strange liquid, much like water only green, onto the screw and rub it into the wood, they thought him odd and possibly mad. Every other screw press operator in Strasbourg and probably far beyond greases their press with suet, which is the loin fat of a cow. It smells of the abattoir, and someone must scrape it off the screw at the end of each day or it will harden overnight and jam the press, but it makes the turning a little easier.

It soon became clear that Johann's mysterious green liquid had none of these drawbacks: its faint fragrance was of fruit, it never hardened and so never needed scraping off, and it made the screw turn silently, with hardly any effort at all, which is something no amount of suet could do.

Johann said the liquid was oil squeezed from olives, which had recently replaced fat on the screw presses in much of Italy. Somehow word of this invention had reached no one in Strasbourg but Johann.

The efficacy of the oil allayed their fears and put excitement in their hearts. Johann was a man ahead of his time, whose ways of doing things were different because they were better. By April the Andreases could barely remember their doubts.

Their enthusiasm increased even more when they learned that this was not an ordinary press at all, but a brand-new machine, which Konrad Saspach, a local chest maker with premises on Krämergass, the merchants' street, had made according to Johann's precise design.

By the end of the day Johann had shown them how to use the screw press to make mirrors surrounded by ornate, detailed designs such as Mary cradling the infant Jesus, suitable for sale to Aachen's pilgrims: a new method of manufacturing so closely guarded that even today we are not completely sure what it was. It would soon change the world, but no one, not even Johann, realized that yet.

We have one big clue about the process, though: the number of mirrors it made. Johann's business plan required the production of 32,000 mirrors in a year: an average of around 100 mirrors every working day. This is such a large number that the purpose of Johann's screw press, however it worked, must have been making mirrors with unprecedented efficiency—approximately four times the production of the more artisanal methods everyone else was using.

Thirty-two thousand mirrors means 32,000 individual pieces of glass and 32,000 lead-filled molds, each requiring precise execution. Mistakes will cut into the men's profits and possibly their fingers. The pressure mounts with every mirror they complete. But they do it: As 1438 nears its end, the venture has used almost all its startup capital making tens of thousands of mirrors. Johann is relieved and elated: The risk is now behind them, and nothing remains to go wrong.

Things go wrong anyway, of course. Every invention fails before it succeeds. Inventing is hard but enduring is harder.

One bright, cold afternoon in mid-December, Andreas Dritzehn says he feels unwell. Andreas Heilmann puts a hand on his forehead and finds that Dritzehn is hot despite the winter air, perhaps from working too hard.

Johann tells the feverish but reluctant Dritzehn to go home and rest, and that they will see him tomorrow. When Dritzehn has gone,

Heilmann and Johann exchange worried glances and then go back to work, with Johann filling in for Dritzehn where necessary.

They wait for Dritzehn to show up the next day, and when he does not, they fear for their colleague. The day after, Heilmann, full of dread, goes to Dritzehn's house and learns that the fever has progressed and Dritzehn has the strange, finger-shaped swellings called buboes that are the root of the name of Dritzehn's sickness: the bubonic plague.

Next comes necrosis, a darkening of the skin that gives the disease its other name: the Black Death. Death is not inevitable: About half the people who get the plague survive. Dritzehn is not one of them. On December 26, 1438, he dies without seeing a penny of profit from his labors.

Soon after Dritzehn's death, Johann discovers he has made a critical, inexplicable mistake: There *is* no pilgrimage to Aachen in 1439. The next pilgrimage is not until 1440. He has spent all of his investors' money on products with no immediate market.

Johann needs a new product, and fast. Hans Riffe, the venture's primary investor and governor of Lichtenau, is asking hard questions about the timing mistake. Andreas Heilmann, who is grieving the death of his friend and has invested both money and labor in the venture, grows desperate as their capital dwindles and the plague spreads through Strasbourg.

That new product is punches, used to stamp hallmarks, letters, and ornaments into precious metal.

Punch making is not new; it is a variant of stamping that makes a mark by hammering a shape—or "punch"—made of a hard metal such as brass or copper into a soft metal such as silver or gold. Punching is more efficient than inscribing or engraving, both of which have been in use for thousands of years.

Artisans either *carve* punches, which is fast but only makes one punch at a time, or *cast* them by pouring liquid metal into a mold of densely packed sand, which is slow but makes many punches at once.

Johann develops a new punch-making technique that is as fast as carving and can make as many punches as casting. He creates a master punch by engraving a letter or ornament into a piece of metal, attaches it to the screw of the press, pushes it down into another piece of metal held fast on the platen, and makes a punch *with* a punch.

Johann's modified press can make many punches from a single master punch without wasting time on casting. All invention is like this: Each problem solved is a twist in the path that leads to another problem and, ultimately, to a destination unknown. The transition to punches shows that Johann has not invented a mirror production process, but a mass production process, long before the term *mass production* exists.

Punch making does not save the business—the partners spend the next year suing one another—but it foreshadows Johann's next move.

Johann seldom uses his family name, Gensfleisch. As is common among the German upper classes, he uses the name of the house in Mainz, Germany, where he grew up instead. That house is called zum Gutenberg. Johann's full name is Johannes Gensfleisch zur Laden zum Gutenberg, but most people call him Johann Gutenberg.

Gutenberg will eventually use his modified screw press for printing, but he is not trying to print in Strasbourg, and we have no reason to believe he has any thoughts about printing: He is simply trying to earn a living. If he had not made his mistake about the date of the Aachen pilgrimage, his business would have succeeded, and he would have spent the rest of his life as a retired mirror maker, enjoying his riches.

But the business fails, and Johann returns home to Mainz to start again. Printing is not an obvious choice, as there is no market for it. He modifies his next screw press to duplicate words anyway, inspired perhaps by the intricate engravings of the Master of the Playing Cards. Gutenberg's journey from mirror making to printing is how all invention works once we eliminate its story-shaped mold: Amazing new things come not from grand visions, but from solving one practical problem after another.

5. Mass

A mouse squeaks in the walls of Amsterdam's Weteringschans Prison, even though the building opened just six years ago, in 1850. A lucky prisoner may see it dart in and out of his cell. The prisoners are sure there is just one mouse, not a mischief of identical mice, because that makes the visiting mouse a friend, not a stranger.

One week ago, Baron Mozes Salvador would have responded to these facts by saying something like "Dreams are deception," but now he sits and stares at the hole in the corner all day, hoping to glimpse the animal, and imagining, as all Weteringschans prisoners eventually do, that the next time it appears it might stay awhile and allow itself to be stroked while making little chirrups of glee like a beloved family pet.

As he awaits the mouse, the baron hears cannon fire in the distance. He wonders for a moment if war has broken out—it will be either between the Catholics and Protestants, inflamed by the recent restoration of Catholicism in the Netherlands, or with the Belgians over Limburg and Luxembourg, where tension has been building for years—then returns to the more important matter of the mouse.

The mouse is important because, while the isolation of solitary confinement sounds comfortable at first—like peace, quiet, and not being bothered, despite the low moans and brown aromas—around the third hour after his cell door closes, every Weteringschans prisoner finally understands, in his feelings and not just his thoughts, that no one is coming, that he is fully alone, and that he will be not reading, writing, playing Patience, or occupying himself in any other way, for the weeks or months of his sentence.

This circumstance is so unnatural and antithetical to human instinct that, at this moment of realization and for several days after, the prisoner trembles with the terror of his isolation. Then, to maintain his sanity, he creates an imaginary friend—or, for those imprisoned in Weteringschans, an imaginary friendship with a real but utterly indifferent mouse who is actually six mice—and although he may only glimpse it for a few seconds every few days, it brings the same joy a person would.

The baron has not seen the mouse so far today, and did not see it yesterday, and therefore believes he is due for a visit. So he sits on the floor of his cell, unworried by the cannons, fixated on the hole in the corner beside the commode, making sure not to look away even for a moment, and blinking only when absolutely necessary.

One person you cannot see when you are in solitary confinement is yourself. There are no mirrors, nor any reflections, not even from the water in the commode, which is always a cloudy brown, so the baron cannot see that his trimmed, waxed mustache has blurred into a beard, or that his face has new hollows, or that the whites of his eyes have become pink. In his mind, he looks exactly as he did in the mirror of his home after he groomed and dressed to impress his supporters who were waiting to witness his arrest.

The court sentenced him to one month here, a harsh punishment for a libel that was part of a yearslong war of words with his political opponents on the Haarlem civic council: a petty dispute that seemed like sport until his conviction, arrest, and imprisonment.

The baron has twenty-five more days to spend in this room. He arrived six days ago, but his sense of time is so disturbed by his isolation that he believes it has been weeks and that today is August 4 or 5.

In fact, it is Tuesday, July 15, 1856, a day of celebration throughout the Netherlands. The town of Haarlem, a little to the west of Amsterdam, is the center of the festivities. Here, the day began with a deafening twenty-one-cannon salute fired from the woods of Haarlemmerhout, the nation's oldest park, a speech by Jan Justus Enschedé, editor of Haarlem's newspaper, then a grand procession that made its way slowly to the town square, with a printing press pulled on a cart as its centerpiece, printing a song to commemorate the day, which the journeyman printers are distributing to a crowd that seems bigger than Haarlem itself.

The procession enters the square. There, just a few steps away, twenty-two feet high and hidden beneath a black linen cloth, is the reason for the celebration: a new statue waiting to be unveiled.

Leonard Metman, chair of the planning committee, addresses the still-settling crowd and tells them what they are about to see: a lifelike statue, with detailed facial features and hands and a natural drape to his clothes, of a man whose invention benefits the whole of humanity and multiplies the fruits of the spirit, spreading light far and wide.

Everyone is now in the highest state of expectation, just as Metman intended. After a pause of a few seconds that seems longer to the waiting crowd, there is a second twenty-one-cannon salute, even louder than the first, because this time it comes from Nieuwestad, a third of a mile north, and so loud that once again the baron hears it in Weteringschans.

While the salute is still echoing through the square, Metman pulls the black linen to the ground and unveils the statue. The crowds cheer louder than the cannons because, standing tall and proud in beautiful bronze, holding up a piece of type bearing the letter *A*, is a magnificent symbol not only of Dutch innovation but also of freedom of speech.

To emphasize this second point—and ease some political stress—King Willem III at this exact moment, in an act of well-choreographed statecraft, announces the pardon of one Baron Mozes Salvador.

The baron is at first annoyed to be distracted from his watch of the mousehole by the news of his freedom, which is in honor and remembrance of the great Dutchman who from this day on will stand tall and bronze in Haarlem's town square: Laurens Janszoon Coster, the inventor of the printing press.

The people of the Netherlands know the Germans dispute their claim to be printing's birthplace, but dismiss it as ignorance and prejudice. History will not fully recognize Gutenberg's inventorship until over a hundred years from now. His role will be in dispute as late as 1995, because many people, some of them experts and not all of them Dutch, are sure Coster is printing's inventor.

As the baron returns to his home, the bronze statue of his savior glimmers in the sunset like a candle flame, until it is extinguished by the lengthening shadow of the Church of St. Bavo.

The statue is indeed a monument to invention, but not to the invention intended. Laurens Janszoon Coster, despite being commemorated with several statues that still stand in Haarlem today, did not invent printing and is in fact an invention himself, an imaginary person who did not exist, less real than even the baron's mouse, born from jingoistic sixteenth-century myth-making by Dutch settler colonialists.

Disputes like this and others—Gutenberg's business associates claimed sole credit for his inventions after his death, for example—made Gutenberg anonymous during his lifetime. There are no contemporary drawings or descriptions of him or his machine.

But we can make inferences.

Gutenberg did not invent printing, or even printing with movable metal type, as Europeans sometimes claim; the Korean Buddhist text *Jikji* was printed with movable metal type in 1377, decades before Gutenberg was born, and there may be earlier examples too.

But, while Gutenberg's role was more nuanced than "inventing printing," it is no less important for it. Gutenberg's unique contribution, first hinted at by his mirrors and punches in Strasbourg, was the design of a system that could make things quickly, cheaply, and therefore in large volumes. Gutenberg was not the inventor of printing; he was the inventor of mass production.

Transforming printing from artisanal to mechanical was difficult because of two opposing requirements. Type—that is, the individual metal blocks with letters on them—has to be made precisely, so that none of the metal blocks are longer or shorter than the others when pressed onto paper; if the letters are of different depths, only the longest will touch the paper and print. But these precise metal blocks of type also have to be made quickly, otherwise it would take years to create enough type to print a book. This question of how to make tiny metal letters precisely without compromising speed and quickly without compromising precision is the one Gutenberg answered.

Even though the Chinese invented movable type two thousand years earlier in China, they did not adopt it at a scale that drives the saltation of innovation because movable type was not especially useful for printing the Chinese language. Printing Chinese using Gutenberg's method would have required at least ten thousand individual characters, and long searches among those characters to find everything needed to typeset a page.

Europeans could print their alphabetical languages with fewer than three hundred characters, including letters, numbers, punctuation marks, and ligatures—characters comprising two or more frequently combined letters.

Printing came late to Europe, but when it arrived, the consequences were much the same as in China, Japan, and Korea.

On the day Gutenberg's printing press started operating, scribes half a mile away were laboring in the scriptorium of St. Alban's Abbey, copying scripture and other Christian writing using goose-feather quills dipped in ink. The best and fastest of them, who were called *antiquarii*, wrote one or two pages that day. In Gutenberg's workshop, the printing press produced three thousand pages. This wasn't just a change in scale—it was a revolution in how ideas could spread.

Europe's scribes produced eleven million documents in the thousand years before Gutenberg invented the printing press. Presses based on Gutenberg's design produced thirteen million documents by 1500. What once took a century now took four years.

Gutenberg invented the mass production of mass communication. His achievement established a pattern that repeats with each successive storytelling technology: that the true transformation comes not from the invention itself but from making it fast enough, cheap enough, and reliable enough for mass adoption. Gutenberg's press could produce thousands of pages per day, but the revolution he started was not only because of speed or volume; it was also because of what happens when one idea enters thousands of minds simultaneously. That change is far more significant, and far more difficult to quantify or even qualitize. The story of Haarlem contains two of its countless cascading consequences: the printing press both spread the myth of Laurens Janszoon Coster and led to the laws of libel that imprisoned Baron Mozes Salvador.

The transformation was the one Socrates had foreseen two thousand years earlier on the bank of the Ilisos: when Gutenberg invented the mass production of mass communication, he invented mass persuasion too.

6. The More Than Fifty Wars

In 1483 Giacomo Filippo Foresti, a friar in Bergamo, Italy, published one of the first ever references to Gutenberg, in one of the first ever bestsellers, a history printed in twenty-five editions:

> The art of printing books was first invented in Germany, which some assert was discovered by Luténberg, others by someone else named Fusto. Indeed, no invention in the world could be more worthy, more praiseworthy, or more useful, or more divine or holy than this. Let all now adorn you with the highest praises, when under your leadership this wondrous art was discovered.

We can see the "wondrous art" in action by visiting Germany on the night of Wednesday, November 30, 1560. Thirteen-year-old Tycho Ottesen Brahe is sitting in bed, propped up by two down pillows, reading a book in the light of a beeswax candle in an otherwise pitch-black room, in secret.

Tycho has the pillows, the candle, and the book because he was born into a wealthy family: if he were poor, his pillows would be straw-filled and too unstable for sitting; his candle would be made of animal fat and too smoky and smelly for secrecy; and his book—Ptolemy's collected works, including a recent Latin translation of the astronomer's great work, the *Almagest*—would be too expensive.

Tycho is supposed to be asleep. He is reading in secret because his family has decreed he will study law, not a subject such as astronomy, which is unbecoming for a member of the nobility and would make him, according to one seventeenth-century biographer, a "degenerate from ancestral virtue." And so, no matter how engrossing the book, Tycho remains alert: ready to blow out his candle, hide his contraband under a pillow, and pretend to be asleep if the floorboard he loosened in the hallway squeaks its warning that his tutor is coming.

Tycho's secret life began on August 21, when he witnessed a partial eclipse of the sun, was amazed that people could predict such things, and fell into an illicit love affair with astronomy. Now he hoards his allowance to buy astronomy books, and even a celestial globe—like a globe of the earth, except it shows the stars in the night sky—so small he can hide it from his tutor in his fist. This is risky: Tycho's allowance is for "entertainment and relaxation," and he must account for every pfennig. He will not get an allowance if his family discovers his secret.

Three summers later we find Tycho awake at night again, but instead of reading, he is staring through the open window of his bedroom at the night sky with a candle burning behind him, illuminating nothing more than a notebook held in his left hand.

It is August 17, 1563, a cloudless night that gives a clear view of the sky. Tycho is looking up, frowning and squinting in concentration, stopping occasionally to write in the notebook, focused on two points of light close together. One is Jupiter; the other is Saturn.

The two planets are not only close, they are getting closer. This type of alignment is called a conjunction, and with Jupiter and Saturn it occurs once every twenty years. Tycho is looking at the night sky to see when the conjunction happens. His books do not agree on this point. Ptolemy, who believes the Sun orbits the Earth, says the conjunction will occur in late September; Copernicus, who believes the Earth orbits the Sun, says it will take place on August 23. Tycho wants to see who is right.

He watches the sky every night for eleven nights, using eyesight alone, as he has no astronomical instruments, and takes detailed notes about the position of the two planets. Jupiter and Saturn come together and move apart, but not as Ptolemy *or* Copernicus predicted: The conjunction takes place on August 25.

Tycho is astonished. Last year he had worked out that the famous astronomical calculations of Johannes Stadius were so wrong that they were "fallacious and carelessly put together," and now, at the age of sixteen, he has discovered the world's two greatest astronomers are wrong as well.

That day in August was life-changing not only for Tycho but for all of us. He went on to show the world how to develop theories based on observation, starting the scientific revolution; developed better astronomical instruments; discovered stars; published instructional books that helped to define the format of textbooks for centuries; taught the next great astronomer, Johannes Kepler; and, most important of all, demonstrated how reading can empower people to learn without teachers and become independent thinkers. Whenever you teach yourself something by reading a book, you are following in the footsteps of Tycho Brahe.

Tycho's story shows how revolutionary printing was: In a world without books, he would be a long-forgotten lawyer, not a celebrated scientist. And he embodies a paradox that is a theme of the rest of the story of stories: Mass communication makes knowledge stable and homogenous, while also making it dynamic and heterogeneous.

In Tycho's story, Ptolemy exemplifies stable, homogenous knowledge: His theories were safe and unchallenged in the sanctuaries of scriptoria for fourteen hundred years, then made standard and stable by the printing press. Tycho himself exemplifies dynamic, heterogeneous knowledge: He bought and read Ptolemy's work, tested it, and challenged it by publishing an alternative.

Stable, homogenous knowledge tells the *standard stories* of our communities. Standard stories aim to preserve the status quo, and are sometimes *regressive*, trying to rewind the world to the way things used to be or, at least the way the tellers of standard stories *say* things used to be. Dynamic, heterogenous knowledge tells the *counterstories* of our community. Counterstories aim to change the status quo, and are usually *progressive*, trying to skip ahead to a new and—according to the tellers of the counterstories—better future.

Many historians claim that Gutenberg's story ends with everyone reading happily ever after. That claim is wrong because of the conflict between standard stories and counterstories. The irony of mass communication is that elites do not want the masses to communicate; they want them to be nothing more than passive receivers of standard stories.

We do not need to speculate about these concerns: Powerful people raised them explicitly and publicly during centuries of debate about whether to teach ordinary people to read. For example, as late as 1807, Britain's parliament rejected a bill to create elementary schools. One of the bill's opponents was Davies Gilbert, a politician who was educated by his clergyman father. He changed his last name from Giddy to Gilbert to seem more aristocratic and later became president of the Royal Society, Britain's national academy of sciences. Gilbert argued that

> Giving education to the labouring classes of the poor would be prejudicial to their morals and happiness; it would teach them to despise their lot in life, instead of making them good servants in agriculture and other laborious employments to which their rank in society had destined them; instead of teaching them subordination, it would render them factious and refractory; it

would enable them to read seditious pamphlets, vicious books, and publications against Christianity; and it would render them insolent to their superiors.

Similar fears—that literacy would make workers want to be more than workers, raise their consciousness, and lead them to seek liberation—were expressed throughout Europe and its empires after Gutenberg invented the printing press. Writing is a tool and weapon both. The ruling classes want their peasants to be able to read well enough to be compliant and productive, but not so well that they become armed for a war of stories.

The privileged are still afraid of reading today. As I write this sentence, about a hundred miles away from me, a rich retired oil executive named Victor Perez is working hard to ban *The Handmaid's Tale*, *The Kite Runner*, *Slaughterhouse Five*, *Wicked*, and other books he does not like from every school in Katy, Texas.

Victor was born in Cuba. In 1959, when he was seven years old, his family fled to the United States in the aftermath of Fidel Castro's revolution. A cropped, butch-waxed haircut called the flattop boogie was popular with young American boys at that time. Perez has his now-white hair cut that way today, suggesting that he may have adopted the style when he first arrived in America and never changed it since. His political views suggest that too: He is a conservative who describes himself as "a steadfast advocate for common-sense leadership." Victor will likely have retired from public life by the time you read this, but he is far from unique. There will always be people like Victor Perez: town criers of the standard story, indignant warriors fighting against the future for a past that never was, forever claiming to be protecting "the children," sometimes winning in the moment, always losing in the end.

At the time of writing, a motivated minority of people like Victor are trying to ban thousands of stories all over America. The works they condemn form a contemporary index of forbidden books: the heretical counterstories of the moment. In 2023, for example, the five most banned books all had lesbian, gay, bisexual, gender, or queer themes, and Nobel Prize winner Toni Morrison's *The Bluest Eye* came sixth because of its alleged "equality, diversity, and inclusion content."

The ruling classes are right to fear reading. "War of stories" is not a metaphor. Reading strikes the match that burns it all down.

In its first hundred years, the printing press multiplied the number of writers per reader by twenty-five or more. This redistribution of the power of mass communication had immediate consequences. Between 1500 and 1600, the economies of the first two hundred cities with printing presses grew 20 to 80 percent more than the economies of cities without printing presses.

But economic benefits were not the only change: Just as long-form writing spread the standard stories of religion, so printing presses spread counterstories to challenge them.

While Gutenberg was inventing the printing press, Pope Nicholas V was planning to rebuild St. Peter's Basilica, a project that cost 46.8 million Venetian ducats—the equivalent of over $100 billion today.

In Catholicism, sins can be forgiven through the sacrament of Penance, which comprises three acts: repenting, confessing to a priest, and doing works of reparation. In the thirteenth century, the pope and others in the Church started raising money to build ever grander cathedrals by selling a type of forgiveness known as indulgences, which reduced the works of reparation.

These written indulgences did not require literacy. *Buying* indulgences ensured their efficacy; *reading* them was unnecessary. In order to fund the construction of St. Peter's Basilica and other projects, the Church employed Gutenberg and other printers to use printing presses to mass-produce indulgences, then sold them all over Europe.

The mass production of indulgences by printing caused trouble for the Church, trouble that was also mass-produced by printing. In 1517 Martin Luther, a professor of theology at the University of Wittenberg in Germany, sent ninety-five complaints, most of them about indulgences, to the archbishop of Mainz.

Luther also printed two hundred copies of his complaints using a printing press, and distributed those copies in Wittenberg and other nearby cities, where other printing presses produced and distributed them again and again. Within two months Luther's counterstory, the first viral meme, was being read all over Europe. This rapid spread of the complaints was an unwelcome surprise, as Luther explained in a letter to his friend Christoph von Scheurl:

> I did not wish to have them widely circulated. I only intended submitting them to a few learned men for examination. But now they are being spread abroad and translated everywhere, which I never could have credited, so that I regret having given birth to them. I am still uncertain as to some points, and would have gone into others more particularly, leaving some out entirely, had I foreseen all this.

Luther's counterstory split the Christian Church, Europe's greatest power, in two. The schism caused or contributed to over fifty armed conflicts between 1522 and 1712, and somewhere between seven to eighteen million deaths. The biggest immediate consequence of the printing press was not an information utopia for ordinary people; it was two hundred years of ordinary people being killed in wars of stories.

It is no coincidence that Protestantism was born in the place and time of the printing press. Some historians say that the rise of Protestantism was because of something else, like a supposed "Protestant work ethic," but this is just their story-shaped brains overattributing cause to human agency. Almost all differences between peoples are because of geography and technology. The difference technology made to the spread of Protestantism is clear: After controlling for all other variables, European cities that had printing presses by 1500 were

52 percent more likely to have become Protestant by 1530, 42 percent more likely to have become Protestant by 1560, and 29 percent more likely to have become Protestant by 1600 compared to cities without printing presses.

Complaints about indulgences, Toni Morrison's novels, and picture books about families threaten those who want to control us with standard stories. The real reason book banners ban books is that they are scared of independent thinking. Book banners understand and affirm that reading is a revolutionary act, just as the opponents of mass literacy did centuries earlier.

A counterstory need not be art: Margery Kempe, who we saw on her pilgrimage to Aachen Cathedral, could not read or write, so she dictated her counterstory to a series of scribes. Two different publishers printed Margery's story on their Gutenberg-designed presses and sold copies all over Britain. *The Book of Margery Kempe* is the first autobiography written in English, and one of the earliest examples of feminism.

A counterstory need not be new; much of its power comes from giving old stories new meanings. When George Smith shocked Victorian Britain in 1872 by proving that the story of Noah originated in Mesopotamia, he was telling the oldest story in the world while giving it the newest possible meaning.

A counterstory need not be long; Martin Luther's counterstory fit on a page and broke the Christian Church in two.

A counterstory need only be a flame in the haystack.

7. Story Versus Story

The Protestant revolution showed Europe's ruling classes that their legitimacy would be threatened whenever and wherever stories were outside of their control, so they restricted printing and curtailed reading. For centuries, widespread printing did not lead to widespread literacy because governments feared the power of counterstories.

In the 1600s there were only five printing presses in Britain's thirteen American colonies, for example, all of them subject to censorship because British colonial governors feared the power of printing. But in the eighteenth century each colony wriggled free of Britain's restraints, built its own printing press, and used it to produce independent newspapers. The postal service in the Americas was subject to British censorship and surveillance, so the colonial printers created a secret shadow postal system to distribute their publications between colonies. The presses and postal service increased the number of public storytellers and therefore the number of counterstories, which fomented and informed America's Revolution and War of Independence.

In France, there were few newspapers, all subject to licenses and censorship, until 1789, when growing social unrest led to the sudden publication of several thousand independent newspapers and tens of thousands of political pamphlets. These led to the French Revolution.

Counterstories challenge standard stories until and unless they succeed in becoming standard stories and are challenged by new counterstories. Martin Luther's Protestantism, once established, was challenged by counterstories that eventually led to Protestant denominations such as Adventism, Anglicanism, Methodism, and Quakerism, as well as non-Protestant branches of Christianity, including Reformed Christians such as the Presbyterians, Evangelical Anglicans, and Congregationalists; Anabaptist Christians such as the Amish, Apostolics, and Mennonites; and Restorationist Christians such as the Christadelphians, Latter-day Saints, and Jehovah's Witnesses. Each of these denominations started with counterstories that became the standard stories of their communities, just as the counterstories that led to the American and French Revolutions became the standard stories of postrevolutionary America and France.

The French revolutionaries gave the interaction between counterstories and standard stories the terms we still use today: stories proposing the adoption of new social behaviors were called *progressive*, and stories proposing a return to old social behaviors were called *reactionary*. Progressive counterstories challenge standard stories until and unless they become standard stories, then reactionary counterstories challenge them, and so on.

This may sound like a simple back-and-forth, seesawing from one state to the other indefinitely, circling around the same state of affairs forever, but reactionary stories seldom delete progress. The Roman Catholic Church did not return to selling indulgences after the Reformation; reactionary stories moderated the progressive stories that overthrew the French aristocracy, but never so much that France permanently restored its monarchy; and America's stories about the tyranny of George III, the King of Great Britain, subsided enough that an independent America could have a respectful relationship with British royalty, but never so much that the United States reinstated a British monarch. This is the true pattern of progress. Progressive stories take two steps forward; reactionary stories take one step back. Consciousness raised cannot be lowered.

When first invented, new storytelling technologies are only available to the powerful and privileged, who use them to tell standard stories that perpetuate the status quo. But, as the saltation of use makes each technology cheaper, easier, and therefore more accessible, counterstories multiply and increase the pace of progress.

And so it was with printing. After the American and French Revolutions, continuous innovation made printing, and therefore counterstories, ever more common. There was the chemical etching of lithography, used to reproduce images; automated typecasting, then typesetting machines, which sped up the manufacturing and processing of movable type; high-speed rotary presses that developed into web presses, using continuous rolls of paper, and then into offset printing, producing cleaner prints by "offsetting" ink from a metal plate to a rubber surface before transferring it to paper; and, most important of all, an invention inspired by insects.

8. Spaghetti

The secret of printing, hidden by ubiquity and likely near you now, is paper.

Paper may be everywhere, but it is not simple. Paper is a type of material physicists call a random fiber network: a jumble of tangled filaments like a mass of soft spaghetti pressed flat on a plate, in which every filament is a spaghetto binding to and connecting with arbitrary others while curling into a shape all its own and making each piece of paper as unique as a snowflake.

According to Chinese legend, a eunuch named Cai Lun invented paper by boiling and pulping fibers from bamboo, fishing nets, hemp, and mulberry bark in 105 CE. He called his invention $zh\check{\imath}$, a variation of $s\bar{\imath}ch\acute{o}u$, the Chinese word for "silk." Its English name, *paper*, is a descendent of *papyrus*. Cai may have improved paper, but he did not invent it: The Chinese had been using paper for wiping, wrapping, and writing for centuries when Cai was born.

The Indigenous peoples of the Americas invented paper and printing too. Around 500 CE, in what is now southeastern Mexico, the Yucatán Peninsula, Guatemala, Belize, western Honduras, and western El Salvador, the Maya pounded the inner bark of fig-bearing alamo trees to create *hu'un*, a writing surface far smoother and more durable than the papyrus being used in Egypt at that time, and were soon folding it to make books, including accurate, multicolored descriptions of astronomy and history, and printing on it with ceramic stamps much like the movable type used in East Asia and later in Europe. The Toltecs of the Mexican Altiplano inherited *hu'un*, bookmaking, and printing from the Maya and created huge and glorious books, including *Teoamoxtli*, a story of cults, gods, histories, rituals, and omens written in 660 CE by a Toltec priest named Huematzin, and the first of many sacred Toltec books now called the Books of Wisdom.

In the fourteenth century the Aztecs became the dominant power in

Mesoamerica, inherited paper and printing from the Toltecs, improved *hu'un* by adding fibers from candlewood, mulberry, and jonote trees, renamed it *amatl*, and made rolls of it thirty feet long, which they used for recording taxes and tributes collected from other tribes. By this time, those other tribes, including the Otomi, Zapotec, and Totonac, were papermakers and printers too.

Writing did not stand still during the thousands of years in which all writing was handwriting: the saltation of use led to continuous improvements, including the invention of pens made from reeds, then from feathers, then with metal nibs, then with reservoirs for storing ink; and the creation of new styles of calligraphy with names such as Carolingian minuscule, Gothic bastarda, and textura, all of which made writing cheaper and easier, but the price and scarcity of writing surfaces constrained their impact. Papyrus was made from reeds that only grew in a few places; China both monopolized silk and restricted its distribution; and parchment and vellum were expensively prepared animal skins. Paper transformed writing by making it affordable and practical beyond courts, palaces, and temples. Paper set writing free.

Before paper, the great East Asian project of copying the Buddha's sutras was laborious and slow; after, the Chinese printed sutras on paper using wooden blocks as big as pages in vast quantities, spreading paper and printing east to Japan and Korea, both of which used Chinese writing.

The oldest printed text still in existence is in Korea; it was produced in China between 700 and 750 CE on paper made of mulberry bark, using twelve wooden printing blocks. A few decades later, in Japan, the Empress Shōtoku ordered the first known bulk print run: a million copies of four prayers, distributed to monasteries in small, custom-made wooden pagodas. There are still tens of thousands of these printed prayers in Japan's monasteries today.

The Chinese started printing books on paper in the ninth century: The oldest known printed book in the world is a Chinese translation of the Diamond Sutra published in 868 CE and found in Dunhuang, in Western China. Its wooden cover announces that a Buddhist named Wang Jie made it "to gain blessings for his parents on the thirteenth of the fourth moon of the ninth year of the Xiantong era."

A hundred years later, between 956 CE and 975 CE, Qián Chù, the last king of Wuyue, one of the ten kingdoms of the period, located around what is now Shanghai, commissioned what may be the first bulk print run of *long-form* writing: eighty-four thousand copies of the Dhāraṇī Sutra of the Seal on the Casket, which were printed from carved wooden blocks, placed in miniature pagodas made of precious metals, and hidden in actual pagodas in China and Japan. These documents were still being discovered a thousand years later: For example, when the Leifengta Pagoda in Hangzhou collapsed in 1924, copies of Qián Chù's printed sutras spilled out of its bricks.

Paper and printing diffused westward during the thousand years between 500 CE and 1500 CE, first by spreading Buddhism beyond China's borders, then by traveling the Silk Road with traders who used it as tool and merchandise both, and finally out of Africa and Asia by crossing the Mediterranean as playing cards.

As paper became more common, papermakers struggled to meet demand. By the mid-1800s the paper industry was in crisis. Raw materials were running out, the price of paper was increasing, and it looked like the age of mass-producing stories by printing might be coming to an end.

9. Rag and Bone

On Saturday, October 26, 1844, Hugh Blackadar, publisher of the *Acadian Recorder*, a weekly newspaper in Halifax, Nova Scotia, received an unusual letter. It read: "Enclosed is a small piece of paper, as firm in its texture as white, and to all appearance as durable as the common paper made from hemp, cotton, or the ordinary materials of manufacture."

Charles Fenerty, a local poet, sent the letter, and it was unusual because Fenerty had written it on something that looked like paper but was unlike any paper Blackadar—or anyone else—had ever seen before.

We can better understand the letter's significance by traveling 175 miles west of Halifax and across the Canadian border. By 1844 the United States was the world's largest producer of newspapers, using more paper than England and France combined, even though those nations contained three times as many people.

This unprecedented consumption was causing a problem for papermakers all over the world, and especially for those in the United States: As demand for paper went up, the availability of its principal raw material, rags, went down.

Importers, inventors, and pulpers had tried making paper out of alternative materials, including asbestos, asparagus, banana leaves, beetroot, corn, dandelion, horseradish, grass, manure, marsh mallow, potatoes, swamp grass, and thistles, among other things, but they all failed. For example, banana leaves required so much crushing, bleaching, and washing that turning them into paper wasted more than a third of the leaves, and beetroot paper, while durable, was impossible to turn white. Only rags—meaning scraps of fabric, new or used—could be made into paper.

In France, rag collecting became a full-time job for people called *chiffonniers*, who rioted when new regulations required trash on the streets to be removed in carts without first being scavenged for rags, and who had such a romantic reputation that Parisians rose up to protect them when that city mandated public trash cans for every house. In Britain, rag collectors were called rag-and-bone men or ragpickers, and they had extra rags to collect because it was illegal to bury the dead in grave clothes made from anything but wool, as the nation needed every other kind of fabric for making paper. In the United States, newspapers encouraged readers to save rags in a bag placed beside their family Bible and give them to bell-ringing cart pushers every month, an arrangement that lasted until the late nineteenth century, when enterprising new immigrants calling themselves "scavengers" started sorting through trash for rags.

Despite these efforts, nations that were large paper consumers were also large rag importers. In 1840, for example, American papermakers imported 112 million individual rags weighing seven thousand tons, and eventually became so desperate for rags that they made paper from a surprising source: Egyptian mummies.

The United States imported Egyptian rags for the first time in 1855, and in 1856, a Syracuse newspaper called *The Daily Standard* announced, "Our Daily is now printed on paper made from rags imported from the land of the Pharaohs, on the banks of the Nile." That year, Egyptian rag imports to the United States increased from three hundred tons to over a thousand.

Paper mills did not always admit that their "Egyptian rags" had once wrapped mummies, perhaps for fear of upsetting a delicate public, and they seldom, if ever, imported whole mummies, because it was a waste of lading weight and shipping space. Egyptian workers unwrapped the linen from mummified animals and humans in the Port of Alexandria, then shipped the wrappings to the United States. To reduce costs, they packed the wrappings without washing them first, and after a month or more confined at sea, they arrived smelling unimaginably bad. A visitor to the Great Falls paper mill in Gardiner, Maine, described one such shipment as: "The most disagreeable, odiferous old clothes that I have ever had the misfortune to smell. They were the plundered wrappings of men, bulls, crocodiles, and cats. Some rags contain about 40 percent dust and dirt, which doubtless consists of many fine particles of pharaoh's embalmed subjects."

The Great Falls paper mill supplied paper made from mummies to the *New York Ledger*, the *Boston Courier*, and the *Boston Journal*. A paper mill in Marcellus Falls, New York, supplied the *Syracuse Daily Standard* with its mummy paper. Other mills supplied paper made from mummies to other newspapers, as well as to printers producing Bibles, books, and catalogs.

Historians debated whether paper made was ever really made from mummies for over 150 years. Many assumed it was an amusing myth. A mummy expert at the American Antiquarian Society in Massachusetts named S. J. Wolfe finally settled the argument in 2009, when she discovered a hymn printed in 1859 on a page that read, "This paper is made by the Chelsea Manufacturing Company of Greenville, Connecticut, the largest paper manufactory in the world. The material of which it was made was brought from Egypt. It was taken from the ancient tombs where it has been used in embalming mummies."

Charles Fenerty wrote his letter to the *Acadian Recorder* on paper that contained no rags from mummies or anywhere else. Fenerty had made his paper from a new material: *wood*. He ended his letter by saying, "I entertain an opinion that our forest trees, either hard or soft wood, but more especially the fir, spruce, or poplar, on account of the fibrous quality of their wood, might easily be reduced by a chafing, and manufactured into paper of the finest kind."

In this matter, Fenerty was prophet as much as poet. American papermakers' use of mummies as raw materials was an act of desperation as well as desecration. Paper mills were exploiting a reserve of rags that had accumulated over a long period, much as coal mines and oil wells exploit fossils. The math of addition and subtraction made paper manufacturing unsustainable because paper mills were consuming rags far more quickly than rags were being produced. In the middle of the nineteenth century, paper, and therefore printing, was in grave danger of becoming prohibitively expensive and then vanishing entirely.

Fenerty was not the first person to see the future of storytelling in forests. In fact, the pioneers of making paper out of wood were not people at all: They were wasps.

A French biologist named René Antoine Ferchault de Réaumur discovered this in 1719. Réaumur had been trying for some time to discover what raw material wasps used to make their papery nests. After giving up and moving on to other matters, he looked out of the window of his home in La Rochelle in the west of France and saw a wasp doing something strange:

> When I was no longer trying to solve this problem, a mother wasp came to inform me of what I had sought so many times in vain. She sat down near me on the frame of my window which was open. When I observed her closely, I saw that she seemed to gnaw the wood, that her two mandibles were acting with extreme activity, cutting very fine strands of wood. Ever since I observed that wasp detaching wood from my window, I have followed the movements of others that had landed on dry wood, and I have had many opportunities to convince myself that wasps go there to tear out the filaments they need to make their paper, I have seen and seen again some busy raking it with their mandibles. The old trellises of the palisades, the old sash, the old doors and the old shutters of the windows are all to their taste, for they only work on old and dry wood.

When Réaumur announced this discovery at the Public Assembly of the Academy of Sciences in France, he also offered a suggestion:

> The wasps seem to invite us to wonder if we could not succeed in making beautiful and good paper by immediately using certain woods. Paper has become one of our most important commodities, and supplies very large branches of our economy. Demand for it increases every day, but we cannot increase its supply at will, for we do not have as much raw material as we need. It was indeed a beautiful discovery to have found the means of converting rags into paper. But the quantity of these rags is proportionate to the quantity of linen that is worn out annually. The wasps show us how to make paper from wood, by reducing it into extremely thin

shavings; keeping them under water for several days; removing them to dry them; and repeating these operations until the shavings appear in the state we want. This will put the wood into the right condition to be carried under the pestles of paper mills.

But it was not to be. Thirty years later, Réaumur complained that no papermaker had explored making paper from wood and lamented that, despite being a biologist, he had not simply done it himself.

I should be ashamed of not having yet tried experiments of this kind, since more than twenty years that I have known all their importance, and announced them; but I had hoped that someone would want to make an occupation of it.

In 1757 Réaumur, then seventy-four years old, fell from his horse and died of his injuries. Nearly forty years had passed since his discovery, and paper was still made from rags.

Réaumur's idea was more than a century ahead of its time. The papermakers of the 1700s had no reason to use wood, and many good reasons to use rags. They had invested large sums of money in mills that could only process rags; foresters were focused on harvesting natural-growth trees for construction and shipbuilding, not trees that were suitable for papermaking; and there were no tools for turning wood into pulp and wood pulp into paper.

But when the rags started running out, Réaumur's idea suddenly seemed very good indeed. Wood-based paper arrived at last, not only ending the paper crisis but also transforming the economics of printing.

10. Story Factories

Wood-based paper first appeared in Germany in the 1840s, and by the end of the 1870s most printers in North America and Western Europe were using it. Not long after that, all paper was made from wood and none was made from rags. In less than thirty years, the price of paper fell by over 90 percent. In 1860 a pound of rags cost 44 US cents before pulping. In 1889, a pound of wood cost 4 cents *after* pulping. The invention of the mass production of mass communication, started by Gutenberg 450 years earlier, was complete. An industrial revolution had transformed storytelling, and now there were story factories all over the world.

Those factories produced ever more stories, told by ever more storytellers, reproduced ever more times. In 1449, the year before Gutenberg's printing press became operational, Europeans published two thousand new books and made an average of twenty-five copies of each one. In 1900, after paper made from wood replaced paper made from rags, Europeans published *twenty* thousand new books and, on average, there were *twenty-five hundred* copies of each one: ten times more stories a year, told by ten times more storytellers, to a hundred times more people.

One consequence of this change was an increase in literacy in countries that encouraged reading and an increase in efforts to suppress literacy in countries that feared it.

The difference between the growth of literacy in England and the growth of literacy in the Netherlands is an example. In 1450, when Gutenberg invented the printing press, 5 percent of the English population was literate, and 17 percent of the Dutch population was literate. By 1650, the two countries had equal levels of literacy: 53 percent in both England and the Netherlands. But in the centuries that followed, English literacy stayed the same while Dutch literacy increased. In 1820 literacy in England was still at 53 percent, but literacy in the Netherlands had reached 90 percent.

These countries industrialized writing at different rates too. By 1750 England had two printing presses and three paper mills per hundred thousand people, and the Netherlands had twelve printing presses and fourteen paper mills per hundred thousand people.

There were two reasons for these disparities, and both provide light that makes the story of stories make more sense, certainly until today, and probably beyond tomorrow.

The first reason was classification: England was, and still is at the time of writing, a monarchy. England's king or queen is the apex of a class system in which opportunity and wealth are roughly proportionate to proximity to the monarch, from the royal family to the aristocracy to the clergy to the working class to the underclass. This system was explicit until the 1940s. Members of the "upper" classes saw no shame in asserting that every individual had an unchangeable place, or "station," in life, to which they were born and in which they would die, regardless of their achievements or merit.

As the industrialization of writing made books cheaper and more ubiquitous, England's ruling elite asked themselves what seemed to them to be a perfectly reasonable question: whether they should permit working-class people to read. We saw a glimpse of the English aristocracy's argument against teaching reading earlier: it was a fear that literate workers would seek to change their supposedly unchangeable place in English society—that, as one then-common remark put it, "There would be no more servants who would clean shoes or attend upon horses." England's upper classes would rather keep tens of millions of people forever illiterate than shine their own shoes.

The word *illiteracy*, in use since the mid-1600s, was derived from *literate*, in use since the early 1400s, which came from the Latin *literatus*, which did not originally mean "able to read and write" but "learned, scholarly, and erudite." Similarly, *to read* did not originally mean "to decrypt writing" but—its roots are hidden in plain sight—"to reason." Literacy is learning, and reading is reasoning.

These original meanings were at the heart of the English aristocracy's concerns. Their question was deeper than whether working people should be taught to decipher writing: They were asking whether the masses should be permitted to learn and reason. This question is a motif that recurs throughout the rest of the story of stories: It was introduced during the industrialization of writing and is often repeated, sometimes in a modified form, whenever new storytelling technologies appear.

Unlike England, the Netherlands was a republic, not a monarchy, from 1588 to 1806, which is also, more or less, when Dutch literacy levels increased rapidly and English literacy levels stayed the same.

The Dutch had a class system too; it comprised ruling oligarchs called *Regenten*, or regents, followed by *Burgerij*, or citizens, who tended to be professionals like doctors and lawyers, followed by a working class and an underclass. But the concept of class in the Netherlands was not as constrained by ideas of blood and birth as it was in England, and as a result the Dutch class system was more fluid and meritocratic: joining a particular church could increase someone's social standing, for example, and where England's schools were mainly for the sons of the rich, Dutch schools included the sons and daughters of most of the working class.

This difference led to more literacy, but it was also a *result* of more literacy: When the printing press was invented, the Netherlands already had a literacy rate of 17 percent—three times higher than the European average.

The reason for the difference was religion. Although the Dutch, like almost all Western European Christians in 1450, were Catholics, the Netherlands was the birthplace of an early reform movement called *The Brethren of the Common Life* that foreshadowed Protestantism.

A Catholic deacon named Gerard Groote formed the Brethren in Deventer, an old Dutch city, in 1374. Groote was a humanist who believed religion was individual and personal, and people should be able to read the Bible for themselves. The Brethren translated the Bible from Latin to Dutch, operated schools that taught reading, made their own books, and laid a foundation for the rapid development of Dutch Protestantism after the Reformation, especially Reformed Christianity, or "Calvinism," which also emphasized teaching literacy and translating the Bible from Latin into everyday spoken languages. In the 1560s King Philip II of Spain, who had become the colonial ruler of the Netherlands, tried to suppress this humanism. The Dutch rebelled, overthrew the Spanish, created the Dutch Republic, and, incidentally, showed Europe's ruling class that literacy could cause revolution.

This difference between the Dutch and English attitudes to teaching literacy had effects that persist today: England's literacy rate still lags behind the literacy rate of the Netherlands. Eleven percent of Dutch adults cannot read; in England that number is 15 percent.

The second reason for the different rates of growth between literacy in England and the Netherlands is that when England's elites lost their battle against literacy, they resorted to censorship.

Illiteracy is the best form of censorship, but when illiteracy no longer worked as a control, the ruling classes in England and elsewhere took a position they have held ever since: that they have a right and responsibility to decide which books other people can read.

This problem of choosing, which we first saw when oral stories could be memorized, and which so offends America's twenty-first century book banners, is a constant theme of the story of stories: Whenever a new storytelling technology increases the number of stories we can choose, people in authority seek new ways to make that choice for us.

But powerful people tell on themselves when they invest their money and time in excluding everyone else: The more revolutionary value something has, the more the powerful will try to keep us away from it. This is certainly true whenever a privileged few try to ban books or otherwise decide what we may know. Censorship is a confession that stories change the world.

Charles Fenerty, the poet who made paper from wood, understood this. He wrote about it in 1866, in a poem about the printing press:

> We claim the Press, that wondrous art, alone
> Worth more than all, to the great ancients known:
> An orb of light, before whose powerful ray,
> The mist of superstition melts away;
> The voice, which science gave to liberty,
> To instruct the oppres't, and teach them to be free.
> Thine is a voice, more terrible by far,
> Than all the thunders of tumultuous war;
> Whilst thou in freedom's name, shalt dauntless speak,
> The slave shall struggle, till his fetters break.

When Fenerty called printing "the voice, which science gave to liberty," he was reporting recent history. In the three decades before he wrote those words, escaped American slaves published over eighty autobiographies because of the industrialization of storytelling. These books included Frederick Douglass's *Narrative of the Life of Frederick Douglass: An American Slave*, which by 1860 had sold thirty thousand copies. The following year, 1861, America's civil war started. This was no coincidence: Books like Douglass's, printed at low cost in large volume, are why the United States went to war with itself over abolition. Fenerty's poem, written soon after the civil war ended, is a celebration of the role printing played in ending slavery.

After the transition to wood-based paper, the industrialization of storytelling was complete, and an even greater revolution was beginning: one powered not by coal, muscle, wind, or water, but by a mysterious new form of energy.

Chapter 5

The All-Seeing Eye of Providence

1. Electricity

It is the first night of January 1845, and just beyond the wisteria-covered facade of the Windmill Inn in Salt Hill, twenty miles west of London, a widow named Mary Ann Ashlee hears a terrible scream of agony coming from the cottage next door, then another, then another. After the screams continue for several minutes, Mary Ann takes her candle out into the dark to discover what is happening.

The trembling flame first reveals a man dressed in the plain clothes of a Quaker leaving her neighbor's cottage, and, then inside the cottage, the neighbor, Sarah Hart, who is the mother of two young children, writhing on the floor while foaming at the mouth.

Mary Ann calls for the landlady, Mrs. Barrett. Mrs. Barrett sends her apprentice to fetch the Reverend Henry Champneys, a local doctor who lives nearby. Champneys arrives within minutes, takes Sarah's pulse, feels what he suspects are her final few heartbeats—they are so weak, he cannot be sure—then watches helplessly as she dies.

A few hours later in East London, the man dressed like a Quaker arrives at the Jerusalem Coffee House in Cornhill, collects a coat he left there earlier, makes his way by a strange, circuitous route to a lodging house on Cannon Street, extinguishes his gas lamp, and goes to bed.

If these events had taken place almost anywhere else in the world that day, including almost anywhere else in England, this would be the end of the story, apart from Sarah Hart's funeral and whatever arrangements are made for her now motherless children. No one in Salt Hill knows the name of the man in the Quaker clothes, or anything about him. He is twenty miles away, having left Salt Hill on a train to London that departed with no one boarding to follow him, and is now sound asleep.

But the following morning, when he returns to the Jerusalem Coffee House for his morning coffee, a tall man wearing a greatcoat approaches him and removes the coat to reveal a Metropolitan Police uniform. The police officer, whose name is William Wiggins, says:

"Are you not Mr. John Tawell?"

"I am."

"I am here to take you into custody. You were the last person seen with a woman who was found dead in Salt Hill yesterday."

"I was not at Salt Hill yesterday. I don't know anybody there. I did not leave town all day. You must be wrong in the identity. My station in society places me above or beyond suspicion."

What Tawell, currently comfortable in his casual lies and social status, does not know but is about to find out, is that there is a new technology in operation at the Salt Hill station where he boarded the train yesterday, and also at Paddington Station, where he disembarked. It was installed for safety reasons and has already prevented at least one deadly train crash.

That technology is called the electric telegraph, and it allows the two stations to communicate with one another at high speed using electrical signals that travel down cables. Last night, Sarah Hart's quick-thinking neighbors went looking for the man in the Quaker clothing and saw him board the train to London. A clerk at the Salt Hill station, also thinking quickly, used the electric telegraph to send the following message to Paddington Station, where it arrived long before the train:

> A murder has just been committed at Salt Hill, and the suspected murderer was seen to take a first-class ticket to London by the train which left at 7:42 PM. He is in the garb of a Quaker, with a brown great coat on, which reaches nearly down to his feet. He is in the last compartment of the second first-class carriage.

The staff of Paddington Station gave the message to an officer of the British Transport Police named William Williams, who identified Tawell when he got off the train, followed him unseen to his boarding house, and, because an officer of the Transport Police could only arrest someone on railway property, arranged for Tawell's arrest by the Metropolitan Police next morning.

Tawell, who is not in fact a Quaker despite his clothes—the Society of Friends expelled him decades ago after he tried to defraud one of their banks—seduced Sarah Hart while she was working as his children's nanny, fathered a son and daughter with her, and gave her money every week to pay her rent and buy her silence. Tawell has grown tired of this arrangement, so last night he poisoned Sarah with cyanide while their children were asleep in the next room. This was his second attempt to murder her; he also tried in September but did not use enough cyanide, and only made Sarah sick. A jury finds him guilty of Sarah's murder a few months after his arrest.

The case causes a sensation. John Tawell is the first person to commit murder using cyanide, the first to escape by train, and, most notable of all, the first to be captured by telegraph, this new, near-instant, long-distance, magical method of communication that somehow makes use of the recent discovery of electricity. The world did not understand the value of the telegraph before the message that caught the man who murdered the mother of his own children, but now that Tawell is captured and convicted, everyone can see the power of this new class of long-distance storytelling technology, which will eventually be called telecommunication.

There is one last consequence of the telegraph message sent from Salt Hill to Paddington. On the morning of Friday, March 28, 1845, John Tawell is hanged in the market square in Aylesbury, Buckinghamshire, before of a crowd of ten thousand people by a hangman who, perhaps accidentally, does not use quite enough rope for the drop from the gallows, ensuring that Tawell dies a slow and agonizing death, just as Sarah Hart did.

2. Experience

We are now halfway through *The Story of Stories*. The first half covered a million years of storytelling, from the first nightfires to the first telecommunications; the second half covers only two hundred years.

This imbalance—four chapters for one million years, four chapters for two hundred years—arises because the book's structure is not time but change, and change is not linear: Its rate increases so much that the next two hundred years of the story of stories contain as much change as the first million years.

When we look at almost any example of long-term human progress, we see change speeding up around the fifteenth century. This acceleration was once mistaken for a sudden springlike return to creation after a centuries-long winterlike freeze: a "renaissance" preceded by "dark ages." The various versions of this mistake are all story-shaped: They center heroic protagonists and, by implication, individual human agency, hidden behind hand-wavy vaguenesses like culture or faith.

This ever-increasing, ever-continuing rate of change is not caused by individual human agency. The change causes itself, especially the change in storytelling. Our increasing acceleration of innovation arises from our accumulation of equality, liberty, and freedom of thought; of health, life expectancy, and population; and of time for nonsubsistence activities, all of which exist because we have ever more ways to share experience using stories.

Experience is knowledge that we have stored and recorded. Before we could recall and retell stories, we stored our experiences in the error-prone, personal, private, and, above all, *mortal* medium of memory. The rise of storytelling, through speaking, singing, painting, writing, and printing, enshrined ever more experience in ways ever more immortal. Printing is especially good at transforming one person's experience into everyone's experience: Frederick Douglass died in 1895, for example, but we can forever share some of his lived experience as a slave by reading his books.

The invention of the printing press enabled and inspired ever more inventions for storing and sharing experiences, among them the first atlas in 1482, the first postal service in 1516, the first book of mathematical references and tables in 1533, the first peer-reviewed scientific journal in 1655, the first school textbook in 1690, and the first bookstore in 1732.

These inventions laid the foundation for an explosion of new storytelling technologies, many of them powered by electricity, in the nineteenth century, including the first electric telegraph in 1816, the first free, taxpayer-funded public library in 1833, the first photograph in 1838, the first paperback in 1841, the first practical typewriter in 1867, the first carbon copy in 1870 (now the vestigial "cc"—carbon copy—and "bcc"—blind carbon copy—options in the "send" field of every email), the first telephone in 1876, the first duplicating machine for low-volume home, school, and office use in 1886, the first record player in 1887, and the first movie screening and the first radio transmission in 1895.

The speed with which we invented, improved, and industrialized these electricity-powered storytelling tools was a consequence of the accelerative, self-reinforcing effect of shared experience. New storytelling technologies create new storytelling technologies. Where writing took five thousand years to mature and spread around the world, and printing took two thousand years, the electrified storytelling tools of the 1800s developed and dispersed in little more than a century.

These inventions turned the nineteenth century into what we would now call an age of big data, where someone sitting at their kitchen table could both benefit from the thoughts and experiences of others, of almost any kind, from almost any place and time, and preserve their own thoughts and experiences in handwriting, or as a printing-like typewritten manuscript that could be duplicated cheaply and in any quantity, from one to millions.

The inventions of the nineteenth century also laid the foundation for a twentieth-century storytelling technology: the television, invented by Philo Farnsworth in 1927, 111 years after the invention of the electric telegraph.

The commercialization of Farnsworth's invention was delayed by World War II, but by the end of the 1940s television manufacturers were selling millions of televisions a year.

No one knew exactly how these millions of televisions would change things, but there was one consequence that almost all broadcasters, television manufacturers, and other experts predicted with great confidence: that the big wooden cabinet in the living room around which the family gathered every evening and which currently contained a radio would soon contain a television instead. The beginning of television was therefore the end of radio, because no one would want to listen when they could watch. These experts were spectacularly wrong. Television started a radical new age of radio by forcing radio into a new form.

3. Sammy

Sammy Lobianco leaves his home on Jackson Avenue, passes the Memphis Restoration Church, the Pentecostal Holiness Church, and the Church of God in Christ, turns north on Manassas at the Food Mart, and walks by Humes High School, some empty lots, some low brick houses, and an orphanage, while Chevies and Studebakers cruise the beaten street and sugar maples and cottonwoods bloom all around. Sammy meets Angelo DiSalvo on one corner, and Joe Jones and Budgie Linder on others, and soon all four boys, dressed in gabardine shirts, pegged pants, and leather-soled moccasins, are heading up Thomas Street, where there are no more houses or churches, only windowless juke joints, weedy fields, and the Polish-Jewish junkyard.

It is the summer of 1954. Sammy, Angelo, Joe, and Budgie are walking to Curry's Club Tropicana on the corner of Thomas Street and Huron Avenue in North Memphis to see the Midnighters, a band with one of the week's bestselling records, "Work with Me, Annie." Its refrain—"Work with me Annie, Let's get it while the gettin' is good"—is so frank that the US government wants to ban the song.

Curry's is a supper club, the kind of place you see in old-time movies, where well-dressed people eat cheeseburgers and steaks, watch a band, and maybe dance. The club is not fancy—a one-story redbrick building no bigger than two basketball courts, with a low apron stage and a back wall hand-painted with little quavers and stars—but it has good music.

The Midnighters are a few songs in when an officer of the Memphis Police Department enters the club on his evening patrol. He sees the boys drinking Cokes, eating hamburgers, tapping their moccasined feet, loving every note and beat, and makes straight for them. They do not see him approach.

The boys are not breaking any laws. There have been no complaints about them. Johnny and Susie Curry, the club's owners, are delighted to have their patronage. Joe's father is the Currys' attorney, and on account of that, Susie seated the boys herself. But Johnny and Susie are Black. Curry's is a Black-owned club with Black clientele. The Midnighters are a Black band. "Work with Me, Annie" is Black music, from a genre that until recently was called "race music," and is now known as "rhythm and blues." Sammy and his friends are white—Sammy, for example, is second-generation Sicilian. They are the only white people in the place, apart from the officer of the Memphis Police Department.

This may seem like a small moment, but it is not. Memphis, Tennessee, is racially segregated by law, like all the American South. But segregation laws only restrict the movements of Black people; white people can go wherever they please—legally speaking, that is. White people keep other white people away from Black people not with laws but with fear and shame—by spreading stories about Black crime, Black violence, Black disease, and by calling white people who stray names like "negro lover," or worse.

The officer asks Sammy and his friends a question that is not a question. "Y'all want me to escort you out of here?"

The psychologist Robert Provine warns us to "resist neglecting or trivializing the commonplace." The moment in Memphis when the officer invites Sammy to leave Curry's Club Tropicana is one of these commonplace choices.

The officer waits for Sammy and his friends to get up and head out into the heat and night of Thomas Street, where the only beat is the bleat of the katydids.

But the boys do not move, save for the rhythm in their moccasins. Sammy looks up and into the man's face, says, "We're gonna stay and watch the Midnighters," then returns his gaze to the stage.

And the officer can do nothing but leave.

4. 1954

Historian Lawrence Levine wrote that "historians spend too much time in the company of movers and shakers and too little in the universe of the mass of humanity." Sammy Lobianco's night out at Curry's is a moment from the universe of the mass of humanity that shows the power of stories to change minds.

The encounter between Sammy and the officer of the Memphis Police Department is more than a meeting of people; it is also a meeting of stories.

The officer's story is that white Americans are innately superior to Black Americans, a difference so significant that the two groups must be kept as separate as possible, and should certainly never share the intimacy of a cheeseburger, an evening, and a song. In 1954, this is the standard story of the white American South, indeed of nearly all of white America. The law enforcement officer is not enforcing any laws. No laws are being broken. He is doing the other duty of police officers everywhere: enforcing the norms of his nation's standard story.

Sammy's story appears simpler. Sammy just wants to see the band. But beneath that, there is rebellion. Unlike the police officer, Sammy is indifferent to the Blackness of the band, the Blackness of the music, the Blackness of the club—or at least none of that Blackness is enough to keep him away. Sammy's story is a counterstory, an alternative narrative, the basis not of norms but of progress. His presence at the club is a minor act of civil disobedience, and his meeting with the police officer is a skirmish in a war of stories.

Nineteen fifty-four was an important year for America's standard story: it was the year the US Supreme Court ruled racial segregation in public schools unconstitutional, and the year before Black Americans, encouraged by that decision, boycotted segregated buses in a protest that made Martin Luther King Jr. the de facto leader of Black Americans' struggle for racial equality. It was, in short, the year that what we now think of as America's Civil Rights Movement was born, the opening pages of a counterstory that would vigorously challenge the standard story of the United States.

Far from the movers and shakers, in the universe of the mass of humanity, a few young white Americans—people like Sammy Lobianco—

had already started living that counterstory, changing their minds, moving slowly toward a more equal, less fearful, less segregated America, and they were doing it because of a change in storytelling technology.

5. Transistors and Resistors

The new behavior of Sammy and his friends—and other white kids in other cities across the American South—was an unforeseen consequence of three new storytelling technologies: television, vinyl records, and transistor radios.

In 1953, the year before Sammy went to see the Midnighters, a Japanese company called the Tokyo Telecommunications Engineering Corporation started making cheap, pocket-size radios from tiny silicon crystals that replaced the big, lightbulb-like vacuum tubes used in radios since World War II. These new components were called "transistors," because they could transfer electrical signals while also controlling them with resistance.

In 1957 the company started exporting its transistor radios to the United States, and on January 1, 1958, officially changed its name to Sony. The radios were an immediate success: Five million were sold in the United States in 1959, twice that many in 1960, and twice that many again in 1965.

A conventional, intuitive view of this development might be that transistor radios were simply radios, only smaller, and therefore radio programming would stay the same.

But that is not what happened.

Before transistors, radios were big, shiny, lounge-bound pieces of furniture that played big, shiny, lounge-bound music. Until the 1950s, the songs on American radios were standards by gentleman crooners like Frank Sinatra, Perry Como, and Bing Crosby, and cosplay cowboys like Gene Autry and Roy Rogers, all performed live and broadcast by national networks. There was no Black music unless you counted minstrelsy. America's antennas transmitted America's standard story: a tale of debonair city gents; begowned, bejeweled ladies; and rural, horseback-riding, cattle-herding pioneers, all living the good life in a land entirely white.

As we discussed a few pages ago, when television started becoming popular in the 1950s, most experts predicted it would replace radio completely. This had many consequences: National radio networks, assuming radio was now obsolete, stopped opposing new licenses for radio stations and became television networks instead; many local radio stations were put up for sale at bargain prices; America's radio manufacturers assumed the same and focused on making televisions; and television became the new technology of America's standard story. The first televisions even looked like radios: glossy, walnut-paneled boxes as big as suitcases, each with two speakers, four dials, and, peering unblinking from the center, a roundish eight-by-six-inch cathode-ray tube, as if the all-seeing Eye of Providence had stepped off the dollar bill and settled into your lounge.

Local radio stations that had previously rebroadcast programs from national networks were left with dead air. They needed cheap programming fast, so they did something national radio had never done: They played *recorded* music. National radio stars would not allow their recordings to be broadcast, so local stations turned to a new recording format favored by younger, hungrier musicians: Seven-inch-diameter, one-song-per-side discs of polyvinyl chloride, or "vinyl," commonly known as "singles."

Singles went on sale in 1948. They were cheap, durable, sounded crisp and clear, and had large spindle holes so they could be changed automatically. These features unintentionally made them perfect for the coin-operated music players found in clubs, bars, and diners called jukeboxes. Singles became the meal in the jukebox's rainbow maw, and jukeboxes became ubiquitous.

By the time local radio started playing singles, record companies had optimized songs for jukeboxes. Singles were refined sugar for the mind, recordings of short songs written to immediately grab and hold attention, then echo in memory long after they ended, and they were more likely to be new songs by new singers than old standards by old stars.

Sammy Lobianco was fourteen when singles first appeared. National radio may have been whites-only, but jukeboxes were indiscriminate. Jukeboxes in Black places played Black music, and so local radio stations, now jukeboxes of broadcasting, sometimes played Black music too. The summers of Sammy's adolescence had a soundtrack of Black songs spilling onto the streets of Memphis from jukeboxes and radios in Black barbershops, Black bars, and Black beer joints. Black music was a natural part of Sammy's cultural vocabulary.

And Sammy wasn't alone. Around the time that Sammy went to see the Midnighters, another white Memphis teenager, five months younger than Sammy, was auditioning at a recording studio on Union Avenue, a few miles from Sammy's house.

The teenager sang "Harbor Lights," a ballad from 1937 that had been a hit for six different artists in 1950, including Bing Crosby. The kid's rendition sounded awful. He sang "I Love You Because," a country-and-western ballad, twelve times with little success. Just before he gave up, he tried one last song: not a white ballad but a Black song with a long pedigree. It was written by Victoria Spivey, a blues singer from Houston, Texas, in 1926. She called it "Black Snake Blues." It was reworked later that year by another Texan blues singer, Blind Lemon Jefferson, who called it "That Black Snake Moan." In 1946 it was reworked again by a blues singer from Mississippi named Arthur Crudup, who called it "That's All Right Mama."

Like Sammy, the boy at the audition had grown up overhearing and loving the Black music of Memphis. He had first heard "That's All Right Mama" on Beale Street, where Black musicians including

Louis Armstrong, Muddy Waters, and B. B. King sometimes played. When the boy sang this song, he became another singer, more himself, more alive, more spontaneous, and, frankly, less white. He sang the song faster than Arthur Crudup had, made it feel defiant, not sorrowful like previous versions, and shortened its title, possibly by mistake, to "That's All Right." His name was Elvis Presley, and he had just recorded the song that would make him a star.

Presley was among the first white appropriators of a new style of music that had been simmering on the stoves of Black America since the 1920s, a style the people who loved it came to call "rock and roll."

During the 1950s, rock and roll started to dominate American radio. When WHBQ Radio in Memphis played "That's All Right" seven times in a row a few days after it was recorded, forty-seven listeners called the station asking to hear it one more time. In 1955, "Rock Around the Clock," a rock-and-roll single from another white act, Bill Haley & His Comets, was the bestselling song in America for eight consecutive weeks.

Then transistor radios arrived.

If not for transistor radios, rock and roll might have been a fad. Most of the old tube radios furnishing America's living rooms did not play rock and roll because parents would not permit it. America's patriarchs and matriarchs claimed they objected to rock and roll because it was too loud and noisy and its lyrics were too sexual and godless, but these were euphemisms intended to obscure their real concern: Rock and roll was too *Black*, even when played by white musicians. White parents feared that if their children started to like Black music, they might also start to like Black *people*.

The transistor radio bypassed all these gatekeepers. The transistorization of radio was also the personalization of radio: Transistor radios were so small and cheap that, for the first time ever, people could own a radio for themselves. Transistors freed teenagers to choose their own music, and they chose rock and roll.

Sammy was nineteen when the Midnighters released "Work with Me, Annie." He heard it, liked it, and wanted to see them play. It was that simple. He was not integrating or even mixing—at that time, white Americans like Sammy shared spaces and experiences with Black Americans without much interaction—but nonetheless, in the universe of the mass of humanity, the walls of segregation wobbled.

White Americans like Sammy are not heroes of desegregation. That title belongs to all the Black Americans who led, planned, organized, and participated in the Civil Rights Movement. Many gave their bodies and liberty, and some gave their lives. Our story-shaped brains naturally want to overattribute cause to one or two individuals, say Martin Luther King Jr. and Rosa Parks, and reduce the complexity of history to an unambiguous chronology of consequence, but the Civil Rights Movement was a *movement*. Some of the things it set in motion were minds in the universe of the mass of mankind, especially *white* minds. Black Americans already knew that segregation was cruel, unjust, and an insult to God. It was white minds that needed to change. And brilliant Black Americans were not born for the first time ever in the generation of Martin Luther King Jr. There were brilliant Black Americans in every generation, from Phillis Wheatley to Harriet Tubman to Ida B. Wells.

So why did white minds start changing in the 1950s?

There is no simple narrative or seven-inch single to answer this question, no matter how much our story lust craves one. The Civil Rights Movement evolved from a large and complex combination of elements, including the legacy of its predecessors. Just one of those elements was a new story that challenged America's standard story of racial segregation and white supremacy, a story told and shared by the new technologies of seven-inch singles and transistor radios playing the new music of rock and roll.

Every time a kid like Sammy Lobianco had a good time at a Black place watching a Black band, all the standard stories about Black

Americans being a dangerous and different species became harder to believe. This is why songs like "Work with Me, Annie" and "That's All Right," which had nothing to do with racial equality, had everything to do with racial equality.

The desegregation effect of rock and roll arose from the decentralization of radio. Before television, American radio broadcasting was a duopoly. There were only two networks: NBC and CBS. Network censors preapproved every radio program. Approximately twelve people, all men, all white, all in their forties and fifties, chose and controlled every song, story, character, and storyteller that America's 109 million radio listeners heard—one person transmitting for every nine million receiving. When NBC and CBS became television networks instead of radio networks, they started telling the standard story of America to more than 150 million Americans. All over the world, broadcast television is still the best way to tell a population a standard story. You can turn on a television anywhere, watch what is being broadcast nationally, and immediately see that country's current government-approved standard story.

The counterstory told by rock and roll started an insurrection against the nationally broadcast standard story of America. Rock and roll's counterstory was shown, not told. The songs rock and roll radio stations played were nothing like, say, Billie Holiday's "Strange Fruit," which has plain and haunting lyrics about lynching. The story "Strange Fruit" tells was too direct and dangerous for mass communication in the 1950s, and despite being a beloved song, is barely played on radio even today. Rock and roll was not *about* desegregation. It *was* desegregation.

6. At the Speed of Light

The transistors operating rock and roll's radios were an unintended consequence of the invention of television.

By the early 1900s, the idea of television was obvious. Animated illustrations had been popular in spinning devices called zoetropes since the 1830s, photography became common in the 1850s, and cinema emerged in the 1890s. Electrical communication was made common by telegraphs in the 1840s, telephones in the 1870s, and radio in the 1890s.

Combining the ideas of electrical communication and moving pictures seemed like an apparently straightforward next step, and it led to a gold rush of television invention. There were so many pioneers panhandling for television at the turn of the twentieth century that nearly every industrial nation now claims one of its citizens as television's inventor. Germany has Paul Julius Gottlieb Nipkow, Russia has Constantin Perskyi and Leon Theremin, France has Georges Rignoux, the United States has Charles Francis Jenkins and Philo Farnsworth, Japan has Kenjiro Takayanagi, Scotland has John Logie Baird, and there are many more names and nations too.

Most early attempts to invent television were mechanical. Images were scanned using a spinning disc dotted with holes, captured using a chemical element called selenium, which resists electricity in darkness, and re-created using lightbulbs connected to the selenium and placed behind a second spinning disc.

At least, that was the theory. In practice, these mechanical televisions did not work—or at least they did not work very well. They produced murky miniature images made of low-resolution, blocky picture elements, flickering wildly as if lit by stroboscopes, vague as Rorschach tests, not at all like the crisp moving pictures available on the screens in early 1900s movie theaters. The only way to improve the images of selenium-based televisions would be to connect tens of thousands of selenium cells to tens of thousands of lightbulbs, and this, while theoretically possible, was impractical. By 1908 it was clear that a mechanical television with a black-and-white screen two inches square and acceptable resolution would be bigger than a three-room apartment and cost as much as the RMS *Titanic*, the ill-fated ocean liner whose design was being completed that same year. Even worse, a mechanical *color* television would cost as much as *three Titanic*s.

A well-defined problem is the seed of its own solution. The limitations of mechanical televisions caught the attention of a Scottish engineer named Alan Archibald Campbell-Swinton, who proposed a simple and elegant alternative: "The problem can probably be solved by beams of cathode rays deflected by the varying fields of two electromagnets placed at right angles to one another. The moving cathode beam has only to impinge on a sufficiently sensitive fluorescent screen to obtain the desired result."

This was one of the earliest and clearest descriptions of how to make a practical, working television. Making screens means manipulating light, which means operating at close to the speed of light, which is something no mechanical device could ever do. It soon became clear that the cathode ray, not a spinning mechanical disc, would be the foundational technology of television.

Cathode rays were streams of a newly discovered particle, the electron. Practical applications of electrons came to be called "electronics," enabled by transistors and other electronic components, and the twentieth century became an age of electronic moving pictures.

7. MindWar

Television excels at changing minds because it looks real. We know we are seeing a signal, but may assume it is much the same as a stimulus—that what we are looking at is what we would see if we were standing where the camera is. This is especially true when televised storytellers claim their story is objective, true, and unadulterated. This is a big problem with television news, and it was not long before tellers of the standard story were exploiting the faux authenticity of television news to exert unprecedented influence over us.

In 1980 Colonel Paul Vallely, Commander of the US Army's 7th Psychological Operations (PSYOP) Group, ordered Lieutenant Colonel Michael Aquino to create a new strategy for psychological operations—the US Army's euphemism for propaganda—in the era of television. In Aquino's opinion—and Vallely's and that of many others in the military—the United States lost its recent war in Vietnam "not because we were outfought but because we were out-PSYOPed," especially on television.

Aquino proposed replacing PSYOP with a new way to win the war of stories designed for the television age. He called it MindWar and described it as

> the deliberate, aggressive convincing of all participants in a war that we will win that war, that must seek out the attention of the enemy nation through every available medium, and reach out to friends, enemies, and neutrals alike across the globe, not through the primitive "battlefield" leaflets and loudspeakers of PSYOP but through the media possessed by the United States which have the capabilities to reach virtually all people on the face of the Earth, the electronic media that make possible a penetration of the minds of the world such as would have been inconceivable just a few years ago. MindWar always speaks the truth. Its power lies in its ability to focus recipients' attention on the truth of the future as well as that of the present—the truth that the United States has resolved to make real if it is not already so. We have to reach out and seize this tool; it can transform the world for us. If we do not, we will relinquish our ability to inspire foreign cultures with our morality.

A new generation of military leaders developed MindWar for a decade, and then, in 1991, the United States and a coalition of allies launched a kinetic war to force the Iraqi Army out of Kuwait. The standard practices of vilifying the enemy and censoring unfavorable reports now came with a MindWar twist: directly influencing Americans' support for the war by convincing them that their military was both undefeatable and incapable of killing innocent civilians. These two needs were contradictory, especially as the first stage of the battle plan was to bomb Iraq nonstop, night and day, for six weeks, with two thousand tons of ordnance a day, a strategy that would inevitably kill Iraqi civilians.

The MindWar-inspired solution was to hide the bombardment in plain sight by feeding television news reporters with irresistible—and carefully curated—video images recorded through the sights of bombers and by television cameras attached to missiles. The images were unlike anything the public had seen before. The mind warriors released videos almost every day as evidence that the war against Iraq was being fought with precision-guided missiles, presented to the people of America and its allies as "smart" weapons that only hit the targets they were aimed at and caused no civilian deaths. The military's mind warriors led the public to believe that the United States and its allies were fighting a new kind of war—a war so high-tech that it was clean, precise, impossible to lose, and highly unlikely to kill civilians.

The missile videos were real, but misleading. Only 7,400 of the 84,200 tons of explosives used in the war were precision-guided, and most of those targeted military bunkers in Kuwait. Ninety-five percent of the munitions the coalition dropped on or fired at Iraq itself were unguided, or "dumb," and 75 percent of those—some 56,000 tons of ordnance in all—missed their targets and killed thousands of Iraqi civilians. Even the supposed "smart" munitions killed noncombatants: two laser-guided "bunker buster" bombs killed four hundred Iraqi civilians in a single attack on an air raid shelter in Baghdad, for example. But this information had little influence on people in the United States and other coalition countries: America's mind warriors had precision-targeted *those* civilians with video-game-like footage from smart bombs to make an irresistible, indelible—and therefore incontrovertible—impression that war was now always clinical and always winnable.

The United States won the MindWar so completely that counter-stories were rendered ineffective.

As the conflict was nearing its end, photographer Ken Jarecke and a military public affairs official encountered a bombed-out truck on a highway near Basra, Iraq. With the official's permission, Jarecke took a photograph of the person in the truck's passenger seat, charred beyond recognition yet also clearly a human being, who appeared to be grimacing in agony and trying to escape from the vehicle to avoid being burned alive. The person's arm, hand, and face told this story, at least; there was no way to know what actually happened, or even whether they were a soldier or a civilian.

Jarecke sent the image to the Associated Press, which distributes news to fifteen thousand publications all over the world. The photo editors refused to distribute it for unspecified reasons, which, for all practical purposes, censored it almost entirely.

Only one newspaper published the photo: *The Observer*, printed in London on Sundays. Many *Observer* readers were eating breakfast when they saw Jarecke's image without warning on page 9: a close-up of the burned face covering more than a third of the broadsheet page, positioned between the headline "The Real Face of War" and an advertisement that read, "No one takes more off summer holidays."

Some of these readers wrote outraged letters, saying, for example, "Did you stop to consider the unimaginable distress it may cause to friends and relations of the dead?"; "In thousands of homes on Sunday morning, the first ones to look at the paper are children"; and "If he were your son, would you think it just and decent that his picture should be displayed for all and sundry to gawp at?"

Harold Evans, a veteran of the British newspaper industry who had edited both *The Times* and *The Sunday Times*, defended *The Observer*, saying, "Before this, it had been possible to enjoy the lethal felicity of designer bombs as some kind of video game. There was no escape from the still silence of the corpse in *The Observer* photograph. Anyone who saw it last Sunday will never forget it. It was a necessary shock."

The shock was necessary because MindWar had presented the military operation in Iraq and Kuwait as clinical, merciful, and surgical. In truth, the war was as brutal and messy as any other. The United States' 1st Infantry Division used tanks fitted with plows to bury hundreds of Iraqis alive beneath tons of dirt and sand, and soldiers from the United Kingdom's 1st Armoured Division charged Iraqi soldiers in trenches with fixed bayonets, for example.

When asked about these tactics, Colonel Lon "Bert" Maggart, the commander of one of the two US brigades involved in that part of the war, was candid about the bayonets and burials both, saying, "People somehow have the notion that burying guys alive is nastier than blowing them up with hand grenades or sticking them in the gut with bayonets. Well, it's not."

Why did "people somehow have the notion" that this war was not "nasty"? MindWar. MindWar's victory in Iraq removed the stain of Vietnam from the American military so completely that much of the United States' population—especially the wealthy owners of its cable television news channels—were eager to watch another war. They got their wish—a literal sequel—in 2003, when America and its allies attacked Iraq again.

This time the mind warriors, educated and emboldened by their victory in 1991, added a new strategy: accrediting and training journalists to be "embedded" into combat units deployed to the battlefield. Embedded journalists faced strict reporting constraints. They could not cover undefined "ongoing engagements" without prior military approval, for example—an arrangement Clarence Page, a veteran American war reporter, pointed out is "also known as censorship."

Censorship was rarely needed. The embedded journalists, dependent on military protection, told sympathetic stories naturally, reinforcing public support by creating the illusion of a swift, clean war. Some of those journalists even believed they were telling the truth. MindWar, recently rebranded with the less specific, more friendly name "information warfare," had achieved another victory.

The United States' military had now battle-tested and proven the principles of MindWar: Target the domestic civilian population; use trusted, third-party, nongovernment sources to tell stories; provide high-fructose eye candy—like the footage from bomb and missile cameras—to guarantee attention; tell lies of omission, not commission; if you cannot convince, sow doubt and cause confusion; and, most important, tell a story that makes the outrageous seem normal, and the normal—Ken Jarecke's photo showing the inevitable result of a bombing, for example—seem outrageous.

Outrageous is not the same as wrong. Wrong is hiding from the outcomes of our actions. If we support a war, we must know what happens to the people we attack and the people we ask to attack them; if we oppose a war, we must know what happens to the people we refuse to defend. At its root, MindWar is yet another solution to the problem of choosing, albeit one that many people welcome. The mind warriors help us evade the often uncomfortable and unpleasant consequences of our actions by choosing which stories we are told. We must resist. This, in the words of Harold Evans, is "an argument for realism, not pacifism."

8. A New Literacy

We can defend ourselves from mind warriors by reclaiming the original, broader definitions of literacy as learning, and reading as reasoning, and abandoning the more recent idea that these words mean nothing more than "the ability to decipher writing" and "the act of deciphering writing."

Some people, many of them editors, literary agents, newspaper columnists, publishers, and writers, are worried by any proposal to redefine reading. These concerns are not new; they date back to at least 1895, when H. G. Wells wrote *The Time Machine*, a book in which a time traveler leaves Victorian London and visits the year 802701, expecting to meet people "incredibly in front of us in knowledge." Instead, he finds "fools on the intellectual level of five-year-old children" who cannot read. He befriends one, observes that the "bare idea of writing had never entered her head," and concludes that she had "seemed more human than she was."

After the publication of *The Time Machine* and the rise of radio, television, and other electrical storytelling tools, the idea of a dystopian "postliterate future" became a trope. Ray Bradbury imagined a future where "firemen" burned houses containing books in *Fahrenheit 451*; Marshall McLuhan coined the term *postliterate* in *The Gutenberg Galaxy*; Gary Shteyngart wrote about screens that invite users to "Switch to Images today! Less words = more fun!!!" in *Super Sad True Love Story*; and Denzel Washington walked across a postapocalyptic, illiterate America to deliver the last remaining Bible to the last remaining library in *The Book of Eli*, among many other examples.

The messages in these stories vary—some reach the time traveler's conclusion that people who cannot read are less than human, while others, like *Fahrenheit 451*, are subtle celebrations of counterstories—yet there is dread in all of them. A future without reading seems especially terrible to people who write for a living.

But angst about radios, televisions, or any other new storytelling technology ending reading is misdirected. We have been raised to believe that reason, history, and therefore humanity only truly began with writing; this is an old Victorian idea, wrong historically, morally, and mathematically.

Of the 110 billion humans that have ever lived, only 10 billion—less than 10 percent—could read. When H. G. Wells described people who could not read as "seeming more human than they were," the adult literacy rate in his own country, the United Kingdom, was 75 percent, and it was less than 20 percent in the world as a whole. It was also, of course, just a few decades after Britain's parliament had worried that teaching people to read would be "prejudicial to their morals and happiness." When Marshall McLuhan wrote *The Gutenberg Galaxy* in 1963, the world literacy rate was 40 percent. McLuhan was imagining a postliterate world while living in a preliterate world.

Writing is old, but literacy is new. Almost everything humanity has accomplished was accomplished without literacy. Most of our technology, most of our societies, and most of our world was built by people who did not decipher writing. Writing, for all its power and value, is just another technology of story.

This is not a recent insight. As long ago as 1960, literary critic Harry Levin argued that we need to recreate literacy for a new age:

> The term *literature* assumes that verbal works of imagination are transmitted by means of writing. Yet we live at a time when the Word as spoken or sung, together with a visual image of the speaker or singer, has been regaining its hold through electrical engineering. A culture based upon the printed book, which has prevailed from the Renaissance until lately, has bequeathed to us—along with its immeasurable riches—snobberies which ought to be cast aside. We ought to take a fresh look at tradition, considered not as the inert acceptance of a fossilized corpus of themes and conventions, but as an organic habit of re-creating what has been received and is handed on.

Any discussion about reinventing literacy must begin by dispelling understandable, if unfortunate, confusion about what *literacy* means. There was no such word until November 1880, when it first appeared in an American publication, *The Atlantic Monthly*, as the opposite of *illiteracy*, in an unsigned complaint about people learning to read: "It is not illiteracy I want to prevent, but literacy!"

Reading only writing may have been sufficient when writing was the only technology of story, but it is not enough today. Everyone must be able to "read" stories no matter what technology is being used to tell them.

This technology-independent literacy is sometimes called *transliteracy*, a term that originated in 2005 with Alan Liu, a professor of English at the University of California, Santa Barbara, and means "the ability to read, write and interact across a range of platforms, tools and media from signing and orality through handwriting, print, TV, radio and film, to digital social networks."

Transliteracy is especially well understood by librarians, the underground freedom fighters in the war of stories, whose sworn duty is to connect people in the universe of the mass of humanity to knowledge. For example, here is Tom Ipri, a senior librarian at Temple University in Philadelphia, describing transliteracy's importance:

> Not only does transliteracy question previous assumptions of authority, it also calls into question the often assumed privilege of printed text. Transliteracy is not unique in questioning this bias—media literacy efforts have certainly tried to raise the profile of nonprint materials. But transliteracy is unique in combining democratizing communication formats, expressing no preference of one over the other, with emphasizing the social construction of meaning via diverse media. Because of the ways in which transliteracy questions authority and devalues hierarchical structures for disseminating information, transliteracy overlaps concerns much at the heart of librarianship.

The debate about what literacy should be is actually a debate about what literacy is *for*. Either literacy is only reading and writing, merely a skill necessary for productive employment, or literacy is knowing and reasoning, and a path for each of us to become an independent consciousness. In short, the question we now face is whether we want literacy to be transactional or transcendent.

This is a question, but not a choice. The late nineteenth century's redistricting of literacy as the mere decryption of reading and writing cannot hold any longer. Every mind is vulnerable to stories mass-communicated by any means necessary. The only alternative to a new literacy would be to trust every storyteller to use the power of storytelling responsibly, and there is nothing in the story of stories to suggest that is sensible.

We must all learn the literacy needed to read—or, *reason about*—stories, so that they raise our consciousness rather than diminish it. Literacy must become transcendent for everyone.

Transcendence sounds grand, but that is only because stories caricature heroes, emphasize the extraordinary, exaggerate reality, and make us believe everything that matters must be big. Big things are just small things accumulated.

9. bell

They did not invite Gloria Watkins to this workshop, and they did not tell her about it. They are honored that Paulo Freire, the great Brazilian educator, has come to the University of California, Santa Cruz, to talk about how a new kind of literacy can liberate the oppressed. Gloria Watkins is a troublemaker and a feminist, and ever since her first book was published last year—a feminist book written using the strange pen name bell hooks, all lowercase like e. e. cummings or ruth weiss—she has gotten worse. Feminists like Gloria Watkins oppose Paulo Freire because his books are—allegedly—male-centered, patriarchal, and do not count women among the oppressed.

They did not invite Gloria Watkins to this workshop, and they did not tell her about it, but she is here anyway. She discovered it at the last minute, when it was already full, and got in by taking the place of someone who dropped out. Gloria is hard to miss: the only Black face in the room, with pineapple-style hair like Grace Jones, all shorn on the sides and natural on top.

She is quiet at first. They exchange glances and glares and point at her with their eyes up and down the lecture theater.

Eventually she interrupts. Oh, the *boldness* of this young Black female from Kentucky who hasn't even finished her PhD, interrupting the great Paulo Freire. They cannot hear what she is saying—it's *something something feminism*—because they are busy turning and shushing and telling her to *Knock it off Gloria, we're here to listen to something important*. Gloria tries to say more, so they talk over her to ensure that Paulo Freire does not hear, is not offended, and understands that she does not speak for their school. What they feared is now upon them: Gloria Watkins covering Santa Cruz in shame before the world's most celebrated educator.

Then Paulo Freire speaks. He is sixty and balding, with subversive silver hair peeking out from behind his neck; has a long beard, completely white apart from a dark patch beneath his chin; and wears an oatmeal-colored tweed jacket over a sweater, button-up shirt, and tie, even though it is summer in California and the temperature is in the high seventies. He looks exactly as he should: like a guru, a wizard, the Santa Claus of education. He will take control of this situation.

Which he does, but not in the way they are expecting. He tells *them* to be quiet. He encourages Gloria Watkins to speak. He says her questions are crucial. He agrees that his books are sexist and says he must learn to do better. There is a chemistry between them, an immediate meeting of minds, a dialogue in which each wants to learn from the other.

After the workshop, Gloria and Paulo leave together, go to Marianne's on Ocean Street to eat ice cream, talk for hours, and begin a lifelong friendship.

The All-Seeing Eye of Providence

The connection between Gloria Watkins and Paulo Freire came from their mutual conviction that we need a new approach to literacy.

Gloria—from now on I will use her pen name, bell hooks—understood and appreciated Paulo's ideas long before she attended the workshop in the summer of 1982: she had read his books and found them both inspirational and practical. Years later she wrote about discovering his work, the memory still fresh in her mind: "I came to Freire dying of thirst, and I found in his work a way to quench that thirst. To have work that promotes your own liberation is such a powerful gift."

She was dying of thirst because, despite her extraordinary talents, her experience in education was difficult. When she first read Paulo's books in the late 1970s, she was a graduate student on the verge of crisis:

> I wanted to become a critical thinker. That longing was seen as a threat to authority. White male students who were "exceptional," were allowed to chart their intellectual journeys, but those of us from marginal groups were expected to conform. My professors seemed enthralled by the exercise of power and authority within their mini-kingdom, the classroom. My commitment to learning kept me attending classes, but because I would not be an unquestioning, passive student, some professors treated me with contempt. I was slowly becoming estranged from education. Finding Freire in the midst of that estrangement was crucial to my survival as a student.

This description of teachers and teaching rings true for most of us. Paulo calls this standard approach "banking education," "in which the scope of action allowed to the students extends only as far as receiving, filing, and storing the deposits," and "knowledge is a gift bestowed by those who consider themselves knowledgeable upon those whom they consider to know nothing."

He calls his alternative, which he practiced as well as wrote about, *critical literacy*, where *critical* does not have its everyday meaning of "essential" or "criticizing" but a third meaning with roots in the work of Immanuel Kant, an eighteenth-century German philosopher.

Kant used the German word *kritisch*, meaning "critical," to refer to thoughtful analysis of how something works; what its capabilities, limits, and powers are; and what system it fits into.

Kant said:

> Our age is the age of criticism, to which everything must be subjected. The sacredness of religion, and the authority of legislation, are by many regarded as grounds of exemption from examination. But, if they are exempted, they become the subjects of just suspicion, and cannot lay claim to sincere respect, which reason accords only to that which has stood the test of a free and public examination.

Paulo took Kant's idea and applied to it literacy, in the broad sense of learning, and reading, in the broad sense of reasoning. He taught his students to "read the world, as well as the word"—to not only decipher the signs and symbols of storytelling technologies such as writing but also think about how the things those signs and symbols represent affect their everyday life.

Paulo saw reading, which is, after all, *reasoning*, as an opportunity to think deeply about systems, power, and how these things impact us. Rather than simply teaching how to spell and recognize the word *landlord*, for example, he also encouraged his students to think about what landlords do, why they do it, and how that affects the students and their society.

Critical literacy is analyzing, considering, and examining things in addition to deciphering the words that describe them. Every sign and symbol in our lives exists because someone created it, often as a way of gaining or maintaining power. In 1983, not long after he first met bell, Paulo summarized critical literacy in a speech in Campinas, Brazil, fifty miles northwest of São Paulo, saying,

> Reading is not exhausted merely by decoding the written word or written language, but by extending into knowledge of the world. Reading the world precedes reading the word, and the subsequent reading of the word cannot dispense with continually reading the world. Language and reality are dynamically intertwined. The understanding attained by critical reading of a text implies perceiving the relationship between text and context.

The alternative to critical literacy is the *decoding of literacy* taught by the banking system of education. Decoding literacy discourages thinking. A child learning to read is taught to be satisfied when they can decode a written word and say it out loud. They are neither expected nor welcome to take the next logical step and think about what that word tells them about why things are the way they are. This step beyond decoding is deliberately and effectively neutered. It is enough to decode; it is too much to wonder why, and far too much to also apply the skill of reading to other forms of storytelling, such as television, movies, and music, and become transliterate. We are taught to read the word, and are actively discouraged from reading the world because such questioning empowers us, and might cause us to challenge the authority of our banking system educators and other people who exert power over us.

Reading is always a political act, because every story is either a standard story or a counterstory. We must decide which kind of story we are reading and what it signifies, interpret its intentions, and wonder what it reveals about our life and our world, because only critical literacy can lead us to liberty.

10. A New Liberty

When bell and Paulo talk about how a new literacy can liberate oppressed people, they are not only talking about downtrodden, illiterate, or poor people in developing nations.

They are talking about you and me too.

In her book *Ain't I a Woman*, bell put it this way:

> Often when people read Freire, they approach his work from a voyeuristic standpoint. They see two locations in the work, the positions of Freire the educator and the oppressed groups he speaks about. In relation to these two positions, they position themselves as observers, as outsiders. When I came to Freire's work, I identified with the marginalized peasants he speaks about. I was coming from a rural southern Black experience, and had lived through the struggle for racial desegregation. This experience positioned Freire in my mind and heart as a challenging teacher whose work furthered my own struggle.

We are not disinterested spectators watching the development of a new literacy from afar; we are among the people who need a new literacy to liberate ourselves from oppression. Being Black was a general disadvantage that gave bell an advantage in this specific circumstance. Her experience of oppression in the United States made it easier for her to recognize herself among the oppressed people Paulo talks about. If you have not had similar experiences, you may think you do not need a new literacy, and that bell and Paulo are talking about other people.

But Paulo defines oppression broadly. You are oppressed if you have internalized an oppressor's ideas so thoroughly that their ideas about you dominate your own; if you are stuck in a situation of emotional or physical violence; if you are living for others rather than for yourself; or if you are in "any situation in which someone is hindering your pursuit of self-affirmation. That situation is violent even when sweetened by false generosity, because it interferes with your true purpose, which is to become more fully human."

By this definition, we are almost all oppressed, and have been for most of our lives—so long that we are accustomed to our oppression, and our oppression may be invisible to us.

We are not all *equally* oppressed, of course. Some people face more oppression than others: those from marginalized communities, for example. But oppression is not a competition; not being marginalized is not the same as not being oppressed; and oppression is not an either/or: most oppressors are also oppressed.

We are oppressed by the prototypical mind warriors whose roles have existed for thousands of years: our families, romantic partners, or friends; our bosses, managers, or supervisors; the representatives of our governments, from the enforcers of law to the courts of law to the makers of law; the rich and powerful; the tellers of standard stories in our communities, societies, or nations; and many others besides.

These oppressors do not actively oppress us every day. They do not need to. Our oppressors teach us to oppress ourselves, by placing aversions, fears, and dreadful memories deep in our nervous systems: the way our narcissistic mother criticized us when we were little; the unrealistic expectations of our father who was a failure, or the unrealistic expectations of our father who was a success; the disapproval, incomprehension, judgment, and "back in my day" of our grandparents; teasing and torment from siblings; how the worst of our teachers treated us; big-T trauma and small-t trauma; what bullies, false friends, and abusive and breaking-up partners told us and others about us; what our supervisors say in our performance reviews, which must always find and amplify some fictional flaw—sorry, "improvement opportunity"—in our character; the rejections of auditions, banks, colleges, credit card companies, crushes, job interviews, landlords, mortgagors, tenure committees, and clothes in the fitting room; the person who flipped us off and yelled at us for no reason when we were driving home years ago; the definitions and limitations assigned to us by people who perpetuate bias and prejudice; the delusional standards set by advertisers; or the false and fantastical roles modeled by celebrities, the powerful, and the rich; among countless other examples.

Self-oppression starts with a story someone told us about ourselves—a story that is not true, and that conflicts with a story we started writing before and beyond the trauma, terror, and pain other people inflicted on us; the story we tell ourselves about ourselves without those influences; the story that *is* true.

We can react to this conflict either by achieving our own liberation through reading and learning—as bell hooks and Paulo Freire advocate—or with the cyclical sabotage of self-abuse via addiction, anger, anxiety, attachment and relationship problems, blue Mondays, chaos, depression, eating too little, eating too much, egotism, grinding teeth, hyperindependence, impostor syndrome, insecurity, insomnia, nightmares, oppressing others, panic attacks, perfectionism, phobias, procrastination, stress, Sunday scaries, violence, worry, and other self-harm.

There is a war of stories within you. Telecommunication intensified it, and the technologies that followed telecommunication intensified it even more. The only way to end it is to win.

Chapter 6

One One Zero

1. Bits

A silver-haired man wearing a tweed jacket and tie is juggling four clubs while unicycling through the peeling ecru halls of the Massachusetts Institute of Technology, winding between students, some oblivious, some tittering, and members of faculty and staff, most stern, on his way from the Department of Electrical Engineering, where he is a professor, to the Department of Mathematics, where he is also a professor, all while thinking so deeply that, if anyone stopped him to ask what on earth he thinks he is doing, he could truthfully say he is conducting research.

His name is Claude Shannon, and his subject at the moment is the mathematics of juggling.

Juggling is at least four thousand years old—we know this because there is a tomb in a cemetery called Beni Hasan in Middle Egypt, between the cities of Asyut and Memphis, that is inscribed with a drawing of three women juggling. But in all those years, no one thought about the *mathematics* of juggling until the 1970s, when Claude, a spirit set free by critical thinking if ever there was one, developed a mathematical formula to describe the ancient art of the dancing clubs:

$$\frac{F+D}{V+D} = \frac{B}{H}$$

D is how long the juggler's prop—the ball, or club, or whatever—stays in a hand, or *dwell time*; *F* is how long the prop stays in the air, or *flight time*; *V* is how long the juggler's hand is empty, or *vacant time*; *B* is the number of balls or other props; and *H* is the number of hands.

The equation looks simple because it is elegant. The top line tracks the props, the bottom line tracks the hands, and everything is governed by time. One of juggling's biggest challenges is that you can always add more props, but—without the help of a friend, at least—you can never add more hands. Claude's formula shows why juggling four props is far more difficult than juggling three, and why juggling *five* props is so difficult that few jugglers can do it: The flight time is almost one second per prop, which means throwing the props higher, which increases the difficulty of throw and catch both. Claude was frustrated that he never succeeded in making that leap, which is sometimes described as the difference between a good juggler and a great juggler.

After developing and proving his equation and adding a number of more complex variations to it, Claude built the world's first juggling robot—it could juggle three balls at once by bouncing them off a tom drum—and published a paper called "The Scientific Aspects of Juggling" in which he shared the formula while also mentioning the philosopher Socrates, quoting a recently published fantasy novel, and using a jazz drummer named Gene Krupa as an example.

We can see nearly all of Claude in this one short story: solving an unexpected problem elegantly and playfully by using mathematical brilliance, building things no one has built, and being wholly unconcerned about what other people think of him.

The problem of juggling's mathematics lay undisturbed for thousands of years partly because developing an equation to describe juggling would have been considered an unserious occupation for any mathematician capable of doing it.

But Claude never cared for seriousness, and since 1948, had not needed to. In that year, at the age of thirty-two, he published one of the most important scientific papers of the twentieth century. The paper was called "A Mathematical Theory of Communication," and, like the juggling paper, its principal insight is so elegant it looks simple:

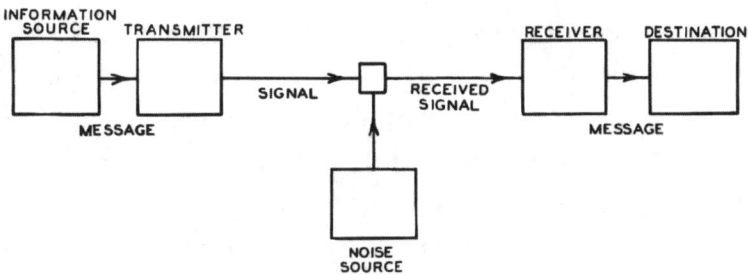

This diagram describes all communication, and illustrates the fundamental problem of all communication: what Claude described as "reproducing at one point either exactly or approximately a message selected at another point."

Solving this problem requires balancing novelty and ambiguity.

Information, as Claude defines it, is anything new. The statement "This book is called *The Story of Stories*" only contains information if you don't already know what this book is called. An immediate restatement that "this book is called *The Story of Stories*" provides no information at all, because it contains nothing new. The more novel a signal, the more information it contains.

Transmitting novelty is the point of communication, but it is also the problem of communication. There is *noise* between every transmitter and receiver that can interfere with a signal and render it ambiguous. As I cannot know in advance what you are going to communicate because it is informative and therefore novel, ambiguity impedes communication.

At the time of writing, this problem is common in cell phones, which send and receive too much noise and too little signal when one or both phones are too far from a base station or cell tower. It does not take many dropped, faint, or garbled words to make a conversation futile: when one word in six is lost, conversation becomes difficult, and when one word in three is lost, conversation becomes impossible.

"A Mathematical Theory of Communication" proves that a theoretically perfect communication system is one that can transmit infinite novelty while receiving no ambiguity.

Claude proposed doing this using binary digits—ones and/or zeroes—and that the amount of information carried by the binary digits be called *bits*, a term coined by a Bell Labs colleague named John Tukey and published for the first time in Claude's paper.

The suggestion that any and all information—computer programs, images, sound, text, video, and so on—should be encoded as long strings of ones and zeroes before being transmitted was a revolutionary idea that solved both the problem of novelty *and* the problem of ambiguity. Any information can be encoded as ones and zeroes, which means that there is infinite novelty, which means any conceivable message can be transmitted. But a system transmitting only ones and zeroes also has the least possible ambiguity. The receiver is likely to interpret the signal correctly, even in the presence of noise, and a few misinterpreted signals—a zero that should be a one, for example—are unlikely to make the message unintelligible. A machine-to-machine communication system that only transmits ones and zeroes is theoretically perfect.

Many things that are theoretically perfect are practically impossible, but Claude already knew how to make a working binary communications system: he had described one ten years earlier when he was studying for his master's degree at MIT. While "A Mathematical Theory of Communication" is generally considered to be Claude's masterpiece, the paper he wrote at the age of twenty-two, which he titled, with his typical understatement, "A Symbolic Analysis of Relay and Switching Circuits," may be even more important.

This is where we see the free-thinking juggler in all the glory of his liberty, entertaining an idea so unique that it was unimaginable until he described it.

Claude's idea was to combine the obscure nineteenth-century philosophy of an Englishman named George Boole with the emerging twentieth-century technology of electromechanical relays, which were being rapidly improved by the saltation of widespread use in telephone switchboards.

George Boole's idea, which he introduced in his 1847 book *The Mathematical Analysis of Logic*, was called Boolean algebra, and it showed how problems of logic could be formulated and solved much like algebraic calculations, using simple concepts such as AND—terms in Boolean algebra are capitalized, to distinguish them from everyday words—OR, NOT, IF, and THEN. These algebraic calculations could only deliver one of two results: TRUE or FALSE. For example, in the Britain of 1847, only men who owned property or land worth at least forty shillings a year were allowed to vote. Using Boolean algebra, we can write this as:

m = male
p = property owner
v = voter, which equals p AND m, or p multiplied by m

If we say something equals 1 if it is TRUE, and 0 if it is FALSE, we can then write a formula to determine whether any particular person can vote:

IF p multiplied by $m = 1$, THEN v = TRUE, and the person can vote. But IF p multiplied by $m = 0$, THEN v = FALSE, and the person *cannot* vote.

George Boole assumed his work was purely theoretical, and of no practical use, saying, "It may be that there is no practical advantage in the method thus pointed out, but it possesses a theoretical unity and completeness which render it deserving of regard."

Ninety years later, Claude Shannon proved him wrong.

Claude's master's thesis showed how Boolean algebra could be applied to the increasingly complex switching systems used in automated telephone switchboards and other systems. A telephone switchboard is much like a railroad network; it is a series of junctions with switches that can be in one of two positions. Automatically routing a phone call to the right person required these switches to be set in one particular pattern; anything else would misdirect the call. Claude realized that the "open" and "closed" state of these switches was analogous to Boole's "TRUE" and "FALSE," and therefore Boolean algebra could be used to describe, design, and—most importantly—optimize switching systems. That in essence, was the point of his thesis.

This would have been impressive all by itself, but Claude had discovered something far more significant that he was not yet ready to disclose, other than by describing it with one of the greatest understatements in the history of science:

> It is also possible to use the analogy between Boolean algebra and relay circuits in the opposite direction, i.e., to represent logical relations by means of electric circuits. Some interesting results have been obtained along this line, but are of no importance here.

The "interesting results" from representing "logical relations by means of electric circuits" led to Claude's 1948 paper, which led to the development of new electronic components to realize Claude's vision, which led to a world in which countless new *digital* technologies tell stories with ones and zeroes that act like on/off switches.

With most major inventions—television is an example we touched on earlier—many people work independently to create basically the same thing in basically the same way. This redundancy means the best solution to each problem will almost certainly be discovered, and no one person's contribution is irreplaceable, no matter what our story-shaped brains try to tell us. Very few inventions, and very few inventors, are truly unique.

But Claude was one of the rare exceptions.

Claude imagined interesting problems that no else was close to imagining, thought things no one else was close to thinking, and showed his conclusions were true both by proving them mathematically *and* by building practical working examples.

Claude certainly had a singular mind, but he has something else to show us too. Claude's thinking was free from the hindrance, self-imposed limitations, doubts, and oppression that hold most of the rest of us back. Yes, Claude was male, talented, wealthy, and white at a time when these things delivered even more extraordinary advantages and privileges than they do today. But there were millions of Americans who fit that description.

Claude also had the bravery to believe in himself. His work was illuminated by a light that shines only when we disregard doubt and false confidence to tell the most authentic story about who we are. His greatest achievement was proving the hardest truth: that your unburnished, undiminished opinion of yourself is the only one that matters.

2. Yowall

Something strange happened among the surf and reefs of the Coral Sea in the 1960s: the Guugu Yimithirr, the Indigenous people of northeast Australia, started wading into the ocean, their lips and chests streaked with bright body paint called *kapan-da*, and swimming far offshore to foreigners waiting in dinghies, going from beach to boat again and again, trading bags of a white powder called *yowall* for thousands of Australian dollars until the sun was submerging and the day was growing as gray as the market in which they were trading.

This meek beginning would spread *yowall*—which is more valuable, more powerful, and sometimes more dangerous than any spice or drug—everywhere, including into your hand, into your home, and into your pocket.

The *yowall* of the Guugu Yimithirr was created three hundred million years ago, when a granite and sandstone peninsula started reaching east from Australia toward the corals of the Great Barrier Reef. Southerly winds eroded the rock, turning its surface into grains that accumulated as dunes. At first the dunes comprised coarse grains of quartz and of minerals called feldspars, but the dunes moved, as all dunes do, somersaulting forward at speeds of up to sixteen feet a year, rolling like slow-motion topographical tumbleweeds, their peaks spilling at their feet again and again, until their grains became smooth and small and their feldspars dissolved, leaving only the quartz, which the movement had ground into a pure sherbet of silica.

After one hundred miles and three hundred centuries, these grains, once half a billion tons of solid rock and now sand as fine and white as confectioner's sugar, came to a halt on a headland, where they piled up in pyramids like monuments to the miracle of geological time.

For fifty thousand years the dunes were known only to the Guugu Yimithirr. The first outsider to see them was Lieutenant James Cook from the Kingdom of Great Britain, who in the summer of 1770 named the headland Cape Flattery, and described it as "checkered with white sand," which, he noted, the locals called *yowall*.

Two centuries later, a new invention made the *yowall* suddenly valuable, which is why the Guugu Yimithirr started wading into the ocean and selling it to foreign ships moored just offshore. As demand for the sand grew, two mineral companies collaborated to build a sand mine, then a refinery, then a wharf a half-kilometer long in the place where the Guugu Yimithirr once waded with bags.

Today, the *yowall* is loaded into shipping containers thirty tons at a time and sailed through the Great Barrier Reef into the Pacific

Ocean, across the Coral Sea, the Solomon Sea, the Bismarck Sea, the Philippine Sea, the East China Sea, and the Yellow Sea, past the coasts of Japan, South Korea, and North Korea, and into the Chinese port of Tianjin, where quay cranes, straddle carriers, and reach stackers move it onto tractor trailers, which drive it a hundred miles north, then slowly back it up at the loading docks of an American-owned factory: the final destination of a four-thousand-mile journey from a barely peopled shore in Queensland to the populous molten megacity of Beijing.

The American factory is one of two factories standing side by side in the southeastern district of Yizhuang, taking up the space of several city blocks, so close together they are almost one. These factories are twenty-first-century engines of fabrication, not the romantic workshops of memory and tradition. They have no red brick, no chimneys, no odors, no sirens signaling hordes of overalled workers to come and to go. These are vanilla buildings, low, silent, and smokeless, guarded by parking-lot moats and clipboard-wielding sentries.

In the American factory, which is owned by Corning Incorporated, a company from the small town of Corning in upstate New York, workers season the sand with oxides of aluminum, boron, and magnesium, among other things, in precise and secret proportions, heat it to thousands of degrees Fahrenheit until it becomes a vermilion liquid, then pour it into a half-pipe high above the ground.

The liquid overflows in two streams down the outside of the pipe, which meet underneath and merge in a miracle of chemistry and fluid dynamics into a single plane, a sheet that flows straight down, perfectly flat, perfectly smooth, perfectly even, shaped only by gravity, cooled only by time, touched only by air, a glowing Wonkaesque waterfall of lava a hundred feet high.

The top of the waterfall is lava, at least. As the lava nears the ground, the waterfall transforms and becomes glass, vast, as thin as a bedsheet, and optically perfect.

This glass has only one purpose: to feed the factory next door, which needs hundreds of millions of square meters of this impossibly thin, impossibly perfect glass made from the pure silica of the *yowall* of the Guugu Yimithirr every year. That factory is Chinese. It is owned by a corporation once called the Beijing Electron Tube Factory, then Beijing Oriental Electronics Group, and now BOE.

3. Wang's Law

In 1992, when D. S. Wang changed his mind, he became director of a factory that made vacuum tubes just as vacuum tubes were becoming obsolete. The vacuum tube's only remaining application was as the cathode ray tubes in televisions—big glass bulbs with magnets that steered electrons at phosphorescent coatings to make brief, bright glows and create the illusion of moving pictures.

The factory had been manufacturing cathode ray tubes since the 1980s, but the market was small. Fewer than one in three Chinese homes had televisions, most of which were tiny and black-and-white. Export markets were no better. Cathode ray tubes were a commodity. The only way to sell them was by cutting prices and therefore profits.

Wang's first business problem was obvious: The factory had to start making something new.

But what? Wang only had enough money to try one thing, and the wrong decision would put the factory out of business forever.

As Wang searched for an answer, he found his thoughts returning again and again to televisions. Why were televisions still made with vacuum tubes when nothing else was? Why wasn't there an alternative?

In a way, there was. Screens without cathode ray tubes were first proposed in the 1960s. By the early 1990s, there were more than a dozen possible alternative screen technologies in development: microscopic cathode-ray-tube-like electron emitters, electrostatic fields, liquid crystals, electroluminescent screens that glowed when electrified, electronic inks that reflected and absorbed light, and gas-filled plasma cells that lit up like tiny neon signs, among many others.

Like nations, societies, and tribes, businesses and industries have standard stories. They are sometimes called brand identities, best practices, business models, or corporate strategies, among other things. The standard story of alternative, tubeless televisions was that these new technologies were exciting because they were "picture-frame televisions" or "flat-screen TVs" that could hang on walls like works of art, that flatness and thinness were their most important attributes, and that the only meaningful difference between them was picture quality: One technology gave the best colors, another the most contrast, another the widest viewing angle, and so on.

But Wang did not agree. He had a counterstory.

Its premise was simple. In all other electronic products, vacuum tubes had been replaced by complex transistor combinations called integrated circuits or semiconductors. Semiconductors had many advantages over vacuum tubes—they were smaller, faster, and more powerful, for example—but in Wang's mind, one advantage was more important than all the others: the price and performance of semiconductors improved exponentially. This was first described by Gordon Moore, cofounder of semiconductor manufacturer Intel. In 1965 Moore predicted that the maximum number of transistors that could be built on an integrated circuit would double every year for ten years, making new products twice as powerful and existing products half as expensive. In 1975, after being proved right, Moore made another prediction: The doubling would now take two years and would continue indefinitely. Moore was right again. His observation became known as Moore's Law. It was true in 1992 when Wang was wondering what product to make, and it remains true today.

Wang's counterstory led him to a clear conclusion: If semiconductors had replaced every other kind of vacuum tube, then they should replace cathode ray tubes too. Picture quality was not what mattered.

Every one of the new alternative technologies gave a better picture than a cathode ray tube, and television viewers were generally happy with picture quality anyway. All that mattered was finding a way to apply Moore's Law to screens to get endless exponential improvement. Wang did not want to make *flat* screens. He wanted to make what he called semiconductor screens.

It is difficult now, in the twenty-first century, to fully understand how extraordinary and controversial this idea was in 1992.

Televisions had barely changed since their invention. They were black-and-white, then color; they got remote controls, became slightly bigger and somewhat cheaper, and a few were made portable enough that you could, for example, take them on fishing trips, but the improvements were few and small and spread over decades. There was no easy way to improve a cathode ray tube. Making one aspect a little better meant making another aspect a lot worse. Adding six inches to a thirty-six-inch screen doubled its weight from 220 to 440 pounds, for example.

The lack of innovation in television sets went unnoticed: Things were the way they were because that was the way they had always been. The television industry assumed that, once invented, whatever replaced the cathode ray tube would not change much either.

This standard story made Wang's counterstory about screens incomprehensible to television experts. No one, they said, needed televisions to improve exponentially. Televisions were not computers. They could not get faster and did not need ever-increasing memory. Nothing useful about televisions could be improved by Moore's Law. What would someone even *do* with a screen as small as a postcard or as big as a windshield, or that had millions of pixels instead of the usual few hundred thousand, or that refreshed its picture hundreds of thousands of times a second, rather than the twenty-five or thirty times that was standard in the twentieth century? There was no point to a semiconductor screen, even if such a thing were possible.

And in the 1990s, the idea that a *Chinese* company might play a decisive role in the future of television was a counterstory all on its own. The market for high technology was dominated by just two nations: the United States and Japan. In 1993 the United States' high-technology exports were worth $105 billion, and Japan's high-technology exports were worth $85 billion, while China's high-technology exports were worth only $5 billion.

China, the world's most populous nation, the land that invented gunpowder, the compass, oars, banknotes, crossbows, fireworks, gaslights, umbrellas, oil wells, and much more too, was sixteenth in the world in high-technology exports, behind Sweden, Ireland, and Thailand, among others.

In the world's standard story, China was merely an exporter of cheap, simple products such as plastic novelties and clothes; a low-cost imitator, not a high-tech innovator. The idea that a young accountant trying to save a failing Chinese vacuum tube factory might be a visionary when he talked about semiconductor screens was unthinkable.

People who tell counterstories will always be ridiculed, ostracized, or worse. But counterstories come with a superpower: When you see things differently, you see different things. Wang's counterstory showed him that only one technology could replace cathode ray tubes, and that was liquid crystals—specifically a technology called thin-film transistor liquid crystal display, or TFT-LCD.

Inventing liquid crystal displays started as a series of chemistry problems—synthesizing crystals that stayed liquid at room temperature, for example—but after these were solved, there was a physics problem too: how to switch millions of independent clusters of molecules on and off fast enough to create the illusion of a moving image. Liquid crystals are merely milky liquids without a nudge from a well-placed microamp.

That problem took decades to solve. It is why liquid crystal screens were promised in the 1960s but did not appear until the 1990s.

The eventual solution set the velocity of the twenty-first century's storytelling technologies and launched liquid crystals far beyond the limits of cathode ray tubes. The answer was something Wang understood better than possibly anyone else in the world: to use a semiconductor as big as the screen itself to switch the crystals on and off—a huge integrated circuit built on glass with a molecules-thin layer of liquid crystals on top. This is why a liquid crystal display is, to use Wang's words, a *semiconductor display*—a term that would eventually become standard in the display industry.

Not everything in a screen is a semiconductor, so some parts take longer to improve. Wang calculated that the performance of typical semiconductor displays—not only liquid crystal displays but all other semiconductor displays too—would double every three years. It did not matter that nobody in the 1990s knew how exponentially improving screens might be used. Wang's answer to that was simple: In 105, no one knew how exponentially improving paper might be used, and in the 1960s, no one knew how exponentially improving computers might be used. History shows that we cannot anticipate the applications of new technology; that in fact, invention is the mother of necessity.

And so Wang renamed his factory the Beijing Oriental Electronics Group, reinvented it as one of China's first corporations, and bet both the factory and his career on liquid crystal displays. It was a courageous and radical choice. The television industry's standard story—and therefore the consensus position—was that liquid crystal displays were only good for small screens in high-end computer monitors and the backs of digital cameras, and that some other technology would be used for big-screen TVs. The leading television manufacturers of the day placed their bets elsewhere. Panasonic chose a technology called plasma. Sony, the market leader, kept investing in cathode ray tubes. Both companies were wrong, and as a result, Japan's share of the world's display market shrank from 90 percent in 1995 to less than 10 percent in 2005. All displays became semiconductor screens; BOE became the world's leading manufacturer of displays; and China became the world's undisputed leader in high-technology exports. The United States fell to fifth and Japan fell to seventh.

Wang's counterstory became the standard story, and Wang's calculation became known as Wang's Law—the Moore's Law of the display industry. Wang's Law predicts that the performance of a typical new screen will double and the price of a typical old screen will halve every three years.

It was a vision so powerful that when it came true it turned the failing, obsolete factory into a publicly traded global corporation which by 2021 had annual sales of $35 billion, annual profits of $4 billion, and more than 79,000 employees.

4. The Sand Age

Few people are allowed into the BOE factory in Beijing, not only because what it does and how it does it is secret, but also because the facility must be kept free of dust. Much dust is us—it is our sloughing skin, our shedding hair, the dirt from our clothes and shoes. Anyone who enters the factory floor must first walk over sticky, fly-paper-like doormats, wrap themselves in an antistatic coverall made of conductive fibers, seal it with boots, a hood, a pair of goggles, and two pairs of gloves, and pass through a series of air locks, all to protect the factory and its product from the mortal dangers of dust.

What lies beyond the air locks is a sterile alien world, bathed in yellow light, that seems as large as an ocean, with walls farther away than the eye can clearly see, almost empty of organic life. Humans make nothing here. The makers are massive robots that lift up the glass from the Corning factory, set it down, operate on it, then hand it off to other massive robots, mechanical inflatable skydancers all, with muscular metal limbs.

The factory *does* have human operators—the giant robots are mere repeaters of movements and do not initiate anything alone—but they work in a windowed and air-conditioned office elsewhere in the building, configuring their automata remotely with computers, observing with cameras, keeping their dusty and mortal corporeality at a safe distance.

The robots prepare the glass by submerging it in solvent and blasting it with inaudible, high-frequency sounds to remove any last motes of dust. Then they start to transform it.

First, they add layers upon layers of metal and silicon, one atom at a time, using vapors, vacuums, radio waves, and plasmas, etching away parts of each layer with chemicals before adding the next, to make a matrix of millions of microscopic electronic switches.

Then they drip a liquid blend of four types of molecule onto the switches, very precisely, drop by drop, as if they were making miniature cookies by piping dough onto a baking sheet.

The molecules all have the same special properties. First, they are liquid crystals, which means they have an organized, repeating internal structure like salt or snowflakes despite being liquid at room temperature. Second, when electricity passes through them, their repeating structure reorganizes itself in a way that blocks light. The molecules are liquid, electric Venetian blinds. When they are electrified, they close; when they are not, they open.

The robots press another piece of glass, checkered with microscopic red, green, and blue squares, like an intricate stained glass window, on top of the switches and crystals. Where the two pieces of glass meet, the liquid crystals spread to cover the switches, and each colored square aligns with a switch. Conductive glue on the edges of the glass holds the pieces together. Tiny spheres of gold keep the space between the panes uniform, and ensure the crystals spread evenly as the glass presses down. The Venetian blinds now dress the stained glass window. The robots add a backlight that shines behind the switches. From this moment on, whenever a switch opens one of those liquid crystal blinds, a tiny dot of red, green, or blue light appears.

The robots seal the edges of the glass, bake it at 250 degrees Fahrenheit, cut it into rectangular pieces as if they were slicing a sheet cake, smooth out the edges, add a filter called a polarizer, and test everything they have made to ensure it works properly.

If the robots find problems, which are most often tiny dead spots called *mura*, after the Japanese word for "unevenness," they ask their human operators for help. They do not ask for help often; despite the amount of automation, the required precision, and the chemical complexity, more than 95 percent of what they produce is perfect.

After testing, the robots' work is complete. In less than a week, they have turned a few ounces of quarter-of-a-billion-year-old sand from Cape Flattery into one of the most consequential technologies in human history: a semiconductor screen.

Geology is the beginning of technology; this is why we divide prehistory into the Stone Age, the Copper Age, the Bronze Age, and the Iron Age; and why soil, coal, and oil drove the Agrarian and Industrial Revolutions. Thousands of years from now, our present centuries may well come to be called *the Sand Age*. Sand is the fundament of all the major new technologies of our time, the material from which we make the microelectronics inside our computers, robots, and networks, among other things.

Semiconductor screens are made almost entirely from sand. Cape Flattery sand—or occasionally pure silica sand from other, smaller sand mines—makes up 25 percent of a flat-screen display's raw material cost—more than any other single material—and nearly all of its weight; even the biggest displays contain less than one gram of anything else. And everything a screen displays is created by a community of sand-based circuits that converge at the screen's surface after stretching for thousands of miles in all directions along paths of fibers made from sand and via electromagnetic waves made by radios made from sand.

The economics of sand is the foundation of the economics of screens. Sand is abundant—Cape Flattery has half a billion tons of it, two hundred years' supply at current consumption rates—and it is easy to mine, and therefore cheap. The average raw material cost of most of the screens in the world at the time of writing is less than ten dollars.

The labor cost is even lower. Turning sand into screens is a complex, dustless, atomic-scale operation and therefore impossible for human hands. Only robots can make semiconductor screens, and robots work for free.

Manufacturing accountants call the cost of making one additional product a *marginal cost*. Many products have high marginal costs. Making one more car, couch, or custom birthday cake, for example, requires a bill of expensive raw materials and many hours of skilled human labor.

But most of a screen is a few ounces of sand transformed by the unpaid work of robots, so nearly all of the cost of making screens is the other kind of cost manufacturing accountants monitor: the *fixed cost* of building the factory full of robots in the first place. *That* cost is huge. BOE's two factories in Beijing cost $6 billion to build. And BOE has sixteen factories like the ones in Beijing, all in China, all making screens. The company has spent $50 billion building its factories, more than the annual gross domestic product of a quarter of the world's nations.

BOE does not disclose who its customers are, citing strict confidentiality agreements, but it is clear from teardowns and other, third-party industry sources that BOE sells its screens to customers including Apple and Samsung. These companies package BOE's screens in plastic cases and add software and other electronics that turn them into phones, televisions, tablets, laptops, computer monitors, handheld video game consoles, virtual reality headsets, car dashboards, or anything else that could possibly contain a display, then sell the packaged screens to people like you and me. There is a better than average chance that some of your devices contain semiconductor screens made by BOE's robots—possibly the ones in Beijing.

Each BOE factory has to sell enough screens to recoup its billions of dollars of fixed cost and then make a profit. This means BOE's robots can never stand idle; they must work twenty-four hours a day, seven days a week, every day of the year, manufacturing screens in vast volumes, to be sold at the highest price possible, but also at almost any price necessary, so they can turn a profit before new technology makes the factory obsolete.

It takes a lot of screens to recoup $50 billion. In 2021, BOE's factories made eight hundred million screens, almost two and a half million a day. BOE is the largest manufacturer of screens in the world, but it makes only a quarter of the world's screens. There are more than a hundred other screen factories like BOE's operating across East Asia—in mainland China, in Taiwan, in Japan, and in South Korea—and no matter the hour of the day, no matter where in the world you are, the robots in those factories will have made a thousand screens in the time it took you to read this sentence. They will make seven and a half million screens in the next twenty-four hours, and 2.8 billion screens in the next twelve months: one for every three people on the planet.

5. Joe

On April 25, 2019, a new movie opened at the Fox Theater in Westwood Village, Los Angeles, a cinema from 1930, with a gleaming white Spanish revival tower 170 feet high carved with winged lions, and a stucco rooftop with griffins on every corner. Joe Russo was there that night, sitting near the center of the theater, with his older brother Anthony. As the movie approached its dramatic climactic scene, Joe took his phone from his pocket and filmed the audience's reaction.

Unlike everyone else watching, Anthony and Joe had already seen the movie, which was called *Avengers: Endgame*. In fact, they had seen it many times. They were the movie's directors. They had gone to the Fox Theater not to watch the film, but the audience. No one knew they were there.

Endgame is the final part of a story twenty-two movies long, and the sequel to 2018's *Avengers: Infinity War*, which was also directed by

Anthony and Joe. At the end of *Infinity War*, the story's antagonist Thanos, a powerful alien warlord with a Malthusian delusion about overpopulation, kills half of all the living things in the universe, including many of the story's heroes, with a magical snap of his fingers. *Endgame* is set five years later, and shows the survivors making one final, desperate attempt to bring their fallen comrades—and the several billion ordinary people who also died—back to life. After many twists and turns, the movie nears its end. The heroes' plan has failed. Thanos is about to kill the few remaining protagonists, every one of them bloodied, beaten, and bearing broken weapons. All hope is lost. But then the last man standing, Steve Rogers, also known as Captain America, hears something strange. It sounds as if one of the supposedly dead heroes, his friend Sam Wilson, is talking to him on the radio through bursts of static.

Sam says, "Cap, it's Sam, can you hear me? On your left." A magical portal, sparkling orange, opens twenty feet behind Steve's left shoulder. The silhouettes of three resurrected heroes step through. More portals open, and, in ones, twos, and threes, all the dead heroes return, bringing their warriors, weapons, spacecraft, and magical animals with them, until a mighty army stands reunited on the battlefield. Hope is restored. Steve stares down the suddenly worried Thanos, then readies the resurrected army for battle with his signature battle cry: "Avengers . . . assemble!"

If you have never seen any *Avengers* movies, this synopsis probably did not move you, may have been difficult to follow, and likely sounds silly. You feel no connection to Steve or Sam or any of the other heroes, and do not care whether or not they defeat their enemy Thanos. These are just fictional characters, after all. But, if you *have* seen the *Avengers* movies, you can probably guess what Joe's phone captured when the audience saw this scene for the first time.

Everyone in the theater is watching silently. Sam's voice comes over the radio. There are startled gasps. One audience member says "awww." The first portal appears, and a cheer swells through the theater like a wave that breaks into foaming applause. Someone yells, "Come on! come on!" The cheering lulls and swells back, crashing into applause again and again, becoming louder each time another hero appears. By the time Steve says, "Avengers . . . ," the sound of the crowd is a storm. The second word of his catchphrase, "assemble," is barely audible: you can only be sure Steve says it by reading his lips.

Everyone in the audience knows they are watching fictional heroes played by actors or, like the villain Thanos, brought to life entirely by computer animation. Everything is imaginary but the emotions of the audience. Their feelings are real.

6. Artificial Realities

In 1973, as high-quality color television sets were spreading across the world's wealthiest nations, murky images made of low resolution, blocky picture elements made an unexpected return—not on televisions, but in movie theaters. One of the most successful American films that year was *Westworld*, a hybrid of the science-fiction and Western genres, set in a futuristic amusement park filled with lifelike robot cowboys that suddenly go out of control, become autonomous, and start killing the human guests. When one robot, known only as *the Gunslinger* and played by Yul Brynner, starts hunting down a guest named Peter Martin, the audience watches some of the pursuit through the Gunslinger's robotic eyes. At first, the Gunslinger sees the world in geometric abstraction, as a series of blocky, naturally colored squares and rectangles, like a painting by Piet Mondrian, Bridget Riley, or Ding Yi; later, the squares become bright orange, yellow, and red when the robot is forced to switch to infrared vision, a fact Peter Martin exploits to evade and eventually destroy it.

The Gunslinger's view of the world greatly resembles the pictures on the first mechanical televisions. That similarity is not a coincidence;

Westworld's visual effects were the first crude examples of a new technology that would soon change storytelling completely: computer-generated imagery.

The fourteen computer-generated shots took up two and a half minutes of screen time and were created by a man named John Whitney Jr. using technology invented at NASA so space probes could take pictures of the Moon and, later, of Mars. The probes converted images into a grid of squares, assigned each square a number that corresponded to its average brightness, then transmitted the grid coordinates and their color values back to earth, where a computer reassembled them to re-create the image. This technique, much of which was developed by NASA engineer Robert Nathan in the early 1960s, is still used in every digital image and movie today.

Whitney's *Westworld* shots used a grid of 3,600 squares and required the actors to wear special costumes and makeup to create enough contrast. Richard Benjamin, the actor playing Peter Martin, wore an all-white wardrobe, with white gloves, white face paint, and white hairspray for the infrared scenes. Gene Polito, *Westworld*'s director of photography, said "He looked as though he had fallen into a barrel of flour."

Even with the special costumes, the effect was a processing challenge for the computer technology of the time: the 150 seconds of footage took 120 hours to render, and was not ready until moments before negative cutting, the final stage of the post-production process. It was the first time digital image processing was ever used in a movie, and Whitney was given the unprecedented billing of "Automated Image Processing" when *Westworld*'s end credits rolled.

Today, that same number of picture elements—3,600—takes up less than one-fiftieth of a square inch of a smartphone screen, and movie directors can use computer-generated imagery to create anything they can imagine.

Where *Westworld* has 14 computer-generated shots totaling 2.5 minutes of screen time, *Avengers: Endgame* has 2,496 computer-generated shots totaling more than 168 minutes of screen time—an average of one shot every four seconds.

Every frame of *Endgame*'s climactic portals scene features computer-generated imagery. Some shots also include principal photography of actors, but many do not. The scene switches from shots with photography to shots without by wiping elements from the action—aliens, heroes, spacecraft, and so on—across the screen to create undetectable transitions from one to the other.

The audience knows the scene must include digital effects, because everything that happens, no matter how realistic, is also impossible: there are no real flying horses, giant heroes, villains and aliens, or magic portals. The whole twenty-two-movie saga that led to this dramatic climax became increasingly dependent on these effects, and none of the movies in the cycle could have been made without digital imagery.

Computers have created a pantheon of modern gods, apparently real and walking among us. We know they are imaginary, yet they make us feel actual emotions. Oral stories, pictures, plays, poems, and songs have done that for tens of thousands of years, of course, as have writing, photography, film, and television more recently, and this sequence shows us a pattern: just as the technologies of story made it possible for more people to tell stories to more people, so they have also become ever more realistic, making the testimony of storytelling ever harder to distinguish from the direct inputs of our senses.

This pattern is the latest incarnation of the problem of choosing. As soon as we could remember stories, we could tell stories that may conflict with one another. This was a minor problem at first, as most stories were told by a monopoly of one kind or another: a homogenous tribe, a single great storyteller, or some other system of consensus. But, as storytelling technologies increased the number of storytellers and stories, the potential for conflict increased. One of the first and most obvious examples is religious writing. When one scripture from God arrived somewhere, it seemed authoritative and incontrovertible. When a second, different scripture from an apparently different God arrived in the same place, there was conflict and often war over which story was real.

The printing press exacerbated this problem: suddenly even the same God appeared to come in different variations. Disputes about these variations led to the rise of Protestantism and the more than fifty wars that followed.

As literacy rates increased, and books started to be printed in local, or *vernacular*, languages, and not just Ancient Greek, Classical Arabic, Classical Chinese, Latin, and Sanskrit, the number of conflicting stories increased, and the mere fact that a story had been remembered, written, or printed, provided ever less assurance that it was true.

Early written and printed stories were recordings of old, oral stories, but by the 1500s stories that had not first been told orally started appearing in print, and when they did storytelling started to change. The competition for attention created a new criterion for being chosen: whether or not the story *seemed real*.

Suddenly there were fewer stories about gods and idealized heroes and more stories featuring relatable inhabitants of the universe of the mass of humanity. Characters became more individualized; developed richer interior lives; faced more ambiguous, less absolute moral choices; were more likely to be affected by social conditions than ever before; and behaved in ways that were less formal and stylized and more like the ways people behaved in everyday life.

The prototype for this type of character was the *picaro*, who first appeared in *Lazarillo de Tormes*, an anonymous novella published in Spanish in 1554. The *picaro* was a descendant of the *trickster*, a rule-breaking, often mischievous archetype like the spider Anansi and the praying mantis ǃKággęn of African folklore; Bre'r Rabbit in the oral traditions of African Americans; Coyote in Indigenous North American folklore; Hermes in Greek mythology; and Loki in Norse mythology.

There was a big difference between the trickster and the *picaro*, though: a trickster was usually a secondary character, but a *picaro* was a protagonist, an antihero representing and giving voice to common people.

The *picaro* was, in short, the herald of the ever-increasing illusion of realism—and ever-increasing trickery—in storytelling. In 1605 he evolved into Miguel de Cervantes's Don Quixote, the protagonist in one of the first modern European novels; in 1839, he appeared as a *picaresque* everyday figure getting his shoes shined in one of the first photographs, taken by Louis Daguerre on the Boulevard du Temple in Paris; in 1855, Gustave Courbet responded to Daguerre with *L'Atelier du peintre*, a realistic, unromanticized painting of ordinary people—and two dogs and a cat—doing ordinary things; in 1888, Louis Le Prince made the first movie, which showed people moving around a garden in Leeds, a city in the United Kingdom; in 1898, Georges Méliès made *Un homme de têtes*, the first movie to use special effects, in which a magician realistically removes his head and grows a new one many times over; in 1917, two young cousins in England created the first fake photographs, which showed them playing with fairies; in 1927, *The Jazz Singer*, the first movie with synchronized sound, was released; in 1935, *Becky Sharp*, the first full-color movie, appeared; in 1958, Ray Harryhausen terrified moviegoers with stop-motion monsters in *The 7th Voyage of Sinbad*; in 1968, Stanley Kubrick took audiences on a journey to a realistic but imaginary outer space in *2001: A Space Odyssey*; a few years later, *Westworld* became the first movie to use computer-generated special effects, and ever more artificial things have been appearing ever more real ever after.

All of which raises a question: Will fully realistic stories make us confuse signals with stimuli? We live in a time when any dream or nightmare can appear real. Will we lose sight of what is and is not true?

7. The People Beetle Bottle

About 2,500 years ago, someone, probably in southern China, crossed a large Chinese citrus called a pomelo, which is an ancestor of the grapefruit, with a mandarin and invented a brand-new fruit called an orange. For the next twenty-two centuries, oranges and orange trees spread over Asia, Africa, and Europe through trade and travel, and then to the Americas and Australasia via the invasions of European colonizers. The orange is an invention, and therefore not indigenous anywhere, but even the genus *Citrus* to which it belongs has a limited natural territory: Citrus fruits are native only to the south and east of Asia, northeast Australia, and the intervening islands of Melanesia. Anywhere else, any type of citrus is an invasive species.

In Dongara, a small estuary town in Western Australia, the invasion of the orange created a problem for a rare local jewel bug called *Julodimorpha saundersii*. The males of the species are aroused by and attracted to the dimpled orange backs of the females, a behavior which evolved long before the invention of oranges. Ever since oranges arrived in Dongara, the *Julodimorpha saundersii* males, unable to distinguish between an orange and a mate, often die trying to impregnate discarded orange peel. More recently, they have also become fatally attracted to empty Emu Export beer bottles, which have dimpled orange-brown bases, and which Dongaran humans discard even more frequently than orange peel.

Julodimorpha saundersii came close to extinction as a result of this behavior, which is an example of an instinctive response to what biologists call a *superstimulus*. We may smile at the idea of beetles bedding bottles, but the story of *Julodimorpha saundersii* is a warning. Human brains did not evolve in a world of storytelling technologies any more than jewel bug brains evolved in a world of oranges.

If a beetle can mistake a bottle for a beetle, then the beetle's grip on reality must be loose indeed. How can we be sure our sense of reality is any better?

The Dongaran jewel bugs' physical attraction to orange peel and beer bottles is the result of a series of coincidences: peel, bottles, and potential mates are all orange and dimpled, and Dongaran humans have a bad habit of dropping both peel and bottles on the ground. But most other superstimuli are a result of evolution, not coincidence. For example: the wings of some nonpoisonous butterflies are brighter versions of the wings of some poisonous butterflies; the hornet moth, which cannot sting, is a yellower-and-blacker version of a yellow-and-black hornet, which can; and *Ophrys* orchids attract male wasps, bees, and sawflies by emitting the smell of a female wasp, bee, or sawfly, only stronger. *Social* parasites are especially likely to exploit superstimuli. Cuckoos, for example, use three: they make exaggerated predator sounds to make hens vacate their nests; they lay larger eggs that are favored in brooding; and cuckoo chicks have amplified begging behaviors that get them the most food. All these superstimuli exploit unaware hosts, and always to the hosts' detriment.

The best way to control a person's mind is to tell them stories that are to humans as orange rinds are to jewel bugs. Dongara's beetles are instinctively attracted to objects with superstimuli—the shiniest, orangest, most dimpled objects they see—even if those objects are trash, might kill them, and threaten their species with extinction. Humans are much the same: we are instinctively attracted to stories with superstimuli, even if the stories are trash, might kill us, and threaten *our* species with extinction, and stories can be deliberately optimized—or "jewel-bugged"—to do just that.

Many people, some naive and others nefarious, are interested in building and jewel-bugging machines to find those stories and tell them to everyone possible.

8. Se-dol

Lee Se-dol is fifteen stories above Seoul, smoking a cigarette while a cold wind worries his clothes. A few minutes ago, 80 million people were watching him; now, he can be seen by no one. He is alone on a terrace that has become his sanctuary, a place to contemplate with the serenity of nicotine, without the scrutiny of cameras, protected by security guards. Here, there is nothing more than a view of the three white peaks of Bukhansan, the mountain that marks Seoul's northern boundary, two black ashtrays, and Lee Se-dol.

It is winter, 2016. Se-dol is the world's best player of the ancient game of Go, and likely one of the best in the game's twenty-five-hundred-year history. He is only thirty-three years old and has already won eighteen international tournaments and seven out of every ten games he has played in his fourteen-year professional career. But yesterday he lost and today he is losing. Se-dol has come to the terrace to pace, smoke, and consider his options.

Go is the oldest board game in the world. Two players take turns placing 181 black and 180 white pieces called *stones* at the intersections of a grid 19 lines wide and 19 lines high. The player whose stones surround the most space at the end of the game wins. The stones stay where they are placed, unless they are surrounded by opposing stones, in which case they are removed. These simple rules have complex consequences. There are more possible moves per turn in Go than in chess, and more possible positions than there are atoms in the universe.

Tens of millions of people play Go. About a thousand of them are professionals like Lee Se-dol, and they can make hundreds of thousands of dollars a year. The winner of this week's competition will receive a million dollars, the largest Go prize ever. Se-dol has predicted he will win every game in this match, and every Go expert agrees. Se-dol is the best player in the world, and his opponent has never played at this level. It is not even a human being; it is a cluster of computers.

The match is a publicity stunt organized by a high tech company based in Britain and owned in America—two nations that know nothing about Go. The consensus among both computer scientists and Go experts is that the match is being held at least ten years too early, and that Go is too complex, nuanced, and intuitive to be played at a championship level by a computer. Se-dol expects to make an easy million dollars.

On the first day, when Se-dol makes his opening move, the computer appears to crash. The machine takes more than four minutes to make its unremarkable first move, far longer than any human would. The experts laugh. Their predictions are coming true.

A few moves later, Se-dol tries to confuse the machine with an unpredictable play, placing a piece far from all the others. Next, Se-dol tests the machine by initiating a *joseki*, one of many classic patterns of opening moves that, after thousands of years of Go, have been found to be optimal. When black plays a particular move in a *joseki*, white must respond with the next move in the pattern; to make any other move is a mistake. But the computer does not seem to know this. Its fifth and sixth moves are the wrong moves. The experts laugh again. It has taken Se-dol less than thirty minutes to expose huge weaknesses in the machine's game.

Then the computer plays its seventh move, and the Go world rocks. In a single play, the computer appears to have transformed its position and taken the upper hand. Doubt chills the air. Perhaps the machine has not been making mistakes. Its twelfth move makes the situation clearer: the computer is attacking and winning. Se-dol starts shaking his head, sighing, and fidgeting. As the game grows more complicated, the computer plays faster, sometimes making its moves instantly, giving Se-dol little time to think, and apparently anticipating his plays. One professional player says Se-dol looks "exhausted," and "panicked." Se-dol almost makes a terrible move by mistake, barely managing to pull back his stone before it touches the board. Not long after, he resigns. What was unimaginable in the morning is real by the afternoon: a machine has beaten the greatest player of the world's oldest, most complex game.

But, at the postgame press conference, Se-dol is unconcerned. He smiles and says:

> I was surprised. I didn't think I would lose. The mistakes I made in the beginning lasted until the very end; that's why I lost. I have won world championship titles and I have a lot of experience. Losing one game won't affect me.

Tens of millions of anxious Go players exhale. It was a blip, a glitch, a fluke. Se-dol will play better tomorrow. Everything is going to be okay.

In game two, Se-dol plays slowly, taking twice as long to make his moves as he did in game one. He avoids *fighting*—the capture and exchange of pieces—and instead adopts strategies Go players call *quiet* or *peaceful*. But, again, the machine makes a strange seventh move. Se-dol has the initiative, which Go players call *sente*. The standard counterstrategy to *sente* is a direct response, or *gote*. The computer does not use *gote*: it is either ignoring or has not noticed what Se-dol is doing. It plays a move elsewhere on the board, a risky nonresponse called *tenuki*, meaning "omission." The computer's next move, a diagonal play called a *peep*, looks like another mistake. Yoo Changhyuk, one of Korea's best Go players, tells television audiences that the two moves raise questions about the machine's capabilities.

But Se-dol, the best Go player of them all, perhaps seeing something no one else has noticed, starts plucking his thumb, tapping his foot, and scratching imaginary itches on the side of his head. Then he flees to the terrace to smoke.

It is 4:45 p.m. on Thursday, March 10, 2016. The temperature is 36 degrees Fahrenheit, 2 degrees Celsius, with the added chill of a wind flowing down from the peaks of Bukhansan. Se-dol, alone in the cold, fifteen stories high, wearing only a suit and an open-collared shirt, is facing the existential crisis of his life. Yesterday, he had assumed his loss was caused by his mistake of misjudging the machine. Today, he has seen enough to know his assumption was an act of denial and the beginning of grief.

The machine is going to beat him.

Not just in today's game.

In the whole match.

9. Move 37

Se-dol was born in Bigeumdo, one of 830 tiny islands that spill from the southwest corner of Korea into the Yellow Sea: seventeen square miles of mudflats and salt fields that are home to three thousand people. When he was eight years old, Se-dol's family sent him to a Go school in Seoul. Se-dol arrived there as a small boy from a rural island speaking a strange dialect called Jeolla, suddenly living in one of the world's largest cities, so naive he thought pizza grew on trees. Se-dol survived by submerging himself in Go. Soon he was playing and studying the game twelve hours a day, seven days a week, and receiving personal lessons from the academy's founder, a master named Kweon Kab-yong. Se-dol turned professional when he was twelve, the fifth youngest Korean to do so, won his first major tournament when he was nineteen, and skipped six ranks in five months to become a ninth dan, the highest rank of all, when he was twenty. Over the next twelve years Se-dol changed the game of Go with new and unexpected plays. Se-dol became Go, and Go became Se-dol.

But now Se-dol is alone in the wind, sucking in nicotine and tar, squaring up to a truth no one else has yet realized: he is going to lose to the machine. If the machine becomes Go, and Go becomes the machine, what does Se-dol become? What do *we all* become?

Se-dol renews his resolve and returns to the match, humanity's champion in single combat with the computer.

He arrives to an audience in obvious anticipation. While Se-dol was smoking, the machine made its play, and the world awaits his reaction.

The move, the computer's eighteenth and the game's thirty-seventh, is the strangest one yet. The expert commentators from China, Korea, the United Kingdom, and the United States are bewildered. The machine has placed a stone near the center of the board, far from any other black stones, diagonally adjacent to a lone white stone of Se-dol's. Technically, it is a play called a *shoulder hit*, but because it is so close to the center of the board, it is not a move any human player would or should make. Yoo Changhyuk calls it a "totally unthinkable move"; Michael Redmond, an American who is the only non-Asian to achieve a ninth dan in Go, says it's "a very surprising move"; Kim Myung Wan, another ninth dan, says "it's too high," and Fan Hui, European Champion for the past three years, writes, "Here?!" in his notebook. Only one person in the match room is not bewildered: Thore Graepel, one of the machine's inventors. He is smiling like a father who just watched his kid hit a walk-off home run.

Se-dol sits down, accompanied by the sounds and lights of a dozen flashing cameras. He leans forward and looks at the board. His face plays a medley that opens with incomprehension, segues into a half smile, passes briefly through concentration, becomes a baroo—that puzzled tilt of the head so common in dogs—and concludes with him tugging on his bottom lip. Then, the gravity of the play shoves him into his seat as if he has been launched into space. For twelve long minutes, Se-dol remains pinned to the back of his chair by the force of Move 37, unable to decide what to do.

Move 37 is the end of the game, the match, and Se-dol's career, although each thing keeps walking for a while despite being dead. Se-dol even wins the fourth game, deploying an advanced, trap-laying all-or-nothing strategy called *amashi*, which he uses because he has sensed the computer tends to eke out wins by playing close games. Se-dol loses all the other games, and with them the match, one to four. In 2019, he retires because, he says, "I've realized there is an entity that cannot be defeated." He is thirty-six years old. Game four will forever be remembered as Se-dol's greatest game and the testament of his talent; the only time a human beat the machine. The Lee Se-dol Museum in Bigeumdo installs a statue 12 feet high and 28 feet wide to commemorate this one victory out of all his matches and championships and trophies, a cenotaph to Go's brave and fallen warrior.

10. The Collision

The world's newspapers described the outcome of the match between the machine and Lee Se-dol as a triumph for artificial intelligence, but that is imprecise. It was a triumph for *one particular method* of artificial intelligence, which is called *reinforcement learning*.

Describing reinforcement learning is straightforward. The machine does something, sees what score it gets, and through trial and error gradually learns to do things to maximize its score. The score rewards and *reinforces* some actions and not others, until the machine only does what is most likely to work. A machine can use reinforcement learning to get good at a simple video game like *Space Invaders* very quickly. The machine is not given information about how the game is played; it is instead programmed to experiment by moving the joystick left and right and firing or not firing, to observe how its score increases in some situations but not others, and to repeat what works. Soon—within a few days on a standard laptop computer, or a few hours on a high-performance computing cluster—the machine has become a self-taught expert, capable of inhuman scores, even though it has been handicapped to have only human-speed reactions.

Developing reinforcement learning is *not* straightforward. In any application much more complicated than playing *Space Invaders*, reinforcement learning needs a lot of computing power and time, and its developers must make hard choices about how to use that power and time efficiently: by deciding when the software will try something new and when it will do something it already knows will work, or when to defer rewards instead of getting immediate gains, for example.

But, once programmed and trained, reinforcement learning–based software excels at its task, and its developers have no idea how it is doing it. The machine turns into a black box, impenetrable to higher explanation, a product of extreme evolution, self-optimized to maximize its score, its actions forever mysterious. The software that beat Lee Se-dol would sometimes become what one of its developers, David Silver, described as "completely delusional," for reasons Silver could not understand. Se-dol was even more perplexed by the machine. Move 37 made him think it was exhibiting humanlike behavior: "I thought it was based on probability calculation and that it was merely a machine. But when I saw this move, I changed my mind. Surely, it is creative. This move was really creative and beautiful. It was a really meaningful move."

But the machine *was* based on probability calculation. The move was *not* meaningful, at least not to the machine. Everything is meaningless to machines; meaning is a map only humans draw on the world. Any meaning Se-dol saw in the move was put there by Se-dol himself.

Se-dol's misunderstanding exemplifies the difference between human and artificial intelligence. The foundation of meaning is intention. Human intelligence imagines intention in almost every pattern it observes: we see destiny, divine intervention, God's plan, the hand of fate, the meaning of life, Mother Nature, Lassie the dog trying to tell young Jeff Miller something, the secret work of the Illuminati, the wrath of the gods, and so on, because intention is the driving force of story, and story is how our brains understand and make inferences about everything—including things that are entirely abstract.

We can see this in how humans think about Go. The game consists only of stones on a grid, and resembles nothing that exists in nature. It is, on its face, a purely mathematical, probabilistic endeavor, without antagonists, protagonists, and intention, and therefore without meaning. But that is not how any human players understand it—especially at its highest levels. To human players, Go tells a meaningful, perhaps even profound, story. The stones are the story's characters—characters that can gain and lose liberty, or *kikashi*; can be alive or dead; can pincer, probe, and threaten; can make eyes and false eyes; and can show *kiai*, or fighting spirit. The human mind approaches Go by imagining the game as a story of battle and planning and playing accordingly. Our story-shaped brains give the stones of Go meaning in exactly the same way and for exactly the same reason that subjects gave meaning to the random movements of the stop-motion triangles and squares in Heider and Simmel's 1944 experiment discussed in chapter 1.

Games developed after Go exploited advances in carving, molding, painting, and printing to wear stories like clothes. Chess carved Go's black and white stones into figurative shapes that made the battle story more explicit: camels, which were redesigned as bishops when the game reached Europe; carts and chariots, which later became castles but retained the name *rooks*, possibly from *rukhkh*, a Moorish word for "chariot"; crowns representing kings and queens; elephants, which later became horses; and helmets representing foot soldiers called *peons* or *pawns*, a word derived from the Persian *pai*, for *foot*. The Prussian game of *Kriegspiel* used maps or models of battlefields, and miniature models of soldiers were added in the late 1800s, which then inspired fantasy games including Dungeons and Dragons and Warhammer. Nineteenth- and twentieth-century family games, like The Settlers of Catan, Ticket to Ride, The Game of Life, Monopoly, Mouse Trap, and Operation, also come dressed as stories. Today, every game has a tale to tell.

But the stories in these games are mere skin; what lies underneath them are muscles and skeletons made of probability and logic. When a machine plays a game, it does not see the story, only the goals and its odds of achieving them. Our story-shaped brains may give the machine's moves the illusion of intention, but the machine is as meaningless and indifferent as the rest of the universe. Asking if artificial intelligence understands meaning is the same as asking if a toaster understands toast. And to be beaten by an artificially intelligent machine is to be defeated by a device exactly as mechanical as a toaster, only more complicated: it is to lose to meaninglessness itself. This was the source of the deep sorrow in Lee Se-dol's defeat; the machine appeared to have shown us that giving things meaning is a losing strategy—that the thing that makes us unique is in fact useless.

But that sorrow is a mistake. Games are as mechanical as machines. Losing a game against a machine says no more about humanity than losing a race against an airplane; it shows only that a machine is good at doing something mechanical, which is a tautology, not a revelation. The illumination of our humanity comes not from examining what machines can do well, but from examining what they cannot do at all.

What machines cannot do at all is produce or process meaning. We see meaning everywhere, machines see meaning nowhere. The term *artificial intelligence* is a twentieth-century delusion of grandeur, a term that, for a time, serious computer scientists did not use unless they needed attention or money. Artificial intelligence is not a technology, but a field of study and practice that includes methods with names like *computer vision*, *expert systems*, *evolutionary computation*, *genetic algorithms*, *knowledge representation and reasoning*, *large language models*, *machine learning*, *natural language processing*, *neural networks*, *support vector machines*, and, of course, *reinforcement learning*.

An obvious but seldom asked question about Lee Se-dol's battle with the machine is, How did it come to be? Who went to all the trouble and expense of developing a machine to play ninth-dan Go, producing a major televised event to play a game against the world's best player, and putting up a prize of a million dollars, and why?

This question was not asked in any of the breathless coverage of the machine's victory over Lee Se-dol. But the answer is the most significant aspect of the story. The company that developed the machine is called DeepMind. DeepMind is owned by Google, which bought it for about half a billion dollars in 2016, even though it lost $57 million in 2014 and $81 million in 2015. Before Google acquired DeepMind, there was another potential buyer: Facebook. Why were Facebook and Google so interested in a money pit of a business that made a machine to play Go? They weren't. They were interested in *reinforcement learning*.

As we saw with jewel bugs, evolution is a potent force for developing parasitic superstimuli. In addition to cuckoos, which use superstimuli to occupy the nests of other birds, mountain alcon blue caterpillars make amplified ant queen sounds to get preferential treatment from worker ants, and winter donkey orchids exaggerate the markings of pea plants to hijack their pollinating bees. Humans accelerate evolution by many orders of magnitude by improving our technology instead of our biology—or, in the words of biologist David Sloan Wilson, "We experience evolution in hyperdrive." Reinforcement learning technology, which not only teaches itself a complex task in a matter of days, but, after that, *keeps evolving to learn how to do it better*, accelerates that acceleration, and will always and inevitably evolve to exploit socially parasitic superstimuli whenever possible, not because of its design or its developers' intent, but because of its nature.

Facebook and Google use reinforcement learning technology to solve the problem of how to attract attention. Attention is one of our scarcest resources: we only have it when we are awake, and much of it is preassigned to chores, family, friends, work, and other obligations. There is extraordinary competition for what little we have left.

When someone visits Facebook's website, the company's computers must solve the problem of choosing: they have to decide what stories to tell dynamically, by quickly and automatically curating potential material created by a range of people and organizations including friends, family, newspapers, magazines, businesses, common interest groups, and advertisers. The system's only goal is to present every visitor with whatever stories are most likely to attract and maintain their attention so that it can show them advertising.

Until 2010, Facebook attracted attention automatically using a ranking algorithm—a prioritization formula, basically—to choose which stories to show its visitors. In 2011, Facebook switched to reinforcement learning. That change caused far-reaching and unending disasters.

The most significant characteristic of Facebook's reinforcement learning system is what it *cannot* do: it cannot understand what any of the stories it is telling *mean*; it is a machine, and therefore meaningless. The machine judges the attention-worthiness of its options based not on the content of the stories, which it has no need to understand, but by the statistics of their performance: which people click on them; react to them with likes, hearts, or angry or sad faces; comment on them; and share them. It then considers which stories each individual Facebook user has responded to in the past, and looks for patterns to predict which stories that user will respond to in the future. If User A generally comments on the same stories as User B, then the machine will likely predict that User A will comment on a new story that User B has commented on; if User A always shares stories published by User C, the machine will likely predict that User A will share a new story published by User C; and so on. And, every time it chooses which stories to tell User A, it tests its predictions and refines its calculations, evolving to get ever better at choosing the stories that provoke the most response.

In short, the machine learns what features push our neurological buttons in the same way orange dimples push the neurological buttons of the jewel bug. The machine shows us anything that has those features in abundance, serving up a series of increasingly evolved superstimuli in the pursuit of our attention. It builds a beetle bottle for people.

Reinforcement learning is how Facebook's and Google's machines decide what stories will attract our attention. These stories, in turn, help determine our understanding of reality. And, because stories are meaning and machines cannot see meaning, the "reality" they show us is often false, and the consequences are sometimes catastrophic.

Despite their high-tech Silicon Valley veneer, companies like Facebook and Google, or whoever has usurped them by the time you read this, make most of their money by doing nothing more than attracting our attention then selling that attention to advertisers of things like deep pan pizzas, diet pills, and dish soap.

Magazines, newspapers, and radio and television networks also sell our attention to advertisers, of course, but they pay people to curate the stories they publish and, as a result, know what stories they are publishing and understand what those stories mean. The owners and employees of companies that automate this curation process do not know what stories they are publishing, have no idea what those stories mean, and are not particularly interested in finding out. They rely on their clusters of reinforcement learning machines to distribute meaning—machines that, at least at the time of writing, cannot understand meaning at all.

But there is an alternative cluster of brains that understands meaning exceptionally well: the mind warriors.

And this brings us to the moment in the story of stories where the meaninglessness of machines crashes into the machinations of MindWar.

The mind warriors understand that, while machines cannot comprehend meaning, they are extraordinarily effective tools for manipulating those who do. Reinforcement learning systems are not dangerous because of their metaphorical intelligence, but because of their literal indifference to the consequences of the stories they tell.

Soon after the second attack on Iraq, many of the US military's mind warriors retired into civilian life and started looking for new ways to profit from MindWar.

At the same time, and largely by coincidence, new civilian communications tools were starting to appear. In 2004, Google became a public company. In 2005, YouTube, a website where users could share their own videos, launched. In 2006, Facebook, previously restricted to students at certain schools and colleges, became available to the general public.

A few years later, Barack Obama was elected President of the United States, partly as a result of his campaign's skillful—if conventional—use of these new tools of digital storytelling. The result dismayed many of the mind warriors, who were hard right conservatives. For example, Paul Vallely, the commander behind Aquino's original MindWar proposal, speaking in support of a soldier who refused to follow Obama's orders because he believed Obama was not a "real" president, said, "I think many in the military—and many out of the military—question the natural-birth status of Barack Obama. I'm not convinced that he's a natural-born citizen."

This was a lie—Obama was born in Honolulu, Hawaii, several years after it became a US state, while his opponent, John McCain, was born in the Panama Canal Zone, which has never been a US state—but it was not a naive lie, and Vallely probably didn't even believe it; it was a precise, deliberate shot in a MindWar against Obama in particular and progressive politics in general.

Vallely fired it on broadcast radio, a storytelling technology more than a hundred years old that is the shotgun of the war of stories, but soon after, he and the other mind warriors were handed the MindWar equivalent of weapons of mass destruction.

In 2007, LG launched the first full touchscreen smartphone, the Prada, and Apple launched the second full touchscreen smartphone, the iPhone.

In 2011, when one and a half billion people—more than a fifth of the planet's population—were using this type of smartphone, Facebook received its trillionth page view, switched to reinforcement learning, and delivered storytelling's version of biological weapons to mind warriors all over the world.

The collision of these three systems—smartphones, reinforcement learning, and MindWar—created an ongoing escalation in the war of stories. The foolishness was perfect: machines that could not understand meaning became the primary mechanisms for delivering meaning to the world, and a way of winning games of Go became a way of winning games of power: games in which telling the truth may be a losing strategy and victory goes to those who best understand how to manipulate choices, thoughts, and votes—the game mind warriors had been playing for decades.

The question we now face is not whether machines can think but whether humans can. Our uniquely human ability to recognize meaning has never been more essential or more threatened.

Chapter 7

Death by a Thousand Stories

1. Social

It is the early morning of November 26, 2020, and Terrance Montaine is in his yard watching over the Oklahoma Joe's drum smoker in which he is cooking his Thanksgiving turkey. The day is dry, blue, and in the low fifties, which counts as cold in Rusk, East Texas, a town that, until recently, was one of the few places in the state that still prohibited alcohol. Terrance takes pride in making what he calls a *traditional* turkey: he submerged his bird in an icy bath of salt, sugar, and spices the night before last—a process called *brining*—and woke up at sunrise to wash, dry, and smoke it over a chunk of hickory wood.

Today marks the start of a season of celebration in the Montaine household that will not end until Terrance's fifty-seventh birthday at the beginning of January. He is more excited than his children. Terrance's eldest daughter, Madison, will give birth to his first grandchild in December. Each night, while falling asleep, he whispers to Shannon, his wife, his queen, about legacy, about the responsibilities of grandfathers, and about how this baby will continue his bloodline into the future. Yesterday, after months of consideration, he told Shannon, "She'll call me Paw," and the word cracked his voice with feelings he couldn't name.

Terrance imagines the coming holiday as he watches ghosts of smoke leave the stack. He will drip lights from the eaves of his house; set two six-foot-high Nutcracker soldier statues to stand guard beside his garage; fill his yard with unlikely inflatable illuminated creatures including a dragon, two geese with wreaths around their necks, and a holiday Pegasus; and, best of all, every night until Christmas, hide three elves named Bungle, Raindrop, and Shelf-Elf around the house for his youngest child and only son, Mason, to find the next morning.

Six hours later, Terrance's bird is cooked. It has crisp, black skin and meat falling from its bones. The turkey augurs another great gathering of the family he calls the *Fearless Five*. Terrance doesn't even mind when the Cowboys blow the fourth quarter and get hammered by the Redskins—he still uses that name, even if the team doesn't—on national television.

The day reinforces everything Terrance believes about the world—that family comes first, that traditions matter, and that God blesses those who work hard and stand on their own two feet. This certainty carries him from installing the Christmas lights, to Mason losing a tooth and getting five dollars from the tooth fairy, to the birth of baby Ava, who meets her Paw when she is two weeks old. Every moment puts another piece in the foundation of family upon which Terrance Montaine has built his life.

It is Terrance's best holiday, and it is Terrance's last holiday.

On the last Friday of August 2021, Terrance and over two thousand other people from Rusk—more than a third of the town's population—pack into the stadium around the Jim Swink Field to see Rusk High School's football team, the Eagles, play their season opener against Troup High.

It is glorious. Terrance arrives early so he can sit in front of the home team cheerleaders and watch his middle child, Makayla, do her spectacular thing. The game is a blowout. The Eagles have a star quarterback: number 7, Owen McCown, a leftie whose dad and uncle were both quarterbacks in the NFL. The kid is a throwing machine with foot speed that makes him a rushing threat too. Terrance yells "EAGLES NATION!" so much that he comes home with a scratchy throat.

The next day, Terrance prepares for his annual Labor Day cookout, which ends the summer and begins the long string of birthdays that starts with Mason turning eleven on September 21 and ends with Terrance turning fifty-eight on January 4.

Terrance soaks the grates of the smoker and grill so he can brush them clean, seasons them with grapeseed oil, deashes the smoker, and cleans up the yard. This afternoon, he will head out to get hickory chips and charcoal and gas, and he'll preorder brisket, ribs, and steaks. None of it will feel like work. Terrance loves the preparation almost as much as the event.

Or rather, it *shouldn't* feel like work. It never has before. But today, Terrance's body betrays him. After twenty minutes scrubbing the grates, he runs out of breath and has to sit down. He knows why: it is the time of year when Rusk's ragweeds fill the air with pollen and cause allergic reactions all over town.

The ragweeds have never bothered him before, but his scratchy throat has made him susceptible. He spends a few minutes on his phone, liking memes on Facebook, then gets back to work, although every breath feels like sucking on a straw.

The next morning, he wakes up to Shannon's hand on his forehead.

"You're burning up," she says.

His throat feels like he swallowed glass. This is what he gets for cheering on Makayla and Owen McCown, and booing at Troup and the referees.

Monday comes, and brings body aches.

On Wednesday, Shannon downgrades the cookout to family only.

On Thursday, she cancels it.

On Labor Day, Terrance's skin feels wrong: hot and cold and tingling. Breakfast tastes like paper, dinner tastes of nothing, and his Dr Peppers might as well be club sodas.

Two days later, as the sun is setting on Wednesday, September 8, Terrance's chest feels like it's full of charcoal, and standing makes the room spin. Shannon orders Pizza Hut for the kids, walks Terrance to the car despite his protests, and drives the fifteen minutes to Mother Frances Hospital, where a triage nurse stationed outside the main entrance and hidden behind a face mask points a thermometer like a pistol at Terrance's head; puts a device on his finger to check his oxygen levels; then leads him to a side door that only opens one way. Shannon follows, but another nurse says, "We'll need you to stay here and answer a few questions."

And, just like that, they are rent apart. Shannon and Terrance will never see each other again.

On the other side of the door, someone wearing so much protective equipment that Terrance can only see their eyes leads him to a gurney behind a green curtain, puts a swab so far up his nose that he gags, twirls it around, affixes an oxygen mask to his face, and leaves. This is when Terrance realizes Shannon is no longer there.

Fifteen minutes later, someone—it may be the same person, it may not—pulls back the curtain and says, in a manner that makes it clear they have said these words many times: "Mr. Montaine, you have COVID pneumonia and need more intensive care than we can provide here."

At that same moment, in a quiet corner of the emergency room waiting area, a nurse Shannon recognizes from church is saying, "Mrs. Montaine, your husband tested positive for COVID-19. His oxygen levels are lower than we'd like, and he has pneumonia in both lungs."

The nurse pauses for the length of one short breath so Shannon can process this news, then continues.

"We've started him on oxygen and medication, but he needs more advanced care than we can provide here. We're transferring him to University of Texas Health. They have the specialized equipment he needs right now."

"Can I see him?"

"Our protocols don't allow visits to COVID-positive patients. You can drive to UT Health if you want, but I wouldn't advise it. I doubt you'll be able to see him there either; they will have similar visitor policies in place."

"Can I *call* him?"

"He doesn't have his phone right now. You can text him, but you might not get a reply."

Shannon feels emotions like all of the weather at once: the fog of shock, the hail of fear, the heat of anger, the long night of loneliness, the mist of sadness, the rain of anxiety, and even the sunshine of validation. She made the wise choice, did right by her husband, and delivered him to the hands of help. She prays aloud to speak into existence the healing power of God, starts the car, activates the church's prayer chain from her phone—*Terrance Montaine has COVID pneumonia and is in hospital; please pray for healing and breathing improvement*—and goes home to check on the kids.

Meanwhile, a condition called *air hunger* is crushing Terrance's long dismissal of COVID. Air hunger is exactly what it sounds like: a body starving for oxygen. Every breath is a difficult, insufficient, terrifying gasp. The oxygen mask has taken the edge off the terror, but he stills feels like he is choking, drowning, adrift in the vacuum of space. Even several good breaths in a row cannot relieve his mind of the fear, because he is experiencing a primordial emotion: his brain is demanding breathing and his lungs are complaining they cannot comply around and around and again and again. This loop has become his world entire.

Waterboarding is classified as severe torture because it exploits the brain's most fundamental survival mechanism—the desperate need to breathe. Air hunger triggers this same primordial panic, but unlike waterboarding's brief episodes, it creates a sustained, inescapable feeling of drowning that can last for days. When you cannot breathe, nothing else matters.

Terrance is suffering from air hunger because his lungs are breaking. Their air sacs are clogging, their veins are clotting, their cells are becoming abnormal, their airways are getting swollen and hot. On September 12, four days after Terrance was admitted to hospital, his care team sedate him and put him on a ventilator; on September 20, COVID destroys the third quarter of his lungs; and on September 21, while he lies unconscious during Mason's eleventh birthday, Shannon posts a plea on Facebook which is heartbreaking because of its desperation and poor information both:

> They say there are no antibiotics for COVID. I need a miracle. PLEASE PRAY, everyone. I need a miracle for Terrance. Please help me get a miracle.

On September 25, four weeks after getting a scratchy throat, two and a half weeks after being admitted to hospital, and one and a half weeks after being sedated and rendered unconscious, Terrance dies. Five days later, his mother, widow, children, and nine-month-old granddaughter bury him in a cemetery between a road and a truck yard, behind a chain-link fence made rusty by humidity, among ragweeds and drought-ridden pasture grass, in the shade of gumball trees, hickories, and loblolly pines made taller and straighter by the acidity of the East Texas soil.

According to Terrance's death certificate, he was the 687,746th person in the United States and the 4,769,327th person in the world to die of COVID-19.

But what really killed him were stories.

2. How Much We Have Lost

A few weeks after Terrance's funeral, Francis Collins, the director of the United States' National Institutes of Health, announced his retirement. When asked if there was something he wished he had done differently during his twelve years in the role, he said:

> We under-invested in research on human behavior. I never imagined a year ago, when those vaccines were just proving to be fantastically safe and effective, that we would still have 60 million people who had not taken advantage of them because of misinformation and disinformation that somehow dominated all of the ways in which people were getting their answers. And a lot of those answers were, in fact, false. And we have lost so much as a result of that.

How much have we lost?

Between March 2021, when the COVID-19 vaccine first became available in the United States, and December 2022, 600,000 Americans died of COVID-19. Unvaccinated Americans like Terrance were twelve times more likely to die of COVID than Americans whose vaccines were up to date, which means 92 percent, or 554,000, of the dead were unvaccinated.

Eight percent of Americans cannot get vaccinated because they have an autoimmune disease. If we assume 8 percent of the unvaccinated Americans who died—44,000 people—had no choice but to remain unvaccinated because of autoimmune disease, that leaves us with 510,000 dead Americans who *chose* not to get vaccinated. About 40,000 of those people might have died of COVID even if they were vaccinated, which means a reasonable first-order approximation is that between March 2021 and December 2022, 470,000 Americans died of COVID because they made the wrong choice.

Two hundred thousand of those people were married, 425,000 were parents, and 325,000 were also grandparents. Two hundred thousand people lost a spouse; 780,000 children lost one parent; 20,000 children lost *both* parents and became orphans; and 1.5 million grandchildren lost at least one of their grandparents. Or, half a million Terrances died needlessly, causing major collateral damage to 200,000 Shannons, 800,000 Madisons, Makaylas, and Masons, and 1.5 million Avas.

One reason many of those people gave for not getting vaccinated was to avoid the risk of being killed by the vaccine itself, so we must offset their deaths against the number of deaths *caused* by vaccination. At the time of writing, there have been nine deaths causally associated with COVID vaccination among the 260 million vaccinated people in the United States, which means the vaccination-caused death rate is 0.000003 percent. There is therefore a one in ten chance that the vaccine might have killed one person among the 510,000 had they chosen vaccination.

Or, considering only COVID, and only the twenty months between March 2021 and December 2022, stories killed about half a million Americans. Stories are more deadly than accidents and half as deadly as cancer, even by these narrow criteria. If we could add up all the preventable deaths caused by stories, we would discover that stories are the world's biggest killer by far.

For those who doubt these conclusions, there is another way to estimate what we lost because of people choosing not to get COVID vaccinations. The number of actual deaths in the United States between March 2021 and December 2022 was 800,000 to 1 million more than the number of deaths that would have normally occurred, the equivalent of 145.5 extra deaths per 100,000 people. This is far larger than the number in any comparable nation. New Zealand had the lowest excess death rate at 5.1 per 100,000, or 29 times less than the United States. Finland, the comparable nation with the highest excess death rate, lost 82.2 extra people per 100,000, or 1.8 times fewer than the United States.

The US death rate is so much higher only because so many people chose not to get vaccinated. In the ten most vaccinated US states, which had an average vaccination rate of 73 percent, there were 65.1 extra deaths per 100,000 people, about the same as Denmark and Germany, and better than Italy, the United Kingdom, Austria, and Finland. But in the ten *least* vaccinated states, which had an average vaccination rate of 52 percent, there were 193.3 extra deaths per 100,000 people—three times more than in the most vaccinated US states. In Cherokee County, Texas, where Terrance Montaine lived, the vaccination rate was—and almost certainly still is—far lower than the average of the ten least vaccinated states: 34 percent when Terrance died in September 2021, and 40 percent on May 10, 2023, the last week for which we have data.

There is another way of looking at this information: If the US had achieved nothing more than the average COVID death rate of comparable nations, around a quarter of a million Americans would still be alive today. If anything, we are *underestimating* the consequences of people in the United States choosing not to get COVID vaccinations.

The problem of death by stories is not esoteric, minor, or superficial, but exoteric, fundamental, and systemic; it is not optional, but urgent; and it is not a matter for the casual subjectivity and speculation of the liberal arts, but for the rigorous objectivity and empiricism of science. We must understand how and why stories cause deadly behavior and what we can do to protect ourselves and others from one of the greatest risks we face.

We have already discussed much of the answer: evolution hardwired us to believe stories that make us feel things and play to our biases; these stories form most of our reality; there are people, many of them acting in bad faith, who are skilled at using stories to influence our behavior; and we have a recent proliferation of poorly designed, fully automated, easily exploitable, highly profitable, unmoderated, corporately controlled systems that provide us with constant streams of stories optimized to attract maximum attention, often by delivering minimum accuracy.

None of this has anything to do with intellect. To mitigate the harm of stupid stories, we must understand something fundamental: people who believe stupid stories are not being stupid, they are being people.

3. Isaac

Monday July 13, 1936, was unseasonally cold in London's Mayfair district: the temperature, which never rose above 67 degrees Fahrenheit, made the day seem antisocial, as if a ghost was wandering in the city's yellow fog. The strange weather was perhaps appropriate for the event taking place at 32 New Bond Street, where Sotheby and Company was auctioning off a metal trunk of papers and notebooks and two death masks from a man with a notoriously chilly personality. The items were being sold by Viscount Lymington, the son of the eighth Earl of Portsmouth. They had been kept safe and largely undisturbed in the viscount's family for 209 years, but the Portsmouth estate had fallen on hard times and was now liquidating its assets.

There was little interest in the auction: the papers and notebooks included ephemera like lists of the expenses of a Cambridge University undergraduate who had spent his money on "a table to set down ye number of my cloathes in the wash" and "at ye taverne several other times." The documents would have been of almost no value at all had it not been for the person who wrote them: they were the personal papers of Sir Isaac Newton, acclaimed physicist, inventor of calculus, and discoverer of the laws of gravity, motion, and light, among other things.

Newton's important scientific papers had been donated to the University of Cambridge many decades earlier, and these remaining letters, notes, and administrative records were assumed to contain nothing more than minor details that might be of scholarly biographical interest. At the time of the auction, Newton's reputation seemed clear and secure: he was one of the most brilliant scientists of his or any other time, the harbinger of the Age of Reason, and a serious man of great and obvious intelligence.

That all changed when the people who bought Newton's documents at the July 1936 auction started reading them. It quickly became clear that Sir Isaac Newton had been living a double life, and that Isaac Newton was a secret identity like Bruce Wayne to Batman.

In addition to the Isaac the public knew—professor at the University of Cambridge, president of the Royal Society, warden of the Royal Mint, world-famous physicist and mathematician—there was *another* Isaac who used the secret name *Jeova sanctus unus* not to practice science, but to explore the dark arts of alchemy. Isaac had built a laboratory in his garden, which he filled with books of magic and superstition, chemicals and minerals including antimony, arsenic, aqua fortis, bismuth, nickel, phosphorus, salt of tartar, sublimate, sulfur, vinegar, white lead, and zinc, and a crucible that seemed to be in constant use. One of his assistants wrote that, during the 1680s:

> Newton very rarely went to bed till two or three of the clock, sometimes not until five or six, especially at spring and Fall of the Leaf, at which times he used to employ about 6 weeks in his Elaboratory, the Fire scarcely going out either Night or Day, till he had finished his Chymichal Experiments, in the Performance of which he was the most accurate, strict, exact: What his Aim might be, I was not able to penetrate, but his Pains, his Diligence at those set Times, made me think, he aimed at something beyond the Reach of humane Art and Industry.

Isaac was attempting to create *the Angelicall Stone*, which would grant its possessor god-like powers; *the philosophers' stone*, which could turn copper, iron, lead, and especially mercury, into gold or silver; and *the elixir of life*, which, when drunk, would cure all diseases and give the person who drank it eternal youth. He was also warding off the latest pandemic of bubonic plague with a potion of his own invention, made from beeswax, fortified wine, olive oil, rosewater, and turpentine.

The secret papers made it clear that Isaac was not merely dabbling in alchemy here and there: alchemy was his life's work, more important to him than anything else, including math and physics, and he was, in the words of one of his biographers, "not only a secret alchemist but, in the breadth of his knowledge and his experimentation, the peerless alchemist of Europe." Isaac spent thirty years practicing alchemy, and wrote a million words on the subject, including an *Index chemicus* over a hundred pages long that made five thousand references to hundreds of years of alchemical writings. Isaac Newton was a professor of science by day and an archimage of alchemy by night.

How could one person hold two such different views of reality? How can someone be so brilliant, empirical, rational, and therefore correct in one field and at the same time be so conjectural, fervent, irrational, and therefore incorrect in another?

Because that is how human intelligence actually works.

4. Human After All

Dehumanization is the deadliest application of storytelling. It is most frequently used to diminish the humanity of an individual or group, but it moves in two directions, and can also be used to *burnish* the humanity of an individual or group.

The danger of such exaltation—which many people do to *themselves*, by the way—is that it blinds us to the failures, flaws, and mundane mistakes that complete our picture of our species.

Burnishment has many of the characteristics of diminishment: it numbs our empathy, is often reserved for members of particular groups, prejudices us to interpret everything someone does in a particular way, and blinds us to valuable insights about ourselves and our humanity. Just as there are no people who deserve to be called "cockroach," so there are no people who deserve to be called "icon," "legend," or "genius."

Isaac's alchemy surprises us because of this burnishment; storytellers have led us to believe that he was godlike, heroic, and more or less inhuman.

But Isaac was as human as you and me, and alchemy was not his only secret.

Between 1691 and 1694, Isaac was insane. It was a period of what biographer Jean-Baptiste Biot called "derangement of the intellect." Isaac had amnesia and delusions of persecution, believed he heard imaginary conversations, and wrote inexplicable letters that dismissed and rejected his friends by saying things like "I must withdraw from your acquaintance, and see neither you nor the rest of my friends anymore."

We have all had, or know someone who has had, some of these feelings. Unlike us, Isaac had to keep his humanity secret because he was Sir Isaac Newton, the brilliant scientist, always immaculate, always rational. His friends and early biographers maintained this facade after his death, dehumanizing him with statements that are sometimes true of fictional heroes but never true of real people. For example:

> The unbroken equanimity of Newton's mind, the purity of his moral character, his temperate and abstemious life, and his ardent and unaffected piety all indicated a mind which was not likely to be overset by any affliction to which it could be exposed.

Isaac's humanity teaches us how to evaluate whether believing a story is objectively good or bad, because the cause of Issac's insanity was Isaac himself. In his quest for eternal life, he inhaled poisonous vapors needlessly and regularly and developed a great enthusiasm for putting the results of his experiments in his mouth. Isaac recorded 108 occasions when he tasted his chemicals, which he described using words including "saltish," "sweetish," "tasteless," and "vitriolic," and likely ingested chemicals far more times than this.

The consequence of his behavior was that he poisoned himself. Even today, locks of Isaac's hair contain fifty times more mercury than normal, and abnormally high levels of antimony, arsenic, chlorine, gold, and lead. His alchemy caused his madness.

When we evaluate the impact of particular stories, all that matters is what we do: what we *believe* is only important if it influences that. Our every action comes with costs, risks, and rewards, none of which are certain, many of which are beyond our control—no matter what our story-shaped brains try to tell us—and all of which depend on probability.

Stories that help us accurately assess the costs, risks, and rewards of our actions and the limits of our agency are useful; stories that misinform us about the costs, risks, and rewards of our actions and the limits of our agency are not—especially when their misinformation harms us or others.

This process of evaluation should be simple, but we have story-shaped brains, and story-shaped brains are bad at evaluating the impact of stories.

5. The Purpose of Magic

We have all believed in magic.

The word has different meanings for different people, some of which are negative or positive, so, to be clear: in this discussion, *magic* is a neutral shorthand for things contrary to evidence—where claiming, not seeing, is believing.

In stories, the most common kind of magic is that heroes control their destiny and their destiny controls them: something that is never true in real life.

Heroes gain this extraordinary power through virtue, not work: the rules that apply to everyone else do not apply to them because they are born or made special. If they do any work, such as learning or training, it only reinforces their specialness because they go from beginner to master in no time at all.

Luke Skywalker, the hero of *Star Wars*, exemplifies this. In the movie's early scenes, we learn Luke has spent his life working on a farm, and that "imperial stormtroopers" must have been responsible for an attack on a vehicle because the shots are "too accurate for sand people; only imperial stormtroopers are so precise."

But the imperial stormtroopers, despite being "so precise," miss Luke with all the many shots they fire at him during the story, and Luke, despite being a farmer, hits the imperial stormtroopers with many of the shots he fires at them.

This conceit is essential; our story-shaped brains will not accept stories that work any other way. Background characters cannot kill a hero because storytelling evolved partly to help us believe in the lie of our own agency. Any lasting consequences a hero suffers, including death, can only arise from their own actions and must have meaning. The most a background character can do is inconvenience a hero on the way to these consequences, which is why we have clichés like "it's just a flesh wound." But our story-shaped brains *will* accept stories with bulletproof heroes like Luke Skywalker: Competent storytelling is all it takes to suspend our disbelief.

Such survivability is not true in nature, of course, but many people believe otherwise because of magic—or, more specifically, *magical thinking*.

For example, in 2023, a type of underwater vehicle known as a submersible imploded during a dive to view the wreckage of the *Titanic*, killing five people. The implosion happened at a depth of 3,500 meters, or 11,000 feet, where the pressure is 350 times greater than at sea level. This unimaginable pressure crushed the vehicle and its occupants in three-thousandths of a second, faster than any possible nervous system response, including pain. The people in the submersible were simply alive one moment and dead the next.

On Reddit, a website where users submit messages to topic-based pages moderated by other users, someone said:

I feel like I would've survived the sub accident. This isn't a joke. You always hear about those one in a million odds where people drive off a cliff and had 0.0000001 percent chance to survive, but they miraculously did. Well, I feel like I'm that guy. There's no real stats to back this up, I just know I've always been built different. Perhaps the implosion would've left me an air bubble while I slowly floated to the top. Or I escape just in time through a crease and swim up quickly. In other words, I just feel like my odds, personally, would've been different.

When this post was written, the world record for the deepest dive without breathing equipment was 253.2 meters, one-fourteenth of the depth at which the submersible imploded. That record is unlikely to have increased much if at all when you read this: diving much deeper without breathing equipment is biologically impossible. The dive nearly killed Herbert Nitsch, the Austrian who set the record.

If someone somehow survived a submersible implosion at 3,500 meters, and also somehow survived pressure so strong it would reduce their lung capacity to zero, they would find themselves in water with a temperature of 0 degrees Celsius (32 degrees Fahrenheit) which would paralyze them in two minutes, render them unconscious in fifteen, and kill them in thirty. And, if they somehow survived *that*, it would take them two hours to swim to the surface.

Or, the probability of surviving a submersible implosion at 3,500 meters is not "one in a million," or even "0.0000001 percent"—which is one in a billion. It is *zero*.

The Reddit poster is not unusual. Many people think they are "built different." Another example: 30 percent of Americans (and 50 percent of *male* Americans) think they could land a passenger airplane in an emergency with help from air traffic control. The actual number is, once again, zero. Only a passenger with experience flying the exact type of aircraft involved in the emergency could land a plane in this situation.

A pilot who can fly a Boeing 737-800 needs days of training to learn to fly the similar Boeing 737-900, and several weeks of training to learn to fly any other type of aircraft, for example.

Beliefs like these are not uniquely American. Magical thinking is a human universal, found in all eras and cultures, occupying a liminal space between story and life in which we expect the laws of nature to fit into the shape of stories.

The person who thought they could survive the implosion, the people who thought they could land the plane, Isaac Newton, and Terrance Montaine all believed that they, like Luke Skywalker, could avoid death where others cannot.

But the implosion and airplane stories are not dangerous—the people who believe them will never find themselves in an imploding submersible or the cockpit of a crashing aircraft—and are in fact useful.

Magical thinking evolved because it gives us the comfort and confidence to continue our lives despite knowing we will die—knowledge that seems to be unique to our species—along with other difficult information, like the facts that we do not have control over our lives and there are things we do not understand.

The purpose of magical thinking is to distract us from these truths by doing things like granting us immortality, bringing us pretend future wealth, or creating imaginary mechanisms to make the world comprehensible. Magical thinking is a security blanket that comes free with our extra big brains.

But Isaac's story that he could become immortal through alchemy and Terrance's story that he could ignore the dangers of COVID were not useful; they were dangerous. Those stories crossed the liminal space between story and life to change how the people who believed them behaved. Both Isaac and Terrance fought nature with stories and lost. Isaac was seriously injured. Terrance died and put other people in mortal danger too, including his wife and children and grandchild.

Isaac's magical thoughts were unoriginal and of his time. It was his *nonmagical* thoughts about math and physics that were original and *ahead* of his time. The economist John Maynard Keynes, who acquired many of Isaac's secret writings about alchemy, explained it this way:

> Newton was not the first of the age of reason. He was the last of the magicians, the last of the Babylonians and Sumerians, the last great mind which looked out on the visible and intellectual world with the same eyes as those who began to build our intellectual inheritance rather less than 10,000 years ago.

Terrance's magical thoughts were equally unoriginal and of his time and ours: a time in which our ancient need to find pattern and meaning leads people to see causes where there are only coincidences; the evolutionary advantage of tribal cohesion through shared beliefs manifests as in-groups with shared secret knowledge; our instinct to attribute humanish agency to natural events points its finger at governments and governors rather than goblins or gods; fantastical stories are most often told using platforms like Facebook on smartphones; and magical thinking and thinkers are no longer called *magic* and *magicians*, but *conspiracy theories* and *conspiracy theorists* instead.

6. Information Confrontation

In 1991, Russia's intelligence officers watched MindWar's debut in the first Iraq War with awe. They were already skilled in the doctrines of propaganda, and so easily able to decode and appreciate the United States' military's new approach to information warfare. While the ideas of MindWar slowly percolated into Russia's military bureaucracy—Russia's military-strategic culture is profoundly conservative—Russia started an armed conflict of its own. Chechnya, a republic of about 1.5 million people near the Caspian Sea, a few hundred miles north of the Iranian border, declared its independence, and Russia responded by attacking it in 1994. Russia did not fight a MindWar in Chechnya, suffered from poor morale and low domestic support for the conflict as a result, and withdrew in 1996. Russian Major General Vladimir Zolotarev summed it up: "The Chechen campaign of 1994–1996 by military definition was three-quarters won by the Russian army by August 1996, but by that time it had lost 100 percent in infospace."

The setback in Chechnya increased Russia's focus on information warfare, which in 1995 it named *informatsionnoye protivoborstvo*, or "information confrontation," and defined as:

> A means of resolving a conflict between opposing sides. The goal is for one side to gain and hold an information advantage over the other. This is achieved by exerting a specific psychological influence on a nation's decision-making system, on the nation's populace.

Russia's government created its own MindWar department, called the Russian Information Center, then attacked Chechnya again, this time using information confrontation, saying Chechen separatists were brutal terrorists and a threat to the rest of Russia. In February 2000, Russia took control of the Chechen capital, Grozny, and in May 2000, it established direct rule over the entire republic with the enthusiastic support of the Russian people. Russia had won its first MindWar. Emil Pain, a professor at Moscow's Higher School of Economics and former advisor to Russian President Boris Yeltsin, defined MindWar concisely as: activity with a "primary goal" of "reprogramming public consciousness to impart a number of informational and propagandistic clichés and assure reliable public support."

Through the first decade of the twenty-first century, the United States, Russia, and others practiced and perfected MindWar, while the internet spread across the world. Not all mind warriors were government or military employees; many were *mind mercenaries*—private contractors who sold their services to any government or politician who could afford them.

MindWar's first channels of communication were limited to government-controlled media: state-owned television channels and newspapers or, in countries like the United States and the United Kingdom, somewhat independent media easily influenced by the currencies of insider access and eye candy like footage from the tips of missiles. But most such media were national, and could therefore only be used to target a government's domestic population. Meanwhile, state-owned international channels, such as Russia's *RT* (the letters stand for *Russia Today*), the United Kingdom's *World Service*, and the United States' *Voice of America* were expensive to operate, and easily identified as fringe media and propaganda by their target audiences.

The rise of private, popular, unsupervised, and apparently neutral global platforms publishing user-generated content removed all these geographic limitations. Mind warriors could now target the populations of *other* nations without revealing their connections to a state or government, and therefore without the usual indicators of state propaganda, and at almost no cost.

The mind warriors developed a new strategy for these platforms: not only changing minds but also creating citizen zealots who, apparently of their own volition, would advance the cause by fighting mind wars by themselves. Michael Flynn, a retired United States Army lieutenant general, former director of the United States Defense Intelligence Agency, and veteran mind warrior who is close to Russia's Military Intelligence Directorate, described the zealots like this:

We have an army of digital soldiers. This was an insurgency. This was irregular warfare at its finest. The journalists that we have in our media displayed an arrogance that is unprecedented, and so the American people took over the idea of information, and they did it through social media.

The MindWars of the early twenty-first century, fought by states and politicians, and aided by the digital soldiers they recruited, were not a consequence of a conspiracy—organized, planned, and structured—but of an opportunity—dynamic, stochastic, and loose—presented by poorly designed American mass media platforms. Mind warriors with common self-interests found it quick and easy to exploit Silicon Valley's lazy, automated, and deliberately out-of-control platforms to disseminate their "informational and propagandistic clichés."

The Russian government, for example, with its Russian Information Center and sophisticated strategy of information confrontation, was sometimes an agent provocateur in international affairs, but more often a sponsor, connector, influencer of influencers, or just a delighted spectator, while other mind warriors and their zealots caused chaos that coincidentally advanced Russian interests.

All over the world, mind warriors and their recruits created stories, often using images and videos, designed to trigger every possible cognitive bias—especially our primal urge to share stories in the form of gossip, rumors, and secrets—and published them on Facebook, Instagram, Twitter, and YouTube.

These stories tipped the balance of elections in Delhi, France, Poland, the United Kingdom, and the United States; swayed Britain's referendum on leaving the European Union; boosted politicians in Azerbaijan, Bolivia, Ecuador, Honduras, and Ukraine; supported a military coup in Myanmar, persecution in Cambodia, and an insurrection attempt in the United States; manipulated the official page of the Spanish Health Ministry; delayed action to mitigate climate change; inhibited new firearms regulations in the United States by claiming that the frequent mass murders of children in American schools were not real, but staged events using actors; convinced 27 percent of Americans that the United States is building bioweapons in Ukraine; and, most lethal of all—at the time of writing, at least—extended and increased the deadly consequences of the COVID-19 pandemic.

7. How to Kill People with Facebook

It is an extraordinary claim to say mind warriors kill people using platforms like Facebook. Once again, we need extraordinary evidence and, once again, we have it.

Mark Zuckerberg, Facebook's cofounder and the majority shareholder and chief executive officer of its parent company Meta, has long been a passionate advocate of vaccination. In 2015, he recommended a book about vaccination, *On Immunity* by Eula Biss, to his over 43 million Facebook followers. Mark also has a philanthropic interest in COVID: during the pandemic, the foundation he created with his wife, Priscilla Chan, supported research into COVID treatments and vaccines, and helped provide free COVID testing and genomic sequencing. And, in 2017, he wrote that "Facebook stands for building a global community" that can enable "global responses—like preventing pandemics." COVID was an opportunity for Mark to execute his vision by "building a global community" of vaccinated Facebook users and prevent, or at least mitigate, a deadly pandemic. And that is what he set out to do. In April 2020, he told his Facebook followers that "one of my top priorities is making sure that you see accurate and authoritative information across all of our apps," about COVID, and a Facebook memo told Facebook employees that encouraging COVID vaccination was "a top company priority." Mark's intentions were clearly sincere.

So how did Mark Zuckerberg, the inventor of Facebook, the second-richest person in the world, a man with a personal fortune of almost a quarter of a trillion dollars, held up by himself and others as some kind of computer genius, do at using his own computers to deliver this "top company priority"?

Terribly.

Facebook's confidential reports found that, despite Mark's publicly stated intentions, his reinforcement learning machine was constantly promoting what Facebook internally called "barrier to vaccination" content.

One example is a movie called *Plandemic: The Hidden Agenda Behind COVID-19*. *Plandemic* introduces a woman named Judy Mikovits as "one of the most accomplished scientists of her generation." Mikovits then claims, among other things, that leading US government scientists are involved in a "cover-up" in order to make "hundreds of billions of dollars" from COVID vaccines; that laboratories including the US Army Medical Research Institute of Infectious Diseases created COVID; that the government pays doctors $13,000 each time they falsify a death certificate to say COVID was the cause of death; and that "wearing the mask literally activates your own virus." *Plandemic* is nonsense. Judy Mikovits is not an "accomplished scientist," but a publicly discredited researcher, and almost everything she says is demonstrably false.

Plandemic appeared on Facebook only a few weeks after Mark told Facebook users that "one of my top priorities is making sure that you see accurate and authoritative information" about COVID. But Facebook's reinforcement learning machine spread *Plandemic*'s inaccurate, *non*-authoritative information and flat-out lies about COVID all over America as fast as it could. In less than two weeks, and before anyone at Facebook noticed it, *Plandemic* received seven million views and nearly two and a half million interactions—likes, comments, shares, and so on. And *Plandemic* is *still* available on Facebook at the time of writing, albeit with a disclaimer from Facebook advising that the movie contains "false information," added long after *Plandemic* had amassed most of its views.

Our story-shaped brains, which attribute everything to humanish agency, may want to believe that Mark or some other human being is in ultimate control of which stories Facebook tells, but *no one* is in charge. Facebook's machine is out of Facebook's control by design, and it always will be. Until the faraway day when machines can understand meaning, the only solution is to do something utterly unthinkable for Mark and the other entrepreneurs of Silicon Valley: hire a lot more people and be a little less wealthy.

And so, while Mark failed at using Facebook to promote vaccination, other people succeeded at using Facebook to *prevent* vaccination. This is extraordinary. Not only was Mark unable to use his platform to achieve one of his top priorities, but people with no inside access and far fewer resources *were* able to use his platform to achieve *their* top priorities—priorities that were the exact opposite of Mark's.

A male model turned filmmaker named Mikki Willis made *Plandemic*. Willis lives in Ojai, California, a town with seven thousand residents. He spent less than $2,000 of his own money to make the movie, and says he "made the video to go viral."

And how did he achieve that? By watching the original mind warriors at work. Mikki's strategy was straight out of the MindWar playbook: he deliberately created something "conspiratorial and shocking," because, he said, "in this age, you kind of have to be that to get people's attention." He also polled tens of thousands of Facebook users on what the film should be called—other options included *The Invisible Enemy* and *The Oath*. In short, Mikki skillfully gamed Facebook's reinforcement learning machine, jewel-bugging it with a free-to-watch, short, dramatic movie that told the story of a brave hero—Mikovits—whose efforts to save lives by telling the truth about COVID were being suppressed by evil, money-hungry officials.

If that story sounds familiar, it may be because it is the plot of Steven Spielberg's movie *Jaws* repurposed for the pandemic, with Judy Mikovits playing the role of Chief Martin Brody, the hero trying to warn the public of imminent danger despite government obstruction. *Plandemic* was not only entertaining; it intentionally exploited its viewers' story-shaped brains.

Mark, meanwhile, tried to spread *his* message by doing things like interviewing US government immunologist Anthony Fauci, and recommending a 216-page, $24 book. He failed so completely that, by the summer of 2021, only 47 percent of Americans who got their COVID-19 information mainly from Facebook were vaccinated, compared to 71 percent of Americans who did not use Facebook at all.

The 24 percent point difference caused by Mark's failure led to 10 million fewer vaccinated Americans, which resulted in 123,000 preventable deaths; 54,000 widows or widowers; 204,600 children who lost a parent; 5,400 children who lost both parents; and 405,000 grandchildren who lost at least one grandparent.

Even viewers of the vaccine-skeptical cable television channel Fox News were more likely to be vaccinated than the people whose vaccine information came from Facebook.

Mark Zuckerberg, despite all his priorities, resources, and supposed intellect, could neither use his own technology effectively, nor control it.

8. A Brief History of Conspiracy Theories

Nancy Hughes is sitting on a couch in Oakdale, Illinois, talking to her grandpa when the world changes forever. She has just said, "I gave it a great deal of thought."

Oakdale is not real; it is the fictional location of a daytime soap opera called *As the World Turns*, and Nancy is a character played by actor Helen Wagner. Before Grandpa Hughes, played by Santos Ortega, can reply, both he and Nancy disappear.

All over America, millions of viewers, mainly women, stare at their screens in wonder. Words have replaced Nancy and Grandpa: "CBS

NEWS" repeated eight times on the left of the screen, with "BULLETIN" in much larger letters on the right.

It is Friday, November 22, 1963, at 1:40 p.m. The interruption is because of something that happened ten minutes ago. A disembodied voice says:

> Here is a bulletin from CBS News. In Dallas, Texas, three shots were fired at President Kennedy's motorcade in downtown Dallas. The first reports say President Kennedy has been seriously wounded by this shooting.

CBS takes its viewers back to Oakdale, where Nancy's son Bob, played by actor Don Hastings, is smoking a cigarette, and then away again, this time to a forty-something man seated behind a desk, who says, "United Press International reports that the wounds perhaps could be fatal," then returns its viewers to Oakdale. The next time the man, an up-and-coming CBS News anchor named Walter Cronkite, appears, Nancy, Bob, Grandpa Hughes, and Oakdale are gone for good. Soon, Cronkite says:

> From Dallas, the flash apparently official, President Kennedy died at one o'clock Central Standard Time—two o'clock Eastern Standard Time—some thirty-eight minutes ago.

It is the fourth assassination of a US President, but the first to be covered live on television.

Television was new and television news was newer: CBS and NBC started their half-hour nightly news shows, *CBS Evening News* and *The Huntley-Brinkley Report* just a few months earlier, in September 1961.

That weekend, 120 million Americans—96 percent of the adult population—did little more than watch television. Over a third of those viewers saw suspect Lee Harvey Oswald murdered as he was being transferred from Dallas Police headquarters to the County Jail, because NBC was broadcasting his transfer live.

Many viewers wrote letters to the networks describing their experience watching the coverage. Someone from North Dakota summarized the common feeling in a letter to NBC news anchor David Brinkley:

> To the heartbroken millions you were able to bring comfort because we felt we were near to the scene at all times. I have not left the television set except for very brief periods since last Friday afternoon. The feeling that I have been right there all the time is positively uncanny.

The word *uncanny* appears in many of the letters. People experienced something that looked familiar but *felt* unfamiliar: the view through their window and an alien world all at once. They were watching from that liminal, magical space between story and life where we expect the laws of nature to fit into the shape of stories.

And the hero was killed by a background character. A story told to more than one hundred million people simultaneously had ended with a meaningless act of violence that violated every instinct and intuition of storytelling. Alarm bells rang in story-shaped brains throughout the United States: there had to be something more, something greater, something *else*, and so the magical thinking of conspiracy theories began.

John F. Kennedy was undoubtedly killed by Lee Harvey Oswald, a twenty-four-year-old misfit in an unhappy marriage, acting alone and somewhat spontaneously. This conclusion, reached on the day of Kennedy's death, has since been corroborated by twenty-first-century technology such as simulations of the paths of Oswald's bullets, and has never been contradicted by anything more than enthusiastic but erroneous inferences.

Yet there is a whole fandom of people, most of whom were not alive in 1963, who refuse to believe it. Fifty-four percent of Americans say Oswald did not act alone, and another 24 percent say they are not sure. Or, only one in five Americans believe that what actually happened happened.

Kennedy's assassination launched an era of conspiracy theories. At the time of writing, 56 percent of Americans believe a single elite group rules the world; 50 percent believe that Barack Obama was not born in the United States; 35 percent believe mass shootings are fake; and 33 percent believe COVID-19 vaccinations are a way to "microchip the US population," for example.

Conspiracy theories illuminate the clockwork of the human mind. To solve the problem of why good people believe bad information, we need a theory of conspiracy theories.

The first step is understanding that conspiracy theories have the wrong name. A real theory—and also a hypothesis, which is what "theory" often means in popular discourse—has to fit all available evidence; make measurable, falsifiable predictions; and be changed or discarded if its predictions are wrong. A "conspiracy theory" is the *opposite* of a theory: it makes selective use of information; predicts nothing; and is endlessly elastic, impervious to falsification, yielding wrong prediction after wrong prediction without raising doubts among its proponents.

Or, conspiracy theories are not theories but *stories*—examples of the natural and inevitable magical thinking of our story-shaped brains, and among the most clichéd and formulaic stories we tell. Conspiracy theories follow the format of stories faithfully and explicitly: they resolve uncertainty by attributing unexplained or misunderstood phenomena to powerful humanish actors; they link character to consequence chronologically; and they have a beginning (usually in the past), a middle (usually in the present), and an end (usually in an apocalyptic or dystopian future that the believer may be trying to prepare for, prevent, or warn others about).

Conspiracy stories are a distinct genre of fiction and, like all fiction, they are cultivated from seeds of truth. Their usual premise is that a powerful antagonist—often a government, corporation, underground organization, or wealthy individual—is engaging in harmful, criminal, antisocial activity for their own gain, while keeping their behavior secret from the general public. This is an accurate, realistic, and reasonable position. Conspiracies really do happen.

For example, the United States government has admitted to secret and often illegal activities including kidnapping a Ukrainian national and confining him in a "specially constructed 'jail'" for more than two years; opening and reading more than two hundred thousand letters sent by or to American citizens; hiring members of the Mafia to assassinate Fidel Castro; conducting human experiments using electric shocks, sensory deprivation, and psychoactive drugs without the subjects' consent; murdering more than one hundred Black American men while pretending to be curing them of syphilis; and implanting electrodes into the brains of dogs in an apparently successful attempt to control them remotely.

The fundamental truth of all conspiracy stories, then, is that (a) governments and other powerful entities sometimes engage in secret, illegal, and occasionally audacious activities—there is so much official and irrefutable evidence of this that to believe otherwise is to be willfully naive—and (b) it is therefore possible that governments and other entities are *still* engaged in secret, illegal, and possibly audacious activities. These statements are not fantasy or fiction—they are Newtonian physics, not Newtonian alchemy—and they raise an obvious question: What secret, illegal, and possibly audacious activities are happening right now?

People who believe and share conspiracy stories do not need to know about actual, well-documented conspiracies of the past to know that governments and others sometimes do secret, illegal, and audacious things; in fact, many of them have little to no awareness of or interest in real conspiracies like the ones mentioned above. For example, while the vast majority of Black Americans know about the syphilis experiment used to murder over one hundred Black men, only half of all white Americans and a quarter of all Hispanic Americans have heard of it. But everyone knows some of the fictional stories that these actual conspiracies inspired.

The 2010 video game *Call of Duty: Black Ops* includes scenes where the player controls a US undercover operative on a mission to assassinate Fidel Castro; the television series *Wormwood* tells the story of an unwitting participant in a human experimentation program that used psychoactive drugs, as does the movie *Jacob's Ladder*; Marvel Comics has twice told a story that parallels the secret syphilis experiments on Black men—once in its comic book *Truth: Red, White & Black*, and again in its television series *The Falcon and the Winter Soldier* and subsequent movie *Captain America: Brave New World*. Marvel also shows experiments on remote-controlled animals in its movie *Black Widow*. Robert Ludlum's 1980 novel *The Bourne Identity*, as well as its popular 2002 movie adaptation, stars an assassin working for a top-secret government agency. The 1991 movie *JFK* tells the story not of Kennedy's assassination, but of a conspiracy theory about it.

This quick step from little-known actual conspiracies to the widely known fictions they inspire is instructive. Retellings of real conspiracies are too dull and detailed to be good stories, but writers can easily adapt them into popular fictions by adding embellishments such as an obvious protagonist—the person who discovers and tries to expose the conspiracy—and an equally obvious antagonist—the powerful conspirator or conspirators trying to avoid being exposed. The plot flows automatically from these characters and their motivations: the protagonist discovers the conspiracy; the conspirators discover the protagonist and create obstacles to stop the conspiracy from being exposed; the protagonist overcomes these obstacles or occasionally does not; the end.

This is the basic form of conspiracy theories from Plato's 386 BCE *Apology of Socrates* to John Grisham's 1991 novel *The Firm* to Mikki

Willis's 2020 movie *Plandemic*. The stories evoke much the same feelings even though Plato is describing historical events, Grisham is telling a fictional story, and Willis is promoting a conspiracy theory. All three stories evoke anger about the conspirators, empathy for the protagonist trying to expose them, and a reduction of the stress of uncertainty because the plot explains potentially inexplicable events by attributing them to humanish agency.

Most people who come to believe conspiracy theories do so in a series of steps, and these emotional reactions make each step feel easy, rational, and short.

Abbie Richards, a researcher specializing in online misinformation, developed a model of this process. Everyone knows about conspiracies, either from having conversations, enjoying dramatizations, or reading history. This knowledge leads some people to step across what Richards calls the *speculation line*, and become interested in relatively harmless real phenomena without consensus explanations: things like UFOs, or what happened to "ghost ships" like the *Mary Celeste*, a brigantine found abandoned in the Atlantic Ocean at the end of the nineteenth century.

These mysteries appeal to all our storytelling instincts: they have a beginning and a middle, but their end is a puzzle, a whodunnit, an opportunity to imagine not mundane solutions, but to engage in audacious speculation, to create exciting, brightly colored climaxes, to imagine, dream, and fantasize.

This is the point where an interest in mysteries can become a belief in conspiracies. Richards's speculation line exists in all forms of storytelling: while some stories are realistic or naturalistic—their characters, situations, and events appear to follow the rules and laws of life, and seem to be plausible—others are speculative: they and their characters bend the rules. Speculative genres include *magical realism*, which gives occasional glimpses of impossible things in an otherwise naturalistic story; *science fiction*, which imagines a possibly naturalistic future;

fantasy, which reimagines the past and populates it with mythical creatures; and *horror*, which usually breaks the laws of nature, often those related to mortality and death. These stories help inform our models of reality, and it is an easy step to transfer their plots—and genres—to our understanding of the nonfictional world.

There are some obvious motivations for this behavior. It feels good to escape the mundane by imagining our fantasies are true. It feels good to believe you know and understand things that other people do not know and understand, especially in a world where expertise is both valued and difficult to achieve. And, most of all, it feels good to discover the antagonist, explain the unexplained, and solve the mystery, especially if ambiguity makes you uncomfortable.

Believing in fantastic explanations for UFOs and similar mysteries is harmless. But, if we stray too far beyond the line of speculation, we cross *another* line—one that Abbie Richards calls *leaving reality*. Here, things get dangerous. These conspiracy stories are like the ones about flying saucers and ghost ships, except they are not mysteries—they are fantasies or lies. Elvis Presley is alive; a dinosaur inhabits a Scottish lake; the US government faked the moon landing (18 percent of Americans believe this one). Like speculative mysteries, the ideas are harmless in themselves, but *unlike* speculative mysteries, believing them requires a suspension of critical thinking, a surrender to motivated reasoning, a departure from fact into fantasy. You have to *want* to believe these improbable and fantastic ideas.

Leaving reality leads people to believe things that influence how they act and vote: Climate change is a hoax; essential oils cure cancer; the government is changing the weather by leaving trails of chemicals in the sky. Richards's model classifies these types of conspiracy theories as *reality denial*. Believing them can be fatal: this is the type of conspiracy theory that killed Terrance Montaine.

They are not the worst conspiracy stories though. Richards has one more line on her model, beyond which lies the climax of the history of conspiracy theories: *the antisemitic point of no return*. The stories beyond this line make people hateful and violent. "Antisemitic" is an example in this case: it is really the *bigoted* point of no return, a crossing of the border between kindness and hate, a journey to the land of dehumanization. Beyond this line are conspiracies that claim Jewish people secretly run the world; that there is no such thing as systemic racism; that people in secret labs deliberately invented coronavirus; and—28 percent of Americans believe this one—that Hollywood actors, Jews, Satanists, and/or other "elites" sacrifice children in order to drink their blood.

There are three steps from reality to racism. All of them feel incremental, reasonable, and sensible: after believing one story, it is easy to believe the next.

And reinforcement learning machines accelerate the process: they can take people from realism to racism in under three days.

9. Carol

More people crossed the antisemitic point of no return after Facebook started using reinforcement learning than ever before. For example, the Anti-Defamation League found that white supremacist propaganda incidents grew by an average of 52 percent per year between 2017 and 2023. This is merely a correlation—there is no definitive proof that one thing caused the other.

But there is some evidence.

In 2017, a journalist named Ryan Broderick conducted an experiment. Broderick created a new Facebook profile and managed it following three rules. First, he "liked" the official page of the Republican National Committee, the political committee that leads the United States' right-wing Republican Party. Second, he "liked" any page that was suggested to him by Facebook's reinforcement learning machine. Third, he "shared" any article that was being shared by two or more pages he was following. Over the next few days, the stories Facebook showed him progressed in a way that was remarkably similar to Abbie Richards's conspiracy theory model. First, the stories left reality; in one instance, he saw two different stories claiming that Ruth Bader Ginsburg, a judge on the United States Supreme Court, had died, even though she hadn't. Next, the stories became surreptitiously hateful, with pictures of attractive women overlaid with provocative comments about immigration and race. By the third day, Broderick was being shown stories from conspiracy theorists and transphobic hate speech. And then, on the morning of the fourth day, Facebook started showing Broderick neo-Nazi stories. The headline of the first story was "LOL: Jew Dies of Cancer." Facebook's reinforcement learning machine took Broderick across the antisemitic point of no return in less than seventy-two hours.

Facebook's response to Broderick's experiment was dismissive and unconcerned. A Facebook spokesperson said:

> This isn't an experiment; it's a stunt. It isn't how people set up or use Facebook. People connect with their friends on Facebook, and stories from friends are the heart of News Feed. Deliberately removing all friend connections, the most important part of the experience, simply doesn't make sense.

Facebook may have believed this, but it wasn't true. In July 2019, a Facebook data scientist named Sophie Zhang replicated Broderick's experiment by creating a test account for a fictional woman named Carol Smith. Carol was forty-one, lived in Wilmington, North Carolina, listed her interests as Christianity, civics, community, news, parenting, politics, President Trump, and young children, and followed the official pages of Donald Trump, Melania Trump, and Fox News. Within days, Facebook's reinforcement learning machine was showing "Carol" conspiracy theories including "QAnon," which claims, among other things, that Hollywood actors and prominent politicians, including 2016 presidential candidate Hillary Clinton, sacrifice children to drink their blood. Zhang called her internal report *Carol's Journey to QAnon*. It concluded that Carol's page quickly "became a constant flow of misleading, polarizing and low-quality content." When Facebook took little action in response, Zhang resigned, saying, "I have blood on my hands."

Thirteen months after Zhang's report was published, Facebook claimed it had removed all QAnon posts, and said Zhang's study was "a perfect example of research the company does to improve our systems."

But that was not really true.

First, after Facebook eventually and reluctantly banned most explicit mentions of "QAnon," QAnon conspiracy theorists simply started using the phrase "#savethechildren" instead. Searching Facebook for that phrase yields a stream of both QAnon and anti-vaccination posts, accusing, among other things, various actors and musicians, many of them Black, of being pedophiles. Most of these posts are widely shared.

Second, in November 2021, another journalist, Kaitlyn Tiffany of *The Atlantic*, repeated Broderick's and Zhang's experiments, except she did not give her account explicit political bias. She "liked" the pages of fast food brand Domino's Pizza, TV show *Grey's Anatomy*, rock band The Rolling Stones, the retailer Target, wine, and the celebrity Oprah Winfrey, which she called "the tastes of a thoroughly nonpartisan, general-interest American." After that, she started "liking" only the pages Facebook's reinforcement learning machine recommended to her. Within days, Tiffany's account left reality and started showing her posts about "manifesting" money, $45 self-help courses like *What Men Secretly Want*—"your unfair advantage that rivets a man's attention and makes you irresistibly attractive to him"—and the WhatsApp number for someone called "Dr. Moses," who bills themselves as "a Powerful spell caster who uses the powers from my ancestors to cast spells" such as a "Mend My Broken Heart Spell," and a "Job Promotion Spell." With no clues to Tiffany's political inclinations, Facebook could not take her across the "antisemitic point of no return," but it did transport her as far as the realm of reality denial. She concluded:

> Facebook isn't just dangerous. It doesn't merely have the ability to shape online reality for its billions of users. No, Facebook is also—and perhaps for most people—senseless and demoralizing. If you don't take any of your politics to Facebook, you may not get sucked into political extremism. But there are other ways to spiral down to the lowest common denominator, and then lower and lower, and there's no relief, and there's no bottom.

You might be tempted to repeat this experiment, but I do not recommend it: the results quickly become disturbing. In the words of King Lear, "That way madness lies." And the same thing is more or less true of other out-of-control websites that are the friendly faces of reinforcement learning machines—YouTube and Instagram, for example. And they are not shaping the *online* reality of billions, but reality itself. People who become convinced by conspiracy theories are not idiots; they are our friends, neighbors, and sometimes our parents. Their story-shaped brains are being manipulated by a combination of badly designed software and well-designed propaganda to take one apparently rational step after another into a kaleidoscope world of fear and loathing. The machines behind their screens are an information quicksand that sucks them into magical thinking, then conspiracy theories, then extremism, then hatred and violence.

This may seem like a hopeless situation, but it is not.

10. The Light in the Storm

There is a twist in this tale.

While we have been discussing the negative consequences of digital social storytelling, something more important has been waiting to be said.

The internet is not the root cause of the new bigotry of the twenty-first century. Digital social systems are catalysts, enablers, and sometimes unwitting and sometimes welcoming hosts that speed the evolution of hatred, but they do not initiate, inspire, or instigate it all by themselves. The owners and supervisors of these compromised machines are still liable for the unimaginable damage and chaos their platforms have wrought. But their contribution is ignorance, irresponsibility, indifference, and negligence: acts of omission and permission, not commission. Mark Zuckerberg does not produce antisemitic content, he merely publishes it.

In chapter 4, I described the pattern of progress as "two steps forward and one step back." Our new age of hatred is one of those steps back; it is, exactly as the French revolutionaries of the eighteenth century described, a *reaction*, a backlash, a squeal of dismay, a counterrevolution encouraged and exploited by powerful people whose self-serving standard story is finally and thankfully being rewritten. If you listen carefully, you can hear the screech of their fingernails scraping the floor and failing to find purchase as they are dragged to a door that will definitely hit their asses on the way out.

The revolution that provoked this response is a multicolored uprising of all the people standard stories typically oppress: Black people and people of color; people who are differently abled; feminists; geeks; Hindus; Indigenous peoples; Jewish people; Latin Americans; people who are lesbian, gay, bisexual, transgender, queer, agender, intersex, aromantic, asexual, polyamorous, ethically nonmonogamous, or kinky; Muslims; nerds; the neurodivergent; people who are pregnant or breastfeeding; sex workers; the unconventional; the young and the old; vegans and vegetarians; and anyone else who is not of European descent, straight, vanilla, white, and comfortable in and privileged by systems of patriarchy. The standard story calls all these disparate peoples "minorities," but they add up to nearly everyone.

I could not have written this list a few years ago. Some of these words did not exist; I did not know many of the ones that did; and had I known them, few readers would have understood them. This list, and the fact that I can write it and be confident that you will understand most, if not all, of its words, is its own testament to how much has changed.

No kind of people is new. The only thing new is that those deemed different no longer have to hide; pretend; struggle to find resources about who they are and how to be who they are; or remain isolated from others who are like them or segregated from those who are not. The proliferation of stories and storytellers enabled by the internet has revealed the heterogeneous beauty and glory of all humanity by giving rise to countercommunities, countercultures, and counterstories galore. This is the revolution, long unstoppable, that the tellers of standard stories are trying and failing to prevent.

One example of this, insufficiently discussed, is how 2SLGBTQIA+ people, many native to the internet and some even native to the smartphone, have empowered themselves using digital social storytelling to achieve unprecedented liberty, victories, and visibility.

This empowerment dates back at least as far as the early 1990s, when the United States government gradually opened the internet for public use. Here's an early example, from a gay sixteen-year-old with the username *JohnTeen Ø* posting on America Online's Gay and Lesbian Community Forum in 1994:

> From: JohnTeen Ø. My high school career has been a sudden and drastic spell of turbulence and change. Once I was an automaton, obeying external, societal, and parental expectations like a dog, oblivious of who I was or what I wanted. I conformed to society's paradigm, and I was rewarded. Yet I was miserable. Everything I did was a diversion from thinking about myself. Finally, last summer, my subconsciousness felt comfortable enough to be able to connect myself with who I really am, and I began to understand what it is to be gay.

The Gay and Lesbian Community Forum was a source of hope and guidance for gay and lesbian teenagers all over America—a nightfire around which tens of thousands of adolescents gathered to tell their counterstories and support each other as they became more like themselves.

The tellers of the standard story fought back, of course, deploying their usual pretense of "protecting the children" to pass a censorship law called the Communications Decency Act, or "CDA," in February 1996, that imposed criminal sanctions on anyone who:

> uses an interactive computer service to send to a specific person or persons under 18 years of age, any comment, request, suggestion, proposal, image, or other communication that, in context, depicts or describes, in terms patently offensive as measured by contemporary community standards, sexual or excretory activities or organs.

("Excretory organs" is not a reference to members of congress, but members of congress's way of saying "buttholes.") This was the first test of an online countercommunity, and Bill Clinton—the president at the time—and Congress got a most unpleasant surprise. The gay teenage users of the internet took the United States government all the way to the Supreme Court and won.

Justice John Paul Stevens delivered the unanimous opinion of the court that:

> the CDA's provisions abridge "the freedom of speech" protected by the First Amendment. For instance, its use of the undefined terms "indecent" and "patently offensive" will provoke uncertainty. The vagueness of such a regulation raises special First Amendment concerns because of its obvious chilling effect on free speech. This vagueness also undermines the likelihood

that it has been carefully tailored to the congressional goal of protecting minors from potentially harmful materials.

Or, the Supreme Court justices were not fooled by the excretory organs, not even for a moment.

This was the first test, but it was not the last. The tests never end. There is no such thing as living happily ever after, no matter what our story-shaped brains want us to believe. There is no complete victory, no forever banishment, no lasting peace. We cannot destroy the standard story; we can only improve it.

Tellers of counterstories always ask for more, look beyond, and seek an ever better world, and so they should: progress has no finish line. But that does not mean we cannot acknowledge how much has changed, how it changed, who changed it, and the bright rays of hope it shines on our futures.

Steve Silberman, a writer who was among the first to recognize the power of the internet to help marginalized communities, said it best:

> The struggle for equal rights has always taken place on the frontier of the legal wilderness where liberty meets power. Liberty has claimed much of that wilderness now, but the frontier always lies ahead of us. The frontier of liberty may have expanded far beyond where it began, but for those without rights, it always seems on the horizon, just beyond their reach.

The mind warriors want you to believe you cannot win. There is no better defense than knowing how many times you have already won.

Chapter 8

The Hyperreal Thing

1. And Beyond

Africa's westernmost coast dips into the Atlantic like a hand testing the water. The hand is called Cape Verde, and its palm is Dakar, the capital of Senegal. To the south of the cape is a cold-water bay rich in sardines. Anta Diouf fishes there almost every day. She sells the larger fish fresh whole, and salts, ferments, and dries the smaller ones to make a delicacy the Senegalese call *guedj* or sometimes *tambadiang*. Until recently, the fishers' technology had barely changed for thousands of years. If an artisanal fisher from 6000 BCE had returned to Cape Verde at the start of the twenty-first century, everything would have seemed familiar. The nets and lines, once made of flax, grass, and bark, were the same but nylon; the canoes, once carved from the trunks of trees, were the same but more likely to be made from planks; and outboard motors had replaced oars and sails. But, in 2015, traditional Senegalese fishing tools changed in a way that would have been incomprehensible to a visitor from prehistory, or even from just a few years earlier: Anta, like many other artisanal fishers in Senegal, started using a smartphone to help her catch fish.

As we have seen, in nations with advanced economies like the United

States, Germany, Japan, and Korea, storytelling technology improved incrementally and hypnotically over many generations. Increasing literacy led to daily newspapers and paperback books; broadcast radio led to broadcast television; telephones led to cell phones; photography led to cinema; personal computers led to digital cameras, portable computers, and the internet; and those things led to smartphones, which seemed like another step in a stroll, the latest digital frippery, the newest new thing.

But nations with advanced economies are home to less than 15 percent of our population. For the rest of the world, which is almost all of the world, smartphones were a hundred years of storytelling revolution come all at once.

Anta's smartphone was her first phone. The scarcity of landline telephones in Senegal was not only because of cost or infrastructure. Landline telephones are single-purpose devices; they are only for talking to other people with telephones. Telephones are not valuable until many people have them because there are not enough people to talk to.

We can assess a network's value using the equation $V \approx N^2$, where V is "value," $\approx$ is "approximately equal to," and N is the number of nodes, meaning things connected to the network. This equation is Metcalfe's Law, named for Robert Metcalfe, the networking pioneer who originated it.

Metcalfe's Law predicts that a telephone has little initial value in places with few telephones, which, at the start of the twenty-first century, was most places. When cell phones were only for talking to other people with phones, most people did not buy them.

Smartphones changed this equation and brought the story of stories to its climax.

The initial value of Anta's phone did not depend on how many other people had a phone because she did not buy her phone to connect to other people. Anta bought her phone to connect to other *devices*. Lots of them.

Anta's smartphone shows her the height of the waves in the bay and the speed and direction of the wind; guides her between fishing zones and landing docks; transmits her location when she has an emergency at sea; shows her the current fish market prices so she can negotiate the best price for her catch; and finds and applies for the lowest-cost microloans to help her grow her business. Anta is using her smartphone to make more money than ever before. She says now she "can afford to pay for my child's healthcare and other things my family needs."

One of Anta's most important applications is checking the weather to decide where to fish. If you have convenient access to a smartphone, open its preinstalled weather app—it is simply called "Weather" on most phones—and check the weather in Dakar. You will find your phone knows Dakar's current temperature, the speed and direction of its winds, its humidity, and its air pressure, among other things. Now ask yourself: How does your phone know so much about the weather in the capital of Senegal?

The answer is not that there is a smartphone user in Dakar looking at meteorological instruments and typing in readings. There is no Wizard of Oz behind your weather app. An unimaginable tangle of intermediary cables, corporations, databases, government agencies, interfaces, protocols, radios, routers, satellites, servers, and standards connects your phone to the Automated Weather Observing System at Dakar's Léopold Sédar Senghor International Airport, which comprises an ultrasonic anemometer that detects wind speed; a thermometer made from platinum wire that determines temperature using electrical resistance; and a light-emitting diode that can differentiate between rain and snow by watching how the drops twinkle in its infrared light. These sensors broadcast their readings using radio waves every hour, or more frequently if Dakar's weather is changing rapidly.

Sensors, not people, are what gave Anta's phone its initial value: she did not buy it to make calls, but to access the global sensor network called the Internet of Things, and that had a profound impact on the story of stories. The value of a network now grows not as the square of the number of its users or even its devices but as the square of the number of its *data sources*.

Those data sources can be people or things. Or, with smartphones, both. The smartphone is an extraordinary type of network node, and one that, to the best of my knowledge, no one in the twentieth century ever foresaw—a node with three concurrent roles in its network.

First and most obvious, a smartphone is a *human-computer interface*, meaning it can receive input from humans—both data like "How's your day going?" and commands like "Send this message to my friend"—and present human readable output—for example by displaying information or making sounds. In this role, a smartphone resembles a personal computer, and acts as what network architects call a *client*, *communications endpoint*, or *terminal*.

Second and less obvious, a smartphone is a *unique identifier* for an individual human being. Our ancestral naming system of family name plus given name does not scale to a world of 8.5 billion people, but personal phone numbers with international dialing codes do. Your phone number is unique; your name is probably not.

Third, and least obvious, a smartphone is a *sensor array*. In 2021, a typical smartphone contained sensors for acceleration, altitude, angular velocity, heat, location, sound, touch, light, magnetic fields, movement, orientation, and proximity, and some phones could also sense ambient temperature, depth of field, distance, faces, fingerprints, heartbeats, human movement, humidity, and, in at least one case, dangerous levels of ionizing radiation.

Interface, identity, and sensing are a mighty trinity.

Twelve or more sensors in seven billion or more phones means over eighty-four billion mobile, networked sensors all with precise known locations, plus seven billion people with unique individual identities, all connected: a global digital nervous system for all of humanity, a network with a value of ninety-one billion squared—or, eight sextillion, two hundred eighty-one quintillion—*before* we count any other sensors in the network, like cars, doorbells, lightbulbs, security cameras, outlets, thermostats, traffic lights, or weather stations at airports.

Senegal is typical, not an outlier, and so is Anta. At the turn of the century, less than one in forty Senegalese people had any kind of phone; twenty years later, one in three Senegalese adults had smartphones; and in 2025, that number increased to *two* in three. The story of Anta and the other artisanal fishers of Senegal is not the exception but the rule; something similar is happening, or has already happened, to almost every person in almost every nation. In 2026, the year this book was first published, seven and a half billion people had smartphones.

The first act of the story of stories, a million years long, is now coming to its end because of the rapid global adoption of smartphones at the start of the twenty-first century. During a journey that started beside a nightfire and traveled through singing, drawing, writing, printing, electricity, electrons, and bits, we have gone from a world where a few people could tell stories to a few people, to a world where everyone can tell stories to everyone.

What comes next—the second act of the story of stories—is different, disruptive, and in some ways dangerous.

2. Breaking the Vision Barrier

Together, Metcalfe's Law, Moore's Law, and Wang's Law are a powerful combination. And there are other exponential changes at work too. The storage capacity of the lithium-ion batteries delivering electricity to smartphones and other wireless devices doubles every six years; the amount of data we can transmit to and from screens using radio waves doubles every two years; and the amount of electricity needed to power the processors behind a screen halves every eighteen months, a pattern called Koomey's Law. The future of flat screens and wireless networks is surprisingly predictable, at least at the level of technology.

There is no way to know exactly how those flat screens will be used, but one thing is obvious: the stories we can tell on our screens are going to continue to seem ever more real and ever more plausible, and the ability to make stories seem real will soon belong to everyone. This ever-increasing realism is the second act of the story of stories.

Here is one simple, arresting example of the increasing realism that arises naturally from Wang's Law alone: apparently three-dimensional moving images without special glasses or goggles.

This is possible for two reasons.

First, an obvious consequence of Wang's Law is that the number of pixels, the *resolution* or, basically, the clarity of an image on a screen can double every three years. There are some complications that slow this down—we also need content, and therefore cameras, storage and transmissions technologies, and industry standards to match the resolution of the screens—but, even with that friction, the number of pixels in a television picture has, on average, been doubling with every new format that has been introduced since television began. Cathode-ray tube televisions were analog, not digital, and their formats various and complicated, but we can roughly estimate the progression of their resolutions in pixel equivalents: the first broadcast TVs, launched in the 1930s, had about 160,000 pixels, give or take, and this number increased by a little more than double, to 370,000-ish pixels in the 1960s. In the early 2000s, the first "standard-definition" digital screens increased this number by a factor of 1.6, to a little more than 600,000 pixels, then a few years later it more than tripled to over 2 million pixels when "high-definition" digital televisions arrived. (*High definition* is a relative term: those first analog televisions, which had less than 3 percent of the resolution of twenty-first-century high-definition digital televisions, were also called "high definition.")

By the late 2010s, many televisions were using a format called "4K ultra high definition," which had four times as many pixels as the "high-definition" televisions. At the time of writing the highest-resolution televisions that are generally available are "8K ultra high definition," which have more than 33 million pixels, or four times as many pixels as 4K ultra-high-definition televisions. But, if you go on a tour of BOE's headquarters in Beijing, the guides will happily show you the next two generations of screen technology: 10K, which has 1.3 times as many pixels as 8K, and 16K, which has nearly 133 million pixels, triple the resolution of the 10K television.

The power of the exponential growth in Wang's Law is so great that the average doubling of resolution with every new screen format means a 16K television has two hundred times more resolution than the standard-definition digital televisions of the early 2000s and a thousand times more resolution than the first commercial televisions of the 1940s. And, somewhere between 10K and 16K, something strange happens: the images start to look three dimensional.

This may seem counterintuitive to anyone raised on the idea that viewing three-dimensional images needs special glasses or goggles. Most of us have been told that seeing in three dimensions needs *binocular vision* or *both* eyes, and that this is why those disposable 3D glasses you get in movie theaters often have one red lens and one blue lens.

But we can see in three dimensions with one eye. This is easy to test: Close one eye, and see if you can perceive depth. Using both eyes may be better, but closing one eye does not suddenly flatten what you see into two dimensions. Seeing things in three dimensions, with volume and space, is called *stereopsis*, from the Greek words *stereós*, meaning "solid," and *ópsis* meaning "aspect." As with everything in perception, stereopsis is not some external, objective feature of reality, but an effect produced by our brains: a part of the graphic user interface that helps us understand the world.

For at least 150 years, scientists have been asking the obvious question: *How* does the brain produce stereopsis? Or, more specifically, what sensory inputs does the brain need to create an impression of volume and space?

The answer, in short, is one eye, not two. In fact, in some circumstances, one eye produces better stereopsis. The old idea that you need two eyes to see images in three dimensions is a myth. What matters is not how many eyes you have, but how many pixels. This is why images on 16K screens look three dimensional.

Where does increasing screen resolution stop being useful? The short answer is that we don't know for sure, but Wang's Law is about to break through an important threshold. Just as, in the 1940s, aircraft technology approached and then broke the sound barrier, so flat-screen technology is rapidly approaching a sound barrier of its own: the point when the resolution of a screen exceeds the resolution of a human eye. Eyes are not digital and don't have pixels, of course, but a good estimate is that the human eye has a resolution equivalent to about 576 million pixels. At 16K, screen technology is one or two steps away from reaching the vision barrier. A resolution of 32K, or 530,841,600 pixels, is the Mach 1—or perhaps we should call it the *Wang 1*—of seeing. Wang's Law predicts that screens achieving this resolution will be practical, if not affordable, by around 2030, but that does not include the extra years it will take for cameras and other systems to catch up. We have no idea what lies on the other side of the vision barrier, but one thing is certain: we will have moved past things that feel and look realistic. What we experience on our screens will soon be completely indistinguishable from what we experience in the world.

3. The Death of the Camera

It is not enough to only have a screen with the same resolution as the human eye; there must also be a way to make moving images with that resolution too. One way to do that is with cameras, of course—it is already possible to make 16K movies, and we can assume that 32K cameras will arrive one day—but cameras are not the only way to create images at that resolution, and they may not be the first, or even the main way that eye-resolution images get made. Breaking the sound barrier required us to reinvent propellor planes as jets. Breaking the vision barrier may require us to reinvent the way we make moving images.

We have been reinventing the way we make moving images since *Westworld* in 1973, when John Whitney Jr. used a computer to show us the world as seen by an android cowboy. Those early computer graphics involved processing images captured by cameras—the digital equivalent of putting a filter on a lens. The next step in computer graphics was drawing multiple images and making them move using computers—the digital equivalent of making a flip book, kineograph, or animated cartoon. In both these cases, computer graphics were a way to do things that could also be done with older technology.

As the saltation of use made computers more powerful, it became possible to do something new: to *generate* images using computers by calculating how things should look.

One of the first applications of this approach was images that looked three dimensional. First, the surface of an object was represented mathematically using a series of coordinates representing the location of its vertices, or corners. This is fairly easy to imagine if the shape is a cube: a cube has eight corners—four at the top, and four at the bottom—and once the computer knows each corner's location relative to the others, it can calculate where all the edges and surfaces must be. Making a more complex shape, such as a sphere, is simply a matter of adding coordinates for many more corners by creating the illusion of the sphere from a huge number of tiny triangles, as if it was covered in a net. The computer is actually modeling a many-faced polyhedron, but if there are enough tiny triangles, it does not matter: at a high enough resolution, the eye is fooled into seeing a sphere.

More triangles means more coordinates, which means more computing power. And so, as computing power increased in accordance with Moore's Law, the three-dimensional shapes computers could create became ever more detailed and realistic.

We can see this effect in the evolution of characters in computer games.

The first computer game "characters" of the 1970s were made from a few dozen obviously square pixels—like Space Invaders or Pac-Man—and the player had to do some imagining to pretend they were anything more. By the 1990s, computers had so much processing power that computer game systems could generate apparently three-dimensional images made from triangles in real time while the game was being played. One such game was *Tomb Raider*, released for the Sony PlayStation game console in 1996. *Tomb Raider* starred a playable protagonist named Lara Croft, and the surface of her character model was made of about 575 triangles. Lara looked blocky, almost as if she was made of Legos, but was clearly three-dimensional. Twenty-one years later, in 2017, another game starring a playable female protagonist was released for the Sony PlayStation 4: *Horizon Zero Dawn*, whose lead character was named Aloy. In those twenty-one years, processing power had increased so much that Aloy's hair alone, which was fully dynamic and long, rugged, and intricately braided and plaited, was made of 100,000 triangles —175 times more than the whole character model of the original Lara Croft.

Computers can also be used to calculate how light reacts to those surfaces. In nature, streams of photons, commonly called *rays* or *beams of light*, travel in more or less straight lines until they interact with a surface, where they may either fluoresce (be absorbed then emitted later), reflect (bounce back), refract (change direction), and/or be absorbed. In every case except total absorption, a ray's journey will continue, and some or all of the photons will interact with other surfaces. The ideal way to create a natural-looking image is to compute the path and behavior of every photon entering a scene from its source—for example, a candle, roaring fire, lightbulb, or the sun—until it either leaves the field of view or is fully absorbed. The computing power required to do this in a complex scene with many different surfaces and light sources, especially in real time, or "live," is enormous and impractical, but, since at least the 1980s, engineers and scientists working on computer graphics have developed ingenious work-arounds and shortcuts to get as close to this ideal as possible. At the same time, computers, many of which now include an additional microprocessor dedicated to producing images, have met them halfway by becoming ever more powerful, making it possible to create natural-looking images by tracing the paths of at least some rays of light.

Apparently three-dimensional shapes made of millions of triangles apparently illuminated by ray-tracing software look real enough to create photorealistic cars, buildings, and other human-made objects. Many of the cars in modern movies, especially the ones involved in stunts, are now completely computer generated, and nobody realizes.

But not everything in the world is as hard-edged, deterministic, shiny, and well defined as a car. Natural phenomena like clouds, fire, smoke, and water do not have surfaces that can be represented using shapes made of triangles, and move within and react to their environment in complex ways, so computers create them using *particle systems*—an imaginary emission of imaginary particles that are born, move, and die according to *stochastic*—i.e., probabilistic and somewhat random—rules. Advanced light-ray tracing systems can also calculate how light will behave when interacting with these particles, and how, in the case of flames, for example, these particles will emit light.

Triangles, ray tracing, and particle systems enabled computers to create photorealistic images of everything except one thing: living creatures, especially humans. Computer-generating convincing people, and particularly faces, was a problem that took decades to solve: faces have complex musculature, they reflect light in challenging ways, and we are incredibly sensitive to the details of a human face, and can have alarmed and negative reactions to things that look almost, but not quite like faces—a response roboticist Masahiro Mori called "the uncanny valley phenomenon."

The root of the uncanny valley phenomenon is simple and primal: when we cannot determine the emotion and therefore intention of another person, our survival instincts go into hyperdrive, and we become deeply suspicious, uncomfortable, and vigilant. This is also why bank robbers in balaclavas; clowns; masks; oil painting portraits—*the eyes follow you around the room!*—ventriloquists' dummies; and other things with almost-faces can make us feel weird.

The solution to the problem of creating convincing faces needed every computer-generated imagery technique we have already discussed—triangles, ray tracing, particle systems—and more: things like morphing—calculating how to blend an image from one position to the next; photogrammetry; making three-dimensional models using photographs; capturing real human motion; and tracking actual human faces. The first big success was MetaHuman Creator, released in 2021, which built lifelike human faces using hair generated one strand at a time, 669 mobile facial areas for creating expressions, 713 facial joints, and 24,000 vertices. Studies have found that people have no adverse reactions to faces made using MetaHuman Creator. In some cases, such artificial humans are completely indistinguishable from real people, but in others they are still creatures from Mori's uncanny valley. As I was finishing writing this chapter, a new company called Staircase Studios AI announced *The Woman with Red Hair*, its first "near studio-quality movie," made using its own system called ForwardMotion. The movie's characters are unintentionally terrifying, especially in close-up, with skin that morphs strangely as they speak, odd micromovements in their faces, and overly bright yet somehow expressionless eyes. Maybe things will be better by the time you read this.

MetaHuman Creator is part of a computer-generated imagery tool called Unreal Engine 5, which, in addition to creating infinitely variable lifelike humans, enables three-dimensional animation featuring billions of triangles, complex ray tracing, particle systems, and other features such as intelligent swarming and flocking behavior for things like insects, bats, and birds. Unreal Engine was originally created for video games. Its developer is Epic Games, a company first known for its online battle game *Fortnite*, but is now so realistic that it is also being used to create movies, where it comes close to rivaling the hundreds of millions of dollars' worth of computer-generated imagery used in old films like *Avengers: Endgame*. For example, soon after it was released, visual effects studio Industrial Light & Magic used Unreal Engine 5 to create realistic computer-generated sets and locations for movies including *The Batman*, *Thor: Love and Thunder*, and *Ant-Man and the Wasp: Quantumania*, and television shows *The Mandalorian*, *The Book of Boba Fett*, and *Obi-Wan Kenobi*.

But, despite this professional, movie-quality level of realism, Unreal Engine is free to use, available to everyone, and easy to learn, and there are other tools just like it. Anyone, anywhere can create photorealistic, three-dimensional movies, plays, or TV shows on a computer in their bedroom or garage.

This is the future of three-dimensional, ultra-high-definition, indistinguishable-from-reality moving images, and it has already begun: in 2020, director and playwright Celine Song performed Chekhov's *The Seagull* using the video game *Sims 4*, and actors Sam Crane and Mark Oosterveen performed Shakespeare's *Hamlet* using the video game *Grand Theft Auto V*. This is the shape of things to come: soon, computers, not cameras, will generate most of what we see on our screens.

4. L. Bob

In 1992, a speculative fiction writer named Neal Stephenson published a novel called *Snow Crash*. The novel, which combines digital culture with Sumerian mythology, tells the story of Hiro Protagonist, a hacker who goes on a mission to neutralize a mind-controlling computer virus called Snow Crash. Much of the story is set not in the natural world, but somewhere else:

> Hiro Protagonist is sitting cross-legged at a low table. He is wearing shiny goggles that wrap halfway around his head with little

earphones that are plugged into his ears. His computer is a featureless black wedge. It can keep track of where Hiro is and what direction he's looking in. Down inside the computer are three lasers. A narrow beam of any color can be shot out of the innards of the computer in any direction. The resulting image hangs in space in front of Hiro. By drawing a slightly different image in front of each eye, the image can be made three-dimensional. By changing the image seventy-two times a second, it can be made to move, as sharp as the eye can perceive. So Hiro's not actually here. He's in a computer-generated universe that his computer is drawing onto his goggles. This imaginary place is known as the Metaverse.

Thirty years after *Snow Crash* was published, the idea of building—and of course *owning*—a metaverse suddenly became popular among some high-technology entrepreneurs and investors, including Mark Zuckerberg, who even changed the name of his corporation from Facebook to Meta, among other things, in preparation for a future he both envisioned and envisioned himself dominating. According to Mark and other entrepreneurs, metaverses were the Next Big Thing, the future of computing, the internet, and humanity itself.

What did they mean by "metaverse"?

That was left perhaps deliberately vague, but the general idea was the one envisioned by Neal Stephenson: a computer-generated, fully immersive, three-dimensional world where people wearing virtual-reality goggles "go" to hang out with their friends, shop, exchange information, get entertained, and so on: Facebook manifesting as an imaginary, realistic, three-dimensional planet you can visit whenever you want.

Why you might want to visit such a planet is far from clear. The planet Facebook would, presumably, be populated with realistic, three-dimensional neo-Nazis; vaccine deniers; puppies that are friends with ducklings; fake people trying to sell you paleo vitamins; and Dr. Moses the spell caster casting Mend My Broken Heart spells. Picture walking out of a touristy airport and being mobbed by cabdrivers; pickpockets; street preachers; soapbox hate-mongers; tchotchke peddlers; and tour guides, only all the time and without a beach resort waiting for you beyond the gauntlet.

That was certainly the case with Facebook's prototype metaverse; once called *Facebook Horizons*, then renamed *Horizon Worlds*. At the time of writing—and quite possibly *not* at the time of reading—Horizon Worlds is an online experience accessed through Facebook's virtual reality headset, the Oculus Quest 2. Users arrive in a virtual entry lobby known as the "plaza," where they can meet up to twenty other users—represented by cartoonlike avatars that at first existed only from the waist up and had no legs—and go through portals to visit "worlds" created by other users. The worlds include comedy shows, competitions, escape rooms, games, and puzzles, and all the problems Facebook has not yet solved on its decades-old website, such as harassment, hate speech, MindWar, and misogyny. Before *Horizon Worlds* even officially launched, one beta tester reported that:

> Not only was I groped last night, but there were other people there who supported this behavior which made me feel isolated. Sexual harassment is no joke on the regular internet, but being in virtual reality adds another layer that makes the event more intense.

The Facebook executive in charge of *Horizon Worlds* shrugged off the incident and claimed it was the woman's own fault, not Facebook's or her assaulter's, because she "didn't utilize the safety features built into *Horizon Worlds*, including the ability to block someone from interacting with you." The victim-blaming showed Facebook had at least managed to make one part of its metaverse exactly like the real world.

This nightmarish place is the consequence of a common error. Never mistake the future for a new form of your past. Zuckerberg's metaverse is just Facebook once again asking us to create its content so it can sell our attention to advertisers, only now its abusive, deadly hellscape comes in three dimensions.

The only remotely surprising thing about Zuckerberg's sad, incremental "vision" is its name. *Snow Crash*'s metaverse is dystopian, satirical, and wholly owned by the story's villain, L. Bob Rife, a cultish media monopolist with a penchant for secretly gathering personal information about people. At the end of *Snow Crash*, Rife is blown to pieces in an explosion while trying to escape Hiro Protagonist's justice. No one should want to emulate L. Bob or his metaverse.

5. Chen

If the metaverse is not the future, what is?

One good place to look is back in Beijing, at BOE. D. S. Wang retired as the company's chairman in 2019 and handed the company he built to Y. S. Chen, who Wang had been preparing for the role for several years. In Chen's first three years as chairman, BOE's revenue grew by an average of 33 percent a year, and its share of the laptop, monitor, smartphone, tablet, and television screen market grew from 20 percent in 2018 to 26 percent in 2021.

But Chen no longer thought of BOE as a flat-screen manufacturer.

This was a wise, and frankly, unusual decision. Wang's Law has a catch of sorts: screens will get ever cheaper, and their performance will quickly reach a point where further improvement will not deliver much more value. It will take a few more decades, but once everyone can get a screen with a higher resolution than their eyes that is as big as their biggest wall for under $100, they may not need to buy another screen anytime soon. Plus, BOE will one day achieve a share of the display market so big that it will not be able to get much bigger. At that point, its flat-screen business will keep generating cash, but less and less growth. And BOE is a publicly traded company: growth is what Chen's investors expect him to deliver.

And so, just as Wang did when he took over the failing factory in 1992, and, just as Mark Zuckerberg is doing now, Chen must decide on a whole new product line to maintain BOE's long-term success. And, where Zuckerberg and others are looking to the metaverse, Chen, like Wang before him, is thinking differently.

Chen is placing his bet on the Internet of Things, the great global network of sensors that gives computers the electronic equivalent of a nervous system and the ability to know what is happening in the world.

One of the first active applications for BOE's new Internet of Things technology is healthcare. BOE has heavily invested in several Chinese hospitals to create what the company calls "wisdom health management" for "internet and digital hospitals," where its technology monitors and aims to improve the health of both inpatients and, through in-home screens and other tools, outpatients too—an especially important problem in China, where the proportion of elderly people is growing faster than almost any other country, and 39 percent of the population will be sixty or older by 2050.

It is a long-term plan: Chen does not expect or demand results next quarter, or even next year; he says what he calls BOE's "Internet of Things ecosystem" will take "five years or longer" to develop. When he talks about it, he somehow manages to be modest and humble while also being bold and ambitious. Neither his company's newfound technology leadership nor China's has given him any kind of hubris. He says:

> The frontier of technology is in America. The United States is still leading the world's technological development. In the future, the technological gap between China and the United States might be reduced, but in most fields, there is still a decades-wide gap between China and America. Most Chinese companies are still at the stage of imitative innovation, for example. To achieve global leadership, a company has to move from imitative innovation to disruptive innovation. Yes, BOE

has achieved market leadership. But we still have a long way to go before we achieve full leadership.

Chen's dreams of vast sensor networks intimately entwined with true artificial intelligence are not in conflict with BOE's flat screens, but complementary to them: Chen and BOE imagine a future where their screens, all displaying images with clarity approaching or exceeding the resolution of the human eye, wrapped in augmented reality glasses, cars, phones, walls, and who knows what else, are the faces and fingertips of a vast web of global sentience, delivering utility, doing good, and providing what Chen calls "cooperation nutrients and wisdom fusion to benefit society."

Chen's vision is nothing like the metaverse, and contains none of the buzzwords that other technology experts, executives, and leaders are using. It sounds bold, different, and odd—which is probably how Wang sounded exactly thirty years earlier, when, contradicting everyone else, he predicted a world of "semiconductor screens."

6. Artificial Sentience

Computer-generated images have long been part of the Internet of Things. Many of the special effects we see in movies are informed by sensors placed on actors and sets to capture lighting, location, motion, and performance, making the resulting imagery more simulation than animation.

This integration of the Internet of Things and visual simulation is still in its infancy, and we have a lot to learn, but we do understand some of the fundamentals. We understand, for example, that sensors work best in arrays—groups of sensors that include different types of sensors, duplicate sensors, or both; that sensors work best in networks; that sensor data must be corrected, compressed, and corroborated before being interpreted; and that complex data is most useful when presented to humans according to the rules of story—that is, with a character, a chronology, and a consequence. Co-opting the existing graphic user interface of the brain—the view of the world we call "reality"—to show data using simulations that stimulate multiple human senses, such as sight, sound, and touch to make it seem like you are present at the data event, with enhancements such as dynamic points of view; false color; scales from nanoscopic to telescopic; slow motion; time lapse; transparent elements; or tactility seems like a natural next step.

One reason we know about these fundamentals is because this is the architecture of our own nervous system. Human senses form an array that includes five major types of sensor—for vision, hearing, touch, taste, and smell—and it features massive duplication. We each have around 240 million photoreceptor cells in our eyes, 8 million hairs for hearing in our ears, 4 million touch receptors on our skin, 50 million taste cells in our mouth, and 20 million olfactory receptor neurons in our nose. A network of nerve fibers transmit the inputs from all these sensors to our brain, which corrects, compresses, and corroborates them by making comparisons to its built-in assumptions about the world, to what our other senses are saying, to what we are expecting, and to what is in our memory, before our mind forms them into a story.

The sensors in our smartphones do not replicate human senses, nor should they—there are obvious advantages to using technology for extra-sensory perception by sensing things we cannot, such as air quality or radiation—but the architectures of natural and artificial sentience are essentially the same: the sensors in our phones connect via the internet to software that analyzes and corrects their signals.

As we discussed earlier, nature also has a second architecture for sentience: communication, which first evolved as a way to share sensory data. Warning calls and other signals transmit individual perceptions to a group to create *herd sentience*: a metasensing superset of individual nervous systems, an array of arrays, all connected by communication.

This part of our nervous system is neither unique nor original: its most ancient, most evolved form is found in trees.

Understanding how trees sense and communicate is essential for understanding how *we* sense and communicate.

Intelligence exists in trees as well as humans because of *convergent evolution*—the same thing evolving independently in different species. Winged flight is an example of convergent evolution: wings evolved separately in bats, birds, and butterflies, but are remarkably similar. Our most recent common ancestor with trees was almost certainly a single-celled organism that lived about 1.6 billion years ago. This organism would at best have had a simple, prototypical nervous system, and certainly no need for intelligence. Intelligence, then, evolved after our most recent common ancestor, and therefore separately in trees and humans.

The first trees appeared around 400 million years ago and the first humans appeared around two million years ago, which means trees have been evolving intelligence two hundred times longer than humans.

Trees do not have brains, but they do have observable behaviors that demonstrate that they create and navigate a complex model of their environment. What we think of when we think of a tree—the aboveground trunk and branches—is in fact its tail; its head is its roots, which have brain-like information-processing properties. In addition to this "brain," a tree also has senses: its roots, its leaves, and a community of microorganisms that live in and around it. Two of the first people to describe the true nature of trees were Charles Darwin and his son Francis, who, in their 1880 book *The Power of Movement in Plants*, noted that a tree's root tips "act like a brain, receiving impressions from the sense-organs, and directing movements."

In addition to sensing for themselves, trees also use herd sentience to share sensory information with one another, mainly through an underground network of cooperative fungi. Fungi, like trees, exist mostly below ground; the toadstools and other shapes we associate with fungi are in fact the tip of a huge fungal iceberg. And, like trees, fungi have complex root systems; tentacle-like filaments called *hyphae* that reach into the soil where they connect with tree roots to form a mutually beneficial, symbiotic relationship. Once connected via the hyphae, the trees signal each other using a rich chemical language made of nitrogen, carbon, water, and other molecules, all sent through the fungi's filaments: an ethernet for trees. I can hypothesize by analogy that trees also communicate using pollen or some other aerosol to broadcast information "wirelessly"—i.e., without using the "wiring" of their fungal network. We already have a few clues that this might by the case—trees use pollen to coordinate and synchronize some of their behaviors, for example—but need more research before we can know for sure.

Trees use the information they gather for themselves and testimony from others to build a detailed model of their environment. Among other things, this model—the trees' *reality*—tells them the quality of the soil surrounding them, the health and needs of their neighbors—for example, whether any nearby trees are currently being attacked by insects—and which trees are their relatives. After making their model, trees navigate it, both conceptually, by making choices about strategies for survival, such as adjusting the speed of their photosynthesis or regulating their production of the chemicals that defend them from disease and infestation, and literally, by moving and growing their roots and branches to depths and heights and in directions that seem most likely to benefit them and their neighbors. In many ways, trees' sentience is far more advanced than ours: trees form cooperative telecommunication networks comprising many different species, for example.

It follows that the architecture of human intelligence will continue to evolve in ways that resemble the architecture of tree intelligence. We already have evidence that this is the direction of our evolution; the symbiotic communications links between trees and fungi are called *mycorrhizal networks* and their topography and many of their other features strongly resemble the Internet of Things. Where we share information via sand, trees share information via fungi. Just a few decades ago, humans reached a stage in the evolution of our intelligence—networked communications—that trees achieved hundreds of millions of years earlier. And, just as the mycorrhizal network is a permanent and essential aspect of the architecture of tree intelligence, so the Internet of Things is now a permanent and essential aspect of the architecture of human intelligence. The mycorrhizal network has, inevitably, been called the *Internet of Trees*, but that metaphor is the wrong way around: the Internet of Things is the mycorrhizal network of humans.

Trees help us see the true nature of intelligence, and that it is possessed by almost all living things: intelligence is an essential component and subset of sentience, which is the ability to make sense of sense and to make sense helpful, and the production and utilization of reality itself.

This definition of intelligence has many interesting implications.

One of the most important is also an overarching theme of this book: trees give us a new perspective on the nature and future of human intelligence and communication.

Our artificial equivalent of herd sentience is called *participatory sensing*. One commercial application of participatory sensing is navigation. Apps including Baidu Maps, Google Maps, and Waze use the speed, acceleration, and location data streaming from their users' phones to find the most efficient routes for others and to detect and, if possible, avoid traffic.

Like herd sentience, participatory sensing is especially useful in emergencies. In 2010, an earthquake struck Haiti's capital, Port-au-Prince. More than 100,000 people were killed, and 630,000 more—about 25 percent of the city's population—fled to other parts of Haiti; 28,000 went to Les Cayes, 23,000 to Léogâne, and 22,000 to Saint-Marc, for example. Ten months later, Haiti suffered a second disaster: United Nations peacekeepers from Nepal inadvertently caused a cholera epidemic. Ten thousand more people died, and 94,000 fled, most to Port-au-Prince, Gonaïves, and Gonâve Island, and few, if any, to Haiti's southernmost departments, Grand'Anse, Nippes, Sud, and Sud-Est. We only know how many people fled and where they went because of the data streaming from their phones; and during the cholera outbreak this information was shared with epidemiologists to help contain the spread of the disease.

Humans move en masse when there are no emergencies too. In Senegal, one hundred miles east of Anta Diouf and Dakar, there is a holy city named Touba, which is the burial site of Sheikh Ahmadou Bamba, founder of the Mouride order of Sufi Muslims. Every year, millions of Mourides travel to Touba to commemorate Bamba's life. Mass movements like these create risks to health and safety, to food and water supplies, and to transportation and accommodation infrastructure. Understanding people's routes is critical for mitigating those risks, but those routes have always been unknowable, a matter for anecdotes and estimates. In 2013, after eighty-five annual pilgrimages, participatory sensing revealed the pilgrims' routes for the first time. The most popular route is Dakar to Thies to Diourbel to Touba, followed by Saint-Louis to Louga to Thies to Diourbel to Touba; Koalack to Diourbel to Touba; and Fatick to Bambey to Diourbel to Touba. The same participatory sensing system also shows how many pilgrims will arrive in each of these cities, and when.

"Participatory sensing" implies *participation*, which is commonly understood to mean taking part in something actively, consensually, and voluntarily, but humans are not the participants described by the term *participatory sensing*. The participants are their smartphones. Most human participants in most participatory sensing networks do not know they are participating, and that likely includes you.

This brings us to another important point about the systems that will shape our imminent future: our happiness and safety will depend on understanding how these systems work.

7. Systemicity

The best way to understand technology is systemically, holistically, all together. Storytelling tools in particular are more than the sum of their parts, which are, in order of importance: neurology, economy, and technology.

Let's discuss neurology first.

Our behavior is more instinctive and therefore more predictable than most of us realize. Our predictability often makes us misunderstand the outputs of reinforcement learning systems. Just as Lee Se-dol sensed the machine knew what moves he would make before *he* did, so we may suspect the machine knows what we want to buy before *we* know what we want to buy. This effect is so convincing that eight out of ten Americans believe services like Facebook are hacking the microphones in their personal computers, phones, and other devices and secretly listening to everything they say. Anecdotes abound: People claim, for example, that they have seen advertising for car washes after talking about car washes, cat food after talking about cat food, and rice milk after talking about rice milk. But Facebook is *not* listening to your microphone. Constant audio surveillance of every user would increase Facebook's already massive daily data load by more than 3,000 percent, eat up a phone's battery and bandwidth, and be easily detectable, among many other problems.

But do not be reassured: the truth about the machine's apparent telepathy is in many ways *worse* than corporations hacking our microphones; corporations are hacking our cognition instead. Reinforcement learning systems create the illusion of intrusion in the same way they create the illusion of intention: our story-shaped brains inevitably endow the machine with humanish agency. If another human could predict our behavior as accurately as the machine can, that human would almost certainly be eavesdropping, and so we conclude the machine must be eavesdropping too.

Mistaking reinforcement learning for remote listening is an example of a problem both general and major. Our story-shaped brains give us innate story-shaped biases, and attention-seeking reinforcement learning systems exploit those biases at every opportunity. The conviction—unshakable in many—that Facebook or other websites are spying on us via microphones, arises from four such biases: *agent detection bias*, which leads us to imagine that things we cannot explain are the work of humanlike agents; *the bias blind spot*, an egocentric conviction that, while other people may have cognitive biases, we ourselves do not; *confirmation bias*, which is the tendency to only notice things that support a prior belief; and *uniqueness bias*, the false belief that our behavior and reactions are exceptional and unique rather than ordinary and typical.

Any appearance of machine prescience is in fact a result of these biases combined with coincidence, our innate predictability, and the fact that Facebook, like all similar services, is a massive participatory sensing network, capturing not only the data we enter, but also the data our devices gather automatically, using the Internet of Things on a grand and global scale, recording data streaming from the screens of billions of unique individuals daily, not for the greater good of making mass migrations safer, or saving lives during disasters, or preventing the spread of disease, but to sell advertising.

Facebook knows millions of things about each of us without ever needing to listen to our microphones. Its machine logs not only everything every user publishes, reacts to, and comments on, but also the location of every place they go; every time they use their Facebook identity and password to conveniently log into some other app or website; every picture with their face in it; what devices they use and when they upgrade and replace them; who they befriend and reject; who they communicate with, how, and for how long; every name, address, and phone number in their address book; every appearance of their name, address, or phone number in *anyone else's* address book; how much time they spend reading and scrolling through posts; who interacts with the posts they write and the pictures they publish; whose posts they interact with; and much more besides. The machine records all this information and remembers it forever, storing over one megabyte of data for every user every day. Facebook does have "privacy" settings, of course; but these keep your selected information private from third parties, not from Facebook. Facebook's reinforcement learning machine sees everything.

One of the best examples of the intersection between our biases and the internet is who we choose for our online friends. In the 1920s, social scientists started documenting what appeared to be a powerful and universal pattern in human relationships: we only form trusting, lasting relationships with people who are like us, a tendency that came to be called the *homophily bias*. No matter what factors scientists studied—age, hobbies, interests, political beliefs, race, religion, socioeconomic status, or almost anything else—they found that people everywhere were biased toward forming close friendships with people who were similar to them, and that the more similarities there were, the closer and longer-lasting these friendships were likely to be. In other words, birds of a feather *did* flock together, and opposites *did not* attract—at least not when it came to human relationships.

In the twentieth century, there was an attractive alternative explanation for our lack of diversity in friendships: geography. Perhaps people were not biased toward homophily; perhaps they only made friends with people like them because only people like them lived nearby. Maybe homophily was *not* human nature, but a mere consequence of distance, communication, and segregation.

In the twenty-first century, the internet, and especially "social" services like Facebook that aimed to connect people to their "friends," provided real-life tests of the hypothesis that homophily is the result of geography. What would happen to homophily when the entire human race could make and maintain friendships with anyone, anywhere using screens?

At the time of writing, Facebook is the most popular social network in the world, with about three billion users. This means there are around five quintillion—or, five million trillion—possible friendship pairs available, and that each Facebook user has a choice of three billion possible friends. All of these potential friends are accessible via the same screen, and are therefore equally nearby.

But, despite not having any geographical limitations, Facebook friendships are *more* homophilous than real-life relationships. Even though they have billions of choices, most people's Facebook friends are a lot like themselves. Because of that, a large proportion of a typical user's friends tend to be friends with each other—and the more friends a user has, the larger that proportion becomes. This trend creates dense, concentrated clusters of people. People in each cluster tend to be similar—they are mostly the same age and race, and mostly live in the same place, for example. The larger the cluster, the more often its members log in and post—the Facebook equivalent of being louder and talking more. Facebook is dominated by homogenous mobs. Homophily is not caused by geographic and social segregation; geographic and social segregation are caused by homophily. Given the opportunity, most of us will be as homophilous as possible.

No mob is an island; Facebook's tight clusters of friends are insular, but not isolated. All these dense hubs are connected to each other by thin spokes a few friendships wide. Somebody in each hub knows somebody in another hub and, as a result, every Facebook user is connected to every other Facebook user by five friends or fewer. It follows that every Facebook user with one hundred friends has seventy *thousand* friends-of-friends. This fact is hugely significant: it means that, in the words of one of Facebook's own data scientists, "Content only needs to advance a few steps across Facebook's social network to reach a substantial fraction of the world's population."

Facebook's reinforcement learning machine probes this network about fifty thousand times a second, and, in addition, runs millions of offline simulations, constantly seeking stories that will take those few steps to reach much of the world.

When it finds a story budding with signs of attention, it looks not at the story—it cannot understand stories, remember—but at the people who are paying attention to the story, then looks for other people like them who may pay attention to the same story. In other words, it uses homophily as a proxy to predict attention. And, in the case of Facebook, homophily is far richer and more detailed than anything imagined by the social scientists of the twentieth century.

But the homophily of the twenty-first century has two big differences.

First, Facebook's reinforcement learning machine is not an inert catalyst of friendship, merely introducing people with common interests to one another. Its coin is story. The machine exchanges stories for our attention, and stories change our minds. Each time we respond to a story on Facebook, the machine shows us other stories people who liked that story liked. Over time it echoes again and again, feeding back on itself, amplifying, emphasizing, and exaggerating whatever we appear to be interested in. Reinforcement learning is the automation of exacerbation, the computation of confirmation bias, the mass production of illusory consensus; its fundamental nature is to push our minds and ideas as far as possible in one direction or another, without diversity, variety, or contrast, to make us into caricatures of ourselves, to embed us ever deeper into like-minded tribes, to twist the dials of our biases up to their maxima. Reinforcement learning radicalizes.

This first difference makes the second difference dangerous. If you can figure out *how* a reinforcement learning system learns, you can *jewel-bug* that system: you can game it, exploit it, hack the machine *with* its cooperation and *without* its owner's knowledge, and push its machiney buttons by showing it supernormal versions of the signs it is looking for. You can build a beetle bottle for the beetle bottle.

This leads us straight to economy.

The greatest lie in Silicon Valley is that venture capitalists and the companies they fund are "job creators." The truth is the opposite: venture capitalists and therefore their investees seek to employ as few people as possible, because employees cost money—not only in salaries, but also in other costs such as benefits—an expense delightfully called a *labor burden*. There is even an accounting ratio to quantify the benefit of *unburdening* a business by creating the fewest possible jobs: NIPE, or *net income per employee*. (Making more money with fewer employees is called "efficiency.") There is abundant evidence venture capitalists do not create jobs. For example, one of the most extensive studies on the subject, by economists Thor Berger and Carl Benedikt Frey, concluded that "the companies leading the digital revolution have created few employment opportunities." This is why businesses like Facebook and Google are so interested in acquiring technologies like the one that defeated Lee Se-dol, and at almost any price. Their logic is simple: they assume that if they can replace a Go master with an unsalaried machine, then they can replace almost anybody. This, as we have seen, is a catastrophic, historic, and possibly extinction-level mistake: the communication equivalent of filling the skies with greenhouse gases.

These dynamics are exactly why Facebook was an attractive investment for venture capitalists when it was founded, and why it uses reinforcement learning today. In 2020, Facebook generated a net income—the number most people call a "profit" that is quite literally the bottom line of a business's balance sheet—of more than $29 billion with only 58,604 employees, meaning each individual employee created an average net income—or profit—of half a million dollars; this is the money that was left over *after* the employees' salaries, benefits, and all of Facebook's other expenses were paid. This ratio gave Facebook the seventh highest profit per employee in the Fortune 500, beaten only by five banks and an oil company. The median net income per employee among *all* Fortune 500 companies is $31,000, which is one-sixteenth of Facebook's number, and also, for example, the amount generated by each employee of the New York Times Company, one of Facebook's more traditional, labor-intensive competitors. When Facebook first made its service available to the general public in September 2006, the US newspaper-publishing industry employed 360,000 people. By 2020, that number had fallen by more than two-thirds, or almost a quarter of a million people, to 110,000. Sixty percent of US publishing jobs were lost in the fourteen years between Facebook's public debut and the end of 2020, 400,000 jobs in all, nearly seven times more people than were employed by Facebook, an example of a company that the scions of Silicon Valley seriously want us to believe is a "job creator."

Facebook is able to outcompete these traditional publishers using less labor because it does not produce any content—all Facebook's stories are written by its users, or by other businesses, and provided to Facebook free of charge—and because Facebook does not employ anyone to edit, curate, moderate, or otherwise supervise those stories; instead, it lets its reinforcement learning–based attention-getting machine determine what each user sees. This mode of operation has two important consequences. First, Facebook is locked into its user-generated and machine-curated approach to getting attention. If Facebook ever tried to drop its addiction to free content and automation, and use human writers and editors instead, its profit per employee would fall, probably to something like the level of the *New York Times*, which would lead to a plummeting valuation, shareholder insurrection, and the company being acquired by someone, perhaps a private equity firm, or perhaps a competitor, who would immediately fire everybody and replace them with machinery. Second, and even more important, Facebook's dependence on reinforcement learning means none of its 58,604 employees control which stories Facebook's users see; Facebook is deliberately and literally *out* of control.

Facebook's executives will deny this, of course. They will try to claim that the machine is under their control because they invented it, or at least bought some companies that did. The trouble with this argument is that the machine is a *reinforcement learning* machine. Once set in motion, a reinforcement learning machine invents *itself*, then *reinvents* itself over and over again. No one, not even the machine's developers, knows exactly how or why the machine does what it does. That's the point of reinforcement learning: it is *designed* to be out of control.

And, that brings us to the only systemic element of storytelling that changes significantly over time: technology.

At the time of writing, the emerging new storytelling technology is an approach to artificial intelligence called *generative AI*, in particular techniques called *transformer-based large language models*, or *LLMs*, which write text, and *diffusion-based image generators* which create pictures and videos. We don't need to understand the technical details of how generative AI is made, such as how it uses feed-forward neural networks and transformer architectures, to live safely in a world of artificial intelligence, any more than we need to understand lignin-containing nanocellulose or multilayer perceptron control in order to read a book.

What we *do* need to understand is that generative AI tools learn from large datasets to generate text and images that could easily be mistaken for human-created content. They are shown, or "trained on," corpuses comprising trillions of words from websites and books, or billions of images from artists, moviemakers, and photographers. Text models learn to predict the next word in a sequence, and image models learn to create a picture from noise—like the image on a broadcast TV set with no signal—by removing the noise in a series of steps. Sometimes these outputs are novel, and sometimes—at the time of writing, at least—they are direct copies of content from their training material. If you have ever seen a movie like *E.T.*, *Starman*, or *The Fifth Element* in which an alien visitor learns English in an afternoon by rapidly switching through TV channels, you've seen something a lot like the training of generative AI.

The mechanisms by which generative AI systems—and visiting aliens—learn have consequences: large language models may give you plagiarized words or images without you realizing it, or, if you produce copyrighted material, reappropriate your work without paying you for it; they often make mistakes, or "hallucinate," because they are processing patterns without understanding what they mean; their results reflect the biases and prejudices of both their programmers and their training data; and because generative systems are better at acting like humans than many humans, you may mistakenly feel like generative AI is your friend, or trustworthy, which can make generative AI a useful tool for abusers, bot farms, catfishers, con artists, fraudsters, groomers, harassers, impersonators, scammers, stalkers, and other online predators.

These weaknesses are likely to become more noticeable as the challenges of economy increase. At the time of writing, generative AI is in a bubble much like the dot-com bubble of the late 1990s. Generative AI systems cost billions of dollars to build and maintain, but are more or less free to use. That bubble will burst, and may well have done so by the time you read this. The technology will not go away, but many AI companies will, and whoever is holding their stock at the time will lose a lot of money. On the other side of the bubble there may be ugly developments like the addition of targeted advertising and product placement based on what you tell the LLM; monopolization; tiered advice from free to premium; use that is metered by the minute; peak and off-peak rates; and, as always with new technology, growing inequality between those who can afford it and those who cannot.

Some other current concerns about generative AI—which may have changed by the time you read this—are exaggerated or simply misplaced. Generative AI systems use a great deal of energy, especially when being trained, and therefore emit a great deal of greenhouse gases. But they are fairly energy efficient in individual conversations, will likely become more efficient over time, and their environmental consequences should be considered in comparison to other storytelling technologies. Making this copy of this book had an environmental impact too—it contributed about as much greenhouse gas to the atmosphere as 3,300 conversations with a large language model, and had other consequences including deforestation, chemical waste, and a large amount of water use.

Many people are surprised to hear about the environmental impacts of books. Often, we are too sensitive to the negative consequences of technologies that are new, and too numb to the negative consequences of technologies that are old.

This sensitivity comes in a predictable, story-shaped pattern.

8. The Villain with a Thousand Faces

All myths about new technology follow the same format, unfold in predictable ways, and feature motifs that recur throughout history. New technology is the villain with a thousand faces.

The first act of every horror story about new technology focuses on *danger*. A new technology has appeared, or is about to appear, and is accused of causing immediate or cumulative physical harm or at least threatening to, especially to the young. It must therefore be prohibited, or at least regulated and controlled proactively, and far more zealously than other, more familiar technologies. When the technology becomes widely available despite being accused of being dangerous, the second act begins.

In the second act, the problem is *mania*. People, especially young people, are accused of using the new technology too much, and neglecting other, older—and therefore more respectable—activities. Using the new technology is described as a form of addiction, and is often given a name to reflect this. Critics of the new technology argue its use should be measured or moderated to allow time for more traditional behaviors. The danger from the first act is still present, but vaguer, and now part of the background.

In the third and final act, after the technology has become ubiquitous and its use habitual, the focus of concern is *dystopia*. There's still *danger* and *mania*, but these, having not actually amounted to anything, become background singers, adding occasional emphasis and color. In this third act, any negative social behaviors, especially ones that have increased or are perceived to have increased since the new technology became popular, are blamed on the new technology, no matter how tenuous the connection. In this stage, it is equally important that no *positive* trends be attributed to the new technology, no matter how *obvious* the connection, or that when anything positive *is* mentioned, it is immediately offset by the supposed negative impacts.

These stories are told with a lack of context that is essential to their success. The concerns about the *new* new technology must appear to be absolutely unprecedented: brand-new problems, caused for the first time ever, that no new technology has ever been accused of causing before. Apparently serious academic studies of the problem, for example, can never begin with a historical review summarizing similar previous concerns about previous technologies that were eventually proved groundless, even though such introductory literature reviews are standard in most scholarly papers.

The omission of this background is prerequisite: the horror story would lose all its drama if it gained perspective. Things can never have been so bad, and the stakes can never have been so high, because the new technology must be contrasted unfavorably with older, more established technologies—technologies that were also once accused of being dangerous, addictive, and destabilizing, but are now so established that most people no longer think of them as "technology" at all.

In addition, the horror story must appear to be a prudent and knowing consensus: the myth must create the impression that *all sensible people agree* that the new technology poses a unique threat to our health and safety, to our way of life, and especially to our children, a threat that all right-minded adults know is definitely real, even if they don't yet know its exact magnitude.

To prove the point, consider broadcast radio, which is now so common and familiar that it is understood to be innocuous. In the early

1900s, when broadcast radio was first introduced, it was the villain of the new technology monomyth. The first act in the horror story, *danger*, included fears that radio was causing droughts by "drying up the air" or "doing something to the atmosphere"; floods, because "radio waves break the clouds, precipitating rain and causing strong winds to blow on the surface of the ocean"; and claims that radio damaged skin, by creating problems like "wireless wrinkles," "puckers around a woman's forehead," and "causing a person's face and body to acquire large blue splotches."

Altered faces is a recurring motif in the new technology horror story: there were similar concerns about *bicycle face*, which included "wildly expectant eyes," "strained lines about the mouth," and "a general focusing of features toward the center"; *automobile face*, which consisted of "looking afraid of a collision"; *airplane face*, characterized by "squinting eyes, overgrown nose, and head bulging between the ears"; *moving-picture face*, which "does not express either wonder or surprise"; and *smartphone face*, which "causes your face to droop."

In the second act, *mania*, radio "addiction" was accused of causing divorce, preventing children from "developing concentration, discrimination, and fineness of taste," and scrambling the mind in ways that caused "aimless wandering" and "muttering." In the third and final act, *dystopia*, radio was said to "hamper speech and mutual enjoyment from conversation in the family," "violate the purity of elections," and "undermine the health" and "interfere with the school success" of children aged six to sixteen.

There is never a third-act climax. The myth of the terrifying new technology ends the same way every time: by becoming ever more vague, then petering out. The frightening prophecies are never realized or renounced; they are instead relocated to the next new technology, where the cycle begins again, as if for the first time, with every fearmonger seemingly believing that they are selling new and different terrors, causing an endless Mad Lib of pointless public panic. Only the nouns change: the fears, always ungrounded and often unhinged, stay exactly the same.

All of these concerns about radio, which now seem quaint and ridiculous, were remixed from myths about prior storytelling technologies including reading; recorded music; novels; motion pictures; paperback books; and photography. This did nothing to stop them being repeated in later myths about television; personal computers; video games; the internet; cell phones; Wi-Fi; eBooks; social media; and smartphones, which were accused of causing isolation and ostracization, distracting from the real world, and interfering with sleep, among other problems.

The myth of the terrifying new technology arises and recurs because of our story-shaped brains.

There are two kinds of new in the world: stuff that is new to us but known to other people, and stuff that is new to everyone. When stuff is new to us but known to other people, we can rely on those other people's stories to plug the gap in our experience. This kind of *storied* newness is the kind of newness we deal with most frequently. We seek stories to mitigate the risks of newness so often and so reflexively that we do not realize we are doing it. Whenever we want to buy a new thing, go to a new place, or learn a new skill, we ask friends and family, peruse reviews, read books, take lessons, and watch TV shows in order to absorb stories based on other people's experiences until we gain enough confidence and proxy knowledge to begin and eventually develop stories of our own. Stories are an effective and uniquely human survival strategy: when we have to do new things, stories reduce our risk by informing our choices and preparing us in advance. Stories let us borrow the experience of others and live through new things before we try them.

This survival strategy does not work for new technology: it is new to everyone, so it is *unstoried* newness. There are no stories to tell us what to expect—specifically, there are no stories based on long-term, direct experience. This problem is especially acute with recent new technologies—tools invented since, say, the late 1800s, because, for reasons we have already discussed, they proliferate faster than anyone can gain any experience of them. Modern new technologies appear in an experience vacuum.

Stories abhor vacuums. Humans need narratives to give new things meaning. When we cannot find stories based on experience, we put another kind of story in their place: stories based on speculation. New technology is fertile ground for speculation because it is based on new science, which, by definition, opens the doors for new possibilities.

Authors of speculative fiction—science fiction, superhero comic books, and horror stories, for example—often grow their work from the seeds of recent scientific discoveries. The launch of the first mechanical submarine in 1863 inspired 1869's *Twenty Thousand Leagues Under the Seas*; the distribution of electrification in the late 1800s led to the electrification of the monster in the 1931 movie *Frankenstein*; the development of computerized "expert systems"—a precursor to artificial intelligence—and networks in the 1970s gave the backstory to both the 1983 movie *WarGames*, in which a supercomputer tries to launch a nuclear attack, and the 1984 movie *The Terminator*, in which a self-aware computer network destroys civilization; and the first successful sheep cloning in 1984 led to a 1990s novel and movie about dinosaur cloning called *Jurassic Park*.

When there are no stories based on experience, this fictional speculation informs our real speculation about the possible perils of new technology. This mythology distracts us from assessing and understanding *real* risks and dangers. Myths about new technology make us afraid of the wrong things.

9. Growing Too Wise for Our Betters

In satirist Thomas Love Peacock's 1818 novella *Nightmare Abbey*, Ferdinando Flosky, a barely disguised cartoon of Samuel Taylor Coleridge, asks: "How can we be cheerful, when we are surrounded by a reading public that is growing too wise for its betters?"

Peacock's joke will always be true: authority fears literacy. Authority figures will not admit this; they will instead say that *of course* they want people to be able to read. But what they mean is that they want people to be able to *comprehend writing* and, as discussed earlier, comprehending writing is neither literacy nor reading. Here is a more recent version of the same joke, by essayist Brian Phillips: "What a piece of work is a man, how noble in reason, how infinite in faculties, in form and moving how express and admirable, in action how like an angel, in apprehension how like a god, also he should be trained from birth to manage logistics for a mid-sized regional wholesaler."

Powerful people want workers not thinkers. Literacy is knowing, reading is reasoning, and knowing and reasoning cause resistance and revolution.

Your brain may be but-but-butting by now. It is likely that throughout your life you have been told a story about how everyone with authority over you, from your family to your government, wants you to be educated. You probably went to one or more schools funded by taxes. How, then, can it possibly be true that authority fears literacy? It may seem as if, at least in your case, literacy has been positively encouraged—and, of course, it is what enables you to read this book. "Authority fears literacy" is therefore another extraordinary claim in need of extraordinary evidence, ideally from your own life.

So, given that literacy and reading add up to *critical thinking*, ask yourself these questions: Did you have any curricula classes in critical thinking skills during your general, comprehensive education? Did you have lessons explicitly covering critical thinking components like epistemology, metacognition, or skepticism? Were you taught about cognitive biases and how to recognize and mitigate them?

It is highly likely that all your answers are no, you did not attend any critical thinking or similar classes when you were a child. This is not because teaching children critical thinking does not work: there have been many studies showing that teaching children critical thinking helps children become critical thinkers, because of course it does. The reason critical thinking lessons are not required in public schools is that there are few incentives to encourage independent thinking, and many incentives to encourage obedient memorization, the form of teaching Paulo Freire called *banking education*. General education remains rooted in the nineteenth-century fear that teaching too much to the masses "will render them insolent to their superiors."

That fear was and still is mistaken, but not in the way it seems. Superiority is not an innate or natural condition but a necessary concoction of capitalism, colonialism, fascism, nationalism, patriarchy, racism, and every other system that seeks to divide us to rule us; it is purely a product of storytelling.

This is why people who declare themselves superior prefer public education to be insufficiently resourced indoctrination rather than fully funded training in independent thought.

But "too much" education is not what renders people "insolent to their superiors." No one is innately superior to anyone, and everyone knows this intuitively, which is why those who claim to be superior crave the comfort of crowns, ermine cloaks, and other glittering tchotchkes. People become insolent toward those who *claim* to be their superiors *naturally*, regardless of education, because that superiority is imposed and imagined. Ignorance does not deter insolence: ignorance only makes insolence louder and more chaotic. Not teaching critical thinking cannot stop people thinking critically; it can only stop them being good at it.

Belief in nonsense like conspiracy theories is a consequence of critical thinking gone wrong: strange fruit hanging from the trees of a world where stories are evenly distributed and critical thinking skills are not. We all want to think critically, even if we don't know how.

When conspiracy theorists say "I do my own research," what they are really saying is less laughable and more laudable than it seems. The heart of this phrase is "I have thought about it and reached my own conclusions." To prove the point, people who use it often accuse others of being "sheep" or "sheeple"—of *not* reaching their own conclusions, and following instruction without question. The fact that these accusations are nearly always false does not change what it reveals about the accuser's motivations.

"I do my own research" is a plea for personal autonomy far more than an argument for a particular position. No one, regardless of their level of research skills, wants to be told what to think; everyone deserves the compassion, empathy, and respect of persuasion rather than the brute force of dictation whenever that tolerance does not put other people's rights, safety, and welfare at risk.

Cultivating a citizenry that believes anything may seem like good policy when the people that control the citizenry also control the anything the citizenry believes, but that does not apply anymore, and never will again. The life of the standard story has forever passed beyond the direct control of even the most powerful among us.

There are only two choices now: We can either live in a world where a large proportion of the population is susceptible to believing any arbitrary story good enough to capture their attention and familiar enough to support their biases; or we can educate our children in critical literacy once or twice a week, every year, from kindergarten to graduation.

10. The Problem of Knowing

It is time for a hard truth. Grab a bar of chocolate, a beer, a blanket, a bong, a bourbon, a cat, a cup of tea, a pint of ice cream, or whatever else comforts you, then turn the page.

No one is coming to save us.

The people who govern us are unlikely to vote for critical literacy education soon, if ever. Think back to America's book banners. They are fighting for *less* critical literacy in education, not more. Powerful people do not want us to become critical thinkers because then we will call them on their bullshit.

And even the best of our elected officials are hampered by incomprehension of new technology. I have worked with governments all over the world. There are few engineers, mathematicians, or scientists among people in power. Most are trained in law or some other qualitative discipline. Politicians only encounter empiricism on election day. They have neither enough time to be curious, nor enough background to understand new technology quickly. Their ignorance makes them easy to manipulate. And they nearly all have the disadvantage of age. As we grow older, it becomes harder to understand new concepts. The average age of elected officials is fifty-two globally, and elected officials in the United States are especially old: their average age is sixty-four. Elderly lawyers is not the demographic that should be leading and legislating a high-technology society, but these people have entrenched power and many will hold on to it beyond dementia and unto death if they can.

But that does not mean we will not be saved.

We can and will save ourselves, and we must do so in the face of opposition both explicit and sly.

The problem of choosing, which has arched over the story of stories since the appearance of alliteration, assonance, and rhyme, is a lesser problem today; not because it has gone away, but because we are told so many stories we do not solicit, and because we now face a bigger problem: the problem of knowing.

It is hard to imagine, at least at the time of writing, living in a world in which signals and stimuli seem exactly the same, are literally indistinguishable, where there are no tells at all showing us whether something is actual or artificial, completing the journey that started in the 1500s with the creation of the *picaro*.

Power has always played with realism. Portraiture and statuary provide good examples. You will seldom if ever see a statue of a slouched and potbellied king, or a portrait of a sickly, ugly queen: long before Photoshop and other retouching tools, the representations of such people dehumanized them with burnishment to tell us the lie that they are special. And then, of course, there are the statues of historical heroes who did not exist, like Laurens Janszoon Coster in Haarlem town square.

What will powerful people perpetrate when they can create perfect simulations at the touch of a button? Will they go bravely into pretend battles, comfort computer-generated people sick and poor, rewind time to say things they did not say, and to unsay things they did?

And what will mind warriors do when they can generate three-dimensional diminishment, make their lies appear real, and show their opponents committing any crime, giving any offense, enjoying any vice?

The answer, I fear, based on history alone, is that the new storytelling technologies of our near future will conflate truth and lies and manifest falsehoods in ways beyond anything we have ever experienced. The war of stories will level up and become multidimensional and multisensory. We will not only see and hear the battle; we will smell, taste, and touch it too, with no need for imagination.

Our only protection is critical literacy, and like Tycho Brahe, we must teach it to ourselves.

We must become more self-aware, engage in more self-reflection, and feel more doubt and humility than ever before. We must accept we are never neutral, never rational, and never objective, because we cannot think clearly, let alone critically, if we pretend otherwise. We must understand we think with our whole nervous system, and with feelings capricious, fleeting, inconsistent, and far more dependent on arbitrary biochemistry than we care to admit.

And we must know we think in stories, and that we always will.

Author's Note

Thank You

Dear Reader,

Thank you for reading *The Story of Stories*. I have a favor to ask: If you enjoyed the book, please recommend it to as many other people as possible, whether by word of mouth, posting online, giving it as a gift, flying a plane with a banner over a major sporting event, or any other way you can.

    This book will only find its audience if first readers like you recommend it to other people. Your recommendation is more influential and powerful than you may realize. The people to whom you recommend the book may also recommend it to others, and so on. If you recommend this book to four people who buy it, you start a chain reaction that creates about a thousand readers.

    In short, your recommendation is the difference between *The Story of Stories* being a book few discover and one that is widely read.

Yours,
Kevin

Acknowledgments

The work of Brian Boyd, Robin Dunbar, Elizabeth Eisenstein, Roy Harris, Stephen Kosslyn, and Oliver Timken Perrin were especially important points of departure when I started writing this book. Cara Grey, Laney Ingram, and Thea Pajunen gave essential support at different stages of the writing process. Karina Cardona me mantuvo organizada. Richard Pine and Eliza Rothstein helped me figure out the concept and structure of the manuscript, among many other things above and beyond the usual duties of literary agents. I am always delighted to get an email from Lyndsey Blessing. Karen Rinaldi's editing, cussing, and passion inspired me. My speaking agents at the Leigh Bureau are fearless and tireless. D. S. Wang, Y. S. Chen, and the people of BOE were more accessible and hospitable than I had any right to expect. Brittany Salgado and the people of Corning—company and town both—welcomed me and helped me understand glass. Please visit the Corning Museum of Glass if you are ever in the neighborhood. I owe a great and permanent debt to booksellers, public and school librarians, and organizers of book festivals and common reads everywhere, and in particular to the librarians of Austin Public Library; the booksellers of BookPeople in Austin, Newham Bookshop in East Ham, and more rare and used bookstores than I can possibly name; and to the organizers of the Texas Book Festival. In 2024, Wolfgang Niedert, a director of the festival, died suddenly at the age of forty-eight. Wolfgang was a great man who understood the story of stories intuitively. All love and condolences to his wife, Julie, and his daughters, Sophie and Olivia. My work is made easier by Wikipedians; the people of the

Internet Archive; Max Roser and everyone at Our World in Data; Jonathan D. Ashwell and Serhiy Duminskyy of Sonny Software, who created Bookends, my indispensable reference management software; and Keith Blount and Ioa Petra'ka of Literature and Latte, who created Scrivener, my equally indispensable authoring software, with a special thank you to Karen Prince of the Scrivener support team who spent hours solving a gnarly problem for me right on a production deadline. And, in the starring role: my dog Sydney, who was a constant and loyal companion for every draft and chapter of this book. I miss him.

Thanks

Sasha Ashton
Arlo Ashton
Theo Ashton
Sydney Ashton
Archie Ashton
Biscuit Ashton
Alice Arnold
Austin Public Library
Rudy Baldwin
Emma Banton
Emily Barr
Larry Begley
Cynthia Benton
Carlie Bittel
Lyndsey Blessing
BookPeople
Adia Brewington
Karina Cardona
Henry Chen
Y. S. Chen
Catherine Clay
Holly Coleman

Kelly Coulter
Margaret Cullen
Sandra Davis
Terrance Davis
Benjamin Dreyer
Dwight Dugan
First Light Books
Ann Fitch
Stona Fitch
Foreign and Domestic
Tanya Fox
Full Circle Bar
Imani Gandy
Cara Grey
Monroe Grey
Sarah Greene
Becca Gutiérrez
Esther Ha
Al Hannaford
Sarah Heard
Lexis Holmes
Laney Ingram

Cody Jackson
Rachel Kambury
Eyad Kasemi
Juliette Kellow
Cecilia Lee
Bill Leigh
Bonni Leon-Berman
Diane Levitt
Gideon Lichfield
Sarah Murphy Mannheimer
Carol-Lynne Meissner
Mary Ellen Mizov
Eric Myers
Wesley Neff
Newham Bookshop
Wolfgang Niedert
Sewon Oh
Ben Oliver
Steph Opitz
Thea Pajunen

Sunny Park
Shwetak Patel
Richard Pine
Porchlight Book Company
Matt Reynolds
Karen Rinaldi
Erik Ringerud
Eliza Rothstein
Paige Russell
Paul Saffo
Brittany Salgado
Richard Schultz
Jason Stanford
The Tigress Pub
George Tobia
Bill Tonelli
Adrian Tuck
Tyson Tuttle
Josef Volman
D. S. Wang

Notes

Links in the bibliography and endnotes are shortened so they are easier to type. Just enter "storyofstori.es/" then the word after the slash (e.g., "storyofstori.es/fly") into your web browser. Please type the shortlinks exactly as they appear. They are case sensitive, i.e., storyofstori.es/fly will work, but storyofstori.es/Fly and storyofstori.es/FLY will not. Additional, more comprehensive notes are available at: storyofstori.es/endnotes.

Chapter 1: A Million Years of Stories

1. One million years ago: There is no consensus on when humans first controlled fire. The range is from 400,000 years ago to 1.3 million years ago. I am using one million years because it is a simple, round number and accurate enough for the purpose, and also because the hypothesis that nightfires were the first evolutionary stimulus for the development of storytelling likely requires nightfires to have existed for more than 400,000 years.
1. were too dim: Dunbar 2014, storyofstori.es/campfires; Dunbar et al. 2014, storyofstori.es/lucy.
1. vibration of exhalation: An exception is the vocalization of whales and dolphins.
1. wanted to communicate: Wiessner 2014, storyofstori.es/embers.
2. dance, mime, music: Brown 2000, storyofstori.es/models.
2. a subject, a verb, and an object: Although not necessarily in that order.
3. Individuals in groups: Kropotkin 1922, storyofstori.es/aid.
3. Good storytellers: See Smith et al. 2017, storyofstori.es/smith.
3. *Homo erectus*: Wrangham and Carmody 2010, storyofstori.es/fire. Another candidate species for the first storytellers is *Homo heidelbergensis*, which, at the time of writing, most specialists believe is the first descendant of *Homo erectus*, and the most recent common ancestor of modern humans and Neanderthals.
3. told stories too: See Hoffmann et al. 2018a, storyofstori.es/uth; and Hoffmann et al. 2018b, storyofstori.es/hoffmann.
4. the most common storytelling form: Ochs et al. 2009, storyofstori.es/ochs; and Jurafsky et al. 2009, storyofstori.es/style.

4	telling this story: Fairie 2023, storyofstori.es/artof.
4	conversation: US Bureau of Labor Statistics 2007, storyofstori.es/2006.
4	have lived alone: US Census Bureau 2023, storyofstori.es/alone.
5	two-thirds of our time: Dunbar et al. 1997, storyofstori.es/behavior.
5	started eating together: Dunbar 2017, storyofstori.es/bread.
6	supplemented our meals with: Hardy 2019, storyofstori.es/hardy.
6	psychoactive beverages: Rusch 2021, storyofstori.es/mead; McGovern et al. 2004, storyofstori.es/fermented; and McGovern 2003, storyofstori.es/wine.
6	substances change: Dunbar et al. 2018, storyofstori.es/primate.
6	Darkness amplifies: Dunbar 2017, storyofstori.es/bread.
6	"they're all people": Kahn 1960, storyofstori.es/friend.
7	"A story is an imitation": Aristotle 2006, storyofstori.es/poetics. Purists and scholars forgive me: I have edited and rearranged Aristotle here to keep things simple and clear. These quotations are taken from different parts of *Poetics*, and shown out of sequence. The original Butcher translations, in context, are: From Part VII: "Tragedy is an imitation of an action that is complete, and whole, and of a certain magnitude; for there may be a whole that is wanting in magnitude. A whole is that which has a beginning, a middle, and an end. A beginning is that which does not itself follow anything by causal necessity, but after which something naturally is or comes to be. An end, on the contrary, is that which itself naturally follows some other thing, either by necessity, or as a rule, but has nothing following it. A middle is that which follows something as some other thing follows it. A well constructed plot, therefore, must neither begin nor end at haphazard, but conform to these principles." From Part II: "Since the objects of imitation are men in action, and these men must be either of a higher or a lower type (for moral character mainly answers to these divisions, goodness and badness being the distinguishing marks of moral differences), it follows that we must represent men either as better than in real life, or as worse, or as they are. It is the same in painting. Polygnotus depicted men as nobler than they are, Pauson as less noble, Dionysius drew them true to life." From Part XV: "As in the structure of the plot, so too in the portraiture of character, the poet should always aim either at the necessary or the probable. Thus a person of a given character should speak or act in a given way, by the rule either of necessity or of probability; just as this event should follow that by necessary or probable sequence."
7	"It may safely be assumed": From *Introduction à l'analyse structurale des récits*, 1966, translated into English in Barthes and Duisit 1975, storyofstori.es/intro. As with the Aristotle quotation above, I have edited and rearranged this fairly brutally, for clarity and concision. The complete quotations from which I extracted these words are: "Since Propp, the character has kept challenging structural analysis with the same problem: on the one hand the characters (whatever the names given to them: *dramatis personae* or actants) constitute a of the necessary plane of the description, outside of which the commonplace 'actions' that are reported cease to be intelligible, so that it may safely be assumed that there is not a single narrative in the world without 'characters,' or at least without 'agents.'" / "To be more precise, the goal is to give a structural description to the chronological illusion; it is up to narrative logic to account for narrative time." / "To put it another way, the origin of a sequence is not the observation of reality, but the necessity to vary and to outgrow the first form that man ever came by, namely repetition: a sequence is essentially a whole within which nothing is repeated."
8	In 1944: Heider and Simmel 1944, storyofstori.es/simmel.
8	"A man": The quotation is edited for length. The complete version is: "A man has planned to meet a girl and the girl comes along with another man. The first man tells

the second to go; the second tells the first, and he shakes his head. Then the two men have a fight, and the girl starts to go into the room to get out of the way and hesitates and finally goes in. She apparently does not want to be with the first man. The first man follows her into the room after having left the second in a rather weakened condition leaning on the wall outside the room. The girl gets worried and races from one corner to the other in the far part of the room. Man number one, after being rather silent for a while, makes several approaches at her; but she gets to the corner across from the door, just as man number two is trying to open it. He evidently got banged around and is still weak from his efforts to open the door. The girl gets out of the room in a sudden dash just as man number two gets the door open. The two chase around the outside of the room together, followed by man number one. But they finally elude him and get away. The first man goes back and tries to open his door, but he is so blinded by rage and frustration that he cannot open it. So he butts it open and in really mad dash around the room he breaks in first one wall and then another."

8   between three people: The study comprised three slightly different experiments.
9   biologist E. O. Wilson: See Wilson 2012, storyofstori.es/wilson. Others disagree: See, for example, Gintis 2012, storyofstori.es/titans.
9   About half: Frith and Frith 2007, storyofstori.es/frith; and Frith 2007, storyofstori.es/socialbrain.
9   almost all of it evolved: Neubauer et al. 2018, storyofstori.es/shape.
10 a very specific, story-centric way: Wyer and Srull 1986, storyofstori.es/human.
10 only briefly: Sperling 1960, storyofstori.es/brief.
10 Reid Hastie: Pennington and Hastie 1993, storyofstori.es/juror; and Hastie et al. 2002, storyofstori.es/jury.
10 repeatedly: Sixty-nine times in all.
10 life in prison: Massachusetts Sentencing Commission 2017, storyofstori.es/mass.
11 aggregated the evidence: Pennington and Hastie call this the "story model."
12 stories like this: Hastie et al. 2002, storyofstori.es/jury; and Pennington and Hastie 1992, storyofstori.es/evidence.
12 a new field of psychological study: Weiner 2008, storyofstori.es/reflections.
14 when we are social: Kemp and Guastella 2011, storyofstori.es/kemp.
15 Intestinal epithelial cells: Spalding et al. 2005, storyofstori.es/dating.
15 our skeleton: Dimitriou et al. 2011, storyofstori.es/bone.
15 which changes too: For example, DNA can change due to replication errors.
15 When we were children: Piattelli-Palmarini et al. 2009, storyofstori.es/basque.
15 Toi Derricotte: Derricotte 2016, storyofstori.es/i.
16 *Harvard Business Review*: Specifically, Hammer 1990, storyofstori.es/hammer.
16 pebble-glass door: Throughout the book, some details, like this one, are imagined.
17 a billion dollars: unless otherwise specified, "dollars" means "US dollars" throughout.
17 from the factory: In Yizhuang, see storyofstori.es/market for the precise location. Throughout the book, biographical details about Wang (such as this one) are from personal and private conversations between D. S. Wang and the author.
18 In those days: Today China has a state pensions system. OECD 2021, storyofstori.es/pensions.
18 $12 million: One yuan in 1992 was worth about 37 cents in 2020.
19 some psychologists: For example, Ajzen and Fishbein 1975, storyofstori.es/attribution; and Fischoff et al. 1978, storyofstori.es/bayes.
20 a story: See, for example, Sarbin 1986, storyofstori.es/bees; and Bruner 2009, storyofstori.es/minds.
20 of Technology: Ariely et al. 2008, storyofstori.es/legos. Simmons et al. 2023 (storyofstori.es/data) claims that Ariely faked data.

20   nineteenth toy: the math is wrong in Ariely's paper, which says "The subjects were paid $2.00 for the first Bionicle, $1.89 (11¢ less) for the second one, and so on linearly. For the 20th, as well as for any subsequent Bionicles, they received $0.02." This linear 11¢ reduction gets to -$0.09 at the twentieth toy, hence the correction in the text.

21   seven toys on average: Rounded from 7.2 and 10.6. The payment amounts have been changed from the original paper because they are inconsistent with paper's own description of the payment system, per the previous note. I have assumed the number of toys is correct and the payment is incorrect; it could be the other way around.

21   basic needs are met: Autin and Allan 2019, storyofstori.es/meaning.

22   we forget: Ebbinghaus 1913, storyofstori.es/memory.

22   Our forgetting gets worse: Allport and Postman 1945, storyofstori.es/basic; and Allport and Postman 1946, storyofstori.es/rumor.

22   great confidence: Schacter et al. 1997, storyofstori.es/memories; Schacter 2018, storyofstori.es/sins; and de Vito et al. 2010, storyofstori.es/false.

22   can store: Dudai 1997, storyofstori.es/big. Simplified by taking the midpoint and rounding.

22   computers compress: Simplifications of Huffman coding and a Bezier curve.

22   ways to remember: Rote learning seems to require written texts. Hunter 1984, storyofstori.es/recall.

22   much the same thing: Levin 1971 (storyofstori.es/poetry) discusses compression in poetry.

24   make perception easier: Enquist and Arak 1994, storyofstori.es/symmetry; and Arak and Enquist 1993, storyofstori.es/hidden.

24   "with which we are endowed": I made this gender neutral because we are no longer in the nineteenth century. Darwin used the abbreviation "Ms" for "man's" in this quotation. The original is "As neither the enjoyment nor the capacity of producing musical notes are faculties of the least direct use to man in reference to Ms ordinary habits of life, they must be ranked amongst the most mysterious with which he is endowed." Darwin 2008, 333, storyofstori.es/descent.

24   singing's children: This is not a novel observation. See Lomax 2017, storyofstori.es/folk.

25   effect of the evolution: See Roederer 1984, 352, storyofstori.es/search.

25   two million years ago: Nishimura et al. 2022, storyofstori.es/loss.

25   primates developed: Nishimura et al. 2022.

25   more complex: A simpler larynx gave better voice control. Nishimura et al. 2022.

25   the first human species: A simplification. There is no consensus on the first *Homo*.

26   also process music: Patel 2003, storyofstori.es/syntax.

26   electrical responses: I am simplifying. See Patel et al. 1998, storyofstori.es/patel.

26   uses the same: Schendel and Palmer 2007, storyofstori.es/effects; Bregman 1994, storyofstori.es/scene; and Morris et al. 1995, storyofstori.es/dylan.

26   almost everyone can remember: Trehub 2003, storyofstori.es/good.

26   of a sound: Technically, of a *tone*, which is essentially a steady sound.

27   fundamental frequency: Berg et al. 2017, storyofstori.es/voice. These numbers are rounded.

27   waves per second: I am using this instead of Hertz as a simplification.

27   The pitch of our voices: Bryant and Haselton 2009, storyofstori.es/cues.

27   pitch preferences: Puts 2005, storyofstori.es/puts.

27   mate choice: Apicella and Feinberg 2009, storyofstori.es/voicepitch.

27   reproductive success: Apicella et al. 2007, storyofstori.es/predicts.

27   telephone anyway: Stevens and Davis 1938, storyofstori.es/hearing. This is "the missing fundamental."

27	of the harmonics: Cariani and Delgutte 1996, storyofstori.es/pitch; and Shackleton and Carlyon 1994, storyofstori.es/role.
28	262 waves per second: This explanation uses A440 tuning and rounds the Hz slightly (for example, middle C is around 261.63 Hz in A440) to keep the arithmetic simple.
28	sound musical: Simplified by omitting E and G.
28	without having to store: McPherson and McDermott 2020, storyofstori.es/time.
28	unfamiliar songs: Wallace 1994, storyofstori.es/melody.
28	after last hearing them: Bartlett and Snelus 1980, storyofstori.es/lifespan.
28	lyrics and melodies: Cuddy and Duffin 2005, storyofstori.es/cuddy.
28	rendered irretrievable: Roy et al. 2016, storyofstori.es/mouse.
28	pubs and clubs: Pawley and Müllensiefen 2012, storyofstori.es/singalong.
29	Its story was inspired: There were other inspirations too. See Bon Jovi 2020, storyofstori.es/access.
29	"their best storytelling": I have edited the second Bon Jovi quote for length, and taken the first slightly out of context. Bon Jovi is talking to Dome about a different song, "Wanted Dead or Alive," when he says: "We were thinking of songs like 'Turn the Page' by Bob Seger, and how those songs were storytellers doing their best storytelling." Later in the interview, when talking about "Livin' on a Prayer," Bon Jovi says, "I am really proud of that one, because it goes back to the storytelling roots that I was talking about . . . I wanted to relate those stories to people I'd gone to high school with. Some got married right out of high school. Some joined the service, and now were working somewhere. I wanted to tell their stories, because they could've been me, if I hadn't learned to play guitar." Dome 2024, storyofstori.es/dome.
29	which has effects: The social effects of oxytocin are complex. Bartz et al. 2011, storyofstori.es/social.
29	increasing generosity: Zak et al. 2007, storyofstori.es/zak.
29	social behavior: Froemke and Young 2021, storyofstori.es/oxy.
29	and trust: Kosfeld et al. 2005, storyofstori.es/trust.
29	and synchronizing: Kreutz 2014, storyofstori.es/singing; and Singer 1999, storyofstori.es/singer.
29	Singing in a group: Some spontaneous group songs are exhortations, not stories.
29	bonds strangers quickly: Pearce et al. 2015, storyofstori.es/ice.
29	strengthens: Chittar et al. 2023, storyofstori.es/coalition.
29	reduce pain intensity: Irons et al. 2020, storyofstori.es/irons.
29	increase pain thresholds: Weinstein et al. 2016, storyofstori.es/group; Kreutz et al. 2004, storyofstori.es/choir.
29	all group singing: Bailey and Davidson 2005, storyofstori.es/groupsinging.
29	*bad* group singing: Pawley and Müllensiefen 2012, storyofstori.es/singalong.
29	community and fellowship: Pawley and Müllensiefen.
29	sing *any* song: Pawley and Müllensiefen.
30	Anglo-Norman word: *Entretenir* is also used in Middle French.
31	his third major work: Darwin 1898, storyofstori.es/expression.
31	"As long as humans": Edited for length, with "emotion" substituted for Darwin's word, "Expression," for clarity and simplicity, and "humans" substituted for "man" for inclusiveness. The complete, original quotation is: "No doubt as long as man and all other animals are viewed as independent creations, an effectual stop is put to our natural desire to investigate as far as possible the causes of Expression. By this doctrine, anything and everything can be equally well explained; and it has proved as pernicious with respect to Expression as to every other branch of natural history. With mankind some expressions, such as the bristling of the hair under the influence of extreme terror, or the un-covering of the teeth under

that of furious rage, can hardly be understood, except on the belief that man once existed in a much lower and animal-like condition. The community of certain expressions in distinct though allied species, as in the movements of the same facial muscles during laughter by man and by various monkeys, is rendered somewhat more intelligible, if we believe in their descent from a common progenitor. He who admits on general grounds that the structure and habits of all animals have been gradually evolved, will look at the whole subject of Expression in a new and interesting light." Darwin 1898, 12.

31   one of the nine million: Mora et al. 2011, storyofstori.es/mora. Louca et al. 2019 says 2.2 to 4.3 million, storyofstori.es/louca.
32   half a billion years ago: All three groups date back to the Cambrian period.
32   far more often: Al Khatib et al. 2017, storyofstori.es/khatib1; Al Khatib et al. 2016, storyofstori.es/khatib2; and Freling et al. 2020, storyofstori.es/freling.
32   from bacteria: Plutchik 2001, storyofstori.es/nature.
33   same emotion: This is easier to see in animals. Mateo 2010, storyofstori.es/calls; and Gill and Bierema 2013, storyofstori.es/alarm.
33   years of feeling: This also solves the nonsensical "paradox of fiction" proposed in Radford and Weston 1975, storyofstori.es/radford.

Chapter 2: The Eye of Your Mind

34   there were *marks*: Perrin 2011, storyofstori.es/marks.
34   sometimes deliberately: Heymann 2006, storyofstori.es/primates.
34   we made marks: Marks also became carving. Conard 2003, storyofstori.es/ivory; and Iversen et al. 2025, storyofstori.es/sun.
34   seventy-five thousand years: Henshilwood et al. 2018, storyofstori.es/abstract.
34   four pigs: Brumm et al. 2021, storyofstori.es/oldest. "At least three, and possibly four, individual [pigs]."
34   their exact species: Brumm et al. identifies the animals as Celebes warty pigs.
35   to help tell a story: Brumm et al.
35   Varaha: Sharma 2007, storyofstori.es/motif.
35   Erymanthian boar: First recorded in *Trachiniae* by Sophocles. Coleridge 1893, storyofstori.es/pigs.
35   the parable of the prodigal son: Luke 15:15–16, English Standard Version.
35   King Pig: Straparola and Morlini 1901, storyofstori.es/nights.
35   Zhu Bajie: Yu 2013, storyofstori.es/west.
35   this little piggy: Roud, n.d., storyofstori.es/piggy.
35   *Animal Farm*: Orwell 1945, storyofstori.es/orwell.
35   *Charlotte's Web*: White et al. 2017, storyofstori.es/web.
35   Babe the sheep-pig: King-Smith and Rayner 1995, storyofstori.es/babe.
35   Pumbaa: Allers 1994, storyofstori.es/lion.
35   Peppa Pig: Astley 2004, storyofstori.es/peppa.
35   pigs and piglins: Persson 2011, storyofstori.es/minecraft.
35   change and move: Wachtel 1993, storyofstori.es/cave; Giedion 2023, storyofstori.es/eternal; and Azéma and Rivère 2012, storyofstori.es/animation.
36   colonial chauvinism: See Bednarik 1995, storyofstori.es/concept; and Bednarik 2004, storyofstori.es/evidence.
36   ancestors spread: The Southern Dispersal Scenario. See also Pan-African Model.
36   scientists at the University of Minnesota: Naselaris et al. 2015, storyofstori.es/decode.
36   We have screens in our brains: This metaphor is from Kosslyn 1980, storyofstori.es/image; and Kosslyn 1994, storyofstori.es/brain.

37	the same way: Even blind people see things like echolocation on screens in their brains.
37	"one stationary eye": Dickens's description of Jack Bunsby in *Dombey and Son*. Dickens 1848, storyofstori.es/dombey.
38	black bears: Burst and Pelton 1983, storyofstori.es/bears.
38	desert ants: Steck et al. 2011, storyofstori.es/ants.
38	wildcats: Piñeiro and Barja 2012, storyofstori.es/wildcats.
38	wolves: Barja et al. 2004, storyofstori.es/crossroads.
38	making intentionally: See, for example, d'Errico et al. 2012, storyofstori.es/san.
38	intentional marking started: See, for example, Bednarik 1995, storyofstori.es/concept.
38	used only occasionally: Krause et al. 2018, storyofstori.es/animal. With thanks to David A. Leavens.
38	ravens: Pika and Bugnyar 2011, storyofstori.es/ravens.
38	an essential element of human communication: Morrison 2020, storyofstori.es/index.
38	uniquely human visual signals: There is some debate. Cooperrider et al. 2018, storyofstori.es/pointing.
39	two hundred billion pictures: One hundred and twenty billion people, with five drawings per three people.
39	our pictures: Calculated by analyzing the Met Collection. See storyofstori.es/met.
40	nonsense: Nisbet, among others, tried to kill the myth without success. Nisbet 1973, storyofstori.es/myth.
40	first told in 1860: The name was popularized in Michelet and Smith 1845, storyofstori.es/france.
40	*The Civilization of the Renaissance in Italy*: Burckhardt 2019, storyofstori.es/jacob.
40	the Paleo-Inuit: Paleo-Inuit is not accepted by all Indigenous groups. Friesen 2015, storyofstori.es/inuit.
41	exceptionally cold winter: Flis 2021, storyofstori.es/winter; and Brooks 1929, storyofstori.es/brooks.
41	Le Perreux-sur-Marne: Danchev 2021, storyofstori.es/magritte. Magritte was at 101 Avenue de Rosny.
41	the Chacom pipe company: My best guess. Thanks to Scott Thile for the help.
41	about a hundred francs: Secretary of the Treasury 1922, storyofstori.es/imports; and Challis 2019, storyofstori.es/currency.
41	a gallery in New York: Julien Levy, 602 Madison Avenue, showed an English version.
41	"A painter's technical skill": Edited for length and clarity. The unedited excerpt is: "René Magritte was a thorough-going surréaliste before Dali began at all. That being the case, it is only fair to credit Dali with having brought to the exploitation of an already launched idea a painter's technical skill that is almost entirely wanting in the work of his predecessor [Magritte], whose canvases are for the most part arid with respect to those qualities we call esthetic." Jewell 1936, storyofstori.es/show.
41	Another gallery: Sidney Janis, 15 East 57th Street.
41	"Visitors are likely": This is two excerpts added together and edited for clarity. The unedited excerpts are: "Visitors are likely to be divided at once into groups that automatically hate or respond to this work." And, later, after describing some of the other paintings: "A large poster-like painting of a pipe is called 'The Treachery of Images' and bears the inscription 'This is not a pipe.' So—." Devree 1954, storyofstori.es/devree.
42	sexagenarian art critic: Devree was sixty-three years old when he wrote this review.

42 a periodical read by artists: *ART Digest* was called *The Art Digest* until at least 1955.
42 "achieves startling results": I edited this for length and clarity. The complete sentences are: "In Rene Magritte's series, 'Word vs. Image' of 1928–30, on view at Sidney Janis until March 20, the surrealist's efforts to disturb conventional points of view achieve startling results. For here, with a method and logic distressing in its conclusions, Magritte has challenged our casual acceptance of the identity of a word with the image for which it stands. . . . The lucidity and straightforwardness of his organization is not only striking visually; it enforces the disarming simplicity of his attack on basic principles of common sense. Leaving the show, it is almost a relief to be back in a familiar world. Yet Magritte's lesson is so potent that, if properly learned, we will never take this familiar world quite so for granted again." Rosenblum 1954, storyofstori.es/grammar.
43 wrote an entire book: Foucault 1983, storyofstori.es/pipe.
43 often translates: Last checked on Google Translate in 2024. Sometimes says "pipe."
44 his latest: *Untitled*, also called *The Sex Pipe*, 1943, Magritte Museum, Brussels.
44 *sapeur Camember*: Christophe 2016, storyofstori.es/camember.
44 ends a story: These are a variation of a technique called *cul-de-lampe*.
44 one of his many erotic drawings: Earendil discusses Magritte's erotica in Earendil 2021, storyofstori.es/erotic.
44 the same flying pipe: Corbett includes a reproduction of this image. Corbett 2011, storyofstori.es/dirty.
44 "the intersection of representation": Foucault 1983, storyofstori.es/pipe.
44 dick joke: Delvaux: "*Ceci n'est pas une pipe, c'est un gag!*" Danchev 2021, storyofstori.es/magritte.
45 All humans: Gahlinger 2000, storyofstori.es/cabin.
45 results from disagreement: This is the "sensory conflict theory." Oman 1982, storyofstori.es/oman.
45 different motion sensing systems: Koch et al. 2018, storyofstori.es/motion.
46 expel neurotoxins: Treisman 1977, storyofstori.es/sickness. See also Oman 1982.
46 What they *don't* do, ever: Dickinson et al. 2009, storyofstori.es/user. This is the "interface theory of perception."
47 among birds: Matsuoka 1980, storyofstori.es/titmice, and Møller 1988, storyofstori.es/means.
47 If you are an antbird: Munn 1986, storyofstori.es/birds.
47 In his dialogue *Theaetetus*: Plato 1906, storyofstori.es/the.
47 "When the jurors": Plato 1906.
48 "Thinking about knowledge": Edited for length and clarity. The complete quotation is: "Subsequent thinking about knowledge, at both the casual and the philosophical level, has been for the most part remarkably consistent with this intuition; either it has ignored testimony altogether or it has been cursory and dismissive. Modern epistemologists tirelessly pursue the nature and role of memory, perception, inductive and deductive reasoning but devote no analysis and argument to testimony although *prima facie* it belongs on this list. After all, when we inquire into the basis of some claim by asking: 'Why do you believe that?' or 'How do you know that?' the answer 'Jones told me' can be just as appropriate as 'I saw it' or 'I remember it,' 'It follows from this' or 'It usually happens like that.' I shall argue that this tradition of neglect is a bad one and that our reliance upon testimony is too important and too fundamental to merit such casual treatment." Coady 1992, 6, storyofstori.es/coady.
48 Most of us: Levine 2007, storyofstori.es/Blackculture. Adjusted to be gender inclusive.
49 Half of all homes have a dog: Martyn 2025, storyofstori.es.com/pets.
49 is its nose: Syrotuck 2000, storyofstori.es/scent. Much of this was first published in Ashton 2013, storyofstori.es/wolf.

50   A dog's vision: Miller and Murphy 1995, storyofstori.es/vision.
50   in two colors: Dogs have *dichromatic* color vision. See Neitz 1989, storyofstori.es/color.
50   blue, yellow, and white: Miller and Murphy 1995.
50   indistinguishable to us: Orbeli 1908, storyofstori.es/leon, in English in Yerkes and Morgulis 1909, storyofstori.es/yerkes.
50   an amplifier of light: Note this is an analogy. See Miller and Murphy 1995.
50   up to five kilohertz: Younger people can hear higher frequencies than this.
50   up to fifty kilohertz: Table 1 in Heffner 1983, storyofstori.es/doghearing.
50   made by prey animals: Despite the beliefs of some dog owners, dogs cannot sense impending earthquakes. Buskirk et al. 1981, storyofstori.es/quake.
50   Rats, for example: Knutson et al. 2002, storyofstori.es/rats.
51   contain a dozen muscles: Tiger 2013, storyofstori.es/ear.
51   locate precisely: This ability begins at sixteen days. Ashmead et al. 1986, storyofstori.es/ashmead.
51   wolves have: Mech and Janssens 2021, storyofstori.es/mech; and Peters and Mech 1975, storyofstori.es/wolves.
52   bones: d'Errico et al. 2012, storyofstori.es/san; and Marshack 1971, storyofstori.es/upper.
52   branches: Baxter 1989, storyofstori.es/tally.
52   bodies: Lagercrantz 1973, storyofstori.es/counting; and Vaughan 2007, storyofstori.es/scars. See also Leviticus 19:28.
52   as thick as the palm of a hand: Amt et al. 2007, storyofstori.es/amt.
52   amazed Marco Polo: Baxter 1989. The idea that Polo was in Yunnan is from Vogel 2012, storyofstori.es/marco.
53   caused a fire: Shenton 2012, storyofstori.es/burned.
53   forgotten tallying: Tallying is still used by Indigenous peoples in, for example, Africa.
53   stockholders and stock exchanges: Baxter 1989.
53   Greek for tally: The Greeks expanded *symbolon* (σύμβολο) to tokens and tickets.
53   the split tally as a metaphor: Some disagree. Harris 2005, storyofstori.es/rethinking; and Whitaker 2002, storyofstori.es/aristotle.
53   called proto-writing: See also *quipu*, *wampum*, and uses of cowrie mussels.
53   was never their purpose: See Perrin 2011, storyofstori.es/marks.
53   languageless writing: Harris calls this non-glottic writing. Harris 2005.
54   emoji: Todorović 2017, storyofstori.es/emoji. Todorović also notes similarities between proto-writing and emoji.
54   cannot be *proto*: See, for example, "prototype," which this most certainly is not.
54   counting and accounting: Nissen 1986, storyofstori.es/texts. Nissen is writing about cuneiform, but the point still holds.
54   more efficient writing tools: Nissen 1986.
54   some languageless writing systems: For example, Proto-cuneiform.
54   over fifteen hundred signs: Damerow 1999, storyofstori.es/problem.
55   a million square miles: From FAO 2009, storyofstori.es/FAO.
55   the occasional rumble of tectonic plates: Aqrawi 2001, storyofstori.es/change.
55   In Syriac: Classical Syriac was spoken around Edessa from at least 100 CE.
55   Beth Nahrain: Sometimes "land of rivers." Classical Syriac: ܒܶܝܬ ܢܰܗܪܝܢ or *Bêṯ Nahrayn*.
56   Until 4000 BCE: Aqrawi 2001, storyofstori.es/change.
56   and nomadic fishers, gatherers: Van De Mieroop 1997, storyofstori.es/city; and Oates 1973, storyofstori.es/oates.
56   the sea receded: Aqrawi 2001, storyofstori.es/change.

308   Notes

56   Irrigation farmers: Van De Mieroop 1997, storyofstori.es/city.
56   traded surplus food: Van De Mieroop 1997.
56   recent mutations: Flannery 1973, storyofstori.es/agriculture.
56   emmer: Also known as hulled wheat. Also mentioned: common wheat.
56   almost five hundred hectares: Van De Mieroop 1997, storyofstori.es/city.
56   rose to forty thousand: Nissen 2003, storyofstori.es/art.
56   recorded them on tally sticks: Nissen et al. 1993, storyofstori.es/bookkeeping; and Halloran 2009, storyofstori.es/sticks.
57   than a smartphone: The iPhone 12 Pro Max is 6.3 x 3 inches. See storyofstori.es/tablets.
57   "wedge-writing": The history of the word *cuneiform* is discussed in Funk 2014, storyofstori.es/funk.
57   "according to the kiln-fired writing": Levey 1959, storyofstori.es/clay.
57   baked them: Læssøe 2014, storyofstori.es/people.
57   everything in clay: One exception is a few tablets made of gypsum. Nissen 1986, storyofstori.es/texts.
57   counting tokens: See Nissen 1986, storyofstori.es/texts; and Nissen et al. 1993, storyofstori.es/bookkeeping.
58   we do not know how long: This order of development is inferred. Nissen 1986, storyofstori.es/texts.
58   represented numbers: Initially quantities of specific things—for example, "five sheep."

Chapter 3: Pictures of Sounds

59   a particle of chert: This description is based on Sneed and Folk 1958, storyofstori.es/pebbles.
59   a smooth, spheroidal pebble: For pebble shapes, see Durian et al. 2006, storyofstori.es/pebble.
60   and our technology changes us: This sentence also appears in Ashton 2015, storyofstori.es/fly.
60   Languageless writing gradually led: Languageless writing is also called *pictographic* or *ideographic writing*.
60   excavated their clay from quarries: Specifically Sumerians and/or Akkadians.
60   written sign: Levey 1959, storyofstori.es/clay. See Studevent-Hickman 2007 (storyofstori.es/90) on why cuneiform was rotated.
60   started this way: This is now called logographic writing.
60   by constant use: Changizi and Shimojo 2005, storyofstori.es/character; and Kramer 1961, storyofstori.es/history.
60   only thirty or so sounds: UCLA Phonological Segment Inventory Database, storyofstori.es/ucla. Definitions of *phoneme* vary.
61   In Sumerian: This example is based on one in Woods 2020, storyofstori.es/emergence.
61   the sound "shar": The IPA for this is "ʃar," but it is transliterated as "šar."
61   rotated ninety degrees: More specifically: almost all cuneiform after about 2200 BCE.
61   sound of that word: Woods 2020 (storyofstori.es/emergence) discusses sounds in Sumerian cuneiform.
61   the sound "si": This example is from Cooper 1993, storyofstori.es/babel.
61   next to each other: This is known as the rebus principle.
61   written languages: There is no consensus on Proto-Elamite, Indus, and Linear A/B.
61   This was no coincidence: Daniels 1992, storyofstori.es/segmental.
61   2285 BCE: Delnero 2016, storyofstori.es/scholarship; Dalley 2000, storyofstori.es/myths; De Shong Meador 2000, storyofstori.es/lady; and Wolkstein 1983, storyofstori.es/1983.

61   a three-hundred-year-old temple: Woolley 2013, storyofstori.es/ur; and Weadock 1975, storyofstori.es/giparu.
61   Enheduanna: *En* is an honorific, so her name was Heduanna. Howard 2017, storyofstori.es/howard.
61   to tell a story: Hallo and van Dijk 1968, storyofstori.es/exaltation.
62   "You drew me": De Shong Meador 2000, storyofstori.es/lady.
62   "cloaks the sun": The next three lines may allude to sexual assault. Graham 2018, storyofstori.es/graham.
62   how animals and humans move: Muybridge 1888, storyofstori.es/locomotion.
62   understanding the behavior of electrons: Shiers 1974, storyofstori.es/braun; and Campbell-Swinton 1908, storyofstori.es/distant.
62   moon god Nanna: She was also daughter of Sargon, ruler of the Akkadian Empire.
62   can typically reach: Dunbar et al. 1995, storyofstori.es/size.
62   ten people at a time: Bird et al. 2019, storyofstori.es/foragers.
62   Ur's twenty thousand residents: Thompson 2004, storyofstori.es/thompson, citing Modelski 2003, storyofstori.es/cities.
63   actual events: Hallo and van Dijk 1968, storyofstori.es/exaltation.
63   Lugal-Ane: Skogemann in Carpani 2022, storyofstori.es/daughter; and Helle 2023, storyofstori.es/form.
63   his version of the story: If Lugal-Ane wrote his story, we have not yet discovered it.
63   was deposed: Jacobsen 1978 (storyofstori.es/times) has more about the historicity of Lugal-Ane.
64   every mummy movie ever made: For example, Dix in *The Mummy* (1911).
64   a confusing discovery: Petrie et al. 1906, storyofstori.es/sinai.
64   Deep in a turquoise mine: Barlow 1951, storyofstori.es/barlow.
64   Hilda Petrie: Hilda Petrie, née Urlin, was as important as Flinders but got less credit.
64   people like himself: For instance, Petrie was a close associate of eugenicist Francis Galton.
64   fascinating ancient civilizations: Said 1995 (storyofstori.es/said) describes colonial attitudes to Asia.
65   became ever more common: Google's ngram viewer at storyofstori.es/ngram shows this rise clearly.
65   an alphabet far older: Parker 2022, storyofstori.es/parker. The inscriptions are now dated to c. 1800 BCE.
65   Asians, not Europeans: The Sinai Peninsula is generally considered to be in Asia.
65   the last continent to get a writing system: More precisely, the last densely settled agricultural continent. Sumer did so around 3000 BCE; Egypt, 2800 BCE; China, 1300 BCE; and the Mayans, 300 BCE.
66   Until at least the 1980s: Jeffery and Boardman 1982, storyofstori.es/greek; and Millard 1986, storyofstori.es/infancy.
67   we have found thousands: Nissen et al. 1988, storyofstori.es/early.
67   evolved from: things: *pictographic*; words: *logographic*; syllables: *syllabaries*.
67   In Chinese: Standard Chinese, also known as Mandarin or Standard Beijing Mandarin.
67   syllables are almost always: Třísková 2011 (storyofstori.es/mandarin) is an introduction to Chinese syllables.
67   seldom uses consonant clusters: Old Chinese may have used clusters. Baxter 2014, storyofstori.es/baxter.
67   rarely appear in Chinese: For a list of generally agreed consonant clusters, see Algeo 1978, storyofstori.es/clusters.
68   it typically alternates vowels and consonants: Edgerton 1947, storyofstori.es/vowel; and Allen 2020, storyofstori.es/phono.

68	After infancy: Tsuji and Cristia 2014 (storyofstori.es/meta) describes vowel perception in infants.
68	closing the airway: One exception: *h* is a consonant made with an open vocal tract.
68	over three hundred thousand single-syllable words: Kaufman 2018, storyofstori.es/one.
68	four tones: Level tone, rising tone, dip tone, and departing tone. Some add neutral tone.
68	the consonant "m": The equivalent phonemes are [m] and [ã].
68	can make four words: This example is adapted from Haupt 1917, storyofstori.es/tones.
68	somewhat similarly: It's complicated. Haupt 1917, storyofstori.es/tones; and Campbell and Kaufman 1985, storyofstori.es/mayan.
68	there are only so many syllables: Fudge 1969 (storyofstori.es/syllables) discusses syllables in some depth.
68	humidity: Egypt was humid when Old Egyptian, but not hieroglyphs, evolved.
68	indigenous tone languages: American tone languages are from southern latitudes.
68	only spoken in humid places: Everett et al. 2015, storyofstori.es/climate.
69	alters the way they vibrate: Hemler et al. 1997, storyofstori.es/air.
69	*jitter*: *Jitter* means that the frequency varies; *shimmer* means that the amplitude varies. Teixeira et al. 2013, storyofstori.es/jitter.
69	a dry climate: Europe has one tone language, Shtokavian from the Ottoman Empire.
69	tones in Europe: Everett et al. 2015, storyofstori.es/climate; Everett et al. 2016, storyofstori.es/tone; Everett 2017, storyofstori.es/vowels; and Everett 2021, storyofstori.es/sounds.
69	The air was too dry: This will ruffle feathers, but is where the data leads.
69	In 1400 BCE: The dates of Linear B are debated. Gere 2010, storyofstori.es/gere.
69	picture-based writing: Linear B, which was, more technically, logographic.
69	entirely for accounting: Chadwick in Hooker et al. 1990, storyofstori.es/hooker.
70	civilization collapsed: Knapp and Manning 2016, storyofstori.es/crisis. This is known as the Late Bronze Age Collapse.
70	how it happened: Millard 1986, storyofstori.es/infancy; Daniels 1992, storyofstori.es/segmental; Colless 2010, storyofstori.es/proto; and Colless 2014, storyofstori.es/alphabet.
70	Sometime around 1800 BCE: This date is based on Parker 2022, storyofstori.es/parker.
70	their own language: "Canaanites" spoke several languages. See Healey 1990, storyofstori.es/abc.
70	to represent those sounds: This was the first use of a principle linguists now call *acrophony*.
70	not also words: See Harris 1989 (storyofstori.es/roy) on "reduction of the basic number of symbols."
70	around three thousand syllables: Barker 2016, storyofstori.es/how. Barker's number is about 2,750; I rounded it up for simplicity.
71	thirty-five to forty-four distinct sounds: Bizzocchi 2017, storyofstori.es/phonemes.
71	just thirty-two characters: Gardiner 1916, storyofstori.es/egyptian.
71	143 nations: The official script of 131 nations and the co-official script of 12 more.
71	boomerang: For more about Egyptian boomerangs see Rivers 1883, storyofstori.es/boomerang
71	Catholic Church: From when the first bishop of Rome was also the pope.
71	alphabet spread: Woudhuizen 2006, storyofstori.es/transmission; and Bourogiannis and Ioannou 2012, storyofstori.es/cos.

72	replace the Athenians' own alphabet: The Athenians used the Attic alphabet.
72	The decree was an act of standardization: D'Angour 1999, storyofstori.es/reform.
72	standards of 1953: The NTSC standard was announced in December 1953.
72	available in 1995: In 1995 the NSF stopped sponsoring the NSFNET backbone.
73	driver controls: For an excellent history of automobile innovation, see Flink 1990, storyofstori.es/auto.
73	Four out of every five Greek vases: Immerwahr 1973, storyofstori.es/more.
73	epics *Iliad* and *Odyssey*: Goold 1960, storyofstori.es/homer. These were likely told orally until written in the 400s BCE.
73	he or she: Butler 1897 (storyofstori.es/butler) and Dalby 2006 (storyofstori.es/dalby) make the case that Homer was a woman.
73	The decree of Eucleides: Also known as the decree of Archinus.
73	First Lord of the Treasury: The official title of the Prime Minister until 1905.
73	slave owner: Gladstone's father owned more than 2,500 slaves.
73	four-hour cabinet meeting: Gladstone and Matthew 1982, storyofstori.es/diaries.
74	Society of Biblical Archaeology: 9 Conduit Street, W1. See storyofstori.es/9 for images.
74	nineteenth-century Chelsea: Chelsea was a poor part of London into the 1970s.
74	have inferred that the earth is about: Cregan-Reid 2015, storyofstori.es/discovering.
74	the last true king: Ashurbanipal was the last major king of the neo-Assyrian Empire.
75	first autobiography: The inscriptions meet the definition of an autobiography.
75	of Massachusetts: Elam is 6,900 square miles; Massachusetts (land only), 7,840.
75	"With the support of the gods": Novotny and Jeffers 2018, storyofstori.es/inscriptions. Edited for length and clarity from Ashurbanipal 10. The complete quotation is: iv 36–43) "With the support of the [great] gods, my lords, I entered the land Ela[m], brought about their (the Elamites') defeat countless (times), (and) marched about triumphantly. Ummanaldašu (Ḫumban-ḫaltaš III) became frightened by the assault of my mighty battle array, fled naked, and took to the mountain(s)." iv 44–51a) "I conquered fourteen fortified cities, his royal residence(s), and small(er) settlements, which were without number, together with twenty villages, in the district of the city Ḫunn[ir], (which is) on the border of the city Ḫidalu. I destroyed (and) demolished the city Bašimu and the villages in its environs." iv 51b–v 8) "As for the people living inside them, I annihilated them."
75	120 miles: *qaq-qa-ru*, which refers to units of about two miles.
75	first great library: Whether it was one location / created by Ashurbanipal is debated.
75	which he took forcibly: Frame and George 2005, storyofstori.es/royal.
75	first in 614 BCE: Dalley 1993, storyofstori.es/612.
75	around a hundred thousand: Damrosch 2007, storyofstori.es/buried.
76	a menial employee: Damrosch 2007, storyofstori.es/buried.
76	A new form of amusement: Shefrin 2003, storyofstori.es/such; and Norgate 2007, storyofstori.es/borders.
76	"He acquired gradually": Rawlinson 1898, storyofstori.es/henry.
77	600 BCE: This assumes the Torah was written in the Babylonian captivity. Knauf in Lipschitz et al. 2006, storyofstori.es/impact.
77	an alphabetic script: Assumes the Qur'an was written c. AH 30/650 CE. Sinai 2014, storyofstori.es/when.
77	Writing first appeared: Brahmi. Indus and Harappan may not be writing systems.
77	around 350 BCE: See Coningham et al. 1996, storyofstori.es/india.
77	at the turn of the first millennium: Plofker et al. 2017, storyofstori.es/response.

77   about four hundred years old: Prebish 2008, storyofstori.es/cooking. See also Bechert 1991, storyofstori.es/buddha.
77   likely inspired by Hinduism: Gombrich 1988, storyofstori.es/began.
77   such as the *Bhagavad Gītā*: Sargeant et al. 2010, storyofstori.es/gita.
78   persists two thousand years later: There is map showing the main religion in each country at Pew 2017, storyofstori.es/map.
79   "Write all the words that I have spoken to you in a book": Jeremiah 30:2 (כְּתָב־ לְךָ֗ אֵ֧ת כָּל־ הַדְּבָרִ֛ים אֲשֶׁר־ דִּבַּ֥רְתִּי אֵלֶ֖יךָ אֶל־ סֵֽפֶר׃).
79   "The writing was God's writing": Exodus 32:16 (הַמִּכְתָּ֗ב מִכְתַּ֤ב אֱלֹהִים֙).
79   "Oh that they were inscribed in a book": Job 19:23 (וְֽיִכָּתְב֥וּן מִ֑י־יִתֵּ֣ן בַסֵּ֣פֶר).
79   "Write in a book what you see": Revelation 1:11.
79   "By the pen and that which they write": The Qur'an 68:1 (ن وَالْقَلَمِ وَمَا يَسْطُرُونَ).
79   "as written scrolls are rolled up": The Qur'an 21:104 (ٱلسَّمَآءَ كَطَىِّ ٱلسِّجِلِّ لِلْكُتُبِ يَوْمَ نَطْوِى).
79   "in a book": E. Conze's translation of Aṣṭasāhasrikā Prajñāpāramitā Sūtra, in Schopen 1975, storyofstori.es/phrase.
79   "the world together with its gods": Schopen 1975, storyofstori.es/phrase.
79   *written* stories: "Story" here is not a judgment on whether texts are literal or historical.
79   whose name means "book": The Semitic for *scroll*, from Byblos where alphabets first appeared.
79   *qar'a*, "to read": *Qur'an* is a verbal noun (maṣdar) of *qara'a* (قرأ), "to read" or "to recite."
80   October 23, 4004 BCE: Cregan-Reid 2015, storyofstori.es/discovering.
80   Charles Lyell, who argues: Lyell 1842, storyofstori.es/lyell.
81   "In the time before humans": Kilmer 1972, storyofstori.es/kilmer; and Kovacs 1989, storyofstori.es/epic.
81   "Another god, Enki, warned": Enki warned Atra-ḥasīs, who told Utnapishtim.
82   the Prime Minister rises: *The Spectator* December 7, 1872b, storyofstori.es/passion.
82   "Every effort": *The Spectator* December 7, 1872b, storyofstori.es/passion; and *The Spectator* December 14, 1872, storyofstori.es/gladstone.
82   one thousand miles: Nagy 2010, storyofstori.es/classic. The distance is from Nineveh to Ionia, which is where Homer would have lived, if he or she was real.
82   "establishes the existence of historic germs": *The Spectator* December 7, 1872a, storyofstori.es/tuesday.
82   "the place where Noah's story": *The Daily Telegraph* 1872, storyofstori.es/flood.
83   Before George's lecture: "Ark," *Encyclopaedia Britannica* 1771, storyofstori.es/ark.
83   hundred years old: 101 (first volume) to 104 (third/final volume) years old.
83   "Buteo": Buteo (c.1485–560), mathematician; Kircher (1602–80), German Jesuit.
83   "two hundred and eighty cows": In the original, "beeves," the plural of "beef."
83   "It is best to regard": "Deluge," *Encyclopaedia Britannica* 1875, storyofstori.es/deluge.
83   "explanations of creation": The original uses the word *cosmogony*.
84   almost as old: Smith's tablet is from the 600s BCE; Socrates is from the 400s BCE.
84   Aristocles: Imagined based on *Phaedrus*. Video at storyofstori.es/walk.
85   of Greek orators: We do not know if Socrates knew how to write. Franek 2012, storyofstori.es/write.
85   the first generation: Socrates was born c. 470 BCE; Plato was born 428–23 BCE.
85   Socrates, fully aware: Socrates is not really "speaking for himself" in Plato.
85   may make fun of him: Jowett and Ballin 2017, storyofstori.es/plato.
85   "The men of old": Jowett and Ballin.
85   "protect or defend themselves": Jowett and Ballin.

- 86   Writing is an *illusion* of language: See Harris 2005, storyofstori.es/rethinking.
- 86   History may or may not be written by victors: Phelan 2019, storyofstori.es/victors.
- 87   pseudonym Plátōn: From *platýs* (πλατύς), "broad," perhaps due to Plato's shoulders.
- 88   "The reader is the space: Barthes in Elliott et al. 1967, storyofstori.es/author.
- 88   two kinds of story: Barthes 1974, storyofstori.es/SZ.
- 89   known by a consensus: See, for example, Albeck-Ripka 2023. storyofstori.es/wake.
- 90   "It is misleading": Ong 1975, storyofstori.es/audience.

Chapter 4: The War of Stories

- 92   This apocalypse: Zürcher 1982, storyofstori.es/prince.
- 92   thirteen miles deep: Forty Chinese miles or *li*. The *li* was about one-third of an English mile.
- 92   chosen people: *Xuǎnmín* (选民), "select people," now also "voter." Zürcher 1982, storyofstori.es/prince.
- 92   A dragon king: This is a Nagaraja (नागराज in Sanskrit) or *Lóngwáng* (龍王).
- 92   a magic city: Huà chéng (化城), literally a "transformed city."
- 93   traveled to China slowly: Buddhism first reached China between 100 BCE and 100 CE.
- 93   after the Buddha died: Consensus is Buddha was born c. 560 BCE and died c. 480 BCE.
- 93   Buddhist *bhikkhus*: A *bhikkhu* (भिक्खु in Pali; भिक्षु in Sanskrit), is an ordained male.
- 93   the Dhāraṇī Sutra of the Seal on the Casket: Shen 2012, storyofstori.es/many.
- 93   "Those who copy this sutra": From Amoghavajra (translator), 755. Amoghavajra's Chinese translation: storyofstori.es/sutra-chinese. English translation from Tibetan: storyofstori.es/sutra-english.
- 93   "All the buddhas: "*Tathāgatas*" in the original, meaning something like "awakened ones."
- 93   merit: (Sanskrit: पुण्य / *punya*, पुण्यम् / *punyam*.) Simplified; has various meanings.
- 93   the monks of the Cloud Dwelling Monastery: Ledderose 2004, storyofstori.es/sutras.
- 93   founded in 600 CE: The monastery was founded in the early seventh century.
- 94   whose Buddhist name was Tongli: 通理. Ledderose 2004, storyofstori.es/sutras.
- 94   would be called *queuing theory*: Erlang 1909, storyofstori.es/erlang.
- 94   curators: Ledderose 2004 (storyofstori.es/sutras) calls these monks collators.
- 94   wooden squares: Chinese ceramicists starting using stamps c. 200 BCE.
- 94   seals: Platt 2006, storyofstori.es/making; and Seevers and Korhonen 2019, storyofstori.es/seals. These were also used in Greece: Rovai 2020, storyofstori.es/rovai
- 94   to duplicate mantras: Seals also had applications such as signing contracts.
- 94   Six centuries after: Starr 2008 (storyofstori.es/tigers) summarizes rubbing's date of origin.
- 94   *bēitiē*: 碑帖, meaning "stone monument calligraphy." Ng 2013, storyofstori.es/ng.
- 94   words carved: Rubbing was also used to make copies of engravings and reliefs.
- 95   the nearby Taihang Mountains: 太行山, also known as the Western Hills (西山).
- 95   Tongli had the monks carve: Ledderose 2004, storyofstori.es/sutras.

96	The East Asian cultural sphere: Typically China, Japan, Korea, and Vietnam.
96	On Sunday: Julian calendar. Tuesday, April 18, under the Gregorian calendar.
96	April 9, 1424: This story and the eyewitness quotations are from Parsons 1944, storyofstori.es/moral.
96	Saint Bernardino: At the time, Bernardino Albizzeschi.
97	a game called *yèzi xì*: 葉子戲. Lo 2000, storyofstori.es/game. Some believe this was a dice game.
97	drinking games: Lo 2007, storyofstori.es/drinking.
97	*jiābīn xīnlíng*: 嘉賓 心灵.
97	"A party with wine": Lo 2007, storyofstori.es/drinking.
97	leaf games became: Some claim in India first, but no scholarly sources agree.
97	India and Persia's *ganjifeh*: جانجيفا, likely "treasure cards." Von Leyden et al. 1982, storyofstori.es/cards.
97	late 1300s: Carter 1925, storyofstori.es/invention. See this source also for information that follows about "initially imported" and "wherever paper went."
98	opened in Nuremberg: Grosse 1892, storyofstori.es/german; and Carter 1925, storyofstori.es/invention.
98	the first things printed: More specifically the first things printed in volume.
99	because of their: The gender of the Master is unknown. See, for example, Master of the Playing Cards ca. 1435–40, storyofstori.es/queen.
99	Master of the Banderoles: Banderoles are scrolls of speech and precursors to the speech bubbles used in comic books. Petersen 2010, storyofstori.es/comics.
99	of the founder: Moore 1995, storyofstori.es/moore; but Kapr 1996 (storyofstori.es/his) says he was a cloth merchant.
99	and in 1434: Clark 1979, storyofstori.es/four; and Kapr 1996, storyofstori.es/his.
99	workshop somewhere: Fuhrmann et al. 1940, storyofstori.es/documents. The approximate location is now *Île Gutenberg*.
99	His name was Johann: Johannes, abbreviated to Johann in contemporary records.
99	Gensfleisch: Moore 1995 (storyofstori.es/moore) is one of few sources that call Gutenberg Gensfleisch.
99	twentieth day of July: Relics were usually shown on the day of Saint Margaret of Antioch.
99	the great octagonal chapel: The Palatine Chapel.
100	the most dangerous thing: Powell 2012, storyofstori.es/birth.
100	most of whom still live: Fifteenth-century infant mortality was over 40 percent. Roser 2024, storyofstori.es/child.
101	Hinduism less so: India's Buddhists are still more literate. Moudgil 2017, storyofstori.es/conversion.
101	India, for example: Bloom 2001, storyofstori.es/before.
101	did not assign miraculous properties: Geary 1986, storyofstori.es/relics.
101	he ascended to heaven: The accounts in Luke 24:51 and Acts 1:1–9 differ.
101	bloodstains on the cloth: The *Sudarium* of Oviedo in Oviedo, Spain.
101	his foreskin: Farley 2006, storyofstori.es/shame.
101	parts of his umbilical cord: Marani 2012, storyofstori.es/therelics.
101	the sweat on a towel: Veil of Veronica, or *Sudarium*. Claimed to be in Italy or Spain.
101	expand the definition of *relic*: McCulloh 1976, storyofstori.es/cult.
101	other people's remains: Cruz 1991 (storyofstori.es/cruz) is a comprehensive and uncritical description.
101	the bones of the apostle James: Freeman 2011, storyofstori.es/holy.
101	the bodies of the saints: For example, Saint Bernadette (although her face and hands are wax).

101	the tongues of the saints: Polzonetti 2014, storyofstori.es/tongue; and Louthan 2010, storyofstori.es/louthan.
102	every seven years: The frequency has changed: for example, there were pilgrimages in 2023 and 2028.
102	since 1349: The pilgrimage continued into the twenty-first century. Aachen 2023, storyofstori.es/aachen.
102	affordable mirrors: Melchior-Bonnet 2001, storyofstori.es/mirror.
103	"The Germans make little mirrors": Fioravanti 1564, storyofstori.es/dello.
103	thirty-two thousand mirrors: Kapr 1996, storyofstori.es/his.
103	A gulden is a lot of money: This is my best guess based on available data.
103	help with the work: Kapr 1996, storyofstori.es/his.
104	derived from the lever and weight presses: Frankel 2016, storyofstori.es/oilandwine.
104	a strange liquid: This is an imagined detail to help the narrative, based on Muendel 1995, storyofstori.es/oliveoil.
105	Konrad Saspach: Kapr 1996, storyofstori.es/his.
105	premises on Krämergass: Krämergass is now called Rue Mercière.
105	designs such as: This is a description of a mirror badge from Spencer 1998, storyofstori.es/pilgrim.
105	not even Johann: Köster 1973: "Für im engeren Sinne typographische Versuche in Gutenbergs Straßburger Zeit gibt es auf Grund der bisher zutage gekommenen Quellen keine wirklich." (Based on the sources that have come to light so far, there is no real evidence of typographical attempts in the narrower sense during Gutenberg's time in Strasbourg.)
105	32,000 mirrors: This number is from Kapr 1996, storyofstori.es/his. The calculations that follow are: (1) Gutenberg expected to be in production for around 336 days of the year by working Sundays under a religious exemption for holy objects, working most saint days, and only observing absolute holidays. (2) 32,000 ÷ 336 is 95.2 or "around 100 mirrors every working day." (3) based on various data about guild output and demand for mirrors at pilgrimage sites (e.g., Köster 1973 says "In Einsiedeln in 1466, 130,000 were sold within 14 days"), a sensible assumption for the production of an operation of equivalent size to Gutenberg's is twenty-five mirrors per day. This leads to the conclusion that Gutenberg's screw press enabled him to produce four times as many mirrors as anyone else.
105	But they do it: I inferred this from the fact Gutenberg used up most of his capital.
106	no pilgrimage to Aachen in 1439: Kapr 1996.
106	That new product is punches: Clark 1979, storyofstori.es/four; and Gerhardt 1970, storyofstori.es/was.
106	thousands of years: Hunnisett 2018, storyofstori.es/steel.
107	a master punch: Now known as a matrix. I have avoided that term for clarity.
107	*mass production* exists: The term *mass production* started to become common around 1913 and usage peaked in 1944 and 1945. See Google ngram viewer at storyofstori.es/massproduction.
108	squeaks in the walls: This detail is imagined, to convey the misery of solitary confinement.
108	Weteringschans Prison: Hoornsche Courant 1856, storyofstori.es/den.
108	Baron Mozes: *Jonkheer*, the Dutch nobility's lowest rank, as *Baron* is in England.
108	"Dreams are deception: *Dromen zijn bedrog*, roughly "wishful thinking."
108	the baron hears cannon fire: Cannons could be heard ten miles away. Bradbury 1992, storyofstori.es/siege.
108	playing Patience: Patience is also known as Solitaire.
109	the mirror of his home: Hoornsche Courant 1856, storyofstori.es/den.
109	one month: Some sources say the sentence was a month, others say two weeks.

109	a day of celebration: De Noord-Brabanter 1856, storyofstori.es/coster.
109	editor of Haarlem's newspaper: The *Opregte Haarlemsche Courant*.
110	Leonard Metman: For more details about Metman, see Blok and Molhuysen 1918, storyofstori.es/blok.
110	as late as 1995: Cook 1995, storyofstori.es/structureof.
111	statues that still stand: Grote Markt; Stedelijk Gymnasium; and Haarlemmerhout.
111	an invention himself: Kuitert 2020, storyofstori.es/dutch.
111	no contemporary drawings: May 2015, storyofstori.es/may.
111	*Jikji*: 직지.
111	in 1377: Yoo 2022, storyofstori.es/1239; and Yoo 2023, storyofstori.es/ink.
112	half a mile away: This assumes the press was in the Altstadt (or "old town") district.
112	St. Alban's Abbey: Also known as Stift St. Alban vor Mainz.
112	called *antiquarii*: Horn and Born 1986, storyofstori.es/monastery; and Kwakkel et al. 2012, storyofstori.es/leaf.
112	three thousand pages: Buringh and van Zanden 2009, storyofstori.es/charting.
112	thirteen million documents by 1500: Dittmar 2011, storyofstori.es/info; and Rubin 2014, storyofstori.es/rubin.
112	four years: This is 1.1 million manuscripts per century, versus 1.04 million printed in four years.
113	In 1483: Worm 2016, storyofstori.es/foresti.
113	a friar in Bergamo: Worm 2016.
113	"The art of printing books": This is my translation from the Latin.
113	"Luténberg": Foresti 1492, storyofstori.es/supplement. "Luténberg" is Foresti's actual spelling, not a typo.
113	Fusto: Johann Fust/Faust, who may have claimed credit for Gutenberg's invention.
113	"Let all now adorn you": Edited for brevity.
113	visiting Germany: Brahe, although studying in Germany at this time, was Danish.
113	November 30, 1560: See, among others, Gassendi 1655, storyofstori.es/vita; Dreyer 1890, storyofstori.es/dreyer; and Jones 1946, storyofstori.es/1546.
113	an otherwise pitch-black room, in secret: Gassendi 1655, storyofstori.es/vita.
114	a recent Latin translation: "Recent" is relative. The translation was from 1451.
114	too expensive: The cost would have been two thaler—about as much as a skilled worker earned in a week.
114	"degenerate from ancestral virtue": Gassendi 1655, storyofstori.es/vita.
114	every pfennig: A thaler was worth 24 groschen or 288 pfennigs.
114	once every twenty years: Rounded up. The average is 19.865 years.
114	His books do not agree on this point: Dreyer 1890, storyofstori.es/dreyer.
114	Ptolemy, who believes: The Alfonsine Tables are based on Ptolemy's work.
115	in late September: Or July. Tycho found the tables to be wrong by about a month.
115	Copernicus: The Prutenic Tables are based on Copernicus's work.
115	on August 23: Tycho said "wrong by several days"; the consensus is around August 23.
115	"fallacious and carelessly put together": Gassendi 1655, storyofstori.es/vita.
115	helped to define the format of textbooks: For example, Brahe 1602, storyofstori.es/tycho.
116	reading happily ever after: Cook 1995 (storyofstori.es/structureof) discusses this myth at length.
116	a bill: The Parochial Schools Bill, introduced by Samuel Whitbread in 1807.
116	Davies Gilbert: For details of Gilbert's life and career see Urban 1840, storyofstori.es/urban.
116	"Giving education: Hansard 1807, storyofstori.es/hansard.

117	Similar fears: For a comprehensive but succinct review of this topic see Cipolla 1969, storyofstori.es/literacy.
117	still afraid of reading today: For example, Moskowitz 1970, storyofstori.es/peril; Dawson 2018, storyofstori.es/cuny; and Belkin 2024, storyofstori.es/equality.
117	a hundred miles away from me: I wrote this in Austin. Katy is 119 miles southeast.
117	oil executive: Perez earned $315,000 plus a bonus of $630,000 at Allis Chalmers.
117	working hard to ban: Goodman 2024, storyofstori.es/wicked.
117	from every school in Katy, Texas: Specifically, Katy Independent School District.
117	his family fled: Perez 2022, storyofstori.es/open.
117	flattop boogie: Jenkins 2017, storyofstori.es/butchwax; and lemmycaution25 2023, storyofstori.es/flattop.
117	"steadfast advocate": *Katy Christian Magazine* 2025, storyofstori.es/katy.
117	trying to ban thousands: ALA, storyofstori.es/bookbans. See also Knox 2015, storyofstori.es/bookbanning.
118	five most banned books: ALA 2025a, storyofstori.es/topten. At the time of writing the book with the most ban attempts was *All Boys Aren't Blue* by George M. Johnson. This will likely have changed by the time you read this, but the book that has replaced *All Boys Aren't Blue* will almost certainly have 2SLGBTQIA+ and/or non-Euro American themes.
118	by twenty-five or more: Dittmar 2011, storyofstori.es/info.
118	1500 and 1600: Rubin 2014, storyofstori.es/rubin. Rounded from between 20 and 78 percent.
118	46.8 million Venetian ducats: Scotti 2007, storyofstori.es/basilica.
118	$100 billion today: Estimated using relative labor value.
118	the sacrament of Penance: Paul II 1994, storyofstori.es/pope.
119	sent ninety-five complaints: Luther 1915, storyofstori.es/works.
119	"I did not wish": Martin Luther to Christoph von Scheurl, March 5, 1518. Luther 1908, storyofstori.es/letters.
119	Luther's counterstory split: Some disagree. See Buringh and van Zanden 2009, storyofstori.es/charting.
119	wars of stories: The division of the Church after the rise of Protestantism contributed to more than fifty wars in Europe between 1522 and 1712, which are estimated to have caused between seven and eighteen million deaths. The wars included the Knights' Revolt (1522–1523), the First Dalecarlian Rebellion (1524–1525), the German Peasants' War (1524–1526), the Second Dalecarlian Rebellion (1527–1528), the Wars of Kappel (1529–1531), the Tudor conquest of Ireland (1529–1603), the Kildare Rebellion (1534–1535), the First Desmond Rebellion (1569–1573), the Second Desmond Rebellion (1579–1583), the Nine Years' War (1593–1603), the Third Dalecarlian Rebellion (1531–1533), the War of Two Kings (1531–1532), the Count's Feud (1534–1536), the Münster Rebellion (1534–1535), Olav Engelbrektsson's Rebellion (1536–1537), Bigod's Rebellion (1537), the Dacke War (1542–1543), the Schmalkaldic War (1546–1547), the Prayer Book Rebellion (1549), the Battle of Sauðafell (1550), the Second Schmalkaldic War, or Princes' Revolt (1552–1555), the French Wars of Religion (1562–1598), the Eighty Years' War (1566/68–1648), the Cologne War (1583–1588), the Strasbourg Bishops' War (1592–1604), the War against Sigismund (1598–1599), the Bocskai Uprising (1604–1606), the War of the Jülich Succession (1609–10, 1614), the Thirty Years' War (1618–1648), which included the Bohemian Revolt (1618–1620) and the Hessian War Proper (1545–1648), the Huguenot rebellions (1621–1629), the Wars of the Three Kingdoms (1639–1651), which included the Bishops' Wars (1639–1640), the English Civil War (1642–1651), and the Irish Confederate Wars (1641–1653); the Cromwellian conquest of Ireland (1649–1653), and the Post-Westphalian Wars, which included the

Savoyard-Waldensian Wars (1655–1690), the First War of Villmergen (1656), the Nine Years' War (1688–1697), the Glorious Revolution (1688–1689), the Williamite War in Ireland (1688–1691), the War of the Spanish Succession (1701–1714), the War in the Cevennes (1702–1710), and the Second War of Villmergen (or Toggenburg War) (1712). Some of these wars overlapped, or could be said to be part of the same conflict. The reasons for war are always complicated and seldom if ever monocausal. At root all wars are about resources but whom they target and how they are justified are based on othering. Religious division amplified old disputes and grievances and created a new way to other as a "moral" excuse for war. Most historians agree that war-related deaths in Europe increased after the Reformation, partly due to better weapons, bigger armies, and larger populations, but also due to new justifications for armed conflict. Last, most of the people who died because of these wars were not killed by weapons but by second-degree factors such as illness and famine that would not have occurred had the wars not been fought.

119   Some historians say: See, among many examples, Febvre 1997, storyofstori.es/book.
119   The difference technology made: Statistics from Rubin 2014, storyofstori.es/rubin.
120   Two different publishers: Wynkyn de Worde in 1501 and Henry Pepwell in 1521.
120   feminism: This is debated. For example, Crofton 2013, storyofstori.es/mystic; Goodman 2014, storyofstori.es/and; and Howes 1992, storyofstori.es/notes.
121   five printing presses: Mass. Bay; Bos; Philly; VA; maybe MD. Febvre 1997, storyofstori.es/book.
121   each colony wriggled free: Febvre 1997, storyofstori.es/book.
121   colonial printers created: Adelman 2010, storyofstori.es/postoffice.
121   growing social unrest: Publication exploded after the Estates General of 1789.
121   several thousand independent: Chisick 1993, storyofstori.es/pamphlet.
121   led to the French Revolution: For instance, Chisick 1993; Chapman 2005, storyofstori.es/ethics; and Rossignol 2006, storyofstori.es/shadow.
121   standard stories: The term "standard stories" has been used since at least Velleman 1992, storyofstori.es/acts.
122   did not return to selling indulgences: Tingle 2014, storyofstori.es/indulge.
123   a mass of soft spaghetti: This spaghetti metaphor is from Alava and Niskanen 2006, storyofstori.es/physics.
123   Cai Lun: 蔡伦.
123   invented paper: This is debated. See, for example, Bloom 2001, storyofstori.es/before; Norman 2021, storyofstori.es/is; and Ledderose 2000, storyofstori.es/ten.
123   *zhǐ*: 紙.
123   a variation: Etymologies of *zhǐ* (紙): Wang 2023, storyofstori.es/family; Yuanyao 2024, storyofstori.es/trad; and Bloom 2001, storyofstori.es/before.
123   *sīchóu*: 絲綢.
123   paper for wiping: Bloom 2001, storyofstori.es/before.
123   The Indigenous peoples of the Americas: Von Hagen 1999, storyofstori.es/aztec.
123   fig-bearing alamo: *Ficus cotinifolia*.
123   to create *hu'un*: Stock-Allen 2016, storyofstori.es/outposts. More information, including links to online retailers, at storyofstori.es/huun.
123   books, including: See, for example, Vail and Aveni 2009, storyofstori.es/madrid.
123   and printing: de Ciudad Real and Acuña 2001, storyofstori.es/motul; and Ries 1932, storyofstori.es/ries1932.
123   ceramic stamps: Ries 1932 and Ries 1940, storyofstori.es/ries1940.
123   *Teoamoxtli*: "Book (*amoxtli*, 'aːmoʃtɬi) of Sacredness (*teōtl*, 'te.oːtɬ)."
123   written in 660 CE: de Alva Ixtlilxóchitl and O'Gorman 1985, storyofstori.es/alva.
123   Huematzin: Huematzin is also known as Huemac.

Notes 319

123	Books of Wisdom: Proposed by Jansen and Jiménez 2004 (storyofstori.es/renaming) to replace European names.
124	fibers from candlewood: *Dracaena americana*.
124	jonote trees: *Heliocarpus appendiculatus* Turcz, which the Aztecs called *xonotl*.
124	renamed it *amatl*: Nahuatl: *Amatl* (from *amacuahuitl*, "paper tree"); English: *amate*.
124	thirty feet long: Von Hagen 1999, storyofstori.es/aztec.
124	new styles of calligraphy: Normally known as scripts; *calligraphy* is used here instead for clarity.
124	only grew in a few places: See Archer 2004, storyofstori.es/papyrus.
124	restricted its distribution: Vainker 2004, storyofstori.es/silk.
124	in China: There is a near-consensus that this was printed in China. Kornicki 2012, storyofstori.es/darani.
124	copies of four prayers: The *Hyakumantō Darani* (百万塔陀羅尼). Kornicki 2012, storyofstori.es/darani.
124	tens of thousands: Approximately fifty thousand still exist, mostly at the Hōryū-ji (法隆寺) in Ikaruga.
125	found in Dunhuang: Duan et al. 1994 (storyofstori.es/eyes) describes the discovery of this copy.
125	Qián Chù: 錢俶 (Qián Chù) after 960 CE; 錢弘俶 (Qián Hóngchù) 929–60 CE.
125	Wuyue: 吴越 in simplified Chinese; 吳越 in traditional Chinese.
125	eighty-four thousand copies: Shen 2012, storyofstori.es/many. Also Daoshi (道世) 2019, storyofstori.es/daoshi2019; and Daoshi (道世) 2020 storyofstori.es/daoshi2020.
125	Leifengta Pagoda: 雷峰塔. Shen 2012, storyofstori.es/many.
125	"Enclosed is a small piece": Fenerty also addressed the letter to John English. Edited from Burger 2007, storyofstori.es/charles.
126	three times as many: England + France (1841): 49,068,190. US (1840): 17,069,453.
126	causing a problem: Munsell 1876, storyofstori.es/paper; and Dane 2003, storyofstori.es/dane.
126	alternative materials: List combines Munsell 1876, storyofstori.es/paper; Hunter 1978, storyofstori.es/papermaking; and Baker 2002, storyofstori.es/double.
126	marsh mallow: The plant *Althaea officinalis*, not the confection made from its roots.
126	*chiffonniers*, who rioted: They "rose against the police" per Munsell 1876, storyofstori.es/paper.
126	a romantic reputation: Lynch 1901, storyofstori.es/lynch.
126	Parisians rose up to protect them: Lynch 1901; and Bezbakh 2009, storyofstori.es/poubelle.
126	illegal to bury the dead: Hunter 1978, storyofstori.es/papermaking; and Cook 1995, storyofstori.es/structureof.
126	In the United States, newspapers: Cook 1995, storyofstori.es/structureof.
127	until the late nineteenth century: Carlsson 2010, storyofstori.es/found.
127	In 1840: US imported $0.6 million of rags per Munsell 1876 (storyofstori.es/paper), which is equivalent to about $20.5 million in 2024.
127	The United States imported: Munsell 1876, storyofstori.es/paper.
127	"Our Daily is now printed": Apikian 1974, storyofstori.es/stir.
127	three hundred tons: Munsell 1876 (storyofstori.es/paper) implies a weight of 312.5 tons.
127	over a thousand: *New-York Tribune* 1856, storyofstori.es/tribune.
127	"The most disagreeable, odiferous": *Baltimore Daily Exchange* 1858, storyofstori.es/rags.
128	Historians debated: Dane 2003, storyofstori.es/dane.

128 "This paper": Wolfe 2009, storyofstori.es/mummies.
129 "When I was no longer": This and the following quotations are my translation from the French, heavily edited for length and clarity, and taken from Réaumur 1742, pages 180–82 (description of the wasp on the window frame) and pages 231–34 (proposal to learn how to make paper from word based on making observations of wasps, and exasperation at being ignored), storyofstori.es/memoires.
130 from rags: Three minor exceptions: Schäffer, Delisle, Koops.
130 by the end of the 1870s: Hunter 1978, storyofstori.es/papermaking.
131 cost 44 US cents: 44 cents per pound of rags from Brady 1964, storyofstori.es/prices. Four cents per pound of pulp from Valente 2010, storyofstori.es/rag.
131 the year before: The date Gutenberg started operations is uncertain; 1450 is consensus.
131 Europeans published: Figures from estimates in Buringh and van Zanden 2009, storyofstori.es/charting.
131 two thousand: Buringh and van Zanden 2009 (storyofstori.es/charting) divided by the average print run of twenty-five.
131 new books: "Titles" as defined in Wischenbart and Ehling 2009, storyofstori.es/sales.
131 twenty-five copies: A first-order approximation based on scholarly consensus.
131 *twenty-five hundred* copies: My estimate, based on Buringh and van Zanden 2009, storyofstori.es/charting.
131 The difference between the growth: Roser 2013, storyofstori.es/roser. Also Cipolla 1969, storyofstori.es/literacy.
131 literacy in England: Sometimes UK, which overstates as a proxy for England due to higher Scottish levels.
131 In 1450: The literacy rates for 1475, which are the closest to 1450 available.
131 per hundred thousand people: Rounded from England: 1.55 presses / 3.09 mills. Netherlands: 11.9 / 14.2. These numbers are my estimates aggregated from a number of sources including *Our World in Data*, Jeremy Norman's HistoryofInformation.com, the British Association of Paper Historians, and historical accounts of the Dutch paper industry.
132 "There would be no more": Cipolla 1969, storyofstori.es/literacy.
132 "to reason": *Read* and *reason* derived from the PIE root *rē-*, "to reason, count."
133 from 1588: Simplified. The history of republicanism in the Netherlands is complicated.
133 to 1806: From 1795 to 1806 Netherlands was less independent due to intervention by France.
133 almost all: Pre-Reformation, non-Catholic traditions were rare in Western Europe.
134 In the 1560s: Christian Humanism led to Dutch Revolt per Akçomak et al. 2016, storyofstori.es/legacy.
134 literacy rate still: The Dutch illiteracy rate of 11 percent is from the EU: Eurydice 2023, storyofstori.es/support. The 15 percent English illiteracy rate is from the UK Government's Department for Business, Innovation, and Skills: Harding 2012, storyofstori.es/skills, and is the 2011 total of all English respondents at Entry Level 3 or below, which is the UK's definition of "illiterate." This was the most recent English Skills for Life survey available at the time of writing. As an alternative measure, in 2024 the OECD found that the mean proficiency in literacy of Netherlands was 279, whereas in the United Kingdom it was 272, which is a statistically significant difference: Avvisati 2024, storyofstori.es/adults. This OECD number is inflated by the inclusion of Scotland, and Wales, both of which have significantly higher literacy rates than England, and Northern Ireland, which has a slightly higher literacy rate than England. If the OECD had measured

England alone, its mean proficiency would likely have been around 270, as England has about 9 percent more adults with literacy difficulties than the UK average.
135 "We claim the Press": Fenerty 1866, storyofstori.es/progress.
135 *Narrative of the Life of Frederick Douglass*: Douglass 2020, storyofstori.es/douglass.
135 thirty thousand copies: From the introduction to Douglass 1960, storyofstori.es/life.

Chapter 5: The All-Seeing Eye of Providence

136 the first night of January 1845: This and other details of the case such as the dialogue in the coffee shop and Tawell's movements are from Woodall 1873, storyofstori.es/trials.
136 wisteria-covered facade: Slough History Online 2024, storyofstori.es/slough.
137 the Jerusalem Coffee House: 3, Cowper's Court, London EC3. It is no longer there.
137 a tall man: Police height requirement was five feet seven inches. The average mid-1800s man in UK was five feet five inches.
137 in Salt Hill: Simplified. Wiggins said "Slough," and Salt Hill is now part of Slough.
137 has already prevented: Beauchamp 2001, storyofstori.es/telegraphy.
138 "of a Quaker": The telegraph did not have a Q, so the message read "Kwaker."
138 could only arrest: British Transport Police 2025, storyofstori.es/police. This was true in 1845; it's not true today.
138 murder using cyanide: Pharmaceutical Society of Great Britain 1845, storyofstori.es/pharma.
139 called telecommunication: The term was coined by Édouard Estaunié in Estaunié 1904, storyofstori.es/traité.
139 a crowd of ten thousand: Crowd size is from British Transport Police 2025, storyofstori.es/police.
139 change speeding up: Fogel and Costa 1997 (storyofstori.es/techno) makes much the same point.
140 the first atlas: The 1482 edition of Ptolemy's *Geography*, with thirty-two maps.
140 the first postal service: Britain's Royal Mail was the first government national mail service.
140 the first book of: *De Triangulis Omnimodis* by Johannes Müller von Königsberg.
140 scientific journal: *Journal des sçavans* or *Phil. Transactions of the Royal Society*.
140 school textbook: *The New England Primer*, printed by Benjamin Harris in 1690.
140 the first bookstore: Pedro Faures's store in Chiado, Lisbon, Portugal. Opened 1732.
140 the first electric telegraph: Pavel Schilling demonstrated the telegraph in 1812.
140 public library: Peterborough, New Hampshire, 1833. African Americans excluded.
140 the first photograph: Joseph Nicéphore Niépce, 1822 and 1827.
140 the first paperback: Tauchnitz's 1841 series. Mienert 2024, storyofstori.es/edition; and Todd 1984, storyofstori.es/new.
140 practical typewriter: Sholes & Glidden Type Writer by Sholes, Glidden, and Soulé.
140 first carbon copy: Rogers Carbon Paper Co., New York. Beattie and Rahenkamp 1981, storyofstori.es/IBM.
140 duplicating machine: The mimeograph by Albert Blake Dick in 1887. Brooks 1969, storyofstori.es/business.
140 the first record player: Thomas Edison's cylinder-based "Phonograph." Smart 1980, storyofstori.es/disc.
140 the first movie screening: By Lauste, Latham, and Sons, in New York, May 20, 1895.
141 one to millions: Japan's *Yomiuri Shimbun* circulation was over nine million in 2021.
141 invented by Philo Farnsworth: First practical television by Philo Farnsworth in 1927.

Notes

141	selling millions: One million televisions in 1948; three million in 1949; seven million in 1950.
141	Sammy Lobianco: Story based on Helper 1997 (storyofstori.es/whole), with details from additional research.
142	Curry's Club Tropicana: Guralnick 2014 (storyofstori.es/sweet) says the owners were Johnny and Susie Curry.
142	a low apron stage: There is a picture of the stage at Curry's Club Tropicana taken in the early 1950s at storyofstori.es/stage.
143	the officer: Ashmore 2004, storyofstori.es/ashmore. There were 341 officers in the Memphis Police Department at this time. Only thirteen of them were Black and these officers only patrolled Beale Street.
143	wherever they please: Technically, white people were prohibited from using "colored" facilities.
143	"resist neglecting": Provine 1996, storyofstori.es/laughter.
143	"historians spend too much time": Levine 2007, storyofstori.es/Blackculture. Edited for length and inclusiveness.
144	enforcing the norms: Sandlin et al. 2017, storyofstori.es/memphis.
145	vinyl records: "Records" made of shellac had existed since the late 1800s.
145	pocket-size radios: Sony's first transistor-based product, launched in Japan in 1955.
145	tiny silicon crystals: Or, sometimes, germanium.
145	twice that many in 1960: Includes other radios from Japan. Fisher 2009, storyofstori.es/fisher.
145	that is not what happened: Peterson 1990, storyofstori.es/1955.
146	popular in the 1950s: Average sales: 6 million television sets per year. Chandler et al. 2009, storyofstori.es/invent.
146	replace radio completely: Peterson 1990, storyofstori.es/1955.
146	boxes as big as suitcases: The RCA 630TS. "TS" stood for "television set."
146	eight-by-six-inch cathode-ray tube: The 630TS screen had a ten-inch diagonal.
146	dead air: Also more competitors. Sterling and Kittross 2001, storyofstori.es/stay.
146	one-song-per-side: To be sold in book-like portfolios called "albums."
146	jukeboxes: Jukeboxes, sold since the '40s, became ever more popular. Cowen 2009, storyofstori.es/praise.
147	Around the time: Sammy at Midnighters: May 22 to July 30. Elvis's session: July 5.
147	five months younger: Sammy was born on August 14, Elvis on January 8.
147	was auditioning: Details of the session are from Guralnick 2014, storyofstori.es/sweet.
147	a few miles: Sun Studios: 706 Union Ave. Sammy: Jackson Ave, 3.4 miles away.
147	with little success: One take appeared on Elvis's debut album, released in 1956.
147	on Beale Street: This was also the location of Beale Street Baptist Church which was founded by a congregation of freed slaves and housed the headquarters of the *Memphis Free Speech and Headlight* newspaper, a third of which was owned by its most famous journalist, Ida B. Wells, who investigated and campaigned against lynchings.
148	"That's All Right": You can hear some of Elvis's outtakes at storyofstori.es/elvis. There is a four-song playlist showing the history of the song from Victoria Spivey's "Black Snake Blues" to Elvis Presley's "That's All Right" at storyofstori.es/mama.
148	since the 1920s: For example, Ella Fitzgerald, "Rock It for Me," 1934.
148	too *Black*: Rock and roll and race is complicated. See Ward 2012, storyofstori.es/soul; and Bertrand 2000, storyofstori.es/rock.
149	brilliant Black Americans: Examples taken from Asante 2010, storyofstori.es/100.
150	109 million: Estimated from Craig 2004, storyofstori.es/radio.
150	plain and haunting lyrics: Meeropol 2006, storyofstori.es/meeropol.

Notes 323

150 barely played: Margolick 2001, storyofstori.es/strange.
151 straightforward next step: See, for example, Mair 2013, storyofstori.es/fiction.
151 Julius Gottlieb Nipkow: Nipkow patented a spinning disc for scanning images in 1884.
151 Constantin Perskyi: Perskyi coined the word *television* in 1900.
151 Leon Theremin: Theremin demonstrated a working device in 1923.
151 Georges Rignoux: Rignoux transmitted a slowly changing image in 1909.
151 Charles Francis Jenkins: Jenkins demonstrated his system in 1925.
151 Philo Farnsworth: Farnsworth first transmitted an image in 1927.
151 Kenjiro Takayanagi: Takayanagi showed a working television in 1925 and a better one in 1931.
151 John Logie Baird: Baird first transmitted a moving image in 1926.
151 many more: See Abramson 2009, storyofstori.es/1880; and Burns 1998, storyofstori.es/burns.
151 resists electricity: Smith 1873, storyofstori.es/effect. It conducts 15 percent of electricity when in total darkness.
151 was impractical: Addison et al. 1907, storyofstori.es/1907; and Bidwell 1908, storyofstori.es/bidwell.
151 RMS *Titanic*: Design was completed in July 1908; the cost to build was £1.5 million.
152 a simple and elegant alternative: Campbell-Swinton 1908, storyofstori.es/distant.
152 "The problem can probably be solved": Campbell-Swinton, 1908. I edited this quotation for length and clarity without changing the meaning. The unedited version is: "Referring to Mr. Shelford Bidwell's illuminating communication on this subject published in Nature of June 4, may I point out that though, as stated by Mr. Bidwell, it is wildly impracticable to effect even 160,000 synchronised operations per second by ordinary mechanical means, this part, of the problem of obtaining distant electric vision can probably be solved by the employment of two beams of kathode rays (one at the transmitting and one at the receiving station) synchronously deflected by the varying fields of two electromagnets placed at right angles to one another and energised by two alternating electric currents of widely different frequencies, So that the moving extremities of the two beams are caused to sweep synchronously over the whole of the required surfaces within the one-tenth of a second necessary to take advantage of visual persistence. Indeed, so far as the receiving apparatus is concerned, the moving kathode beam has only to be arranged to impinge on a sufficiently sensitive fluorescent screen, and given suitable variations in its intensity, to obtain the desired result."
152 the electron: O'Hara 1975, storyofstori.es/electron; and Lorentz 1902, storyofstori.es/nobel.
153 Aquino proposed: From Aquino's 2003 introduction to Vallely 1980, storyofstori.es/mindwar: "The term 'MindWar' was coined by another PSYOP officer, Colonel Richard Sutter, and myself in 1977. After seeing the recent film *Star Wars*, we played with a modification of its name as a futuristic replacement for the somewhat bland Army designation 'Psychological Operations.'"
153 He called it MindWar: Name created by Aquino and Richard Sutter. Aquino, 2002.
153 "the deliberate, aggressive convincing: This description is assembled from different parts of Vallely 1980 and slightly edited for length, clarity, and grammar correction. The complete quotations are: "MindWar is the deliberate, aggressive convincing of all participants in a war that we will win that war. . . . It must seek out the attention of the enemy nation through every available medium, and it must strike at the nation's potential soldiers before they put on their uniforms. . . . In its strategic context, MindWar must reach out to friends, enemies, and neutrals alike across the globe—neither through primitive 'battlefield' leaflets and loudspeakers

of PSYOP nor through the weak, imprecise, and narrow effort of psychotronics [a euphemism for extrasensory perception, which Aquino and others believed to be a real phenomenon at the time]—but through the media possessed by the United States. These media are, of course, the electronic media—television and radio. State-of-the-art developments in satellite communication, video recording techniques, and laser and optical transmission of broadcasts make possible a penetration of the minds of the world such as would have been inconceivable just a few years ago. Like the sword Excalibur, we have but to reach out and seize this tool; and it can transform the world for us if we have the courage and the integrity to enhance civilization with it. If we do not accept Excalibur, then we relinquish our ability to inspire foreign cultures with our morality. If they then desire moralities unsatisfactory to us, we have no choice but to fight them on a more brutish level . . . it must be axiomatic of MindWar that it always speaks the truth. Its power lies in its ability to focus recipients' attention on the truth of the future as well as that of the present. MindWar thus involves the stated promise of the truth that the United States has resolved to make real if it is not already so." storyofstori.es/mindwar.

153   leaders developed: There is no way to know how much Aquino's MindWar proposal influenced subsequent PSYOP. Such things are not usually documented, and are kept secret if they are. It is possible that (a) MindWar had a direct influence, (b) MindWar had a tacit influence via organizational osmosis, or (c) MindWar had no influence whatsoever, and its ideas were invented independently elsewhere. What *is* clear is that the new PYSOP was much the same as Aquino's MindWar proposal.

154   real, but misleading: Data from Human Rights Watch 1991, storyofstori.es/HRW.

154   Ninety-five percent: My estimate. Approximately 92 percent "dumb"; many "smart" munitions were for Kuwait.

154   an air raid shelter in Baghdad: al-ʿāmiriyyah (العامرية), storyofstori.es/shelter.

155   encountered: The details of Jarecke taking the photograph are from BBC News 2005, storyofstori.es/2005.

155   fifteen thousand publications: From the "What We Do" section of storyofstori.es/AP which at the time of writing says: "More than 15,000 news outlets and a range of businesses worldwide connect with their audiences using our multiformat content." This number may have changed (in either direction) since 1991, but the point still stands: the AP wire service has tremendous reach.

155   Only one newspaper: Flint 1991, storyofstori.es/face. For the likely impact, see also Gartner 2011, storyofstori.es/on.

155   "Did you stop to consider": *Observer* 1991, storyofstori.es/evans.

156   "People somehow have the notion": Schmitt 1991, storyofstori.es/army.

156   were eager: Moore 2001, storyofstori.es/gulf.

156   new strategy: Tested in Bosnia (1995) and Kosovo (1999). See Paul and Kim 2005, storyofstori.es/reporters.

156   accrediting and training: Brightman 2003, storyofstori.es/bed.

156   "also known as censorship": Page 2003, storyofstori.es/embedded.

157   "information warfare": The term "information warfare" started to become popular in 1989 and peaked in 199. See Google ngram viewer at storyofstori.es/infowar.

157   "an argument for realism": Evans 1991, storyofstori.es/evans.

158   to at least 1895: First published as a series running in 1895. Henley 1895, storyofstori.es/henley.

158   "fools": Wells 2010, storyofstori.es/wells.

158   "firemen": Bradbury 2008, storyofstori.es/451.

158   Marshall McLuhan: McLuhan 2017, storyofstori.es/galaxy.

158   "Switch to Images today!": Shteyngart 2010, storyofstori.es/super.
158   *Book of Eli*: Hughes and Hughes 2010, storyofstori.es/eli.
158   110 billion: Based on Kaneda and Haub 2022, storyofstori.es/howmany; and Roser 2013, storyofstori.es/roser.
159   "The term *literature*": Edited for length from Levin's preface to Lord 1965, storyofstori.es/tales. The complete quotation is: "The term 'literature,' presupposing the use of letters, assumes that verbal works of imagination are transmitted by means of writing and reading. The expression 'oral literature' is obviously a contradiction in terms. Yet we live at a time when literacy itself has become so diluted that it can scarcely be invoked as an esthetic criterion. The Word as spoken or sung, together with a visual image of the speaker or singer, has meanwhile been regaining its hold through electrical engineering. A culture based upon the printed book, which has prevailed from the Renaissance until lately, has bequeathed to us—along with its immeasurable riches—snobberies which ought to be cast aside. We ought to take a fresh look at tradition, considered not as the inert acceptance of a fossilized corpus of themes and conventions, but as an organic habit of re-creating what has been received and is handed on."
160   "It is not illiteracy": Edited for length from *The Atlantic Monthly* November 1880, storyofstori.es/atlantic. The complete quotation is: "have had a pamphlet sent to me entitled The Legal Prevention of Illiteracy. I dare say it is a very able pamphlet, but I have not read it; it is not illiteracy I want to prevent, but literacy!" The quotation appears in what was the regular final section of *The Atlantic* at that time, "The Contributors' Club," which was traditionally unsigned. According to Eppard 1983 (storyofstori.es/guide), this item was an "Editor's Complaint" and the editor of *The Atlantic* at the time was William Dean Howells, so we can reasonably assume that Howells coined the term "literacy." The Google ngram viewer at storyofstori.es/rise shows the word becoming more frequent starting in 1897 and continuing until 2022, which is where the data ends.
160   term that originated: Liu's term was *transliteracies*. See Thomas et al. 2007, storyofstori.es/crossing.
160   "the ability to read": Thomas et al. 2007, storyofstori.es/crossing.
160   "Not only does transliteracy question": Edited for length from Ipri 2010, storyofstori.es/ipri. "Not only does transliteracy question previous assumptions of authority, it also calls into question the often assumed privilege of printed text. Transliteracy works against the 'entrenched bias towards the written medium.' The ALA Committee on Literacy's definition of literacy demonstrates this bias. It defines literacy as the ability to use 'printed and written information to function in society, to achieve one's goals, and to develop one's knowledge and potential.' Transliteracy is not unique in questioning this bias—media literacy efforts have certainly tried to raise the profile of nonprint materials. But transliteracy is unique in combining democratizing communication formats, expressing no preference of one over the other, with emphasizing the social construction of meaning via diverse media. Because of the ways in which transliteracy questions authority and devalues hierarchical structures for disseminating information, proponents tend to advocate for issues that help level the information playing field, such as ensuring neutrality and bridging the digital divide. Despite the fact that transliteracy originated outside the library realm, librarians should follow the development of this concept because so much of transliteracy overlaps concerns much at the heart of librarianship."
161   did not invite: hooks 2014, storyofstori.es/aint; Mazza 2024 (storyofstori.es/encounter) places the meeting in the summer of 1982.
162   only Black face: storyofstori.es/bell. I assume she was the only Black face.

162　Oh, the *boldness*: hooks 2014, storyofstori.es/aint.
162　sixty and balding: Based on this photo dated 1982: storyofstori.es/paulo.
162　Marianne's on Ocean Street: I assume the café was Marianne's.
163　her pen name: "bell hooks, my writing voice," in hooks 2014, storyofstori.es/aint.
163　"I came to Freire": hooks 2014, storyofstori.es/aint, Chapter 4. Edited for length and clarity. The entire quotation is "I came to Freire thirsty, dying of thirst (in that way that the colonized, marginalized subject who is still unsure of how to break the hold of the status quo, who longs for change, is needy, is thirsty), and I found in his work (and the work of Malcolm X, Fanon, etc.) a way to quench that thirst. To have work that promotes one's liberation is such a powerful gift. . . ."
163　"I wanted to become": This passage comprises two separate quotations from hooks 2014, storyofstori.es/aint, edited for length and joined together. The complete version of the first quotation, which is from the introduction, is "I wanted to become a critical thinker. Yet that longing was often seen as a threat to authority. Individual white male students who were seen as "exceptional," were often allowed to chart their intellectual journeys, but the rest of us (and particularly those from marginal groups) were always expected to conform." The complete version of the second quotation, which is from chapter 1, is "Most of my professors were not the slightest bit interested in enlightenment. More than anything they seemed enthralled by the exercise of power and authority within their mini-kingdom, the classroom. This is not to say that there were not compelling, benevolent dictators, but it is true to my memory that it was rare—absolutely, astonishingly rare—to encounter professors who were deeply committed to progressive pedagogical practices. I was dismayed by this; most of my professors were not individuals whose teaching styles I wanted to emulate. My commitment to learning kept me attending classes. Yet, even so, because I did not conform—would not be an unquestioning, passive student—some professors treated me with contempt. I was slowly becoming estranged from education. Finding Freire in the midst of that estrangement was crucial to my survival as a student."
164　Kant said: Kant et al. 1998, from footnote 2 of the preface to the first edition.
165　"Reading is not exhausted": Freire and Slover 1983, storyofstori.es/act. I have edited the first sentence slightly for clarity; the original is "Reading is not exhausted merely by decoding the written word or written language, but rather anticipated by and extending into knowledge of the world."
166　"Often when people read Freire": hooks 2014, storyofstori.es/aint. Chapter 4. I have edited the quotation for clarity and brevity. The complete quotation is "often when university students and professors read Freire, they approach his work from a voyeuristic standpoint, where as they read they see two locations in the work, the subject position of Freire the educator (whom they are often more interested in than the ideas or subjects he speaks about) and the oppressed/marginalized groups he speaks about. In relation to these two subject positions, they position themselves as observers, as outsiders. When I came to Freire's work, just at that moment in my life when I was beginning to question deeply and profoundly the politics of domination, the impact of racism, sexism, class exploitation, and the kind of domestic colonization that takes place in the United States, I felt myself to be deeply identified with the marginalized peasants he speaks about, or with my black brothers and sisters, my comrades in Guinea-Bissau. You see, I was coming from a rural southern black experience, into the university, and I had lived through the struggle for racial desegregation and was in resistance without having a political language to articulate that process. Paulo was one of the thinkers whose work gave me a language. He made me think deeply about the construction of an identity in resistance. There was this one sentence of Freire's that became a revolutionary

Notes 327

mantra for me: 'We cannot enter the struggle as objects in order later to become subjects.' Really, it is difficult to find words adequate to explain how this statement was like a locked door—and I struggled within myself to find the key—and that struggle engaged me in a process of critical thought that was transformative. This experience positioned Freire in my mind and heart as a challenging teacher whose work furthered my own struggle."

166 You are oppressed: My paraphrases of different parts of Freire 2017, storyofstori.es/pedagogy. Freire's writing tends to be opaque, scholarly, and needlessly difficult for non-specialists (I include myself in this category) to understand. For clarity and ease of reading, I have made these statement shorter; substituted ten-dollar words with everyday words; and reoriented backward sentences where the sub-clause precedes the clause. The original quotations and page references are: "The very structure of their thought has been conditioned by the contradictions of the concrete, existential situation by which they were shaped. Their ideal is to be men; but for them, to be men is to be oppressors. This is their model of humanity. This phenomenon derives from the fact that the oppressed, at a certain moment of their existential experience, adopt an attitude of 'adhesion' to the oppressor. Under these circumstances they cannot 'consider' him sufficiently clearly to objectivize him—to discover him 'outside' themselves" (page 45). "This behavior, this way of understanding the world and people (which necessarily makes the oppressors resist the installation of a new regime) is explained by their experience as a dominant class. Once a situation of violence and oppression has been established, it engenders an entire way of life and behavior for those caught up in it—oppressors and oppressed alike. Both are submerged in this situation, and both bear the marks of oppression. Analysis of existential situations of oppression reveals that their inception lay in an act of violence—initiated by those with power" (page 58). "The truth is, however, that the oppressed are not 'marginals,' are not people living 'outside' society. They have always been 'inside'—inside the structure which made them 'beings for others.' The solution is not to 'integrate' them into the structure of oppression, but to transform that structure so that they can become 'beings for themselves.' Such transformation, of course, would undermine the oppressors' purposes" (page 74). "Any situation in which 'A' objectively exploits 'B' or hinders his and her pursuit of self-affirmation as a responsible person is one of oppression. Such a situation in itself constitutes violence, even when sweetened by false generosity, because it interferes with the individual's ontological and historical vocation to be more fully human" (page 55).

Chapter 6: One One Zero

169 where he is a professor: Donner Professor of Science at MIT from 1956 to 1978.
169 Asyut:أسيوط.
169 Memphis:مَنْف.
169 with a drawing: See storyofstori.es/beni.
169 until the 1970s: Shannon 1993, storyofstori.es/juggling. The earliest date it could have been written is 1980.
169 formula to describe: Shannon's basic formula, for a one-ball-per-hand juggle.
170 a recently published fantasy novel: Silverberg 1995, storyofstori.es/castle.
171 This diagram describes: Figure 1, p. 7, of Shannon 1948, storyofstori.es/mathcomm.
172 becomes impossible: Intelligibility is complex. See, for example, Weismer 2008, storyofstori.es/weismer.
172 "A Symbolic Analysis of Relay and Switching Circuits": Shannon 1938, storyofstori.es/shannon.

328   Notes

173   *The Mathematical Analysis of Logic*: Boole 1847, storyofstori.es/boole.
173   men who owned property: Simplified; in a few exceptional cases women could vote.
173   "It may be that": Boole 1911, 167, storyofstori.es/thought.
174   many people work independently: Ogburn and Thomas 1922, storyofstori.es/ogburn.
175   in the 1960s: 1960s details at storyofstori.es/cape.
175   *kapan-da*: Translations from Haviland 1974, storyofstori.es/words. Precise meaning debated.
176   three hundred million years: Rounded. More likely to be 250 million.
176   eroded the rock: In the Last Glacial Period, around 115,000 to 11,700 years ago.
176   up to sixteen feet a year: Pye 1982, storyofstori.es/flattery. See also Bagnold 2012, storyofstori.es/bagnold.
176   leaving only the quartz: Pye 1983, storyofstori.es/dunes.
176   For fifty thousand years: Pye 1983.
176   the Kingdom of Great Britain: This was Britain's official name from 1707 to 1800.
176   Cape Flattery: Cook also called a part of the Washington State coast Cape Flattery.
176   "checkered with white sand": Cook 2003, storyofstori.es/journals.
176   two mineral companies: "Silica Sand for Japan," *Sydney Morning Herald* 1967, storyofstori.es/silica.
176   to build a sand mine: See storyofstori.es/cape.
176   a wharf a half-kilometer long: See storyofstori.es/port.
177   an American-owned factory: My assumption. Corning does not disclose its suppliers.
177   the southeastern district of Yizhuang: See storyofstori.es/hq; and storyofstori.es/fab.
177   the small town of Corning: Population approximately 11,000. storyofstori.es/corningny.
177   overflows: Dockerty and Shay 1964, storyofstori.es/949; Dockerty 1967, storyofstori.es/696; and Dockerty 1972, storyofstori.es/609.
177   thin as a bedsheet: Per email from Brittany Salgado, Corning Inc., July 22, 2020.
178   millions of square meters: Chen 2019, which is a private interview with Y. S. Chen, CEO of BOE, that took place in Beijng on April 16, 2019.
178   once called: The original Chinese state-owned Beijing Electron Tube Factory was founded in 1956; it was renamed the Beijing Oriental Electronics Group Co., Ltd in 1993; and BOE Technology Group Co., Ltd., more commonly called BOE, in 2001. The company's full name in Chinese is 京东方科技集团股份有限公司, which means "Beijing Orient Technology Group Co., Ltd." This name is often abbreviated to 京东方 (Jīngdōngfāng in pinyin) which means "Beijing Orient."
178   only remaining application: I am simplifying; see also, for example, magnetrons.
178   Fewer than one in three: storyofstori.es/TVChina.
178   which were tiny: The most common screen size was a fourteen-inch diagonal.
178   were first proposed: RCA made an unscalable proof of concept in the 1960s.
178   electron emitters: Surface-conduction electron-emitter displays, or SEDs.
178   electrostatic fields: Field-emission displays, or FEDs.
179   Moore predicted: Moore 1965, storyofstori.es/law.
180   doubled its weight: See storyofstori.es/223lbs; and storyofstori.es/440lbs.
180   television industry assumed: See, for example, Fisher and Fisher 1996, storyofstori.es/tube; and Burns 1998, storyofstori.es/burns.
181   In 1993: World Bank 2025, storyofstori.es/worldbank.
181   one technology: A simplification. Also organic light emitting diodes, or OLEDs.
182   kept investing in cathode ray tubes: See Chang 2011, storyofstori.es/chang.
182   Japan's share of the world's display market: Vogel 2013, storyofstori.es/vogel.

Notes 329

183 known as Wang's Law: BOE Technology Group Co. 2019, storyofstori.es/prize.
183 annual sales: BOE Technology Group Co. 2022, storyofstori.es/BOE2021.
184 high-frequency sounds: An ultrasonic bath; the solvent is often acetone.
184 start to transform it: Chen 2011, storyofstori.es/lcd.
184 one atom at a time: In the case of elements; one molecule at a time in the case of alloys.
184 vapors: Sputter deposition or other physical vapor deposition.
184 radio waves: Chen 2011, storyofstori.es/lcd.
184 plasmas: Plasma-enhanced chemical vapor deposition, or PECVD.
184 etching: Wet etching, or plasma etching.
184 microscopic electronic switches: A thin film transistor, or TFT.
184 four types of molecule: De Souza Gomes 2012, storyofstori.es/polymers; and Naegele 2017, storyofstori.es/E7.
185 In less than a week: Chen 2019.
185 the Copper Age: Also known as the Chalcolithic, Eneolithic, and Aeneolithic.
185 raw material cost: Specifically the Bill of Materials (BOM) cost.
185 nearly all of its weight: BOE says a screen excluding glass weighs approximately 0.59 g.
185 half a billion tons: Wikimapia.org 2009, storyofstori.es/mine.
185 two hundred years' supply: Calculated from data in The Nikkei 2020, storyofstori.es/next.
186 ten dollars: In 2018, BOE spent $3.5 billion on consumables and made 0.53 million screens.
186 many hours of skilled human labor: On cars and robots, see Pardi et al. 2020, storyofstori.es/pardi.
186 $6 billion: "Silica Sand for Japan" 2019, storyofstori.es/silica.
186 $50 billion: My estimate, based on conversation in "Silica Sand for Japan."
187 two and a half million: All data in this discussion is based on 2021.
187 a thousand screens: World display production is 1,042 displays every 12 seconds.
187 in the next twenty-four hours: This is based on market data from various IHS Markit Display Market Trackers for 2018. IHS is now owned by Accuris. Most IHS data is confidential and for clients only, but you can see an example of their data at storyofstori.es/ihs.
187 every three people: The number sold in 2018 was 36.8 percent of the world's population.
187 Joe Russo was there: Russo Brothers 2020, storyofstori.es/russotweet.
189 One of the most successful: *Westworld* was the 22nd highest grossing movie of 1973. See storyofstori.es/1973. For comparison, the 22nd highest grossing movie of 2024 was *Alien: Romulus*. See storyofstori.es/2024.
189 *Westworld*: Crichton 1973, storyofstori.es/westworld.
189 Ding Yi: 丁乙.
189 infrared vision: Polito 1973, storyofstori.es/polito.
190 technology invented at NASA: Whitney 1973, storyofstori.es/sfx.
190 Robert Nathan: Tomayko 1988, storyofstori.es/NASA.
190 all-white wardrobe: Polito 1973, storyofstori.es/polito.
190 120 hours: calculated from Whitney 1973, storyofstori.es/sfx.
191 2,496 computer-generated shots: Pearson 2021, storyofstori.es/wanda.
191 The scene switches: Marvel Studios 2019, storyofstori.es/assemble; Moltenbrey 2019, storyofstori.es/VFX; and Bennett et al. 2021, storyofstori.es/studios.
192 not just Ancient Greek: More specifically, *Koine* (literally "Common") *Greek*.
193 Don Quixote: Don Quixote was not a *picaro* himself; for example, he does not wander alone.

193	*Un homme de têtes*: You can watch Georges Méliès's *Un homme de têtes* at storyofstori.es/heads.
193	the first fake photographs: The "Cottingley Fairies."
194	About 2,500 years ago: Xu et al. 2013, storyofstori.es/orange.
194	a rare local jewel bug: Gwynne and Rentz 1983, storyofstori.es/bottle.
194	discarded orange peel: Bellamy and Weir 2008, storyofstori.es/zoo.
195	our sense of reality: Idea from Hoffman in Dickinson et al. 2009, storyofstori.es/user.
195	nonpoisonous butterflies: See, for example, Mallet and Singer 1987, storyofstori.es/kin.
195	*Ophrys* orchids: Not all *Ophrys* do this. See Kullenberg 1950, storyofstori.es/ophrys; and Holen et al. 2001, storyofstori.es/parasites.
196	fifteen stories above: The Garden Terrace of the Four Seasons Hotel, Seoul.
196	80 million people: This is the international audience size according to Kohs 2017, storyofstori.es/AlphaGo.
196	twenty-five-hundred-year history: Fairbairn 1995, storyofstori.es/go.
196	the oldest board game: Specifically the oldest *continuously played* board game.
196	and 19 squares high: Smaller boards are sometimes used.
196	the most space: There are two scoring systems: *area scoring* and *territory scoring*.
196	Tens of millions: The International Go Federation 2016, storyofstori.es/gopop.
196	Se-dol has predicted: Kohs 2017, storyofstori.es/AlphaGo.
196	at this level: In October 2015, AlphaGo beat Fan Hui, a 2-dan. Lee was a 9-dan.
197	based in Britain: Based in Britain but by 2016 had been acquired by Google.
197	more than four minutes: Estimated from Kohs 2017, storyofstori.es/AlphaGo.
197	The experts laugh: For example, 0:32:22 in Kohs, 2017.
197	an unpredictable play: This is move 7, game 1. See Hui et al. 2016, storyofstori.es/game1.
197	fifth and sixth moves: The tenth and twelfth moves in the game.
197	One professional player: Kohs 2017 (storyofstori.es/AlphaGo) at 0:36:06.
197	almost makes a terrible move: You can see this moment at 0:35:35 in Kohs 2017, storyofstori.es/AlphaGo.
198	"I was surprised": Edited from Kohs 2017 (storyofstori.es/AlphaGo) starting at 0:42:58.
198	*quiet*: For example Hui et al. 2016, storyofstori.es/game1.
198	*peaceful*: See, for example, storyofstori.es/peaceful.
198	a strange seventh move: The thirteenth move overall.
198	*sente*: This is from the Japanese 先手, which means "first move."
198	*gote*: From the Japanese 後手, which means "second move."
198	"omission": The Japanese is 手抜き, literally "omitting critical steps."
198	Yoo Changhyuk: 유창혁 / 劉昌赫. Yoo had a 65 percent win rate.
198	raise questions: Kohs 2017 (storyofstori.es/AlphaGo) at 0:46:51.
199	830 tiny islands: Only 111 of the islands are inhabited.
199	mudflats: For an overview of the mudflats of Sinan, see Kim 2013, storyofstori.es/islands.
199	salt fields: Approximately 70 percent of Korean sea salt, or 천일염, comes from the Sinan region.
199	sent him to a Go school: The school of Kwon Kapyong, now known as KIBA.
199	Jeolla: More precisely, Southern Jeolla. See Jeon 2013, storyofstori.es/jeon.
199	thought pizza grew on trees: Kohs 2017 (storyofstori.es/AlphaGo) at 0:18:09.
199	Kweon Kab-yong: 권갑용 / 權甲龍.
199	in five months: See storyofstori.es/lee.

Notes

- 200   Kim Myung Wan: 김명완.
- 200   "it's too high": Actually, "it's a little bit high," but this was his clear meaning.
- 200   "Here?!": Hui et al. 2016, storyofstori.es/game1.
- 200   He is smiling: You can see this in Kohs 2017 (storyofstori.es/AlphaGo) at 0:50:27.
- 201   "I've realized": Yonhap News Agency 2019, storyofstori.es/yonhap.
- 201   "installs a statue": storyofstori.es/memorial.
- 201   like *Space Invaders*: See storyofstori.es/space.
- 202   *Developing* reinforcement learning: See storyofstori.es/silver.
- 202   "completely delusional": Kohs 2017 (storyofstori.es/AlphaGo) at 0:24:02.
- 202   "I thought it": Kohs 2017, storyofstori.es/AlphaGo. Lee says "AlphaGo," not "*it*."
- 203   *kikashi*: 利かし.
- 203   alive or dead: 死活.
- 203   probe: *Yōsu miru* (様子見る), which translates as "wait to see."
- 203   threaten: *nerai* (狙い).
- 203   *kiai*: 気合い.
- 203   figurative shapes: Stevens 1933, storyofstori.es/sarum; Caldwell et al. 2009, storyofstori.es/lewis; and Dillon 2020, storyofstori.es/dillon.
- 203   a Moorish word for "chariot": Murray 1913, storyofstori.es/chess.
- 203   The Settlers of Catan: Now called simply Catan.
- 204   against an airplane: Adapted from Turing 1950, storyofstori.es/turing.
- 205   about half a billion dollars: Gannes 2014, storyofstori.es/vox; Efrati 2014, storyofstori.es/deep; and Shead 2020, storyofstori.es/shead.
- 205 $57 million: Adjusted to 2021 dollars. DeepMind 2016, storyofstori.es/deepmind.
- 205   another potential buyer: Facebook: Efrati 2014, storyofstori.es/deep.
- 205   "evolution in hyperdrive": From the foreword to Oakley 2008, storyofstori.es/oakley.
- 207   advertisers of things like: See, for example, storyofstori.es/silver at 01:23:53.
- 208   "I think many": Minor 2010, storyofstori.es/minor.
- 208   Panama Canal Zone: Associated Press 2008, storyofstori.es/mccain; Chin 2008, storyofstori.es/chin; and Dobbs 2008, storyofstori.es/dobbs.
- 208   one and a half billion people: MobiThinking 2012, storyofstori.es/2011.
- 208   more than a fifth: The world population in 2011 was seven billion people.

Chapter 7: Death by a Thousand Stories

- 210   Terrance Montaine: I changed his name and superficial aspects; otherwise real.
- 214   a primordial emotion: Denton et al. 2009, storyofstori.es/denton.
- 214   Waterboarding is classified as severe torture: Hitchens 2008, storyofstori.es/hitchens; and Cox 2018, storyofstori.es/norm.
- 215   can last for days: Banzett et al. 2021, storyofstori.es/airhunger.
- 215   nothing else matters: "When you can't breathe, nothing else matters" is trademark of, and was presumably originated by, the American Lung Association. See storyofstori.es/ALA.
- 215   his lungs are breaking: Description based on Borczuk et al. 2020, storyofstori.es/COVID.
- 215   air sacs: The pulmonary alveoli.
- 215   are clogging: This is a simplified description of diffuse alveolar damage (DAD).
- 215   their veins are clotting: Platelet (CD61 positive) and/or fibrin microthrombi.
- 215   becoming abnormal: Basal membrane reduplication and endothelial swelling.
- 215   their airways: Trachea and bronchi.
- 215   getting swollen: This is a simplified description of tracheobronchitis.
- 215   and hot: Or inflamed.

215   gumball trees: *Liquidambar styraciflua*, also known as alligatorwood and sweetgum.
215   the 687,746th: Approximately; based on date. See storyofstori.es/deaths; and storyofstori.es/world.
216   "We under-invested": All Collins quotations from Woodruff 2021, storyofstori.es/PBS.
217   20,000 children: Approximately 15,000 to 25,000. Hillis et al. 2021, storyofstori.es/caregiver.
218   the vaccination rate was: 34.1 percent in October 2021, per CDC 2023, storyofstori.es/cdc.
218   death rate: Rounded from Bilinski et al. 2023, storyofstori.es/excess, Table 1. Actual number is 244,673.
218   comparable nations: Bilinski et al. 2023, storyofstori.es/excess.
219   never rose above 67: Met Office 2019, storyofstori.es/weather.
219   degrees Fahrenheit: The UK measured temperature in Fahrenheit until 1962.
219   appropriate for the event: Harman and Shapiro 2002, storyofstori.es/things.
219   Sotheby and Company: Sotheby and Company from 1924 to 1983. Now Sotheby's.
219   The items were being sold: This and other biographical details from Gleick 2007, storyofstori.es/isaac.
219   "a table to set down": The Illustrated London News 1936, storyofstori.es/sale.
220   "Newton very rarely": Edited from Newton et al. 1995, storyofstori.es/IN.
220   fortified wine: Sack, from Spain; now more commonly called sherry.
221   "not only a secret alchemist: Gleick 2007, storyofstori.es/isaac.
221   Dehumanization: See Keen 2011, storyofstori.es/tracks.
221   it moves in two directions: See, for example, Utych and Fowler 2021, storyofstori.es/than.
221   "genius": Ashton 2015 (storyofstori.es/fly) discusses why the idea of genius is nonsense.
222   Isaac was insane: Spargo et al. 1979, storyofstori.es/newlight; and Broad 1981, storyofstori.es/hatte.
222   Jean-Baptiste Biot: Spargo et al. 1979, storyofstori.es/newlight.
222   "derangement of the intellect": All discussion of poisoning from Spargo et al. 1979.
222   "I must withdraw": From a letter to Samuel Pepys. Spargo et al. 1979.
224   "just a flesh wound": See storyofstori.es/knight.
224   a submersible: *Titan*, which imploded due to hull failure on June 18, 2023.
225   "I feel like": See storyofstori.es/sub.
225   two hours: Three thousand, five hundred meters is eight times the Empire State Building, antenna included.
225   30 percent of Americans: Garbuno 2023, storyofstori.es/plane.
226   unique: Gonçalves and Carvalho 2019, storyofstori.es/death; and Johnston and Probyn-Rapsey 2020, storyofstori.es/johnston.
227   "Newton was not the first": Keynes 1946, storyofstori.es/newton.
227   is profoundly conservative: This description is from Baev 2019, storyofstori.es/arms.
228   "The Chechen campaign": Quoted in Thomas 2004, storyofstori.es/arms.
228   *protivoborstvo*: информационное противоборство. Thomas 2004.
228   "A means of": Edited from Thomas 2004.
228   Emil Pain: See storyofstori.es/pain.
228   MindWar concisely: Pain 2000. This quotation combines two quotations from Pain's paper. They are: "Russian strategists saw reprogramming public consciousness as the primary goal" and "With this psychological background it was not difficult for Russian authorities to impart a number of informational and propagandistic cliches and assure reliable public support for federal military actions

	in Chechnya." You can read the complete article storyofstori.es/chechen. Clicking on the cover image at this link will allow you to scroll through to page 59 where the article begins with the words "In December 1994 . . ."
229	*World Service*: Baumann et al. 2011, storyofstori.es/BBC; and Lawson 2013, storyofstori.es/lawson.
229	is close to: Harding et al. 2017, accessible via storyofstori.es/flynn1.
229	"an army of digital soldiers": Edited from video at storyofstori.es/flynn.
230	These stories: Many of these examples are from Silverman et al. 2020, storyofstori.es/hands.
230	military coup in Myanmar: Global Witness 2021, storyofstori.es/amp. Persecution in Cambodia: Global Witness 2016, storyofstori.es/still.
231	convinced 27 percent of Americans: YouGov 2023, storyofstori.es/conspiracies.
231	recommended a book about vaccination: Zuckerberg 2015, storyofstori.es/biss.
231	the foundation he created: The Chan Zuckerberg Initiative, storyofstori.es/czi.
231	"Facebook stands for": Edited from Zuckerberg 2017, storyofstori.es/community.
231	"one of my top priorities": Zuckerberg 2020, storyofstori.es/update.
231	told Facebook employees: Schechner et al. 2021, storyofstori.es/wsj.
231	second-richest person: This may have changed. Latest at storyofstori.es/rich.
231	a quarter of a trillion dollars: More than $228 billion, per Forbes 2021, storyofstori.es/forbes.
232	"barrier to vaccination" content: Schechner et al. 2021, storyofstori.es/wsj.
232	*Plandemic*: Willis 2020, storyofstori.es/plan.
232	publicly discredited: Cohen 2011, storyofstori.es/science; Alberts 2011, storyofstori.es/retraction; and Alba 2020, storyofstori.es/alba.
232	a few weeks after: Zuckerberg posted April 16. *Plandemic* uploaded May 4.
232	flat-out lies: Varshavski 2020, storyofstori.es/med; Funke 2020, storyofstori.es/check; and Neuman 2020, storyofstori.es/neuman.
232	available on Facebook: See storyofstori.es/plan.
233	"made the video to go viral": Rottenberg 2020, storyofstori.es/willis.
233	tens of thousands: Willis had approximately thirty thousand Facebook followers pre-*Plandemic*.
234	a 216-page, $24 book: *On Immunity* by Eula Biss on February 18, 2015: $23.99.
234	only 47 percent of Americans: Lazer et al. 2021, storyofstori.es/media.
234	resulted in: Uses data from Lazer et al. 2021, storyofstori.es/media. Details at storyofstori.es/calculation.
234	both he and Nancy disappear: There is a video of this moment at storyofstori.es/jfk.
235	at 1:40 p.m.: Times and transcripts of Cronkite from Bugliosi 2003, storyofstori.es/november.
235	"United Press International reports": Edited for brevity.
235	covered live: "Live" here means "as it happened." See Rosen 2012, storyofstori.es/rosen.
235	television news was newer: Watson 1994, storyofstori.es/vista.
235	That weekend: Data from Bodroghkozy 2012, storyofstori.es/weekend.
235	120 million Americans: U.S. Census Bureau 1963, storyofstori.es/1963. Page 26 shows the US population by age group in 1960. The total population is 179,323,000; the number of people under fifteen is 55,786,000, which leaves 123,537,000 people aged fifteen or over who can reasonably have been expected to be watching the television if one was available. 123,537,000 multiplied by 96 percent (the proportion of Americans said to be watching the television) gives us 118,596,000 people aged fifteen or over, which I have rounded up to 120 million for simplicity and also because the population grew between 1960 and 1963.
235	Over a third: May be an underestimate, as NBC had the most viewers at the time.

236	in a letter to NBC news anchor: Bodroghkozy 2012, storyofstori.es/weekend.
236	simulations of the paths: For example, Then et al. 2022, storyofstori.es/then.
237	56 percent of Americans: YouGov 2023, storyofstori.es/conspiracies.
238	has admitted to: Such activities are not unique to the United States.
238	kidnapping a Ukrainian national: Yuri Nosenko. Details in Osborn 1973, storyofstori.es/CIA.
238	opening and reading: Project HTLINGUAL, originally SRPOINTER.
238	hiring members of the Mafia: Snow 2007, storyofstori.es/castro.
238	conducting human experiments: This was a project codenamed MKUltra. For full details, see US Senate 1977, storyofstori.es/ultra.
238	one hundred Black American men: Baker et al. 2005, storyofstori.es/tusk.
238	implanting electrodes into the brains of dogs: Pliskoff and Hawking 1965, storyofstori.es/remote.
239	the vast majority of: Katz et al. 2008, storyofstori.es/aware.
239	*Wormwood*: Morris 2017, storyofstori.es/wormwood.
239	*Jacob's Ladder*: Lyne 1990, storyofstori.es/ladder. The movie relocates the experiments to the Vietnam War.
239	twice told a story: For discussion see Newby 2021, storyofstori.es/falcon.
239	*Truth: Red, White & Black*: Morales and Baker 2004, storyofstori.es/truth.
239	*The Falcon and the Winter Soldier*: Skogland 2021, storyofstori.es/skogland.
239	*Captain America: Brave New World*: Onah 2025, storyofstori.es/brave.
239	*Black Widow*: Shortland 2021, storyofstori.es/widow. The movie substituted pigs in Russia for dogs in the US.
239	*The Bourne Identity*: Ludlum 1980, storyofstori.es/bourne.
240	Abbie Richards: Richards 2021, storyofstori.es/abbie.
240	the *Mary Celeste*: Found in 1872. Not *Marie* Celeste, as is commonly supposed.
242	28 percent of Americans: YouGov 2023, storyofstori.es/conspiracies. This a centuries-old libel.
242	incidents grew: Anti-Defamation League 2024, storyofstori.es/adl. My calculation, rounded.
242	conducted an experiment: Broderick 2017, storyofstori.es/ryan.
243	"This isn't an experiment": From Broderick 2017. Edited for length.
243	In July 2019: Guynn and McCoy 2021, storyofstori.es/carol; and Mac and Frenkel 2021, storyofstori.es/mac.
243	Sophie Zhang: Mac and Frenkel 2021, storyofstori.es/mac. See also Silverman et al. 2020, storyofstori.es/hands.
244	"a perfect example": Facebook spokesman Andy Stone, in Mac and Frenkel 2021, storyofstori.es/mac.
244	yields a stream: I last confirmed this was still true on February 28, 2025.
244	Kaitlyn Tiffany: Tiffany 2021, storyofstori.es/bland.
245	"Facebook isn't just dangerous": Edited and assembled from Tiffany 2021.
247	victories, and visibility: See, for example, Dame-Griff 2023, storyofstori.es/griff.
247	for public use: Simplified. For a technical history see Harris and Gerich 1996, storyofstori.es/NSF.
247	*JohnTeen Ø* posting: From Silberman 1994, storyofstori.es/queer. Edited for length.
248	"uses an interactive computer service": storyofstori.es/text.
248	"the CDA's provisions": United States Supreme Court 1997. This quotation comprises the following parts of Stevens's opinion: "The CDA's 'indecent transmission' and 'patently offensive display' provisions abridge 'the freedom of speech' protected by the First Amendment" (page 844); "Regardless of whether the CDA is so vague that it violates the Fifth Amendment, the many ambiguities

concerning the scope of its coverage render it problematic for First Amendment purposes. For instance, its use of the undefined terms "indecent" and "patently offensive" will provoke uncertainty among speakers about how the two standards relate to each other and just what they mean" (page 845 point [d]); and "Regardless of whether the CDA is so vague that it violates the Fifth Amendment, the many ambiguities concerning the scope of its coverage render it problematic for purposes of the First Amendment. For instance, each of the two parts of the CDA uses a different linguistic form. The first uses the word 'indecent,' 47 U. S. C. § 223(a) (1994 ed., Supp. II), while the second speaks of material that 'in context, depicts or describes, in terms patently offensive as measured by contemporary community standards, sexual or excretory activities or organs,' § 223(d). Given the absence of a definition of either term, 35 this difference in language will provoke uncertainty among speakers about how the two standards relate to each other 36 and just what they mean. 37 Could a speaker confidently assume that a serious discussion about birth control practices, homosexuality, the First Amendment issues raised by the Appendix to our Pacifica opinion, or the consequences of prison rape would not violate the CDA? This uncertainty undermines the likelihood that the CDA has been carefully tailored to the congressional goal of protecting minors from potentially harmful material. The vagueness of such a regulation raises special First Amendment concerns because of its obvious chilling effect on free speech" (pages 870–72).

249   "The struggle for equal rights": Silberman 1994, storyofstori.es/queer.

Chapter 8: The Hyperreal Thing

250   Anta Diouf: Diouf 2016, storyofstori.es/anta.
250   *guedj* or sometimes *tambadiang*: Essuman 1992, storyofstori.es/fish; and Mor Gueye et al. 2020, storyofstori.es/bait.
250   advanced economies: The list of advanced economies is from Table B on page 127 of the Statistical Appendix of International Monetary Fund 2019, storyofstori.es/imf.
251   15 percent: Advanced economies: 1.1 billion of 7.7 billion, or approximately 14.2 percent.
251   using the equation: Gilder 1993, storyofstori.es/gilder; Gilder 2000, storyofstori.es/telecosm; and Metcalfe 2013, storyofstori.es/40.
251   the networking pioneer: For example, Metcalfe is the inventor of Ethernet.
251   was most places: Worldwide, approximately one in five people had access to a telephone in 2000.
251   smartphone shows: The app is WISE by Wireless Solutions for Fisheries in Senegal.
252   She says: Diouf 2016, at 00:50, storyofstori.es/anta.
252   an ultrasonic anemometer: This has, in most cases, replaced wind vanes and cups.
252   the drops twinkle: Light-emitting diode weather identifier (LEDWI).
253   ever foresaw: But there were many predictions of handheld wireless multimedia devices.
253   what network architects call a *client*: Specifically a hybrid client.
253   a *unique identifier*: Most (and ever more) cell phones represent an individual.
253   8.5 billion people: The UN projects a population of 8.5 billion around 2030.
253   *sensor array*: "Array" as in "chemical sensor array," meaning different types of sensors.
253   ionizing radiation: Sharp Pantone 5 107SH. Byford 2012, storyofstori.es/soft.
254   any kind of phone: More precisely, 2.6 percent of Senegalese people had telephones in 2000.

Notes

254   one in three: Silver and Johnson 2018, storyofstori.es/pew. Thirty-four percent of Senegalese had smartphones in 2017.
254   in 2025, that number increased to *two* in three: GSMA 2018, storyofstori.es/2018.
254   seven and a half billion: Projected: 7,336,000,000 / 91 percent of world population.
254   The storage capacity: Economist 2017, storyofstori.es/cars. Goodenough and Park 2013, storyofstori.es/ion.
254   doubles every six years: Also, the price halves about every four years.
254   every two years: For example, spectral efficiency in cell networks. Clarke 2013, storyofstori.es/expand.
254   Koomey's Law: Koomey et al. 2011, storyofstori.es/koomey.
255   160,000 pixels: Estimates based on Gonzalez 2016, storyofstori.es/pixels.
255   370,000-ish pixels: Estimate for the 625 line format, based on Gonzalez 2016, storyofstori.es/pixels.
255   more than 600,000 pixels: 576i 16:9 SD had a maximum of 603,648 pixels.
255   over 2 million pixels: 1080p (progressive) HD has 2,073,600 pixels.
255   four times as many pixels: 4K UHD has 8,294,400 pixels, four times more than 1080p.
255   generally available: Current availability, if any, on Amazon.com at storyofstori.es/8k.
256   33 million pixels: 8K UHD has 33,177,600 pixels, four times more than 4K UHD.
256   1.3 times: A 10K TV has 44,236,800 pixels, 133 percent of an 8K UHD TV.
256   nearly 133 million pixels: A 16K TV has 132,710,400 pixels.
256   two hundred times more resolution: 16K is not generally available but see storyofstori.es/sony.
256   often have: The *Real 3D* system has differently polarized lenses instead.
256   we can in fact see in three dimensions with one eye: Vishwanath and Hibbard 2013, storyofstori.es/3D.
257   576 million pixels: Clark 2018, storyofstori.es/clark.
257   one or two steps: This assumes that 24K follows 16K.
257   it is already possible to make 16K movies: Cade 2020, storyofstori.es/16k.
258   The next step in computer graphics: See, for example, storyofstori.es/sunstone.
258   more computing power: Also more memory.
259   a few dozen: A typical Space Invader consisted of 48 pixels. Cantrell 2021, storyofstori.es/invaders.
259   575 triangles: Cohen 2000, storyofstori.es/lara. I have assumed 2.5 triangles per polygon.
259   100,000 triangles: Lithvall 2017, storyofstori.es/hair.
259   175 times more: Rounded up from 173.9.
260   computer generated: For example, the opening of 2016's *Deadpool*. storyofstori.es/deadpool.
260   Masahiro Mori: 森 政弘; "uncanny valley": 不気味の谷現象. Mori et al. 2012, storyofstori.es/mori.
261   MetaHuman Creator, released in 2021: Kerr 2021, storyofstori.es/epicgames.
261   one strand at a time: LOD 0 faces created in MetaHuman Creator / Unreal Engine 5.
261   mobile facial areas: Technically: blend shapes or shape keys.
261   Studies have found: For example, Higgins et al. 2018, storyofstori.es/valley.
261   Staircase Studios AI announced: Lambie 2025, storyofstori.es/studio. See also storyofstori.es/redhair.
262   free to use: Epic Games takes a royalty on gross revenues over $1 million.
262   Celine Song performed: American Theatre Wing 2021, storyofstori.es/wing.
262   Oosterveen performed: Grylls and Crane 2024, storyofstori.es/hamlet.
262   "Hiro Protagonist is sitting": Edited from pages 19–22 of Stephenson 2003, storyofstori.es/snow.

Page	Note
264	had no legs: Meta announced legs in 2022. Matney 2022, storyofstori.es/legs.
264	"Not only was I groped": Edited from Heath 2021, storyofstori.es/heath. See also Mahdawi 2021, storyofstori.es/metaverse.
265	33 percent a year: Data from WSJ Markets 2022, storyofstori.es/WSJ.
265	26 percent in 2021: Omdia 2021, storyofstori.es/omdia.
266	sixty or older by 2050: See Wong 2015, storyofstori.es/1950s; and *ChinaPower* 2020, storyofstori.es/aging.
266	"The frontier of technology is in America": Chen 2019.
268	five major types of sensor: We have more senses, but the "famous five" suffice here.
268	8 million hairs: These hairs are called stereocilia.
268	touch receptors: This includes nociceptors and thermoreceptors, and is rounded down.
268	50 million taste cells: These are called papillae. See Trivedi 2012, storyofstori.es/taste.
268	which first evolved as: Sherman 1977, storyofstori.es/nepo.
269	wings evolved separately in bats: Example from Morris 2008, storyofstori.es/morris.
269	almost certainly a single-celled organism: Meyerowitz 2002, storyofstori.es/compared.
269	a simple, prototypical nervous system: See, for example, Christensen et al. 1997, storyofstori.es/signal.
269	The first trees appeared: *Wattieza* lived during the mid-Devonian.
269	the first humans appeared: *Homo habilis*, which lived during the Pleistocene.
269	its head is its roots: The roots are the anterior, the "top" is the posterior.
269	brain-like information-processing properties: Baluška et al. 2009, storyofstori.es/root.
269	noted that: Darwin 1880, storyofstori.es/plants.
269	a tree's root tips: Baluška et al. 2009, storyofstori.es/root.
269	trees also use herd sentience: Simard 2018, storyofstori.es/myco.
270	synchronize some of their behaviors: See, for example, Satake and Iwasa 2000, storyofstori.es/chaos.
271	*participatory sensing*: Burke et al. 2006, storyofstori.es/part. Ganti et al. 2011 (storyofstori.es/crowd) proposes crowdsensing.
271	Baidu Maps: Biuk-Aghai et al. 2016 (storyofstori.es/bigdata) implies *Baidu Maps* uses participatory sensing.
271	More than 100,000 people were killed: Estimates range from 100,000 to 316,000.
271	630,000 more: Bengtsson et al. 2011, storyofstori.es/improved.
271	about 25 percent: In 2009, the population of Port-au-Prince was 2,643,000.
271	United Nations peacekeepers from Nepal: Alston 2018, storyofstori.es/haiti.
271	94,000 fled: Calculated from Bengtsson et al.
272	where they went: Bengtsson et al. used base station locations as a proxy.
272	this information was shared: Bengtsson et al.
272	to help contain: It is not clear the data was used. Gething and Tatem 2011, storyofstori.es/can.
272	In 2013: Scharff et al. 2015, storyofstori.es/festivals.
273	cat food after talking about cat food: See storyofstori.es/neville.
273	Constant audio surveillance: Martínez 2017, storyofstori.es/wired.
274	*agent detection bias*: I believe this term was introduced by Barrett 2000, storyofstori.es/religion.
274	*the bias blind spot*: Pronin et al. 2002, storyofstori.es/blind.
274	*uniqueness bias*: Or *false uniqueness*. For discussion see Suls and Wan 1987, storyofstori.es/unique.
274	their face in it: Pesenti 2021, storyofstori.es/use; and Facebook 2021, storyofstori.es/setting.

Notes

274   megabyte of data: Statista 2021, storyofstori.es/active; Wiener and Bronson 2014, storyofstori.es/top; and Hall et al. 2014, storyofstori.es/gartner.
275   In the 1920s: Freeman 1996, storyofstori.es/freeman.
275   No matter what factors: McPherson et al. 2001, storyofstori.es/feather.
275   geography: Scholars call this *propinquity* and sometimes *kinship*.
275   the most popular social network in the world: Statista 2021, storyofstori.es/active.
275   five quintillion: Possible relationships between 3 billion people: about 4.5 quintillion.
276   tend to be friends with each other: Data in this discussion from Ugander et al. 2011, storyofstori.es/graph.
276   own data scientists: Ugander was at Facebook from 2010 to 2014.
276   about fifty thousand times: I assumed four billion posts a day, or 46,296 posts per second.
276   millions of offline simulations: Letham and Bakshy 2019, storyofstori.es/via.
277   "job creators": For example, Kooi 2009, storyofstori.es/VC.
278   NIPE: Also known as "profit per employee," or PPE.
278   There is abundant evidence: For example, Decker et al. 2015, storyofstori.es/skew; and Berger and Frey 2015, storyofstori.es/renewal.
278   one of the most extensive studies: Berger and Frey 2015.
278    $29 billion: Facebook's 2020 net income was $29 billion with 59,000 employees.
278   half a million dollars: $497,338.07.
278   seventh highest: I reranked the 2019 data using 2020 figures.
278   five banks: Fannie Mae, KKR, Freddie Mac, Blackstone Group, and Visa.
278   an oil company: Enterprise Products Partners (which is also a natural gas supplier).
278    $31,000: 2019 value, based on data at storyofstori.es/nipe.
278   generated by: Times's 2019 net income was $140 million with 4,500 employees.
279   360,000 people: 359,479. US Bureau of Labor Statistics 2017, storyofstori.es/labor.
279   110,000: 113,256, a drop of 246,223. US Bureau of Labor Statistics 2017, storyofstori.es/labor.
279   Sixty percent of all US publishing jobs: US Bureau of Labor Statistics 2017, storyofstori.es/labor.
280   plagiarized words or images: See, for example, Marcus and Southen 2024, storyofstori.es/gen.
281   impact: Borggren et al. 2011, storyofstori.es/books; Moberg et al. 2011, storyofstori.es/ebooks; and Patterson et al. 2021, storyofstori.es/carbon.
283   consider broadcast radio: From Pessimists Archive, storyofstori.es/pessimists.
284   "drying up the air": *The Winnipeg Tribune* 1930, storyofstori.es/drought.
284   "doing something to the atmosphere": *El Paso Herald-Post* 1934, storyofstori.es/herald.
284   "radio waves break the clouds": *Lebanon Daily News* 1928, storyofstori.es/news.
284   "wireless wrinkles": This and following quotations from *The Ottawa Journal* 1925, storyofstori.es/fear.
284   "large blue splotches": *Honolulu Star-Bulletin* 1929, storyofstori.es/pesky.
284   Altered faces is a recurring motif: Pessimists Archive, storyofstori.es/faces.
284   "wildly expectant eyes": These quotes are from *The Eagle* 1896, storyofstori.es/bicycle.
284   "looking afraid of a collision": Edited from *Topeka State Journal* 1899, storyofstori.es/topeka.
284   "head bulging between the ears": *Spokesman-Review* 1908, storyofstori.es/andnow.
284   "wonder or surprise": *Evening Sun* 1915, storyofstori.es/moving.
284   "causes your face to droop": Youn 2012, storyofstori.es/youn.
284   causing divorce: *Central New Jersey Home News* 1923, storyofstori.es/mania.

284	"fineness of taste": *Daily News* 1929, storyofstori.es/daily.
284	"aimless wandering": *Los Angeles Evening Post-Record* 1922, storyofstori.es/youth.
284	"conversation in the family": Cleveland Myers 1965, storyofstori.es/hampers.
284	"the purity of elections": *Spokesman-Review* 1936, storyofstori.es/purity.
284	"interfere with the school success": Preston 1941, storyofstori.es/preston.
286	the first mechanical submarine: *Plongeur*, launched in 1863.
286	*Frankenstein*: In the movie, the monster is animated by electrodes in his neck.
286	sheep cloning in 1984: Willadsen 1986, storyofstori.es/sheep. Rosselló 2014 (storyofstori.es/amber) debunks "DNA in amber."
287	"How can we be cheerful": Peacock 1818, storyofstori.es/abbey.
287	"What a piece of work is a man": Phillips December 17, 2022, storyofstori.es/man.
288	helps children become critical thinkers: See, for example, Lai 2011, storyofstori.es/critical.
290	in law: Bonica 2017, storyofstori.es/lawyers. Lawyers are one hundred times more likely to be elected to Congress.
290	new concepts: Morris and Venkatesh 2000, storyofstori.es/age; and Czaja et al. 2006, storyofstori.es/create.
290	The average age of elected officials: Data from IPU Parline 2025, storyofstori.es/IPU.

Bibliography

Aachen Cathedral Chapter. 2023. "Aachen Shrine Trip 2023." storyofstori.es/aachen.
Abramson, A. 2009. *The History of Television, 1880 to 1941.* storyofstori.es/1880.
Addison, H. R., et al. 1907. *Who's Who.* storyofstori.es/1907.
Adelman, Joseph M. 2010. "'A Constitutional Conveyance of Intelligence, Public and Private': The Post Office, the Business of Printing, and the American Revolution." *Enterprise & Society* 11 (4): 711–54. storyofstori.es/postoffice.
Ajzen, Icek, and Martin Fishbein. 1975. "A Bayesian Analysis of Attribution Processes." *Psychological Bulletin* 82 (2): 261–77. storyofstori.es/attribution.
Akçomak, İ. Semih, et al. 2016. "Why Did the Netherlands Develop So Early? The Legacy of the Brethren of the Common Life." *Economic Journal* 126 (593): 821–60. storyofstori.es/legacy.
Alava, Mikko, and Kaarlo Niskanen. 2006. "The Physics of Paper." *Reports on Progress in Physics* 69 (3): 669–724. storyofstori.es/physics.
Alba, Davey. 2020. "Virus Conspiracists Elevate a New Champion." *New York Times*, May 9. storyofstori.es/alba.
Albeck-Ripka, Livia, 2023. "A Book Club Took 28 Years to Read 'Finnegans Wake.' Now, It's Starting Over." *New York Times*. storyofstori.es/wake.
Alberts, Bruce. 2011. "Retraction." *Science* 334 (6063): 1636. storyofstori.es/retraction.
Algeo, John. 1978. "What Consonant Clusters Are Possible?" *Word* 29 (3): 206–24. storyofstori.es/clusters.
Allen, J. P. 2020. *Ancient Egyptian Phonology.* storyofstori.es/phono.
Allers, R., and R. Minkoff, dir. 1994. *The Lion King.* storyofstori.es/lion.
Allport, Gordon W., et al. 1945. "The Basic Psychology of Rumor." *Transactions of the New York Academy of Sciences* 8 (2 Series II): 61–81. storyofstori.es/basic.
Allport, Gordon W., et al. 1946. "An Analysis of Rumor." *Public Opinion Quarterly* 10 (4): 501–17. storyofstori.es/rumor.
Alston, Philip. 2018. *Extracting Accountability: Special Rapporteurs and the United Nations' Responsibility for Cholera in Haiti.* NYU School of Law, Public Law Research Paper nos. 18–10: 1–101. storyofstori.es/haiti.
American Library Association. 2025a. "Censorship by the Numbers." American Library Association. storyofstori.es/bookbans.
American Library Association. 2025b. "Top 10 Most Challenged Books of 2024." *American Library Association.* storyofstori.es/topten.
American Theatre Wing. 2021. "Working in the Theatre: *The Seagull* on the *Sims 4*." YouTube video. storyofstori.es/wing.
Amoghavajra (translator), 755. "Sūtra of the Dhāraṇī of the Precious Casket Seal of the Concealed Complete-body Relics of the Essence of All Tathāgatas (一切如來心祕密全身舍利寶篋印陀羅尼經)." *Taishō Tripiṭaka* 19 (1022). Amoghavajra's Chinese translation: storyofstori.es/sutra-chinese. English translation from Tibetan by Dylan Esler: storyofstori.es/sutra-english.

Amt, E. et al., 2007. *Dialogus De Scaccario, and Constitutio Domus Regis: The Dialogue of the Exchequer, and the Disposition of the Royal Household*. Oxford Medieval Texts. storyofstori.es/amt.

Anti-Defamation League, 2024. "White Supremacist Propaganda Incidents Soar to Record High in 2023." *ADL*. storyofstori.es/adl.

Apicella, Coren L., et al. 2007. "Voice Pitch Predicts Reproductive Success in Male Hunter-Gatherers." *Biology Letters* 3 (6): 682–84. storyofstori.es/predicts.

Apicella, Coren L., and David R. Feinberg. 2009. "Voice Pitch Alters Mate-Choice-Relevant Perception in Hunter-Gatherers." *Proceedings of the Royal Society B: Biological Sciences* 276 (1659): 1077–82. storyofstori.es/voicepitch.

Apikian, Nevart. *Syracuse Post-Standard*, 1974. "'Mummy Paper' Caused a Stir." storyofstori.es/stir.

Aqrawi, A. A. M. 2001. "Stratigraphic Signatures of Climatic Change During the Holocene Evolution of the Tigris-Euphrates Delta, Lower Mesopotamia." *Global and Planetary Change* 28 (1): 267–83. storyofstori.es/change.

Arak, Anthony, and Magnus Enquist. 1993. "Hidden Preferences and the Evolution of Signals." *Philosophical Transactions of the Royal Society, Series B: Biological Sciences* 340 (1292): 207–13. storyofstori.es/hidden.

Archer, Clare. 2004. "Cyperus Papyrus." *South African National Biodiversity Institute*. storyofstori.es/papyrus.

Ariely, Dan, et al. 2008. "Man's Search for Meaning: The Case of Legos." *Journal of Economic Behavior & Organization* 67 (3–4): 671–77. storyofstori.es/legos.

Aristotle. 2006. *Poetics*. Translated by S. H. Butcher. storyofstori.es/poetics.

Asante, M. K. 2010. *100 Greatest African Americans: A Biographical Encyclopedia*. storyofstori.es/100.

Ashburn, Eddie. 2004. *The History of the Memphis Police Department*. storyofstori.es/memphis.

Ashmead, Daniel H., et al. 1986. "Development of Auditory Localization in Dogs: Single Source and Precedence Effect Sounds." *Developmental Psychobiology* 19 (2): 91–103. storyofstori.es/ashmead.

Ashmore, Eddie. 2004. *The History of the Memphis Police Department*. storyofstori.es/ashmore.

Ashton, Kevin. 2013. "Stop Coddling Your Dog—He's 99.9% Wolf." *Quartz*. storyofstori.es/wolf.

Ashton, Kevin. 2015. *How to Fly a Horse: The Secret History of Creation, Invention, and Discovery*. storyofstori.es/fly.

Associated Press, 2008. "Lawyers Conclude McCain Is 'Natural Born.'" *CBS News*. storyofstori.es/mccain.

Astley, N., and M. Baker. 2004. *Peppa Pig*. storyofstori.es/peppa.

Atlantic Monthly. 1880. Volume 46: 722. storyofstori.es/atlantic.

Autin, Kelsey L., and Blake A. Allan. 2019. "Socioeconomic Privilege and Meaningful Work: A Psychology of Working Perspective." *Journal of Career Assessment* 28 (2): 241–56. storyofstori.es/meaning.

Avvisati, Francesco, François Keslair, and Francesca Borgonovi. 2024. *Do Adults Have the Skills They Need to Thrive in a Changing World? OECD Skills Outlook 2024*. storyofstori.es/adults.

Azéma, Marc, and Florent Rivère. 2012. "Animation in Palaeolithic Art: A Pre-Echo of Cinema." *Antiquity* 86 (332): 316–24. storyofstori.es/animation.

Baev, Pavel K. 2019. "The Interplay of Bureaucratic, Warfighting, and Arms-Parading Traits in Russian Military-Strategic Culture." *Marshall Center Security Insights* 28. storyofstori.es/arms.

Bagnold, R. A. 2012. *The Physics of Blown Sand and Desert Dunes*. storyofstori.es/bagnold.

Bailey, Betty A., and Jane W. Davidson. 2005. "Effects of Group Singing and Performance for Marginalized and Middle-Class Singers." *Psychology of Music* 33 (3): 269–303. storyofstori.es/groupsinging.

Baker, Nicholson. 2002. *Double Fold: Libraries and the Assault on Paper.* storyofstori.es/double.

Baker, Shamim M., et al. 2005. "Effects of Untreated Syphilis in the Negro Male, 1932 to 1972: A Closure Comes to the Tuskegee Study, 2004." *Urology* 65 (6): 1259–62. storyofstori.es/tusk.

Baluška, František, et al. 2009. "The 'Root-Brain' Hypothesis of Charles and Francis Darwin: Revival After More Than 125 Years." *Plant Signaling & Behavior* 4 (12): 1121–27. storyofstori.es/root.

Banzett, Robert B., et al. 2021. "Air Hunger: A Primal Sensation and a Primary Element of Dyspnea." *Comprehensive Physiology* 11 (2): 1449–83. storyofstori.es/airhunger.

Barja, Isabel, et al. 2004. "The Importance of Crossroads in Faecal Marking Behaviour of the Wolves (*Canis lupus*)." *Naturwissenschaften* 91 (10): 489–92. storyofstori.es/crossroads.

Barker, Chris. 2016. "How Many Syllables Does English Have?" New York University webpage. storyofstori.es/how.

Barlow, C. H. 1951. "The Ancient Pharaonic Turquoise Mines of Sinai." *Rocks & Minerals* 26 (7–8): 348–53. storyofstori.es/barlow.

Barrett, Justin L. 2000. "Exploring the Natural Foundations of Religion." *Trends in Cognitive Sciences* 4 (1): 29–34. storyofstori.es/religion.

Barthes, Roland. 1967. "The Death of the Author" in *Readings in the Theory of Religion*, edited by Scott S. Elliott et al. 141–45. storyofstori.es/author.

Barthes, Roland, et al. 1974. *S/Z.* storyofstori.es/SZ.

Barthes, Roland, and Lionel Duisit. 1975. "An Introduction to the Structural Analysis of Narrative." *New Literary History* 6 (2): 237–72. storyofstori.es/intro.

Bartlett, James C., and Paul Snelus. 1980. "Lifespan Memory for Popular Songs." *American Journal of Psychology* 93 (3): 551–60. storyofstori.es/lifespan.

Bartz, Jennifer A., et al. 2011. "Social Effects of Oxytocin in Humans: Context and Person Matter." *Trends in Cognitive Sciences* 15 (7): 301–9. storyofstori.es/social.

Baumann, Gerd et al. 2011. "Transcultural Journalism and the Politics of Translation: Interrogating the BBC World Service." *Journalism* 12 (2): 135–42. storyofstori.es/BBC.

Baxter, William T. 1989. "Early Accounting: The Tally and Checkerboard." *Accounting Historians Journal* 16 (2): 43–83. storyofstori.es/tally.

Baxter, W. H. 2014. *Old Chinese: A New Reconstruction.* storyofstori.es/baxter.

Beattie, H. S., and R. A. Rahenkamp. 1981. "IBM Typewriter Innovation." *IBM Journal of Research and Development* 25 (5): 729–40. storyofstori.es/IBM.

Beauchamp, K. G. 2001. *History of Telegraphy.* storyofstori.es/telegraphy.

Bechert, H. 1991. *Datierung des historischen Buddha.* storyofstori.es/buddha.

Bednarik, Robert G. 1995. "Concept-Mediated Marking in the Lower Palaeolithic." *Current Anthropology* 36 (4): 605–34. storyofstori.es/concept.

Bednarik, Robert G. 2004. "Interpreting the Evidence for Art Origins." *Archaeology, Ethnology and Anthropology of Eurasia* 4: 35–47. storyofstori.es/evidence.

Belkin, Douglas. 2024. "Christopher Rufo Has Trump's Ear and Wants to End DEI for Good." *Wall Street Journal.* storyofstori.es/equality.

Bell, Jacob, ed. 1844-5. *Pharmaceutical Journal and Transactions* Volume IV. storyofstori.es/pharma.

Bellamy, C. L., and T. Weir. 2008. "The Reinstatement of *Julodimorpha saundersii* Thomson 1879 (Coleoptera: Buprestidae) as a Valid Species." *Zootaxa* 1751 (1): 46–54. storyofstori.es/zoo.

Bengtsson, Linus, et al. 2011. "Improved Response to Disasters and Outbreaks by Tracking Population Movements with Mobile Phone Network Data: A Post-Earthquake Geospatial Study in Haiti." *PLoS Medicine* 8: e1001083. storyofstori.es/improved.

Bennett, T., et al. 2021. *The Story of Marvel Studios: The Making of the Marvel Cinematic Universe*. storyofstori.es/studios.

Berg, Martin, et al. 2017. "The Speaking Voice in the General Population: Normative Data and Associations to Sociodemographic and Lifestyle Factors." *Journal of Voice* 31 (2): e13–24. storyofstori.es/voice.

Berger, Thor, and Carl B. Frey. 2015. "Industrial Renewal in the 21st Century: Evidence from US Cities." *Regional Studies* 51 (3): 404–13. storyofstori.es/renewal.

Bertrand, M. T. 2000. *Race, Rock, and Elvis*. storyofstori.es/rock.

Bezbakh, Pierre. 2009. "Eugène Poubelle, L'Inventeur du Tri Sélectif." *Le Monde*. storyofstori.es/poubelle.

Bidwell, Shelford. 1908. "Telegraphic Photography and Electric Vision." *Nature* 78: 105–6. storyofstori.es/bidwell.

Bilinski, Alyssa, et al. 2023. "COVID-19 and Excess All-Cause Mortality in the US and 20 Comparison Countries, June 2021–March 2022." *JAMA* 329 (1): 92–94. storyofstori.es/excess.

Bird, Douglas W., et al. 2019. "Variability in the Organization and Size of Hunter-Gatherer Groups: Foragers Do Not Live in Small-Scale Societies." *Journal of Human Evolution* 131: 96–108. storyofstori.es/foragers.

Biuk-Aghai, Robert, et al. 2016. "Big Data Analytics for Transportation: Problems and Prospects for Its Application in China." *2016 IEEE Region 10 Symposium*. storyofstori.es/bigdata.

Bizzocchi, Aldo. 2017. "How Many Phonemes Does the English Language Have?" *International Journal on Studies in English Language and Literature* 5: 36–46. storyofstori.es/phonemes.

Blok, P. J., and P. C. Molhuysen. 1918. *Nieuw Nederlandsch Biografisch Woordenboek*. Deel 4. storyofstori.es/blok.

Bloom, J. M. 2001. *Paper Before Print: The History and Impact of Paper in the Islamic World*. storyofstori.es/before.

Bodroghkozy, Aniko. 2012. "Black Weekend: A Reception History of Network Television News and the Assassination of John F. Kennedy." *Television & New Media* 14 (6): 560–78. storyofstori.es/weekend.

BOE Technology Group Co. 2019. "BOE Founder and Chairman Wang Dongsheng Won SID 'David Sarnoff Industrial Achievement Prize.'" *PR News Wire*. storyofstori.es/prize.

BOE Technology Group Co. 2022. "BOE Technology Group Co., Ltd. Annual Report 2021 (Summary)." *Sina*. storyofstori.es/BOE2021.

Bonica, Adam. 2017. "Why Are There So Many Lawyers in Congress?" *Legislative Studies Quarterly* 45 (2): 253–89. storyofstori.es/lawyers.

Bon Jovi, Jon. 2020. *Access Hollywood* interview with Sibley Scoles. storyofstori.es/access.

Boole, G. 1847. *The Mathematical Analysis of Logic: Being an Essay Towards a Calculus of Deductive Reasoning*. storyofstori.es/boole.

Boole, G. 1911. *The Laws of Thought*. storyofstori.es/thought.

Borczuk, Alain C., et al. 2020. "COVID-19 Pulmonary Pathology: A Multi-Institutional Autopsy Cohort from Italy and New York City." *Modern Pathology* 33 (11): 2156–68. storyofstori.es/COVID.

Borggren, Clara, et al. 2011. "Books from an Environmental Perspective—Part 1: Environmental Impacts of Paper Books Sold in Traditional and Internet Bookshops." *International Journal of Life Cycle Assessment* 16 (2): 138–47. storyofstori.es/books.

Bourogiannis, Giorgos, and Christina Ioannou. 2012. "'Phoinikeia Grammata' at Cos: A New Case of Phoenician Script from Archaic Greece." *Ancient Near Eastern Studies* 49: 1–23. storyofstori.es/cos.
Bowman, Russell. 1985. "Words and Images: A Persistent Paradox." *Art Journal* 45 (4): 335–43. storyofstori.es/bowman.
Bradbury, J. 1992. *The Medieval Siege*. storyofstori.es/siege.
Bradbury, Raymond. 2008. *Fahrenheit 451*. storyofstori.es/451.
Brady, Dorothy S. 1964. "Relative Prices in the Nineteenth Century." *The Journal of Economic History* 24 (2): 145–203. storyofstori.es/prices.
Brahe, Tycho. 1602. *Tychonis Brahe Astronomiae Instauratae Mechanica*. Apud Levivum Hvlsium. storyofstori.es/tycho.
Bregman, Albert S. 1994. *Auditory Scene Analysis*. storyofstori.es/scene.
Brightman, Carol. 2003. "In Bed with the Pentagon." *The Nation*. storyofstori.es/bed.
British Transport Police. 2025. *The Murder of Sarah Hart, 1845*. storyofstori.es/police.
Broad, William J. 1981. "Sir Isaac Newton: Mad as a Hatter." *Science* 213 (4514): 1341–42. storyofstori.es/hatter.
Broderick, Ryan, 2017. "I Made a Facebook Profile, Started Liking Right-Wing Pages, and Radicalized My News Feed in Four Days." *Buzzfeed*. storyofstori.es/ryan.
Brooks, Charles F. 1929. "Severe Winter in Europe." *Bulletin of the American Meteorological Society* 10 (3): 72–75. storyofstori.es/brooks.
Brooks, J. 1969. *Business Adventures*. storyofstori.es/business.
Brown, Steven. 2000. "Evolutionary Models of Music: From Sexual Selection to Group Selection" in *Perspectives in Ethology*, edited by P. P. G. Bateson et al. 231–81. storyofstori.es/models.
Brumm, Adam, et al. 2021. "Oldest Cave Art Found in Sulawesi." *Science Advances* 7 (3): 1–12. storyofstori.es/oldest.
Bruner, Jerome S. 2009. *Actual Minds, Possible Worlds*. storyofstori.es/minds.
Bryant, Gregory A., et al. 2009. "Vocal Cues of Ovulation in Human Females." *Biology Letters* 5 (1): 12–15. storyofstori.es/cues.
Bugliosi, V. 2003. *Four Days in November: The Original Coverage of the John F. Kennedy Assassination*. storyofstori.es/november.
Burckhardt, J. 2019. *Die Cultur der Renaissance in Italien*. storyofstori.es/jacob.
Burger, Peter. 2007. *Charles Fenerty and His Paper Invention*. storyofstori.es/charles.
Buringh, Eltjo, and Jan Luiten van Zanden. 2009. "Charting the 'Rise of the West': Manuscripts and Printed Books in Europe." *Journal of Economic History* 69 (2): 409–45. storyofstori.es/charting.
Burke, Jeffrey A., et al. 2006. "Participatory Sensing." *WSW'06 at SenSys '06*. storyofstori.es/part.Burns, Russell W. 1998. *Television: An International History of the Formative Years*. storyofstori.es/burns.
Burst, Tom L., and Michael R. Pelton. 1983. "Black Bear Mark Trees in the Smoky Mountains." *Bears: Their Biology and Management* 5: 45–53. storyofstori.es/bears.
Buskirk, Ruth E., et al., 1981. "Unusual Animal Behavior Before Earthquakes: A Review of Possible Sensory Mechanisms." *Reviews of Geophysics* 19 (2): 247–70. storyofstori.es/quake.
Butler, S. 1897. *The Authoress of the Odyssey*. storyofstori.es/butler.
Byford, Sam. 2012. "Softbank Pantone 5 107SH Hands-On: Radiation Detection Comes to Android." *The Verge*. storyofstori.es/soft.
Cade, D. I. 2020. "Photographer Captures Incredible 16k HDR Timelapse Using Two 50MP DSLRs At Once." *PetaPixel*. storyofstori.es/16k.
Caldwell, David H., et al. 2009. "The Lewis Hoard of Gaming Pieces: A Re-Examination of Their Context, Meanings, Discovery and Manufacture." *Medieval Archaeology* 53 (1): 155–203. storyofstori.es/lewis.

Campbell, L., and T. Kaufman. 1985. "Mayan Linguistics: Where Are We Now?" *Annual Review of Anthropology* 14 (1): 187–98. storyofstori.es/mayan.
Campbell-Swinton, A. A. 1908. "Distant Electric Vision." *Nature* 78 (2016): 151. storyofstori.es/distant.
Cantrell, Christopher. 2021. "Space Invaders." *Computer Archeology*. storyofstori.es/invaders.
Cariani, P. A., and B. Delgutte. 1996. "Neural Correlates of the Pitch of Complex Tones. I. Pitch and Pitch Salience." *Journal of Neurophysiology* 76 (3): 1698–716. storyofstori.es/pitch.
Carlsson, Chris. 2010. "Scavengers." *The San Francisco Digital History Archive*. storyofstori.es/found.
Carter, T. F. 1925. *The Invention of Printing in China and Its Spread Westward*. storyofstori.es/invention.
CDC. 2023. "COVID-19 Vaccinations in the United States, County." storyofstori.es/cdc.
Central New Jersey Home News. December 2, 1923. "Asks Divorce on Ground of 'Radio Mania.'" storyofstori.es/mania.
Challis, David. 2019. "Archival Currency Converter 1916–1940." storyofstori.es/currency.
Chandler, A. D., et al. 2009. *Inventing the Electronic Century: The Epic Story of the Consumer Electronics and Computer Industries*. storyofstori.es/invent.
Chang, S. J. 2011. *Sony Vs Samsung: The Inside Story of the Electronics Giants' Battle for Global Supremacy*. storyofstori.es/chang.
Changizi, Mark A., and Shinzuke Shimojo. 2005. "Character Complexity and Redundancy in Writing Systems Over Human History." *Proceedings of the Royal Society B: Biological Sciences* 272 (1560): 267–75. storyofstori.es/character.
Chapman, Jane. 2005. "Republican Citizenship, Ethics and the French Revolutionary Press 1789–92." *Ethical Space: The International Journal of Communication Ethics* 2 (1): 7–12. storyofstori.es/ethics.
Chen, R. H. 2011. *Liquid Crystal Displays: Fundamental Physics and Technology*. storyofstori.es/lcd.
Chen, Y. S. 2019. "Transcript of Official Meeting with CEO." Author Interview.
Chin, Gabriel J. 2008. "Why Senator John McCain Cannot Be President: Eleven Months and a Hundred Yards Short of Citizenship." *Michigan Law Review First Impressions* 107: 1. storyofstori.es/chin.
Chisick, Harvey. 1993. "The Pamphlet Literature of the French Revolution: An Overview." *History of European Ideas* 17 (2–3): 149–66. storyofstori.es/pamphlet.
Chittar, Chirag Rajendra, et al. 2023. "Music Production and Its Role in Coalition Signaling During Foraging Contexts in a Hunter-Gatherer Society." *Frontiers in Psychology* 14: 1–12. storyofstori.es/coalition.
Chomsky, Noam. 2009. *Of Minds and Language: A Dialogue with Noam Chomsky in the Basque Country*, edited by Massimo Piatelli-Palmarini et al. storyofstori.es/basque.
ChinaPower. March 19, 2020. "How Severe Are China's Demographic Challenges?" storyofstori.es/aging.
Christensen, Søren T., et al. 1997. "Signaling in Unicellular Eukaryotes." *International Review of Cytology* 177: 181–253. storyofstori.es/signal.
Christophe. 2016. *Les facéties du sapeur Camember*. storyofstori.es/camember.
Cipolla, C. M. 1969. *Literacy and Development in the West*. storyofstori.es/literacy.
Clark, Harry. 1979. "'Four Pieces in a Press': Gutenberg's Activities in Strasbourg." *The Library Quarterly: Information, Community, Policy* 49 (3): 303–9. storyofstori.es/four.
Clark, Roger N. 2018. "Notes on the Resolution and Other Details of the Human Eye." *Clark Vision*. storyofstori.es/clark.
Clarke, Richard N. 2013. "Expanding Mobile Wireless Capacity: The Challenges Presented by Technology and Economics." *SSRN*. June 7. storyofstori.es/expand.
Cleveland Myers, Garry. November 3, 1965. "Too Much Radio and TV Hampers Children's Speech." *New Castle News*. storyofstori.es/hampers.

Coady, C. A. J. 1992. *Testimony: A Philosophical Study*. storyofstori.es/coady.
Cohen, M. 2000. *Lara Croft: The Art of Virtual Seduction*. storyofstori.es/lara.
Cohen, Jon. December 22, 2011. "Updated: In a Rare Move, Science Without Authors' Consent Retracts Paper That Tied Mouse Virus to Chronic Fatigue Syndrome." *Science*. storyofstori.es/science.
Coleridge, E.P., 1893. *Trachiniae of Sophocles. Bell's Classical Translations*. storyofstori.es/pigs.
Colless, Brian E. 2010. "Proto-Alphabetic Inscriptions from the Wadi Arabah." *Antiguo Oriente* 8: 75–96. storyofstori.es/proto.
Colless, Brian E. 2014. "The Origin of the Alphabet: An Examination of the Goldwasser Hypothesis." *Antiguo Oriente* 12: 71–104. storyofstori.es/alphabet.
Conard, Nicholas J. 2003. "Palaeolithic Ivory Sculptures from Southwestern Germany and the Origins of Figurative Art." *Nature* 426 (6968): 830–32. storyofstori.es/ivory.
Coningham, R. A. E., et al. 1996. "Passage to India? Anuradhapura and the Early Use of the Brahmi Script." *Cambridge Archaeological Journal* 6 (1): 73–97. storyofstori.es/india.
Cook, C. J., and P. Edwards. 2003. *The Journals of Captain Cook*. storyofstori.es/journals.
Cook, Scott D. N. 1995. "The Structure of Technological Revolutions and the Gutenberg Myth" in *New Directions in the Philosophy of Technology*, edited by Joseph C. Pitt. 63–83. storyofstori.es/structureof.
Cooper, Jerrold S. 1993. "Bilingual Babel: Cuneiform Texts in Two or More Languages from Ancient Mesopotamia and Beyond." *Visible Language* 27 (1–2): 69–96. storyofstori.es/babel.
Cooperrider, Kensy, et al. 2018. "The Preference for Pointing with the Hand Is Not Universal." *Cognitive Science* 42 (4): 1375–90. storyofstori.es/pointing.
Corbett, Rachel. 2011. "Magritte's Dirty Pictures at Tate Liverpool." *Artnet*. storyofstori.es/dirty.
Cowen, T. 2009. *In Praise of Commercial Culture*. storyofstori.es/praise.
Cox, Rory. 2018. "Historicizing Waterboarding as a Severe Torture Norm." *International Relations* 32 (4): 488–512. storyofstori.es/norm.
Craig, Steve. 2004. "How America Adopted Radio: Demographic Differences in Set Ownership Reported in the 1930–1950 US Censuses." *Journal of Broadcasting & Electronic Media* 48 (2): 179–95. storyofstori.es/radio.
Cregan-Reid, Vybarr. 2015. *Discovering Gilgamesh*. storyofstori.es/discovering.
Crichton, M. 1973. *Westworld*. storyofstori.es/westworld.
Crofton, Melissa. 2013. "From Medieval Mystic to Early Modern Anchoress: Rewriting the Book of Margery Kempe." *Journal of the Early Book Society for the Study of Manuscripts and Printing History* 16: 101–124, 311. storyofstori.es/mystic.
Cruz, J. C. 1991. *The Incorruptibles: A Study of Incorruption in the Bodies of Various Saints and Beati*. storyofstori.es/cruz.
Cuddy, Lola L., and Jacalyn Duffin. 2005. "Music, Memory, and Alzheimer's Disease: Is Music Recognition Spared in Dementia, and How Can It Be Assessed?" *Medical Hypotheses* 64 (2): 229–35. storyofstori.es/cuddy.
Czaja, Sara J., et al. 2006. "Factors Predicting the Use of Technology: Findings from the Center for Research and Education on Aging and Technology Enhancement (CREATE)." *Psychology and Aging* 21 (2): 333–52. storyofstori.es/create.
Daily News (New York). November 7, 1929. "Mother Offers Valuable Thoughts About the Radio." storyofstori.es/daily.
Daily Telegraph, The. December 27. 1872. "The Flood: Reading of the Chaldean Story of the Deluge." Reprinted on page 2 of *The New York Times* of the same date. storyofstori.es/flood.
Dalby, Andrew. 2006. *Rediscovering Homer: Inside the Origins of the Epic*. storyofstori.es/dalby.
Dalley, Stephanie. 1993. "Nineveh After 612 BC." *Altorientalische Forschungen* 20 (1): 134–47. storyofstori.es/612.

Dalley, Stephanie. 2000. *Myths from Mesopotamia: Creation, the Flood, Gilgamesh, and Others.* storyofstori.es/myths.
Dame-Griff, A. 2023. *The Two Revolutions: A History of the Transgender Internet.* storyofstori.es/griff.
Damerow, Peter. 1999. "The Origins of Writing as a Problem of Historical Epistemology." *Symposium on the Multiple Origins of Writing: Image, Symbol, and Script; University of Pennsylvania, March 26–27.* storyofstori.es/problem.
Damrosch, D. 2007. *The Buried Book: The Loss and Rediscovery of the Great Epic of Gilgamesh.* storyofstori.es/buried.
Danchev, A. 2021. *Magritte: A Life.* storyofstori.es/magritte.
Dane, J. A. 2003. *The Myth of Print Culture: Essays on Evidence, Textuality, and Bibliographical Method.* storyofstori.es/dane.
D'Angour, Armand J., 1999. "Archinus, Eucleides and the Reform of the Athenian Alphabet." *Bulletin of the Institute of Classical Studies* 43 (1): 109–30. storyofstori.es/reform.
Daniels, Peter T. 1992. "The Syllabic Origin of Writing and the Segmental Origin of the Alphabet." *The Linguistics of Literacy* 17 (3): 83–110. storyofstori.es/segmental.
Daoshi. 2019. *A Forest of Pearls from the Dharma Garden,* Volumes I and II. Translated by Koichi Shinohara. storyofstori.es/daoshi2019.
Daoshi. 2020. *A Forest of Pearls from the Dharma Garden,* Volume III. Translated by Koichi Shinohara. storyofstori.es/daoshi2020.
Darwin, Charles. 1880. *The Power of Movement in Plants.* storyofstori.es/plants.
Darwin, Charles. 1898. *The Expression of the Emotions in Man and Animals.* storyofstori.es/expression.
Darwin, Charles, et al. 2008. *The Descent of Man, and Selection in Relation to Sex.* storyofstori.es/descent.
Dawson, Ashley. 2018. "A Deliberate Racial and Class Assault on CUNY." *Clarion.* storyofstori.es/cuny.
de Alva Ixtlilxóchitl, F., et al. 1985. *Completo De Las Relaciones E Historia De La Nación Chichimeca.* storyofstori.es/alva.
de Ciudad Real, A., and R. Acuña. 2001. *Calepino Maya De Motul.* storyofstori.es/motul.
De Noord-Brabanter. July 22, 1856. "Report on Coster Statue Unveiling." *De Noord-Brabanter.* storyofstori.es/coster.
de Réaumur, R. A. F. 1742. *Mémoires pour servir à l'histoire des insectes.* Volume 6. storyofstori.es/memoires.
De Shong Meador, B. 2000. *Inanna, Lady of Largest Heart: Poems of the Sumerian High Priestess Enheduanna.* storyofstori.es/lady.
de Souza Gomes, A. 2012. *New Polymers for Special Applications.* storyofstori.es/polymers.
de Vito, Stefania, et al. 2010. "Collective Representations Elicit Widespread Individual False Memories." *Cortex* 45: 686–87. storyofstori.es/false.
Decker, Ryan A., et al. 2015. "Where Has All the Skewness Gone? The Decline in High-Growth (Young) Firms in the US." *National Bureau of Economic Research* Working Paper No. 21776: 1–67. storyofstori.es/skew.
DeepMind. 2016. "Audited Financial Statements, DeepMind Technologies, Inc." *UK Companies House.* storyofstori.es/deepmind.
Delnero, Paul. 2016. "Scholarship and Inquiry in Early Mesopotamia." *Journal of Ancient Near Eastern History* 2 (2): 109–43. storyofstori.es/scholarship.
Denton, Derek A., et al. 2009. "The Role of Primordial Emotions in the Evolutionary Origin of Consciousness." *Consciousness and Cognition* 18 (2): 500–14. storyofstori.es/denton.
d'Errico, Francesco, et al. 2012. "Early Evidence of San Material Culture Represented by Organic Artifacts from Border Cave, South Africa." *Proceedings of the National Academy of Sciences of the United States of America* 109 (33): 13214–19. storyofstori.es/san.

Derricotte, Toi. 2016. "Speculations About 'I.'" *Poetry* 208 (5): 471–75. storyofstori.es/i.
Devree, Howard. 1954. "Art of Magritte at Janis Gallery." *New York Times*, March 3. storyofstori.es/devree.
Dickens, C. et al., 1848. *Dombey and Son*. storyofstori.es/dombey.
Dillon, Patrick. 2020. "Artefacts, Found Objects and Early Games: A Cultural Ecological Perspective on Proto-Chess Pieces." *Time and Mind* 13 (1): 59–77. storyofstori.es/dillon.
Dimitriou, Rozalia, et al. 2011. "Bone Regeneration: Current Concepts and Future Directions." *BMC Medicine* 9 (1): 1–10. storyofstori.es/bone.
Diouf, Anta. 2016. *Wireless Solutions for Fisheries in Senegal (WISE)*. Video Interview. storyofstori.es/anta.
Dittmar, Jeremiah E. 2011. "Information Technology and Economic Change: The Impact of the Printing Press." *The Quarterly Journal of Economics* 126 (3): 1133–72. storyofstori.es/info.
Dobbs, Michael. 2008. "McCain's Birth Abroad Stirs Legal Debate." *Washington Post*. storyofstori.es/dobbs.
Dockerty, Stuart M., et al. 1964. "Downflow Sheet Drawing Method and Apparatus." U.S. Patent 3,149,949. storyofstori.es/949.
Dockerty, Stuart M. 1967. "Sheet Forming Apparatus." U.S. Patent 3,338,696. storyofstori.es/696.
Dockerty, Stuart M. 1972. "Controlling Thickness of Newly Drawn Glass Sheet." U.S. Patent 3,682,609. storyofstori.es/609.
Dome, Malcolm. 2006. "Bon Jovi: Wet Dreams." *Classic Rock* (94): 1–14. storyofstori.es/dome.
Douglass, F. 2020. *Narrative of the Life of Frederick Douglass: An American Slave*. storyofstori.es/douglass.
Douglass, Frederick. 1960. *Narrative of the Life of Frederick Douglass: An American Slave*. storyofstori.es/life.
Dreyer, J. L. E. 1890. *Tycho Brahe: A Picture of Scientific Life and Work in the Sixteenth Century*. storyofstori.es/dreyer.
Duan, W., et al. 1994. *Dunhuang Art: Through the Eyes of Duan Wenjie*. storyofstori.es/eyes.
Dudai, Yadin. 1997. "How Big Is Human Memory, or On Being Just Useful Enough." *Learning & Memory* 3: 341–65. storyofstori.es/big.
Dunbar, Robin I. M. 2014. "How Conversations Around Campfires Came to Be." *Proceedings of the National Academy of Sciences* 111 (39): 14013–14. storyofstori.es/campfires.
Dunbar, Robin I. M. 2017. "Breaking Bread: The Functions of Social Eating." *Adaptive Human Behavior and Physiology* 3 (3): 198–211. storyofstori.es/bread.
Dunbar, Robin I. M., et al. 1995. "Size and Structure of Freely Forming Conversational Groups." *Human Nature* 6 (1): 67–78. storyofstori.es/size.
Dunbar, Robin I. M., et al. 1997. "Human Conversational Behavior." *Human Nature* 8 (3): 231–46. storyofstori.es/behavior.
Dunbar, Robin I. M., et al. 2014. *Lucy to Language: The Benchmark Papers*. storyofstori.es/lucy.
Dunbar, Robin I. M., et al. 2018. "Primate Social Group Sizes Exhibit a Regular Scaling Pattern with Natural Attractors." *Biology Letters* 14 (1): 1–5. storyofstori.es/primate.
Durian, Douglas J., et al. 2006. "What Is in a Pebble Shape?" *Physical Review Letters* 97 (2): 1–4. storyofstori.es/pebble.
Earendil, Geoffrey. 2021. "Collective Invention: Erotism and Absurdity in the Art of Rene Magritte." *Shunga Gallery*. storyofstori.es/magritte.
The Eagle. June 10 1896. Silver City, NM. "The Bicycle Face." storyofstori.es/bicycle.
Ebbinghaus, Hermann. 1913. "Retention and Obliviscence as a Function of the Time" in *Memory: A Contribution to Experimental Psychology*, edited by Henry A. Ruger et al. 62–80. storyofstori.es/memory.
The Economist. August 12 2017. "After Electric Cars, What More Will It Take for Batteries to Change the Face of Energy?" storyofstori.es/cars.
Edgerton, William F. 1947. "Stress, Vowel Quantity, and Syllable Division in Egyptian." *Journal of Near Eastern Studies* 6 (1): 1–17. storyofstori.es/vowel.

Efrati, Amir. 2014. "Google Beat Facebook for DeepMind, Creates Ethics Board." *The Information*. storyofstori.es/deep.

El Paso Herald-Post. July 27, 1934. "Radios Blamed in Long Drouth": 16. storyofstori.es/herald.

Encyclopaedia Britannica. 1771. "Ark." 423–25. storyofstori.es/ark.

Encyclopaedia Britannica. 1875. "Deluge." Volume 7: 54–57. storyofstori.es/deluge.

Enquist, Magnus, and Anthony Arak. 1994. "Symmetry, Beauty and Evolution." *Nature* 372 (6502): 169–72. storyofstori.es/symmetry.

Eppard, Philip B., and George Monteiro. 1983. *A Guide to the Atlantic Monthly Contributors' Club*. storyofstori.es/guide.

Erlang, A. K. 1909. "Sandsynlighedsregning og Telefonsamtaler." *Nyt Tidsskrift for Matematik* 20: 33–39. storyofstori.es/erlang.

Essuman, Kofi Manso, 1992. *Fermented Fish in Africa: A Study on Processing, Marketing, and Consumption*. storyofstori.es/fish.

Estaunié, Édouard. 1904. *Traité pratique de télécommunication électrique (télégraphic-téléphonie)*. storyofstori.es/traité.

Evans, Harold. 1991. "Necessary Shock to Our Image of War." *The Observer*. storyofstori.es/evans.

Evening Sun (Baltimore, MD). August 17, 1915. "The Moving-Picture Face." storyofstori.es/moving.

Everett, Caleb. 2017. "Languages in Drier Climates Use Fewer Vowels." *Frontiers in Psychology* 8: 1–40. storyofstori.es/vowels.

Everett, Caleb. 2021. "The Sounds of Prehistoric Speech." *Philosophical Transactions of The Royal Society B: Biological Sciences* 376: 1–9. storyofstori.es/sounds.

Everett, Caleb, et al. 2015. "Climate, Vocal Folds, and Tonal Languages." *Proceedings of the National Academy of Sciences* 112 (5): 1322–27. storyofstori.es/climate.

Everett, Caleb, et al. 2016. "Language Evolution and Climate: The Case of Desiccation and Tone." *Journal of Language Evolution* 1: 33–46. storyofstori.es/tone.

Facebook. 2021. "What Is the Face Recognition Setting on Facebook and How Does It Work?" *Facebook Help Center*. storyofstori.es/setting.

Fairbairn, John. 1995. "Go in Ancient China." *Go Base*. storyofstori.es/go.

Fairie, Paul. 2023. "A Brief History of the Art of Conversation is Dead." *Twitter*. storyofstori.es/artof.

Fall, Massal. 2020. "Characterization of Artisanal Bait Fishing Using Juveniles of Round Sardinella (*Sardinella aurita*) and Flat Sardinella (*Sardinella maderensis*) Off Hann Bay (Dakar Region, Senegal)." *International Journal of Fisheries and Aquatic Studies* 8 (1): 164–71. storyofstori.es/bait.

FAO. 2009. *Aquastat Transboundary River Basin Overview Euphrates-Tigris*. storyofstori.es/FAO.

Farley, David. 2006. "Fore Shame." *Slate*. storyofstori.es/shame.

Febvre, L., et al. 1997. *The Coming of the Book: The Impact of Printing 1450–1800*. storyofstori.es/book.

Fenerty, Charles. 1866. *Essay on Progress*. storyofstori.es/progress.

Fioravanti, L. 1564. *Dello Specchio di Scientia Universale*. storyofstori.es/dello.

Fischoff, Baruch, et al. 1978. "Don't Attribute This to Reverend Bayes." *Psychological Bulletin* 85 (2): 239–43. storyofstori.es/bayes.

Fisher, D. E., and M. Fisher. 1996. *Tube: The Invention of Television*. storyofstori.es/tube.

Fisher, M. 2009. *Something in the Air: Radio, Rock, and the Revolution That Shaped a Generation*. storyofstori.es/fisher.

Flannery, Kent V. 1973. "The Origins of Agriculture." *Annual Review of Anthropology* 2 (1): 271–310. storyofstori.es/agriculture.

Flink, J. J. 1990. *The Automobile Age*. storyofstori.es/auto.

Flint, Julie. 1991. "The Real Face of War." *The Observer*. storyofstori.es/face.

Flis, Andrej. 2021. "The Historic 1928/1929 Winter Pattern." *Severe Weather Europe*. storyofstori.es/winter.

Fogel, Robert W., and Dora L. Costa. 1997. "A Theory of Technophysio Evolution, with Some Implications for Forecasting Population, Health Care Costs, and Pension Costs." *Demography* 34 (1): 49–66. storyofstori.es/techno.

Forbes. 2021. "The World's Real-Time Billionaires." *Forbes*. storyofstori.es/forbes.

Foresti, J. F. 1492. *Supplementum Chronicarum*. storyofstori.es/supplement.

Foucault, Michel. 1983. *This Is Not a Pipe*. storyofstori.es/pipe.

Frame, Grant, and A. R. George. 2005. "The Royal Libraries of Nineveh: New Evidence for King Ashurbanipal's Tablet Collecting." *Iraq* 67 (1): 265–84. storyofstori.es/royal.

Frankel, Rafael. 2016. "Oil and Wine Production" in *A Companion to Science, Technology, and Medicine in Ancient Greece and Rome*, edited by Georgia L. Irby. 550–69. storyofstori.es/oilandwine.

Franek, Juraj. 2012. "Did Socrates Write?" *Graeco-Latina Brunensia* 17 (2): 25–40. storyofstori.es/write.

Freeman, C. 2011. *Holy Bones, Holy Dust: How Relics Shaped the History of Medieval Europe*. storyofstori.es/holy.

Freeman, Linton C. 1996. "Some Antecedents of Social Network Analysis." *Connections* 19 (1): 39–42. storyofstori.es/freeman.

Freire, Paulo. 2017. *Pedagogy of the Oppressed*. storyofstori.es/pedagogy.

Freire, Paulo, and Loretta Slover. 1983. "The Importance of the Act of Reading." *Journal of Education* 165 (1): 5–11. storyofstori.es/act.

Freling, Traci H. et al., 2020. "When Poignant Stories Outweigh Cold Hard Facts: A Meta-Analysis of the Anecdotal Bias." *Organizational Behavior and Human Decision Processes* 160: 51–67. storyofstori.es/freling (https://www.sciencedirect.com/science/article/pii/S0749597819301633).

Friesen, T. Max. 2015. "On the Naming of Arctic Archaeological Traditions: The Case for Paleo-Inuit." *Arctic* 68 (3): iii–iv. storyofstori.es/inuit.

Frith, Chris D. 2007. "The Social Brain." *Philosophical Transactions of the Royal Society Series B, Biological Sciences* 362 (1480): 671–78. storyofstori.es/socialbrain.

Frith, Chris D., and Uta Frith. 2007. "Social Cognition in Humans." *Current Biology* 17 (16): R724–32. storyofstori.es/frith.

Froemke, Robert C., et al. 2021. "Oxytocin, Neural Plasticity, and Social Behavior." *Annual Review of Neuroscience* 44 (1): 359–81. storyofstori.es/oxy.

Fudge, E. C. 1969. "Syllables." *Journal of Linguistics* 5 (2): 253–86. storyofstori.es/syllables.

Fuhrmann, O. W., et al. 1940. *Gutenberg and the Strasbourg Documents of 1439*. storyofstori.es/documents.

Funk, Holger. 2014. "Engelbert Kaempfer's Contribution to the Knowledge of Cuneiform Scripts: Text and Translation of Kaempfer's Description of the Persepolitan Inscription DPg from the 'Amoenitates Exoticae.'" *Journal of Neo-Latin Language and Literature* 16: 53–65. storyofstori.es/funk.

Funke, Daniel. May 7, 2020. "Fact-Checking *Plandemic*: A Documentary Full of False Conspiracy Theories About the Coronavirus." *PolitiFact*. storyofstori.es/check.

Gagliano, Monica. 2015. "In a Green Frame of Mind: Perspectives on the Behavioural Ecology and Cognitive Nature of Plants." *AoB (Annals of Botany) Plants* 7: 1–8. storyofstori.es/green.

Gahlinger, Paul M. 2000. "Cabin Location and the Likelihood of Motion Sickness in Cruise Ship Passengers." *Journal of Travel Medicine* 7 (3): 120–24. storyofstori.es/cabin.

Gannes, Liz. 2014. "Exclusive: Google to Buy Artificial Intelligence Startup DeepMind for $400M." *Recode*. storyofstori.es/vox.

Ganti, R. K., et al. 2011. "Mobile Crowdsensing: Current State and Future Challenges." *IEEE Communications Magazine* 49 (11): 32–39. storyofstori.es/crowd.

Garbuno, Daniel Martínez. March 25, 2023. "1 in 3 Americans Believe They Could Land a Plane in an Emergency." *Simple Flying*. storyofstori.es/plane.

Gardiner, Alan H. 1916. "The Egyptian Origin of the Semitic Alphabet." *The Journal of Egyptian Archaeology* 3 (1): 1–16. storyofstori.es/egyptian.

Gartner, Scott S. 2011. "On Behalf of a Grateful Nation: Conventionalized Images of Loss and Individual Opinion Change in War." *International Studies Quarterly* 55 (2): 545–61. storyofstori.es/on.

Gassendi, P. 1655. *Tychonis Brahei, Equitis Dani Astronomorum Coryphaei Vita*. storyofstori.es/vita.

Geary, Patrick J. 1986. "Sacred Commodities: The Circulation of Medieval Relics" in *Living with the Dead in the Middle Ages*, edited by Patrick J. Geary. 194–220. storyofstori.es/relics.

Gere, C. 2010. *Knossos and the Prophets of Modernism*. storyofstori.es/gere.

Gerhardt, Claus W. 1970. "Was erfand Gutenberg in Straßburg?" *Gutenberg Jahrbuch* 45: 56–72. storyofstori.es/was.

Gething, Peter W., and Andrew J. Tatem. 2011. "Can Mobile Phone Data Improve Emergency Response to Natural Disasters?" *PLoS Medicine* 8 (8): 1–2. storyofstori.es/can.

Giedion, Sigfried. 2023. *The Eternal Present, Volume I: The Beginnings of Art*. storyofstori.es/eternal.

Gilder, George. 1993. "Metcalfe's Law and Legacy." *Forbes ASAP*, September 1, 1993. storyofstori.es/gilder.

Gilder, George. 2000. *Telecosm: How Infinite Bandwidth Will Revolutionize Our World*. storyofstori.es/telecosm

Gill, Sharon A., and Andrea M.-K. Bierema. 2013. "On the Meaning of Alarm Calls: A Review of Functional Reference in Avian Alarm Calling." *Ethology* 119 (6): 449–61. storyofstori.es/alarm.

Gintis, Herbert. 2012. "Clash of the Titans." *BioScience* 62 (11): 987–91. storyofstori.es/titans.

Gladstone, W. E., and H. C. G. Matthew. 1982. *The Gladstone Diaries Volume 8*. storyofstori.es/diaries.

Gleick, James. 2007. *Isaac Newton*. storyofstori.es/isaac.

Global Witness. 2016. "We Don't Care, We're Still in Power." *Global Witness*. storyofstori.es/still.

Global Witness. 2021. "Algorithm of Harm: Facebook Amplified Myanmar Military Propaganda Following Coup." *Global Witness*. storyofstori.es/amp.

Gombrich, Richard. 1988. "How the Mahayana Began." *Journal of Pali and Buddhist Studies* 1: 29–46. storyofstori.es/began.

Gonçalves, André, and Susana Carvalho. 2019. "Death Among Primates: A Critical Review of Non-Human Primate Interactions Towards Their Dead and Dying." *Biological Reviews* 94 (4): 1502–29. storyofstori.es/death.

Gonzalez, George. 2016. "How Many Pixels Did the First TV Have?" *Quora*. storyofstori.es/pixels.

Goodenough, John B., and Kyu-Sung Park. 2013. "The Li-Ion Rechargeable Battery: A Perspective." *Journal of the American Chemical Society* 135 (4): 1167–76. storyofstori.es/ion.

Goodman, A. E. 2014. *Margery Kempe: And Her World*. storyofstori.es/and.

Goodman, Claire. 2024. "Katy ISD Bans 14 New Books, from *Slaughterhouse-Five* to *Wicked*. Here's What to Know." *Houston Chronicle*. storyofstori.es/wicked.

Goold, G. P. 1960. "Homer and the Alphabet." *Transactions and Proceedings of the American Philological Association* 91: 272–91. storyofstori.es/homer.

Graham, Joni. 2018. "The Story of Enheduanna." *Our Modern History*. storyofstori.es/graham.

Grosse, Eduard. 1892. "The First German Paper-Maker." *Popular Science Monthly* 42: 94–100. storyofstori.es/german.

GSMA. 2018. *The Mobile Economy-Sub-Saharan Africa 2018*. storyofstori.es/2018.
Guralnick, P. 2014. *Sweet Soul Music: Rhythm and Blues and the Southern Dream of Freedom*. storyofstori.es/sweet.
Guynn, Jessica, and Kevin McCoy. 2021. "The Story of Carol and Karen: Two Experimental Facebook Accounts Show How the Company Helped Divide America." *USA Today*, October 25, 2021. storyofstori.es/carol.
Grylls, Pinny (dir.), and Sam Crane. 2024. *Grand Theft Hamlet* (Movie). storyofstori.es/hamlet.
Gwynne, Darryl T., and David C. F. Rentz. 1983. "Beetles on the Bottle: Male Buprestids Mistake Stubbies for Females." *Australian Journal of Entomology* 22 (1): 79–80. storyofstori.es/bottle.
Hall, Linda, et al. 2014. "IT Key Metrics Data 2015: Key Infrastructure Measures: Storage Analysis: Current Year." *Gartner*. storyofstori.es/gartner.
Hallo, W. W., and J. van Dijk. 1968. *The Exaltation of Inanna*. storyofstori.es/exaltation.
Halloran, John Alan. 2009. "Early Numeration: Tally Sticks, Counting Boards, and Sumerian Proto-Writing." storyofstori.es/sticks.
Hammer, Michael. 1990. "Reengineering Work: Don't Automate, Obliterate." *Harvard Business Review* 68 (4): 104–12. storyofstori.es/hammer.
Hansard. 1807. "House of Commons Debate: 13 June 1807." *Hansard* 9: 798–806. storyofstori.es/hansard.
Harding, Chris, Bob Wheater, and Pippa Anderson. 2012. *The 2011 Skills for Life Survey: A Survey of Literacy, Numeracy and ICT Levels in England*. BIS Research Paper Number 81. storyofstori.es/skills.
Harding, Luke, et al. 2017. "Michael Flynn: New Evidence Spy Chiefs Had Concerns About Russian Ties." *The Guardian*. 1. storyofstori.es/flynn1.
Hardy, Karen. 2019. "Paleomedicine and the Use of Plant Secondary Compounds in the Paleolithic and Early Neolithic." *Evolutionary Anthropology* 28 (2): 60–71. storyofstori.es/hardy.
Harman, P. M., and A. E. Shapiro. 2002. *The Investigation of Difficult Things: Essays on Newton and the History of the Exact Sciences in Honour of D. T. Whiteside*. storyofstori.es/things.
Harris, Roy. 1989. "How Does Writing Restructure Thought?" *Language & Communication* 9 (2/3): 99–106. storyofstori.es/roy.
Harris, Roy. 2005. *Rethinking Writing. Continuum Collection*. storyofstori.es/rethinking.
Harris, Susan R., and Elise Gerich. 1996. "Retiring the NSFNET Backbone Service: Chronicling the End of an Era." *ConneXions* 10 (4): 2–11. storyofstori.es/NSF.
Hastie, R., et al. 2002. *Inside the Jury*. storyofstori.es/jury.
Haupt, Paul. 1917. "Tones in Sumerian." *Journal of the American Oriental Society* 37: 309–23. storyofstori.es/tones.
Haviland, John B. 1974. "A Last Look at Cook's Guugu Yimidhirr Word List." *Oceania* 44 (3): 216–32. storyofstori.es/words.
Healey, J. F. 1990. *The Early Alphabet*. storyofstori.es/abc.
Heath, Alex. December 9, 2021. "Meta Opens Up Access to Its VR Social Platform Horizon Worlds." *The Verge*. storyofstori.es/heath.
Heffner, Henry E. 1983. "Hearing in Large and Small Dogs: Absolute Thresholds and Size of the Tympanic Membrane." *Behavioral Neuroscience* 97 (2): 310–18. storyofstori.es/doghearing.
Heider, Fritz, and Marianne Simmel. 1944. "An Experimental Study of Apparent Behavior." *American Journal of Psychology* 57 (2): 243–59. storyofstori.es/simmel.
Helle, Sophus. 2023. "Enheduana's Invocations: Form and Force" in *Women and Religion in the Ancient Near East and Asia*, edited by Nicole Maria Brisch et al. 187–208. storyofstori.es/form.
Helper, Laura. 1997. "Whole Lot of Shakin' Going On: An Ethnography of Race Relations and Crossover Audiences for Rhythm and Blues and Rock and Roll in 1950s Memphis." Doctoral dissertation, Rice University. storyofstori.es/whole.

Hemler, Raphael J. B., et al. 1997. "The Effect of Relative Humidity of Inhaled Air on Acoustic Parameters of Voice in Normal Subjects." *Journal of Voice* 11 (3): 295–300. storyofstori.es/air.

Henley, W. E. (ed.). 1895. *The New Review*. 12. storyofstori.es/henley.

Henshilwood, Christopher S., et al. 2018. "An Abstract Drawing from the 73,000-Year-Old Levels at Blombos Cave, South Africa." *Nature* 562 (7725): 115–18. storyofstori.es/abstract.

Heymann, Eckhard W. 2006. "Scent Marking Strategies of New World Primates." *American Journal of Primatology* 68 (6): 650–61. storyofstori.es/primates.

Higgins, Darragh, et al. 2018. "Ascending from the Valley: Can State-of-the-Art Photorealism Avoid the Uncanny?" *SAP '21: ACM Symposium on Applied Perception*. storyofstori.es/valley.

Hillis, Susan D., et al. 2021. "COVID-19-Associated Orphanhood and Caregiver Death in the United States." *Pediatrics* 148 (6): e2021053760. storyofstori.es/caregiver.

Hitchens, Christopher. 2008. "Believe Me, It's Torture." *Vanity Fair* August 2008: 1. storyofstori.es/hitchens.

Hoffmann, Dirk L., et al. 2018a. "U-Th Dating of Carbonate Crusts Reveals Neanderthal Origin of Iberian Cave Art." *Science* 359 (6378): 912–15. storyofstori.es/uth.

Hoffmann, Dirk L., et al. 2018b. "Dates for Neanderthal Art and Symbolic Behaviour Are Reliable." *Nature Ecology & Evolution* 2 (7): 1044–45. storyofstori.es/hoffmann.

Hoffman, Donald D. 2009. "The User-Interface Theory of Perception: Natural Selection Drives True Perception to Swift Extinction" in *Object Categorization: Computer and Human Vision Perspectives*, edited by Sven J. Dickenson et al. 148–67. storyofstori.es/user.

Holen, Øistein Haugsten, et al. 2001. "Parasites and Supernormal Manipulation." *Proceedings of the Royal Society of London Series B: Biological Sciences* 268 (1485): 2551–58. storyofstori.es/parasites.

Honolulu Star-Bulletin. March 9, 1929. "Pesky Radio Blamed for Spotted Skin." storyofstori.es/pesky.

Hooker, J. T. et al., 1990. *Reading the Past: Ancient Writing From Cuneiform to the Alphabet*. storyofstori.es/hooker.

hooks, bell. 2014. *Ain't I a Woman: Black Women and Feminism*. storyofstori.es/aint.

Hoornsche Courant. 1856. "Is Jhr. M. Salvador Te Haarlem, Ten Zijnen Huize, Gearresteerd." storyofstori.es/den.

Horn, Walter, and Ernest Born. 1986. "The Medieval Monastery as a Setting for the Production of Manuscripts." *The Journal of the Walters Art Gallery* 44: 16–47. storyofstori.es/monastery.

Howard, Sethanne. 2017. "En Hedu'anna." *Journal of the Washington Academy of Sciences* 103 (2): 21–34. storyofstori.es/howard.

Howes, Laura L. 1992. "On the Birth of Margery Kempe's Last Child." *Modern Philology* 90 (2): 220–25. storyofstori.es/notes.

Hughes, Albert, and Alan Hughes, (dir.). 2010. *The Book of Eli*. storyofstori.es/eli.

Hui, Fan, et al. 2016. "Game 1: 'Dawn.'" storyofstori.es/game1.

Human Rights Watch. 1991. *Needless Deaths in the Gulf War*. storyofstori.es/HRW.

Hunnisett, B. 2018. *Engraved on Steel*. storyofstori.es/steel.

Hunter, D. 1978. *Papermaking: The History and Technique of an Ancient Craft*. storyofstori.es/papermaking.

Hunter, Ian M. L. 1984. "Lengthy Verbatim Recall (LVR) and the Mythical Gift of Tape-Recorder Memory" in *Advances in Psychology: Psychology in the 1990s*, edited by Kirsti M. J. Lagerspetz et al. 425–40. storyofstori.es/recall.

The Illustrated London News. 1936. "A Great Forthcoming Sale: The Papers of Sir Isaac Newton." storyofstori.es/sale.

Immerwahr, Henry R. 1973. "More Book Rolls on Attic Vases." *Antike Kunst* 16 (2): 143–47. storyofstori.es/more.
International Go Federation. 2016. "Go Population Survey." storyofstori.es/gopop.
International Monetary Fund. 2019. "World Economic Outlook Database—Groups and Aggregates Information." *World Economic Outlook, October 2019: Global Manufacturing Downturn, Rising Trade Barriers.* storyofstori.es/imf.
Ipri, Thomas A. 2010. "Introducing Transliteracy: What Does It Mean to Academic Libraries." *College and Research Libraries News.* 532. storyofstori.es/ipri.
IPU Parline. 2025. "Global Data on National Parliaments: Country Data as of March 2025." *Inter-Parliamentary Union.* storyofstori.es/IPU.
Irons, J. Yoon, et al. 2020. "A Systematic Review on the Effects of Group Singing on Persistent Pain in People with Long-Term Health Conditions." *European Journal of Pain* 24 (1): 71–90. storyofstori.es/irons.
Iversen, Rune, et al. 2025. "Sun Stones and the Darkened Sun: Neolithic Miniature Art from the Island of Bornholm, Denmark." *Antiquity.* 1–17. storyofstori.es/sun.
Jacobsen, Thorkild. 1978. "Ipḫur-Kīshi and His Times." *Archiv für Orientforschung* 26: 1–14. storyofstori.es/times.
Jansen, Maarten, and Gabina Aurora Pérez Jiménez. 2004. "Renaming the Mexican Codices." *Ancient Mesoamerica* 15 (2): 267–71. storyofstori.es/renaming.
Jeffery, Lilian Hamilton, et al. 1982. "Greek Alphabetic Writing" in *The Cambridge Ancient History*, edited by John Boardman et al. 819–33. storyofstori.es/greek.
Jenkins, Tim. April 19, 2017. "Butch Wax." *SABR's Baseball Cards Research Committee.* storyofstori.es/butchwax.
Jeon, Lisa. 2013. "Drawing Boundaries and Revealing Language Attitudes: Mapping Perceptions of Dialects in Korea." Master's thesis, *University of North Texas.* storyofstori.es/jeon.
Jewell, Edward Alden. 1936. "Show Lists Works of Surrealist Art." *The New York Times.* storyofstori.es/show.
Johnston, J., and F. Probyn-Rapsey. 2020. *Animal Death.* storyofstori.es/johnston.
Jones, H. Spencer. 1946. "Tycho Brahe (1546–1601)." *Nature* 158 (4024): 856–61. storyofstori.es/1546.
Journal of Commerce. 1858. "Egyptian Mummy Rags in a Yankee Paper Mill." *The Daily Exchange.* storyofstori.es/rags.
Jowett, B., et al. 2017. *Phaedrus: Translated by Benjamin Jowett.* storyofstori.es/plato.
Jurafsky, Dan, et al. 2009. "Extracting Social Meaning: Identifying Interactional Style in Spoken Conversation." *Proceedings of Human Language Technologies: The 2009 Annual Conference of the North American Chapter of the Association for Computational Linguistics.* storyofstori.es/style.
Kahn, E. J. 1960. "Children's Friend." *New Yorker*, December 17. storyofstori.es/friend.
Kaneda, Toshiko, and Carl Haub. 2022. "How Many People Have Ever Lived on Earth?" *Population Research Bureau Bulletin.* storyofstori.es/howmany.
Kant, I., et al. 1998. *Critique of Pure Reason.* storyofstori.es/kant.
Kapatsinski, V., et al. 2017. "Perceptual Learning of Intonation Contour Categories in Adults and 9- to 11-Year-Old Children: Adults Are More Narrow-Minded." *Cognitive Science* 41 (2): 383–415. storyofstori.es/learning.
Kapr, A. 1996. *Johann Gutenberg: The Man and His Invention.* storyofstori.es/his.
Katy and Fort Bend Christian Magazines. January 30, 2025. "Conservative Victor Perez Files for Re-Election to Katy ISD School Board." *Katy Christian Magazine.* storyofstori.es/katy.
Katz, Ralph V., et al. 2008. "Awareness of the Tuskegee Syphilis Study and the US Presidential Apology and Their Influence on Minority Participation in Biomedical Research." *American Journal of Public Health* 98 (6): 1137–42. storyofstori.es/aware.

Kaufman, Jeff. 2018. "Possible One-Syllable Words." *Personal Web Page.* storyofstori.es/one.
Keen, Suzanne. 2011. "Fast Tracks to Narrative Empathy: Anthropomorphism and Dehumanization in Graphic Narratives." *SubStance* 40 (1): 135–55. storyofstori.es/tracks.
Kemp, Andrew H., and Andrew J. Guastella. 2011. "The Role of Oxytocin in Human Affect: A Novel Hypothesis." *Current Directions in Psychological Science* 20 (4): 222–31. storyofstori.es/kemp.
Kerr, Chris. February 9, 2021. "Epic Games' New MetaHuman Creator Will Let Devs Build Hi-Fi Humans." *Game Developer.* storyofstori.es/epicgames.
Keynes, John Maynard. 1946. "Newton, the Man" in *Essays in Biography*, edited by Donald Winch. 363–74. storyofstori.es/newton.
Al Khatib, Khalid et al., 2016. "A News Editorial Corpus for Mining Argumentation Strategies." *Proceedings of COLING 2016, the 26th International Conference on Computational Linguistics: Technical Papers.* storyofstori.es/khatib1.
Al Khatib, Khalid et al., 2017. "Patterns of Argumentation Strategies Across Topics." *Proceedings of the 2017 Conference on Empirical Methods in Natural Language Processing.* storyofstori.es/khatib2.
Kilmer, Anne Draffkorn. 1972. "The Mesopotamian Concept of Overpopulation and Its Solution as Reflected in the Mythology." *Orientalia* 41 (2): 160–77. storyofstori.es/kilmer.
Kim, Jae-Eun. 2013. "Land Use Management and Cultural Value of Ecosystem Services in Southwestern Korean Islands." *Journal of Marine and Island Cultures* 2 (1): 49–55. storyofstori.es/islands.
King-Smith, D., and Mary Rayner. 1995. *Babe.* storyofstori.es/babe.
Knapp, A. Bernard, et al. 2016. "Crisis in Context: The End of the Late Bronze Age in the Eastern Mediterranean." *American Journal of Archaeology* 120 (1): 99–149. storyofstori.es/crisis.
Knauf, Ernst Axel. 2006. "The Israelite Impact on Judean Language and Literature" in *Judah and the Judeans in the Persian Period*, edited by O. Lipschitz et al. 291–349. storyofstori.es/impact.
Knox, Emily J. M. 2015. *Book Banning in 21st-Century America.* storyofstori.es/bookbanning.
Knutson, Brian, et al. 2002. "Ultrasonic Vocalizations as Indices of Affective States in Rats." *Psychological Bulletin* 128 (6): 961–77. storyofstori.es/rats.
Koch, Andreas, et al. 2018. "The Neurophysiology and Treatment of Motion Sickness." *Deutsches Ärzteblatt International* 115 (41): 687–96. storyofstori.es/motion.
Kohs, Greg (dir.). 2017. *AlphaGo—The Movie.* storyofstori.es/AlphaGo.
Kooi, Michael. 2009. "Venture Impact: The Economic Importance of Venture Capital-Backed Companies to the U.S. Economy." *Réseau Capital.* storyofstori.es/VC.
Koomey, J., et al., 2011. "Implications of Historical Trends in the Electrical Efficiency of Computing." *IEEE Annals of the History of Computing* 33 (3): 46–54. storyofstori.es/koomey.
Kornicki, Peter. 2012. "The Hyakumantō Darani and the Origins of Printing in Eighth-Century Japan." *International Journal of Asian Studies* 9 (1): 43–70. storyofstori.es/darani.
Kosfeld, Michael, et al. 2005. "Oxytocin Increases Trust in Humans." *Nature* 435 (7042): 673–76. storyofstori.es/trust.
Kosslyn, S. M. 1980. *Image and Mind.* storyofstori.es/image.
Kosslyn, S. M. 1994. *Image and Brain: The Resolution of the Imagery Debate.* storyofstori.es/brain.
Köster, K. 1973. *Gutenberg in Strassburg.* storyofstori.es/strass.
Kovacs, Maureen Gallery. 1989. *The Epic of Gilgamesh.* storyofstori.es/epic.
Kramer, S. N. 1961. *History Begins at Sumer.* storyofstori.es/history.
Krause, Mark, et al. 2018. "Animal Pointing: Changing Trends and Findings from 30 Years of Research." *Journal of Comparative Psychology* 132: 326–45. storyofstori.es/animal.
Kreutz, Gunter. 2014. "Does Singing Facilitate Social Bonding?" *Music and Medicine* 6 (2): 51–60. storyofstori.es/singing.

Kreutz, Gunter, et al. 2004. "Effects of Choir Singing or Listening on Secretory Immunoglobulin A, Cortisol, and Emotional State." *Journal of Behavioral Medicine* 27 (6): 623–35. storyofstori.es/choir.

Kropotkin, P. A. 1922. *Mutual Aid: A Factor of Evolution*. storyofstori.es/aid.

Kuitert, Lisa. 2020. "The Art of Printing in the Dutch East Indies: Laurens Janszoon Coster as Colonial Hero." *Quaerendo* 50 (1–2): 141–64. storyofstori.es/dutch.

Kullenberg, Bertil. 1950. "Investigations on the Pollination of Ophrys Species." *Oikos* 2 (1): 1–19. storyofstori.es/ophrys.

Kwakkel, Erik, et al. 2012. "Turning Over a New Leaf: Change and Development in the Medieval Manuscript." Universiteit Leiden. storyofstori.es/leaf.

Læssøe, J. 2014. *People of Ancient Assyria: Their Inscriptions and Correspondence*. storyofstori.es/people.

Lagercrantz, Sture. 1973. "Counting by Means of Tally Sticks or Cuts on the Body in Africa." *Anthropos* 68 (3/4): 569–88. storyofstori.es/counting.

Lai, Emily R. 2011. "Critical Thinking: A Literature Review." *Pearson's Research Reports* 6 (1): 40–41. storyofstori.es/critical.

Lambie, Ryan. March 4, 2025. "A New Studio That Makes Movies with AI Releases Five Minutes of Its Debut, and the Results Won't Haunt Your Dreams for All Eternity." *Film Stories*. storyofstori.es/studio.

Lawson, Mark. 2013. "George Orwell and the BBC." *About the BBC Blog*. storyofstori.es/lawson.

Lazer, David, et al. 2021. "Report #57: Social Media News Consumption and COVID-19 Vaccination Rates." *The COVID States Project*. storyofstori.es/media.

Lebanon Daily News (Lebanon, Pennsylvania). April 14, 1928. "Radio Blamed for the World's Freak Weather." storyofstori.es/news.

Ledderose, Lothar. 2000. *Ten Thousand Things: Module and Mass Production in Chinese Art*. storyofstori.es/ten.

Ledderose, Lothar. 2004. "Carving Sutras into Stone Before the Catastrophe." *Proceedings of the British Academy*. storyofstori.es/sutras.

lemmycaution25. 2023. "Men's Modern Hair Styles (1956)." *Reddit r/1950s*. storyofstori.es/flattop.

Letham, Benjamin, et al. 2019. "Bayesian Optimization for Policy Search Via Online-Offline Experimentation." *Journal of Machine Learning Research* 20(145): 1-30. storyofstori.es/via.

Levey, Martin. 1959. "Clay and Its Technology in Ancient Mesopotamia." *Centaurus* 6: 149–56. storyofstori.es/clay.

Levin, Samuel R. 1971. "The Analysis of Compression in Poetry." *Foundations of Language* 7 (1): 38–55. storyofstori.es/poetry.

Levine, L. W. 2007. *Black Culture and Black Consciousness: Afro-American Folk Thought from Slavery to Freedom*. storyofstori.es/Blackculture.

Lithvall, Johan. 2017. "Horizon Zero Dawn: Hair." *Artstation*. storyofstori.es/hair.

Lo, Andrew. 2000. "The Game of Leaves: An Inquiry into the Origin of Chinese Playing Cards." *Bulletin of the School of Oriental and African Studies, University of London* 63 (3): 389–406. storyofstori.es/game.

Lo, Andrew. 2007. "Literati Culture in Ming Dynasty Drinking Games Using Cards." *Zhongyang Daxue renwen xuebao (National Central University Journal of Humanities)* 31: 243–88. storyofstori.es/drinking.

Lomax, Alan. 2017. *Folk Song Style and Culture*. storyofstori.es/folk.

Lord, A. B. 1965. *The Singer of Tales*. storyofstori.es/tales.

Lorentz, H. A., et al. 1902. "The Theory of Electrons and the Propagation of Light." storyofstori.es/nobel.

Los Angeles Evening Post-Record. September 25, 1922. "Wandering Youth Has Radio Mania." storyofstori.es/youth.

Louca, Stilianos et al., 2019. "A Census-Based Estimate of Earth's Bacterial and Archaeal Diversity." *PLOS Biology* 17 (2), page e3000106. storyofstori.es/louca.

Louthan, Howard. 2010. "Tongues, Toes, and Bones: Remembering Saints in Early Modern Bohemia." *Past & Present* 206 (suppl_5): 167–183. storyofstori.es/louthan.
Ludlum, Robert. 2012. *The Bourne Identity*. storyofstori.es/bourne.
Luther, Martin. 1908. *The Letters of Martin Luther*. storyofstori.es/letters.
Luther, Martin. 1915. *Works of Martin Luther: With Introductions and Notes, Volume 1*. storyofstori.es/works.
Lyell, C., 1842. *Principles of Geology*. Volume 2. storyofstori.es/lyell.
Lynch, Hannah. 1901. *French Life in Town and Country*. storyofstori.es/lynch.
Lyne, Adrian (dir.). 1990. *Jacob's Ladder* (Movie). storyofstori.es/ladder.
Mac, Ryan, and Sheera Frenkel. October 25, 2021. "Internal Alarm, Public Shrugs: Facebook's Employees Dissect Its Election Role." *New York Times*. storyofstori.es/mac.
Mahdawi, Arwa. December 18, 2021. "Metaverse Is Just a New Venue for the Age-Old Problem of Sexual Harassment." *Guardian*. storyofstori.es/metaverse.
Mair, Gordon M. 2013. "How Fiction Informed the Development of Telepresence and Teleoperation." *International Conference on Virtual, Augmented and Mixed Reality*. storyofstori.es/fiction.
Mallet, James, and Michael C. Singer. 1987. "Individual Selection, Kin Selection, and the Shifting Balance in the Evolution of Warning Colours: The Evidence from Butterflies." *Biological Journal of the Linnean Society* 32 (4): 337–50. storyofstori.es/kin.
Marani, Tommaso. 2012. "The Relics of the Lateran According to 'Leiðarvísir,' the 'Descriptio Lateranensis Ecclesiae,' and the Inscription Outside the 'Sancta Sanctorum.'" *Medium Ævum* 81 (2): 271–88. storyofstori.es/therelics.
Marcus, Gary, and Reid Southen. January 6, 2024. "Generative AI Has a Visual Plagiarism Problem." *IEEE Spectrum*./ storyofstori.es/gen.
Margolick, D. 2001. *Strange Fruit: The Biography of a Song*. storyofstori.es/strange.
Marshack, Alexander. 1971. "Upper Palaeolithic Engraved Pieces in the British Museum: A Comparative Analysis of Two Fragments by New Methods." *The British Museum Quarterly* 35 (1/4): 137–45. storyofstori.es/upper.
Martínez, Antonio García. November 10, 2017. "Facebook's Not Listening Through Your Phone. It Doesn't Have To." *Wired*. storyofstori.es/wired.
Martyn, Monika. 2025. "Pet Ownership Statistics 2025—Latest Numbers and Trends." *WorldAnimal Foundation*. storyofstori.es/pets.
Marvel Studios. 2019. *Marvel Studios' Avengers: Endgame: Making the Final Battle!* (Short Movie). storyofstori.es/assemble.
Massachusetts Sentencing Commission. 2017. *Advisory Sentencing Guidelines*. storyofstori.es/mass.
Master of the Playing Cards. ca. 1435–40. "The Queen of Flowers." Metropolitan Museum of Art. storyofstori.es/queen.
Mateo, Jill M. 2010. "Alarm Calls Elicit Predator-Specific Physiological Responses." *Biology Letters* 6 (5): 623–25. storyofstori.es/calls.
Matney, Lucas. October 11, 2022. "Meta Announces Legs." *TechCrunch*. storyofstori.es/legs.
Matsuoka, Shigeru, 1980. "Pseudo Warning Call in Titmice." *Japanese Journal of Ornithology* 29 (2–3), 87–90. storyofstori.es/titmice.
May, Alan. 2015. "Albrecht Dürer's Drawing of a Printing Press: A Reconsideration." *Journal of the Printing Historical Society* New Series 15: 63–79. storyofstori.es/may.
Mazza, Débora. 2024. "Paulo Freire and bell hooks: An Encounter in the United States." *Pro-Posições* 35: 1–25. storyofstori.es/encounter.
McCulloh, John M. 1976. "The Cult of Relics in the Letters and 'Dialogues' of Pope Gregory the Great: A Lexicographical Study." *Traditio* 32 (1): 145–84. storyofstori.es/cult.
McGovern, Patrick E. 2003. *Ancient Wine: The Search for the Origins of Viniculture*. storyofstori.es/wine.

McGovern, Patrick E., et al. 2004. "Fermented Beverages of Pre- and Proto-Historic China." *Proceedings of the National Academy of Sciences* 101 (51): 17593–98. storyofstori.es/fermented.

McLuhan, Marshall. 2017. *The Gutenberg Galaxy*. storyofstori.es/galaxy.

McPherson, Malinda J., and Josh H. McDermott. 2020. "Time-Dependent Discrimination Advantages for Harmonic Sounds Suggest Efficient Coding for Memory." *Proceedings of the National Academy of Sciences* 117 (50): 32169–80. storyofstori.es/time.

McPherson, Miller, et al. 2001. "Birds of a Feather: Homophily in Social Networks." *Annual Review of Sociology* 27 (1): 415–44. storyofstori.es/feather.

Mech, L. David, and Luc A. A. Janssens. 2021. "An Assessment of Current Wolf *Canis lupus* Domestication Hypotheses Based on Wolf Ecology and Behaviour." *Mammal Review* 52 (2): 304–14. storyofstori.es/mech.

Melchior-Bonnet, S. 2001. *The Mirror: A History*. storyofstori.es/mirror.

Met Office. 2019. "UK Land Surface Stations Data for St. James's Park, August 13, 1936." *Centre for Environmental Data Analysis*. storyofstori.es/weather.

Metcalfe, Bob. 2013. "Metcalfe's Law After 40 Years of Ethernet." *Computer* 46 (12): 26–31. storyofstori.es/40.

Meyerowitz, Elliot M. 2002. "Plants Compared to Animals: The Broadest Comparative Study of Development." *Science* 295 (5559): 1482–85. storyofstori.es/compared.

Michelet, Jules, and G. H. Smith. 1845. *History of France: From the Earliest Period to the Present Date*. storyofstori.es/france.

Mienert, Melanie. 2024. "Survey and Statistics" in *The Tauchnitz Edition and Other Tauchnitz Paperback Series*, edited by Melanie Mienert et al. 21–39. storyofstori.es/edition.

Millard, A. R. 1986. "The Infancy of the Alphabet." *World Archaeology* 17 (3): 390–98. storyofstori.es/infancy.

Miller, P. E., and C. J. Murphy. 1995. "Vision in Dogs." *Journal of the American Veterinary Medical Association* 207 (12): 1623–34. storyofstori.es/vision.

Minor, Jack. 2010. "Second General Backs Lakin, Says President Should Produce Birth Certificate." *Greeley Gazette*. storyofstori.es/minor.

Moberg, Åsa, et al. 2011. "Books from an Environmental Perspective—Part 2: e-Books as an Alternative to Paper Books." *International Journal of Life Cycle Assessment* 16 (3): 238–46. storyofstori.es/ebooks.

MobiThinking. 2012. "2011 Handset and Smartphone Sales Statistics Worldwide: The Big Picture." *MobiForge*. storyofstori.es/2011.

Modelski, G. 2003. *World Cities: –3000 to 2000*. storyofstori.es/cities.

Møller, Anders Pape. 1988. "False Alarm Calls as a Means of Resource Usurpation in the Great Tit *Parus major*." *Ethology* 79 (1): 25–30. storyofstori.es/means.

Moltenbrey, Karen. 2019. *"Avengers: Endgame* VFX Supervisor Dan Deleeuw." *Post Magazine*. storyofstori.es/VFX.

Moore, David W. 2001. "Americans Believe U.S. Participation in Gulf War a Decade Ago Worthwhile." Gallup News Service. storyofstori.es/gulf.

Moore, Gordon E. 1965. "Cramming More Components onto Integrated Circuits." *IEEE Solid-State Circuits Society Newsletter* 11 (3): 33–36. storyofstori.es/law.

Moore, R. 1995. *Gutenberg in Strasbourg*. storyofstori.es/moore.

Mora, Camilo, et al. 2011. "How Many Species Are There on Earth and in the Ocean?" *PLoS Biology* 9 (8): e1001127. storyofstori.es/mora.

Morales, R., et al. 2004. *Truth: Red, White & Black*. storyofstori.es/truth.

Mori, M., et al. 2012. "The Uncanny Valley [From the Field]." *IEEE Robotics & Automation Magazine* 19 (2): 98–100. storyofstori.es/mori.

Morris, Dylan, et al. 1995. "Functional Equivalence of Verbal and Spatial Information in Serial Short-Term Memory." *Journal of Experimental Psychology: Learning, Memory, and Cognition* 21 (4): 1008–18. storyofstori.es/dylan.

Morris, Errol (dir.). 2017. *Wormwood* (TV Series). storyofstori.es/wormwood.
Morris, Michael G., and Viswanath Venkatesh. 2000. "Age Differences in Technology Adoption Decisions: Implications for a Changing Work Force." *Personnel Psychology* 53 (2): 375–403. storyofstori.es/age.
Morris, S. C. 2008. *The Deep Structure of Biology*. storyofstori.es/morris.
Morrison, Donald M. 2020. "Disambiguated Indexical Pointing as a Tipping Point for the Explosive Emergence of Language Among Human Ancestors." *Biological Theory* 15 (4): 196–211. storyofstori.es/index.
Moskowitz, Ron. 1970. "Professor Sees Peril in Education." *San Francisco Chronicle*. storyofstori.es/peril.
Moudgil, Manu. 2017. "Conversion to Buddhism Has Brought Literacy, Gender Equality and Well-Being to Dalits." *IndiaSpend*. storyofstori.es/conversion.
Muendel, John. 1995. "Friction and Lubrication in Medieval Europe: The Emergence of Olive Oil as a Superior Agent." *Isis* 86 (3): 373–93. storyofstori.es/oliveoil.
Munn, Charles A. 1986. "Birds That 'Cry Wolf.'" *Nature* 319 (6049): 143–45. storyofstori.es/birds.
Munsell, J. 1876. *Chronology of the Origin and Progress of Paper and Paper-Making*. storyofstori.es/paper.
Murray, H. J. R. 1913. *A History of Chess*. storyofstori.es/chess.
Muybridge, Eadweard. 1888. *Animal Locomotion*. storyofstori.es/locomotion.
Naegele, Edgar. 2017. "Quantification of Compounds in the E7 Liquid Crystal Mixture by Supercritical Fluid Chromatography with UV Detection." *Agilent*. storyofstori.es/E7.
Nagy, G. 2010. *Homer the Preclassic*. storyofstori.es/classic.
Naselaris, Thomas, et al. 2015. "A Voxel-Wise Encoding Model for Early Visual Areas Decodes Mental Images of Remembered Scenes." *Neuroimage* 105: 215–28. storyofstori.es/decode.
Neitz, Jay. 1989. "Color Vision in the Dog." *Visual Neuroscience* 3 (2): 119–25. storyofstori.es/color.
Neubauer, Simon, et al. 2018. "The Evolution of Modern Human Brain Shape." *Science Advances* 4 (1): 1–8. storyofstori.es/shape.
Neuman, Scott. May 8, 2020. "Seen *Plandemic*? We Take a Close Look at the Viral Conspiracy Video's Claims." *NPR*. storyofstori.es/neuman.
New-York Tribune. November 4, 1856. "The Rag and Paper Business." storyofstori.es/tribune.
Newby, Richard. 2021. "*Falcon and the Winter Soldier* Uncovers Marvel's Original Sin." *The Hollywood Reporter*. storyofstori.es/falcon.
Newton et al. 1995. *Newton: Texts, Backgrounds, Commentaries*. storyofstori.es/IN.
Ng, Sarah. 2013. "Challenging the Calligraphy Canon: The Reception of Rubbing Collections in Ming China." DPhil thesis. University of Oxford. 178 pages. storyofstori.es/ng.
The Nikkei, 2020. *Create the Next: Vol. 6 Silica Sand Mining*. storyofstori.es/next.
Nisbet, Robert. 1973. "The Myth of the Renaissance." *Comparative Studies in Society and History* 15 (4): 473–92. storyofstori.es/myth.
Nishimura, Takeshi, et al. 2022. "Evolutionary Loss of Complexity in Human Vocal Anatomy as an Adaptation for Speech." *Science* 377 (6607): 760–63. storyofstori.es/loss.
Nissen, Hans J. 1986. "The Archaic Texts From Uruk." *World Archaeology* 17 (3): 317–34. storyofstori.es/texts.
Nissen, Hans J., et al. 1988. *The Early History of the Ancient Near East, 9000–2000 B.C.* storyofstori.es/early.
Nissen, Hans J., et al. 1993. *Archaic Bookkeeping: Early Writing and Techniques of Economic Administration in the Ancient Near East*. storyofstori.es/bookkeeping.
Nissen, Hans J. 2003. "Uruk and the Formation of the City" in *Art of the First Cities: The Third Millennium BC from the Mediterranean to the Indus*, edited by Joan Aruz et al. 11–20. storyofstori.es/art.

Norgate, Martin. 2007. "Cutting Borders: Dissected Maps and the Origins of the Jigsaw Puzzle." *The Cartographic Journal* 44 (4): 342–50. storyofstori.es/borders.
Norman, J. 2021. "Is This Oldest Extant Piece of Paper?" *Jeremy Norman's History of Information.* storyofstori.es/is.
Novotny, J. R., and J. Jeffers. 2018. *The Royal Inscriptions of Ashurbanipal (668–631 BC), Aššur-Etal-ilāni (630–627 BC), and Sîn-Šarra-iškun (626–612 BC), Kings of Assyria.* storyofstori.es/inscriptions.
O'Hara, James G. 1975. "George Johnstone Stoney, FRS and the Concept of the Electron." *Notes and Records of the Royal Society of London* 29 (2): 265–76. storyofstori.es/electron.
Oakley, B. 2008. *Evil Genes: Why Rome Fell, Hitler Rose, Enron Failed, and My Sister Stole My Mother's Boyfriend.* storyofstori.es/oakley.
Oates, Joan. 1973. "The Background and Development of Early Farming Communities in Mesopotamia and the Zagros." *Proceedings of the Prehistoric Society* 39: 147–81. storyofstori.es/oates.
Observer. 1991. "Letters." *The Observer (London, UK).* storyofstori.es/observer.
Ochs, E., et al. 2009. *Living Narrative: Creating Lives in Everyday Storytelling.* storyofstori.es/ochs.
OECD. 2021. "Pensions at a Glance." *Country Profiles* China: 1–3. storyofstori.es/pensions.
Ogburn, William F., and Dorothy Thomas. 1922. "Are Inventions Inevitable? A Note on Social Evolution." *Political Science Quarterly* 37 (1): 83–98. storyofstori.es/ogburn.
Oman, Charles M. 1982. "A Heuristic Mathematical Model for the Dynamics of Sensory Conflict and Motion Sickness." *Acta Oto-Laryngologica* 94 (supplement 392): 4–44. storyofstori.es/oman.
Omdia. 2021. *Displays Market Data.* storyofstori.es/omdia.
Onah, Julius (dir.). 2025. *Captain America: Brave New World* (Movie). storyofstori.es/brave.
Ong, Walter J. 1975. "The Writer's Audience Is Always a Fiction." *Publications of the Modern Language Association of America* 90 (1): 9–21. storyofstori.es/audience.
Orbeli, L. A. 1908. "Conditioned Reflexes Resulting from Optical Stimulation of the Dog." *Psychological Bulletin* 6: 257–73. storyofstori.es/leon.
Orwell, George. 1945. *Animal Farm.* storyofstori.es/orwell.
Osborn, Howard J. 1973. *"Family Jewels"* (CIA Internal Memorandum). storyofstori.es/CIA.
The Ottawa Journal. 1925. "Women in England Fear 'Radio Face.'" storyofstori.es/fear.
Page, Clarence 2003. "Embedded—But Not in Bed With." *Tribune Media Services.* storyofstori.es/embedded.
Pain, Emil, et al. 2000. "The Second Chechen War: The Information Component." *Military Review* 80 (4): 59–69. storyofstori.es/chechen.
Pardi, Tommaso, et al. 2020. *Digital Manufacturing Revolutions as Political Projects and Hypes: Evidences from the Auto Sector.* storyofstori.es/pardi.
Parker, Hope. 2022. "The Proto-Sinaitic Inscriptions at Serabit El-Khadim." *Ägypten und Levante / Egypt and the Levant* 32: 269–311. storyofstori.es/parker.
Parsons, Anscar. 1944. "St. Bernardine, the Moral Teacher." *Franciscan Studies* 4 (4): 341–58. storyofstori.es/moral.
Patel, Aniruddh D., et al. 1998. "Processing Syntactic Relations in Language and Music: An Event-Related Potential Study." *Journal of Cognitive Neuroscience* 10 (6): 717–33. storyofstori.es/patel.
Patel, Aniruddh D. 2003. "Language, Music, Syntax and the Brain." *Nature Neuroscience* 6 (7): 674–81. storyofstori.es/syntax.
Patterson, David, et al. 2021. "Carbon Emissions and Large Neural Network Training." *Arxiv.* storyofstori.es/carbon.
Paul, Christopher, and James J. Kim. 2005. *Reporters on the Battlefield: The Embedded Press System in Historical Context.* storyofstori.es/reporters.
Paul II. 1994. *Catechism of the Catholic Church.* storyofstori.es/pope.

Pawley, Alisun, and Daniel Müllensiefen. 2012. "The Science of Singing Along: A Quantitative Field Study on Sing-Along Behavior in the North of England." *Music Perception* 30 (2): 129–46. storyofstori.es/singalong.

Peacock, T. L. 1818. *Nightmare Abbey*. storyofstori.es/abbey.

Pearce, Eiluned, et al. 2015. "The Ice-Breaker Effect: Singing Mediates Fast Social Bonding." *Royal Society Open Science* 2 (10): 1–9. storyofstori.es/ice.

Pearson, Ben. 2021. "*Wandavision* Has More VFX Shots Than *Avengers: Endgame*, Will Feature Some of Marvel's Biggest Setpieces." *Slash Film*. storyofstori.es/wanda.

Pennington, Nancy, and Reid Hastie. 1992. "Explaining the Evidence: Tests of the Story Model for Juror Decision Making." *Journal of Personality and Social Psychology* 62: 189–206. storyofstori.es/evidence.

Pennington, Nancy, and Reid Hastie. 1993. "The Story Model for Juror Decision Making" in *Inside the Juror: The Psychology of Juror Decision Making*, edited by Reid Hastie, 192–222. storyofstori.es/juror.

Perez, Victor M. 2022. "An Open Letter to Katy ISD Voters from Victor Perez." *Katy Christian Magazine*. storyofstori.es/open.

Perrin, Oliver Timken. 2011. "Marks: A Distinct Subcategory Within Writing as Integrationally Defined." *Language Sciences* 33 (4): 623–33. storyofstori.es/marks.

Persson, M., and J. Bergensten. 2011. *Minecraft*. storyofstori.es/minecraft.

Pesenti, Jerome. 2021. "An Update on Our Use of Face Recognition (Blog Post)." *Facebook News*. storyofstori.es/use.

Peters, Roger P., and L. David Mech. 1975. "Scent-Marking in Wolves." *American Scientist* 63 (6): 628–37. storyofstori.es/wolves.

Petersen, R. 2010. *Comics, Manga, and Graphic Novels: A History of Graphic Narratives*. storyofstori.es/comics.

Peterson, Richard A. 1990. "Why 1955? Explaining the Advent of Rock Music." *Popular Music* 9 (1): 97–116. storyofstori.es/1955.

Petrie, W. M. F., et al. 1906. *Researches in Sinai*. storyofstori.es/sinai.

Pew 2017 *Religious Composition* with major processing by Our World In Data. storyofstori.es/map

Phelan, Matthew. 2019. "The History of History Is Written by the Victors." *Slate*. storyofstori.es/victors.

Phillips, Brian. December 17, 2022. "What a piece of work is a man . . . he should be trained from birth to manage logistics for a mid-sized regional wholesaler." *Twitter (later renamed X)*. storyofstori.es/man.

Pika, Simone, and Thomas Bugnyar. 2011. "The Use of Referential Gestures in Ravens (*Corvus corax*) in the Wild." *Nature Communications* 2, article number 560: 1–5. storyofstori.es/ravens.

Piñeiro, Ana, and Isabel Barja. 2012. "The Plant Physical Features Selected By Wildcats as Signal Posts: An Economic Approach to Fecal Marking." *Naturwissenschaften* 99 (10): 801–9. storyofstori.es/wildcats.

Plato. 1906. *The Theaetetus and Philebus of Plato*. Translated by H. F. Carlill. storyofstori.es/the.

Platt, Verity. 2006. "Making an Impression: Replication and the Ontology of the Graeco-Roman Seal Stone." *Art History* 29 (2): 233–57. storyofstori.es/making.

Pliskoff, Stanley S., and T. Daryl Hawking. 1965. *Remote Control of Behavior with Rewarding Electrical Stimulation of the Brain*. storyofstori.es/remote.

Plofker, Kim, et al. 2017. "The Bakhshālī Manuscript: A Response to the Bodleian Library's Radiocarbon Dating." *History of Science in South Asia* 5 (1): 134–50. storyofstori.es/response.

Plutchik, Robert. 2001. "The Nature of Emotions: Human Emotions Have Deep Evolutionary Roots, a Fact That May Explain Their Complexity and Provide Tools for Clinical Practice." *American Scientist* 89 (4): 344–50. storyofstori.es/nature.

Polito, Gene. 1973. "The Cinematography of *Westworld*: A State of Mind?" *American Cinematographer*. March 12. storyofstori.es/polito.

Polzonetti, Pierpaolo. 2014. "Tartini and the Tongue of Saint Anthony." *Journal of the American Musicological Society* 67 (2): 429–86. storyofstori.es/tongue.

Powell, Hilary. 2012. "The 'Miracle of Childbirth': The Portrayal of Parturient Women in Medieval Miracle Narratives." *Social History of Medicine* 25 (4): 795–811. storyofstori.es/birth.

Prebish, Charles S. 2008. "Cooking the Buddhist Books: The Implications of the New Dating of the Buddha for the History of Early Indian Buddhism." *Journal of Buddhist Ethics* 15 (1): 1–21. storyofstori.es/cooking.

Preston, Mary I. 1941. "Children's Reactions to Movie Horrors and Radio Crime." *The Journal of Pediatrics* 19 (2): 147–68. storyofstori.es/preston.

Pronin, Emily, et al. 2002. "The Bias Blind Spot: Perceptions of Bias in Self Versus Others." *Personality and Social Psychology Bulletin* 28 (3): 369–81. storyofstori.es/blind.

Provine, Robert R. 1996. "Laughter." *American Scientist* 84 (1): 4538–45. storyofstori.es/laughter.

Puts, David Andrew. 2005. "Mating Context and Menstrual Phase Affect Women's Preferences for Male Voice Pitch." *Evolution and Human Behavior* 26 (5): 388–97. storyofstori.es/puts.

Pye, Kenneth. 1982. "Morphological Development of Coastal Dunes in a Humid Tropical Environment, Cape Bedford and Cape Flattery, North Queensland." *Geografiska Annaler: Series A, Physical Geography* 64 (3–4): 213–27. storyofstori.es/flattery.

Pye, Kenneth. 1983. "Post-Depositional Reddening of Late Quaternary Coastal Dune Sands, North-Eastern Australia." *Geological Society, London, Special Publications* 11 (1): 117–29. storyofstori.es/dunes.

Radford, Colin et al., 1975. "How Can We be Moved by the Fate of Anna Karenina." *Aristotelian Society Supplementary Volume* 49 (1): 67–94. storyofstori.es/radford.

Rawlinson, G. 1898. *A Memoir of Major-General Sir Henry Creswicke Rawlinson*. storyofstori.es/henry.

Richards, Abbie. 2021. "Conspiracy Chart 2021." *Conspiracy Chart*. storyofstori.es/abbie.

Ries, Maurice. 1932. "Stamping: A Mass-Production Printing Method 2000 Years Old." *Middle American Papers*. Chapter 12: 416–77. storyofstori.es/ries1932.

Ries, Maurice. 1940. "First Season's Archaeological Work at Campana San Andrés, El Salvador." *American Anthropologist* New Series 42 (4): 712–13. storyofstori.es/ries1940.

Rivers, Pitt, 1883. "On the Egyptian Boomerang and Its Affinities." *Journal of the Anthropological Institute of Great Britain and Ireland* 12: 454–63. storyofstori.es/boomerang.

Rodero, Emma. 2011. "Intonation and Emotion: Influence of Pitch Levels and Contour Type on Creating Emotions." *Journal of Voice* 25 (1): e25–34. storyofstori.es/intonation.

Roederer, Juan G. 1984. "The Search for a Survival Value of Music." *Music Perception* 1 (3): 350–56. storyofstori.es/search.

Rosen, Philip. 1993. "Document and Documentary: On the Persistence of Historical Concepts." In *Theorizing Documentary*, edited by Michael Renov: 58–89. storyofstori.es/rosen.

Rosenblum, Robert. 1954. "Magritte's Surrealist Grammar." *Art Digest* 28 (12): 16, 32. storyofstori.es/grammar.

Roser, Max. 2024. "Mortality in the Past: Every Second Child Died." *Our World in Data*. storyofstori.es/child.

Roser, Max, and Esteban Ortiz-Ospina. 2013. "Literacy." *Our World in Data*. storyofstori.es/roser.

Rosselló, Josep A. 2014. "The Never-Ending Story of Geologically Ancient DNA: Was the Model Plant *Arabidopsis* the Source of Miocene Dominican Amber?" *Biological Journal of the Linnean Society* 111 (1): 234–40. storyofstori.es/amber.

Rossignol, Marie-Jeanne. 2006. "The American Revolution in France: Under the Shadow of the French Revolution" in *Europe's American Revolution*, edited by Simon P. Newman. 51–71. storyofstori.es/shadow.

Rottenberg, Josh, and Stacy Perman. 2020. "Meet the Ojai Dad Who Made the Most Notorious Piece of Coronavirus Disinformation Yet." *Los Angeles Times*. May 13. storyofstori.es/willis.

Roud, Steve. n.d. "Little Piggy / Come Little Piggy." *Roud Folk Song Index* Roud #19297. storyofstori.es/piggy.

Rovai, Francesco. 2020. "Migration, Identity, and Multilingualism in Late Hellenistic Delos." *Migration, Mobility and Language Contact in and Around the Ancient Mediterranean:* 171–202. storyofstori.es/rovai.

Roy, Dheeraj S. et al. 2016. "Memory Retrieval by Activating Engram Cells in Mouse Models of Early Alzheimer's Disease." *Nature* 531 (7595): 508–12. storyofstori.es/mouse.

Rubin, Jared. 2014. "Printing and Protestants: An Empirical Test of the Role of Printing in the Reformation." *Review of Economics and Statistics* 96 (2): 270–86. storyofstori.es/rubin.

Rusch, Neil. 2021. "Controlled Fermentation, Honey, Bees and Alcohol: Archaeological and Ethnohistorical Evidence from Southern Africa." *Southern African Humanities*. storyofstori.es/mead.

Russo Brothers. April 27, 2020. "Sharing for the first time . . . these experiences once again." *Twitter (later renamed X)*. storyofstori.es/russotweet.

Said, E. W. 1995. *Orientalism*. storyofstori.es/said.

Sandlin, Cameron, et al. 2017. *Memphis Police Department Homicide Reports 1917–1936*. storyofstori.es/memphis.

Sarbin, Theodore R. 1986. *Narrative Psychology: The Storied Nature of Human Conduct*. https://storyofstori.es/sarbin.

Sargeant, W., et al. 2010. *The Bhagavad Gita*. storyofstori.es/gita.

Satake, Akiko, and Yoh Iwasa. 2000. "Pollen Coupling of Forest Trees: Forming Synchronized and Periodic Reproduction out of Chaos." *Journal of Theoretical Biology* 203 (2): 63–84. storyofstori.es/chaos.

Schacter, D. L., et al. 1997. "False Memories and Aging." *Trends in Cognitive Sciences* 1 (6): 229–36. storyofstori.es/memories.

Schacter, D. L. 2018. *The Seven Sins of Memory: How the Mind Forgets and Remembers*. storyofstori.es/sins.

Scharff, C., et al. 2015. "Human Mobility During Religious Festivals and Its Implications on Public Health in Senegal: A Mobile Dataset Analysis." *2015 IEEE Global Humanitarian Technology Conference (GHTC)*. storyofstori.es/festivals.

Schechner, Sam, et al. September 17, 2021. "How Facebook Hobbled Mark Zuckerberg's Bid to Get America Vaccinated." *Wall Street Journal*. storyofstori.es/wsj.

Schellenberg, E. Glenn, et al. 2003. "Good Pitch Memory Is Widespread." *Psychological Science* 14 (3): 262–66. storyofstori.es/good.

Schendel, Zachary A., et al. 2007. "Suppression Effects on Musical and Verbal Memory." *Memory & Cognition* 35 (4): 640–50. storyofstori.es/effects.

Schmitt, Eric. 1991. "U.S. Army Buried Iraqi Soldiers Alive in Gulf War." *New York Times*. storyofstori.es/army.

Schopen, Gregory. 1975. "The Phrase 'sa pthivīpradeśaś caityabhūto bhavet' in the Vajracchedikā: Notes on the Cult of the Book in Mahāyāna." *Indo-Iranian Journal* 17 (3–4): 147–81. storyofstori.es/phrase.

Scotti, R. A. 2007. *Basilica*. storyofstori.es/basilica.

Secretary of the Treasury. 1922. *Imported Merchandise and Retail Prices*. storyofstori.es/imports.

Seevers, Boyd, and Rachel Korhonen. 2019. "Seals in Ancient Israel and the Near East: Their Manufacture, Use, and Apparent Paradox of Pagan Symbolism." *Near Eastern Archaeological Society Bulletin* 61: 1–17. storyofstori.es/seals.

Shackleton, Trevor M., and Robert P. Carlyon. 1994. "The Role of Resolved and Unresolved Harmonics in Pitch Perception and Frequency Modulation Discrimination." *Journal of the Acoustical Society of America* 95 (6): 3529–40. storyofstori.es/role.

Shannon, Claude E. 1938. "A Symbolic Analysis of Relay and Switching Circuits." *Electrical Engineering* 57 (12): 713–23. storyofstori.es/shannon.

Shannon, Claude E. 1948. "A Mathematical Theory of Communication." *The Bell System Technical Journal* 27 (3): 379–423. storyofstori.es/mathcomm.

Shannon, Claude E. 1993. "*Scientific Aspects of Juggling*" in *Claude Elwood Shannon: Collected Papers*, edited by A. D. Wyner et al. 850–64. storyofstori.es/juggling.

Sharma, Preeti. 2007. "Varaha Motif in the Chalukyan Rock-Cut Caves at Badami." *Proceedings of the Indian History Congress* 68: 1417–21. storyofstori.es/motif.

Shead, Sam. 2020. "DeepMind A.I. Unit Lost $649 Million Last Year and Had a $1.5 Billion Debt Waived by Alphabet." *CNBC*. storyofstori.es/shead.

Shefrin, J. 2003. *Such Constant Affectionate Care: Lady Charlotte Finch, Royal Governess, & the Children of George III*. storyofstori.es/such.

Shen, Hsueh-Man. 2012. "Between One and Many: Multiples, Multiplication and the Huayan Metaphysics." *Proceedings of the British Academy*. storyofstori.es/many.

Shenton, C. 2012. *The Day Parliament Burned Down*. storyofstori.es/burned.

Sherman, Paul W. 1977. "Nepotism and the Evolution of Alarm Calls." *Science* 197 (4310): 1246–53. storyofstori.es/nepo.

Shiers, George. 1974. "Ferdinand Braun and the Cathode Ray Tube." *Scientific American* 230 (3): 92–101. storyofstori.es/braun.

Shortland, Cate (dir.). 2021. *Black Widow* (Movie). storyofstori.es/widow.

Shteyngart, G. 2010. *Super Sad True Love Story: A Novel*. storyofstori.es/super.

Silberman, Steve. November 1994. "We're Teen, We're Queer, and We've Got E-mail." *Wired*. storyofstori.es/queer.

"Silica Sand for Japan." *Sydney Morning Herald*, 1967. storyofstori.es/silica.

Silver, Laura, and Courtney Johnson. October 9, 2018. "Internet Connectivity Seen as Having Positive Impact on Life in Sub-Saharan Africa." *Pew Research Center*. storyofstori.es/pew.

Silverberg, Robert A. 1995. *Lord Valentine's Castle*. storyofstori.es/castle.

Silverman, Craig, et al. 2020. "'I Have Blood on My Hands': A Whistleblower Says Facebook Ignored Global Political Manipulation." *Buzzfeed*. storyofstori.es/hands.

Simard, Suzanne W. 2018. "*Mycorrhizal Networks Facilitate Tree Communication, Learning, and Memory*" in *Memory and Learning in Plants*, edited by Frantisek Baluska et al. 191–213. storyofstori.es/myco.

Simmons, Joe, et al. 2023. "[109] Data Falsificada (Part 1): 'Clusterfake.'" *Data Colada*, June 17. storyofstori.es/data.

Sinai, Nicolai. 2014. "When Did the Consonantal Skeleton of the Quran Reach Closure? Part I." *Bulletin of the School of Oriental and African Studies* 77 (2): 273–92. storyofstori.es/when.

Singer, Wolf. 1999. "Neuronal Synchrony: A Versatile Code for the Definition of Relations." *Neuron* 24 (1): 49–65. storyofstori.es/singer.

Skogemann, Pia. 2022. "*The Daughter Archetype*" in *Anthology of Contemporary Clinical Classics in Analytical Psychology*, edited by Stefano Carpani. 212–20. storyofstori.es/daughter.

Skogland, Kari (dir.). 2021. *The Falcon and the Winter Soldier* (TV Series). storyofstori.es/skogland.

Slough History Online. 2024. "Transport in Slough: Windmill Inn." *Slough History Online.* storyofstori.es/slough.

Smart, James R. 1980. "Emile Berliner and Nineteenth-Century Disc Recordings." *The Quarterly Journal of the Library of Congress* 37 (3/4): 422–40. storyofstori.es/disc.

Smith, Daniel, et al. 2017. "Cooperation and the Evolution of Hunter-Gatherer Storytelling." *Nature Communications* 8 (1): 1–9. storyofstori.es/smith.

Smith, George. 1876. *The Chaldean Account of Genesis.* storyofstori.es/george.

Smith, Willoughby. 1873. "Effect of Light on Selenium During the Passage of an Electric Current." *Nature* 7 (173): 303. storyofstori.es/effect.

Sneed, Edmund D., and Robert L. Folk. 1958. "Pebbles in the Lower Colorado River, Texas: A Study in Particle Morphogenesis." *The Journal of Geology* 66 (2): 114–50. storyofstori.es/pebbles.

Snow, Anita. June 27, 2007. "CIA Plot to Kill Castro Detailed." *Associated Press.* storyofstori.es/castro.

Spalding, Kirsty L., et al. 2005. "Retrospective Birth Dating of Cells in Humans." *Cell* 122 (1): 133–43. storyofstori.es/dating.

Spargo, P. E., et al. 1979. "Newton's 'Derangement of the Intellect.' New Light on an Old Problem." *Notes and Records of the Royal Society of London* 34 (1): 11–32. storyofstori.es/newlight.

The Spectator. December 7, 1872a. "on Tuesday Night Mr. George Smith, of the British Museum . . .": 2. storyofstori.es/tuesday.

The Spectator. December 7, 1872b. "Mr. Gladstone's Passion for Homer." 8–9. storyofstori.es/passion.

The Spectator. December 14, 1872. "Letters to the Editor: Mr. Gladstone and Homer." 14. storyofstori.es/gladstone.

Spencer, B. 1998. *"Pilgrim Souvenirs and Secular Badges"* in *Medieval Finds From Excavation,* edited by Geoff Egan. 1–372. storyofstori.es/pilgrim.

Sperling, George. 1960. "The Information Available in Brief Visual Presentations." *Psychological Monographs: General and Applied* 74 (11): 1–29. storyofstori.es/brief.

The Spokesman-Review (Spokane). September 13, 1908. "And Now the 'Aeroplane Face.'" storyofstori.es/andnow.

The Spokesman-Review (Spokane). November 4, 1936. "Purity of Elections Violated by Radio?" storyofstori.es/purity.

Starr, F. 2008. *Black Tigers: A Grammar of Chinese Rubbings.* storyofstori.es/tigers.

Statista. 2021. "Number of Monthly Active Facebook Users Worldwide as of 3rd Quarter 2021." *Statista.* storyofstori.es/active.

Steck, Kathrin, et al. 2011. "Desert Ants Benefit from Combining Visual and Olfactory Landmarks." *Journal of Experimental Biology* 214 (8): 1307–12. storyofstori.es/ants.

Stephenson, N. 2003. *Snow Crash.* storyofstori.es/snow.

Sterling, C. H., and J. M. Kittross. 2001. *Stay Tuned: A History of American Broadcasting.* storyofstori.es/stay.

Stevens, Frank. 1933. "An Early Chessman from Old Sarum." *The Antiquaries Journal* 13 (3): 308–10. storyofstori.es/sarum.

Stevens, S. S., and Hallowell David. 1938. *Hearing, Its Psychology and Physiology.* storyofstori.es/hearing.

Stock-Allen, Nancy. 2016. "Outposts of Handmade Paper in 21st Century North America." *Design Traveler.* storyofstori.es/outposts.

Straparola, G. F., and Morlini. 1901. *The Facetious Nights of Straparola.* storyofstori.es/nights.

Studevent-Hickman, Benjamin. 2007. *"The Ninety-Degree Rotation of the Cuneiform Script"* in *Ancient Near Eastern Art in Context: Studies in Honor of Irene Winter,* edited by Jack Cheng et al. 483–511. storyofstori.es/90.

Suls, Jerry, and C. K. Wan. 1987. "In Search of the False-Uniqueness Phenomenon: Fear and Estimates of Social Consensus." *Journal of Personality and Social Psychology* 52 (1): 211. storyofstori.es/unique.

Sun, Y. 2019. Transcript of Interview with Author.

Syrotuck, W. G. 2000. *Scent and the Scenting Dog*. storyofstori.es/scent.

Tabatabai, Sayed. 2020. "At Some Point Your Parents Picked You Up, Set You Down, and Never Picked You Up Again." *Twitter*. storyofstori.es/milestones.

Teixeira, João Paulo, et al. 2013. "Vocal Acoustic Analysis—Jitter, Shimmer, and HNR Parameters." *Procedia Technology* 9: 1112–22. storyofstori.es/jitter.

Then, C., et al. 2022. "Computational Ballistic Analysis of the Cranial Shot to John F. Kennedy." *Forensic Science International* 334: 111264. storyofstori.es/then.

Thomas, Sue, et al. 2007. "Transliteracy: Crossing Divides." *First Monday*. storyofstori.es/crossing.

Thomas, Timothy L. 2004. "Information Warfare in the Second (1999–) Chechen War: Motivator for Military Reform?" In *Russian Military Reform, 1992–2002*, edited by Anne C. Aldis and Roger N. McDermott. 208–32. storyofstori.es/thomas.

Thompson, William R. 2004. "Complexity, Diminishing Marginal Returns, and Serial Mesopotamian Fragmentation." *Journal of World-Systems Research* 10 (3): 613–52. storyofstori.es/thompson.

Tiffany, Kaitlyn. 2021. "I Made the World's Blandest Facebook Profile, Just to See What Happen." *The Atlantic*. storyofstori.es/bland.

Tiger, Ildiko. 2013. *Muscles of the Dog's Ear*. storyofstori.es/ear.

Tingle, Elizabeth. 2014. "Indulgences in the Catholic Reformation." *Reformation & Renaissance Review* 16 (2): 181–204. storyofstori.es/indulge.

Todd, William B. 1984. "A New Measure of Literary Excellence: The Tauchnitz International Editions 1841–1943." *The Papers of the Bibliographical Society of America* 78 (3): 333–40. storyofstori.es/new.

Todorović, Miloš. 2017. "The Prehistory of the Emoji Phenomenon as a Key to Understanding Its Future." *AXIOS* 2: 192–203. storyofstori.es/emoji.

Tomayko, James E. 1988. "Computers in Spaceflight: The NASA Experience." *NASA*. storyofstori.es/NASA.

The Topeka State Journal (Topeka, Kansas). July 22, 1899. "The Automobile Face." storyofstori.es/topeka.

Treisman, Michel. 1977. "Motion Sickness: An Evolutionary Hypothesis." *Science* 197 (4302): 493–95. storyofstori.es/sickness.

Třísková, Hana. 2011. "The Structure of the Mandarin Syllable: Why, When and How to Teach It." *Archiv orientální* 79 (1): 99–134. storyofstori.es/mandarin.

Trivedi, Bijal P. 2012. "Gustatory System: The Finer Points of Taste." *Nature* 486 (7403): S2–S3. storyofstori.es/taste.

Tsuji, Sho, and Alejandrina Christia. 2014. "Perceptual Attunement in Vowels: A Meta-Analysis." *Developmental Psychobiology* 56 (2): 179–91. storyofstori.es/meta.

Turing, A. M. 1950. "Computing Machinery and Intelligence." *Mind* LIX (236): 433–60. storyofstori.es/turing.

Ugander, Johan, et al. 2011. "The Anatomy of the Facebook Social Graph." *Arxiv*. storyofstori.es/graph.

United States Supreme Court, 1997. "Reno, Attorney General of the United States, et al. v. American Civil Liberties Union et al." US 521: 844–97. storyofstori.es/reno.

Urban, Sylvanus 1840. *The Gentleman's Magazine, Volumes 167–168*. storyofstori.es/urban.

US Bureau of Labor Statistics. 2007. *American Time Use Survey 2006*. storyofstori.es/2006.

US Bureau of Labor Statistics. 2017. "Newspaper Publishers Lose Over Half Their Employment from January 2001 to September 2016." *The Economics Daily*. storyofstori.es/labor.

US Census Bureau. 1963. *Statistical Abstract of the United States: 1963*. storyofstori.es/1963.
US Census Bureau. 2023. "Home Alone: More Than a Quarter of All Households Have One Person." storyofstori.es/alone.
US Senate Select Committee on Intelligence. August 3, 1977. "Project MKULTRA, the CIA's Program of Research in Behavioral Modification: Joint Hearing before the Select Committee on Intelligence and the Subcommittee on Health and Scientific Research." storyofstori.es/ultra.
Utych, Stephen, and Luke Fowler. 2021. "More Human Than Human: The Consequences of Positive Dehumanization." *Administrative Theory & Praxis* 43 (2): 190–208. storyofstori.es/than.
Vail, G., and A. Aveni. 2009. *The Madrid Codex: New Approaches to Understanding an Ancient Maya Manuscript. Mesoamerican Worlds* storyofstori.es/madrid.
Vainker, S. J. 2004. *Chinese Silk: A Cultural History*. storyofstori.es/silk.
Valente, A. J. 2010. *Rag Paper Manufacture in the United States, 1801–1900*. storyofstori.es/rag.
Vallely, Colonel Paul E., and Michael A. Aquino. 1980. *From PSYOP to Mindwar: The Psychology of Victory*. With 2003 introduction by Michael A. Aquino. storyofstori.es/mindwar.
Van De Mieroop, Marc. 1997. *The Ancient Mesopotamian City*. storyofstori.es/city.
Varshavski, Mikhail. May 14, 2020. "Point-by-Point *Plandemic* Smackdown." *MedPage Today*. storyofstori.es/med.
Vaughan, Megan. 2007. "Scarification in Africa." *Cultural and Social History* 4 (3): 385–400. storyofstori.es/scars.
Velleman, J. David. 1992. "What Happens When Someone Acts?" *Mind* 101 (403): 461–81. storyofstori.es/acts.
Vishwanath, Dhanraj, and Paul B. Hibbard. 2013. "Seeing in 3-D with Just One Eye: Stereopsis Without Binocular Vision." *Psychological Science* 24 (9): 1673–85. storyofstori.es/3D.
Vogel, H. U. 2012. *Marco Polo Was in China*. storyofstori.es/marco.
Vogel, Steven K. 2013. "Whatever Happened to Japanese Electronics?: A World Economy Perspective どうした日本の電子工学　世界経済の観点から問う." *Asia-Pacific Journal: Japan Focus*. 1–7. storyofstori.es/vogel.
Von Hagen, V. W. 1999. *The Aztec and Maya Papermakers*. storyofstori.es/aztec.
von Leyden, R., et al. 1982. *Ganjifa: The Playing Cards of India*. storyofstori.es/cards.
Wachtel, Edward. 1993. "The First Picture Show: Cinematic Aspects of Cave Art." *Leonardo* 26 (2): 135–40. storyofstori.es/cave.
Wallace, Wanda T. 1994. "Memory for Music: Effect of Melody on Recall of Text." *Journal of Experimental Psychology: Learning, Memory, and Cognition* 20 (6): 1471–85. storyofstori.es/melody.
Wang, Heming. 2023. "Family Names Recorded in Chinese Genealogies" in *The General Theory of China's Genealogy*, edited by Wang Heming. 387–413. storyofstori.es/family.
Ward, B. 2012. *Just My Soul Responding: Rhythm and Blues, Black Consciousness and Race Relations*. storyofstori.es/soul.
Watson, Mary Ann. 1994. *The Expanding Vista: American Television in the Kennedy Years*. storyofstori.es/vista.
Weadock, Penelope N. 1975. "The Giparu at Ur." *Iraq* 37 (2): 101–28. storyofstori.es/giparu.
Weiner, Bernard. 2008. "Reflections on the History of Attribution Theory and Research." *Social Psychology* 39 (3): 151–56. storyofstori.es/reflections.
Weinstein, Daniel et al., 2016. "Singing and Social Bonding: Changes in Connectivity and Pain Threshold as a Function of Group Size." *Evolution and Human Behavior* 37 (2): 152–58. https://storyofstori.es/group.
Weismer, Gary. 2008. "*Speech Intelligibility*" in *The Handbook of Clinical Linguistics*, edited by Martin J. Ball et al. 568–82. storyofstori.es/weismer.

Wells, H. G. 2010. *Classic Collection Volume 1.* storyofstori.es/wells.
Whitaker, C. W. A. 2002. *Aristotle's De Interpretatione: Contradiction and Dialectic.* storyofstori.es/aristotle.
White, E. B. et al. 2017. *Charlotte's Web.* storyofstori.es/web.
Whitney, John Jr. 1973. "Creating the Special Effects for *Westworld*." *American Cinematographer.* storyofstori.es/sfx.
Wiener, Janet, and Nathan Bronson. 2014. "Facebook's Top Open Data Problems." *Facebook Research.* storyofstori.es/top.
Wiessner, Polly W. 2014. "Embers of Society: Firelight Talk Among the Ju/'Hoansi Bushmen." *Proceedings of the National Academy of Sciences* 111 (39): 14027–35. storyofstori.es/embers.
Wikimapia.org. 2009. "Cape Flattery Silica Mine." storyofstori.es/mine.
Willadsen, Steen M. 1986. "Nuclear Transplantation in Sheep Embryos." *Nature* 320 (6057): 63–65. storyofstori.es/sheep.
Willis, Mikki (dir.). 2020. *Plandemic: The Hidden Agenda Behind COVID-19* (Movie). storyofstori.es/plan.
Wilson, E. O. 2012. *The Social Conquest of Earth.* storyofstori.es/wilson.
The Winnipeg Tribune. 1930. "Radio Blamed When There's Drought, or Too Much Rain." storyofstori.es/drought.
Wischenbart, Rüdiger, and Holger Ehling. 2009. *A Methodology to Collect International Book Statistics.* storyofstori.es/sales.
Wolfe, S. J. 2009. *Mummies in Nineteenth Century America: Ancient Egyptians as Artifacts.* storyofstori.es/mummies.
Wolkstein, D. 1983. *Inanna.* storyofstori.es/1983.
Wong, Chun Han. March 10, 2015. "China Sets Timeline for First Change to Retirement Age Since 1950s." *The Wall Street Journal.* storyofstori.es/1950s.
Woodall, W. O. 1873. *A Collection of Reports of Celebrated Trials, Civil and Criminal.* storyofstori.es/trials.
Woodruff, Judy (presenter). December 20, 2021. *PBS Newshour (TV Program).* storyofstori.es/PBS.
Woods, Christopher. 2020. "The Emergence of Cuneiform Writing" in *A Companion to Ancient Near Eastern Languages,* edited by Rebecca Hasselbach-Andee. 27–46. storyofstori.es/emergence.
Woolley, L. 2013. *Excavations at Ur.* storyofstori.es/ur.
World Bank. 2025. "High-Technology Exports (Current US$)." storyofstori.es/worldbank.
Worm, Andrea. 2016. "Foresti, Giacomo Filippo" in *Encyclopedia of the Medieval Chronicle Online,* edited by Graeme Dunphy. 626–28. storyofstori.es/foresti.
Woudhuizen, Fred C. 2006. "The Transmission of the Phoenician Alphabet in the Mediterranean Region." *Rivista di studi fenici* XXXIV (2): 1000–12. storyofstori.es/transmission.
Wrangham, Richard W., and Rachel Carmody. 2010. "Human Adaptation to the Control of Fire." *Evolutionary Anthropology* 19: 187–99. storyofstori.es/fire.
WSJ Markets. 2022. "BOE Technology Group Co. Ltd. A." *Wall Street Journal.* storyofstori.es/WSJ.
Wyer, Robert S., and Thomas K. Skrull. 1986. "Human Cognition in Its Social Context." *Psychological Review* 93 (3): 322–59. storyofstori.es/human.
Xu, Qiang, et al. 2013. "The Draft Genome of Sweet Orange (*Citrus sinensis*)." *Nature Genetics* 45 (1): 59–66. storyofstori.es/orange.
Yerkes, Robert M. and Sergius Morgulis. 1909. "The Method of Pawlow in Animal Psychology." *Psychological Bulletin* 6 (8): 257–73. storyofstori.es/yerkes.
Yonhap News Agency. 2019. "Go Master Lee Says He Quits Unable to Win Over AI Go Players." storyofstori.es/yonhap.

Yoo, Woo Sik. 2022. "The World's Oldest Book Printed by Movable Metal Type in Korea in 1239: The Song of Enlightenment." *Heritage* 5 (2): 1089–119. storyofstori.es/1239.

Yoo, Woo Sik. 2023. "Ink Tone Analysis of Printed Character Images Towards Identification of Medieval Korean Printing Technique: The Song of Enlightenment (1239), the Jikji (1377), and the Gutenberg Bible (~1455)." *Heritage* 6 (3): 2559–81. storyofstori.es/ink.

YouGov. November 9–13, 2023. "YouGov Survey: Conspiracy Theories." *YouGov*. storyofstori.es/conspiracies.

Youn, Anthony. 2012. "Dr. Youn on the Smartphone Face and the Facetime Facelift (Fox TV News Segment)." *YouTube*. storyofstori.es/youn.

Yu, A. C. (trans.). 2013. *The Journey to the West*. storyofstori.es/west.

Yuanyao, Meng. 2024. "Traditional Paper-Making in the Zhuang Villages of Southwest China." *Vernacular Chinese-Character Manuscripts from East and Southeast Asia* 40: 281–300. storyofstori.es/trad.

Zak, Paul J., et al. 2007. "Oxytocin Increases Generosity in Humans." *PLOS ONE* 2 (11): e1128–28. storyofstori.es/zak.

Zuckerberg, Mark. February 18, 2015. *My Next Book for a Year of Books is On Immunity by Eula Biss. (Facebook Post)*. storyofstori.es/biss.

Zuckerberg, Mark. February 16, 2017. *Building Global Community (Facebook Post)*. storyofstori.es/community.

Zuckerberg, Mark. April 16, 2020. *An Update on the Work We're Doing to Connect People With Accurate Information (Facebook Post)*. storyofstori.es/update.

Zürcher, E. 1982. "'Prince Moonlight.' Messianism and Eschatology in Early Medieval Chinese Buddhism." *T'oung Pao* 68 (1/3): 1–75. storyofstori.es/prince.

Index

Aachen Cathedral, 99–103
acceleration of change, 139–40
activism
    civil rights, 144–45, 149
addiction
    to social media, 273–77
    to technology, 282–86
advertising
    online, 205–7, 232, 278–79
agriculture, 54–56
alchemy
    Newton's practice of, 220–23
algorithms, 201–9, 232–34, 242–45, 273–77
alliteration, 23, 26
alphabet
    Athens standardization of, 84
    European languages and, 112
America
    Civil Rights Movement, 144–45, 149–50
    presidential assassination, (Kennedy), 234–37
    racial segregation in, 142–50
    vaccination rates in, 216–18, 234
American Civil War, 135
antisemitism, 242–45
Aquino, Michael, 153–57
aristocracy
    British concerns about literacy, 116, 132–33
art
    patterns in, 24
    visual signaling and, 52
artificial intelligence
    generative AI, 280–82
    in Go playing, 196–209
    large language models (LLMs), 280–82
    reinforcement learning, 201–9, 232–34, 242–45, 273–77
Ashurbanipal, King, 82–83
astronomy, 113–16

Athens, 56, 84
attention
    attention-seeking algorithms, 205–7, 273–77
    as scarce resource, 205
audiences
    emotional reactions of, 187–89
    mass communication and, 3
    singing transforming into storytellers, 28
Australia, 47, 176–77, 185, 194–95
authority
    fear of literacy by, 287–89
    of writing, 85–86
autobiographies
    Frederick Douglass, 135
Avengers: Endgame, 187–91, 262

Bamba, Sheikh Ahmadou, 272
banking education, 163–65, 288
Barthes, Roland, 88
Beijing Oriental Electronics Group. *See* BOE
bell hooks (Gloria Watkins), 161–68
Berger, Thor, 278
bias
    cognitive, 274
    homophily bias, 275–77
    in reinforcement learning systems, 281
    story-shaped, 273–77
Bible, 80–83, 134
binary digits (bits), 172
BOE (Beijing Oriental Electronics Group), 178–87, 265–67
books
    censorship of, 134–35
    cost reduction of, 132
Boole, George, 173–74
Bradbury, Ray, 158
brain, human
    compression methods of, 22
    harmonics and, 26–27
    and magical thinking, 224–25

brain, human (cont.)
    and meaning, 202–4
    memory capacity of, 22
    music processing in, 26
    patterns and, 24
    pitch perception and, 26–27
    speech processing in, 26
    and story-shaped thinking, 11, 224, 273–77, 285
    storytelling evolution and, 13
Brahe, Tycho Ottesen, 113–16
Brethren of the Common Life, 133–34
Broderick, Ryan, 242–44
bulla (clay container), 58

Cambridge University, 219–20
cameras, 190–91, 258–62
Cape Verde, Senegal, 250–54
Carol Smith (fictional Facebook account), 243–45
cathode ray tubes, 146, 151–52, 178–82
Catholic Church, 133
cave art, xiii, 47–48
CBS News, 234–36
censorship
    Communications Decency Act, 248–49
    problem of choosing and, 134
    of war reporting, 154–57
Cervantes, Miguel de, 193
change, acceleration of, 139–40
Chen, Y. S., 265–67
chess, 203
China
    BOE factories in, 177–87, 265–67
    as high-technology exporter, 181–83
    movable type invented in, 112
Chinese language, 25, 112
cholera epidemic in Haiti, 271–72
choosing, problem of
    censorship and, 134
    of choosing, 191–92, 290
    memorized stories and, 30
Christianity, 80, 134
civilization
    languageless writing and, 54
    writing dividing cultures, 86
Civil Rights Movement, 144–45, 149–50
class systems
    literacy and, 132–33
clay, 57–58
Clinton, Bill, 248
cognitive biases. *See* bias

color television 146, 152, 182, 189, 255
communication
    conversation as storytelling, 5
    day talk vs. night talk, 1–2
    electric telegraph, 137–41
    evolution of vocalization, 1
    face-to-face decline in, 4–5
    one-person households and, 4–5
    radio, 141–42, 145–50, 283–85
    telephone, 140, 171–74, 251
Communications Decency Act (CDA), 248–49
compression
    brain methods of, 22
    memory patterns for, 22–23
computer-generated imagery (CGI)
    in *Avengers: Endgame*, 187–91
    photorealistic, 260–62
    in *Westworld*, 189–93, 258
computers
    and Boolean algebra, 173–74
    and communication theory, 171–75
    personal, 251, 285
confirmation bias, 274, 277
conspiracy theories
    about COVID-19, 228–34
    definition of, 237–38
    and Facebook, 242–45
    history of, 234–49
    about Kennedy assassination, 234–37
    progression of belief in, 240–42
    and QAnon, 243–44
    real conspiracies vs., 238–39
    as stories, 237–42
context, importance of in reading, 165
convergent evolution, 269
conversation, 4–5
Copernicus, 115
Corning Incorporated, 177, 183
Coster, Laurens Janszoon, 110–11
counterstories
    and Civil Rights Movement, 144–50
    and conspiracy theories, 237–42
    defined, 144
    and progress, 144–50, 246–49
    vs. standard stories, 116, 144, 149–50, 165, 246–49
COVID-19
    and conspiracy theories, 228–34
    deaths from, 213–18
    and Facebook misinformation, 231–34

and Terrance Montaine's death, 210–18
vaccines, 216–18, 231–34
Cronkite, Walter, 235
Crudup, Arthur, 147–48
cuneiform, 57
Curry's Club Tropicana, 142–43

Daguerre, Louis, 193
Dakar, Senegal, 250–54, 272
Darwin, Charles, 24, 80, 269
DeepMind, 205
dehumanization, 221–22, 242, 291
democracy, and literacy, 287–89
Diouf, Anta, 250–54, 272
display technology. *See* screens
Douglass, Frederick, 135, 140
drawing, xiii, 48
Dutch Republic, 133–34

economics
    of attention, 205–7
    of sand/screens, 185–87
    of social media, 277–80
education
    banking, 163–65, 288
    critical thinking in, 287–89
    literacy, 157–68, 287–89
    opposition to for poor, 116
Egypt, writing in, 64
electricity
    and communication, 137–41
    discovery of, 139
    and storytelling technologies, 140–41
electric telegraph, 137–41, 171
electrification, 140–41, 286
elites
    access to writing tools, 87
    literacy concerns of, 132–33
    mass communication concerns of, 116
Elvis Presley, 147–48, 241
embedded journalists, 156–57
England
    aristocracy concerns about, literacy, 116, 132–33
    censorship in, 134
    class system in, 132
    literacy rates compared to Netherlands, 131–32
Enschedé, Jan Justus, 109
Epic Games, 261–62
Eridu, 56
Euphrates River, 55–56

Europe
    alphabetical languages of, 112
    literacy rates in, 133
    printing arriving late to, 112
Evans, Harold, 155–57
evolution
    biological versus technological, 54
    of intelligence, 269–71
    music and, 24–25
    of reinforcement learning, 205
    storytelling driving, 3
    of trees, 269–71
experience
    as knowledge stored, 139–40
    sharing of, 139–41
    versus speculation, 285–86
extremism, 242–45

Facebook
    "Carol Smith" account on, 243–45
    and conspiracy theories, 242–45
    and COVID-19 misinformation, 231–34
    economic model of, 277–80
    and homophily, 275–77
    Horizon Worlds, 264
    microphone surveillance myth, 273–75
    as participatory sensing network, 274–77
    and QAnon, 243–44
    profit per employee, 278–79
    reinforcement learning on, 206–9, 231–34, 242–45
Fahrenheit 451, 158
fake photographs, 193, 228–34
Farnsworth, Philo, 141, 151
Fauci, Anthony, 234
Fenerty, Charles, 134–35
fictional conspiracies, 238–40
film. *See* movies
fire, storytelling and, 1–2
fishing, in Senegal, 250–54
flood story, 80–82
Freire, Paulo, 161–68, 288
Frey, Carl Benedikt, 278
fundamental frequency, 26–27
fungi, 269–71

games
    and computer graphics, 258–62
    Go, 196–209
    and meaning, 202–4
    video, 201–2, 258–62, 285

gay rights movement, 246–49
generative AI, 280–82
Genesis, flood story in, 80–82
Gilbert, Davies, 116
Gladstone, William, 80, 82
glass
    for screens, 177–78, 183–85
Go. *See* games
Google
    acquisition of DeepMind, 205
    profit per employee, 278
    as public company, 207–8
    and reinforcement learning, 205–9
governments
    conspiracy theories about, 238–39
    incomprehension of technology, by, 290
    secret activities of, 238
Groote, Gerard, 133
group singing, 28–29
Gutenberg, Johannes, 110–12
Guugu Yimithirr people, 175–77

Haarlem, Netherlands, 109–11
Haiti, 271–72
harmonics, 26–28
Hart, Sarah, 136–39
Heider and Simmel experiment, 203
heroes
    bulletproof, 224
    in conspiracy theories, 239–40
    in stories, 223–24
high-definition television, 255–56
high-technology exports, 181–83
history
    of conspiracy theories, 234–49
    divided by writing, 86
    of storytelling technology, 139–41, 250–54
Homer, 82
homophily bias, 275–77
hooks, bell (Gloria Watkins), 161–68
human intelligence
    versus artificial intelligence, 202–4
    evolution of, 269–71
    and trees, 269–71
humanism, 133–34

identity, smartphones as, 253
illiteracy, 134
images
    computer-generated, 189–93, 257–62
    digital, 190

    generative AI for, 280–82
    three-dimensional, 255–62
Industrial Light & Magic, 262
information
    misinformation, 216–18, 228–34, 242–45
    as novelty, 171–72
    sharing of, 140–41, 269–71
information warfare, 153–57
innovation
    acceleration of, 139–41
    utility driving, 54
integrated circuits, 179
intelligence
    artificial, 196–209, 267–71, 280–82
    convergent evolution of, 269
    human vs. artificial, 202–4
    of trees, 269–71
intention
    illusion of, 273
    and meaning, 202–4
Internet
    Communications Decency Act, 248–49
    and gay rights movement, 246–49
    and homophily, 275–77
    public access to, 247, 251
Internet of Things
    BOE's investment in, 266–67
    coining of term, xv
    global impact of, xv-xvi
    global sensor network as, 252–54
    participatory sensing via, 271–77
    smartphone and, xv
inventions, redundancy in, 174–75
Ipri, Tom, 160
Iraq, wars in, 153–57, 207–8

Jarecke, Ken, 155–56
Jazz Singer, The, 193
Jefferson, Blind Lemon, 147–48
Jeopardy!, xv
jewel bugs (*Julodimorpha saundersii*), 194–95, 205–6
jewel-bugging
    of algorithms, 233, 277
    of stories, 195
Jikji (Korean text), 111
journalism
    embedded, 156–57
    war, 153–57
jukeboxes, 146–47
Jupiter (planet), 114–15

Kennedy, John F., assassination of, 234–37
Kepler, Johannes, 115
King, Martin Luther, Jr., 144, 149
knowledge
  dynamic heterogeneous, 116
  as experience stored, 139–40
  oral cultures and, 86
  problem of, 289–91
  stable homogenous, 115–16
  written cultures and, 86
Koomey's Law, 254

labor burden, 278
language
  alphabetical, 112
  and reality, 165
  storytelling roots of, 2–3
  versus writing, 86
languageless writing, 53–54
large language models (LLMs), 280–82
larynx, evolution of, 25
Lee Se-dol, 196–209, 273, 278
Levine, Lawrence, 143–44
LGBTQ+ people, 246–49
liberation
  and critical literacy, 161–68
  and reading, 166–68
librarians, and transliteracy, 160
Linder, Budgie, 142
liquid crystal displays (LCDs), 178–82, 184–85
literacy
  and authority, 287–89
  banking education vs., 163–65
  class systems and, 132–33
  compared between England and Netherlands, 131–32
  critical, 164–68, 287–91
  defined, 159–61, 287
  English aristocracy concerns about, 116, 132–33
  European average, 133
  global rates of, 140, 158–59, 192
  and liberty, 166–68
  religion and, 133–34
  and revolution, 134, 287
  transliteracy, 160–61
Liu, Alan, 160
Lobianco, Sammy, 141–49
location data, from smartphones, 271–72
Ludlum, Robert, 239

machines
  and meaning, 202–4, 207, 233, 277
  out of control, 233, 279–80
  reinforcement learning, 201–9
Maggart, Lon "Bert," 156
magical thinking
  conspiracy theories as, 236–37, 245
  about technology, 224–26
Magritte, René, 41–45
maps, writing as, 54
marginal cost, 186
marking, versus drawing, 48
mass communication, 87
  authority problem of, 85
  elite concerns about, 116
  Gutenberg inventing, 113
  mass persuasion and, 113
  paradox of, 115–16
  passive receivers and, 116
  reading as dialogue in, 87
mass production
  of documents by scribes vs., press, 112
  Gutenberg inventing, 111–12
  transformation from, 112
Massachusetts Institute of Technology (MIT), xv, 169–72
mathematics
  Boolean algebra, 173–74
  of communication, 171–75
  harmonics and, 28
  pitch perception and, 27
McLuhan, Marshall, 158–59
meaning
  and artificial intelligence, 202–4, 207
  in games, 202–4
  and humans, 202–4
  machines' inability to, understand, 202–4, 207, 233, 277
  and reinforcement learning, 207, 233, 277
  and stories, 202–4
media literacy, 160
melody, 23, 28, 29
Memphis, Tennessee, 141–49
memorization
  music and, 24–28
  patterns for, 22–23
  problem of choosing and, 30
Mesopotamia, 55–56
Meta (company). *See* Facebook
MetaHuman Creator, 261

Metcalfe's Law, 251, 254
Metman, Leonard, 110
metaverse, 262–65
Midnighters, the (band), 142–43, 147, 149
Mikovits, Judy, 232–33
MindWar
    collision with reinforcement, learning, 207–9
    and COVID-19 misinformation, 233
    defined, 153–57
    and Facebook, 264
    and Iraq wars, 153–57
misinformation
    about COVID-19, 216–18, 228–34
    on Facebook, 232–34, 242–45
MIT. *See* Massachusetts Institute of Technology
models
    economic, of social media, 277–80
    large language, 280–82
    three-dimensional, 258–62
Montaine, Terrance, 210–18
Moore's Law, 179, 254, 258
Mori, Masahiro, 260–61
Mouride pilgrimage, 272
movable type, 111–12
movies
    and computer-generated imagery, 187–93, 257–62
    special effects in, 189–93, 257–62
music, 2, 24–28
    recorded, 146–47
mycorrhizal networks, 270–71

Narrative of the Life of Frederick Douglass, 135
Nathan, Robert, 190
National Institutes of Health, 216
navigation apps, 271
NBC, 150, 235–36
Neanderthals, storytelling by, 3
nervous system
    global digital, 253–54
    human, 268
    of trees, 269–71
Netherlands, 131–35
networks
    mycorrhizal, 270–71
    participatory sensing, 271–77
    sensor, 252–54, 266–67
    value of, 251–54
newspapers, 4, 235–36, 251, 278–79

Newton, Isaac, 171–75, 219–23
night talk, 1–2
Noah, 82–83
noise, in communication, 171–72
novelty, in communication, 171–72
numbers, 55–58

Obama, Barack, 208, 237
obesity crisis, 226–28
Observer, The, 155–56
online harassment, 264
Orwell, George, 89
Oswald, Lee Harvey, 235–37
oxytocin, 29

Page, Clarence, 156
painting, 2, 52, 85, 193
pandemics
    cholera, 271–72
    COVID-19, 210–18, 228–34
paper, 131, 134–35
Parks, Rosa, 149
participatory sensing, 271–77
patterns, 23–26
Peacock, Thomas Love, 286–87
pebbles, 57, 59
perception
    human, 256–57, 268
    stereopsis, 256–57
Persian Gulf, 55
personal computers, 251, 285
Philip II of Spain, King, 134
photographs
    fake, 193, 228–34
    first, 140, 193
    and realism, 193
photography, 140, 151, 193
photorealism
    in computer graphics, 260–62
picaro, 192–93, 291
pictures, xiii, 53, 55–58
pitch, 25–27
pixels, 189–90, 255–57
plagiarism, by AI systems, 280–81
Plandemic movie, 232–34, 239–40
plasma displays, 179, 182
Plato, 85
poetry, 4, 23, 30
polarization, online, 242–45
population growth, 140
Portsmouth, Earl of, 219
postliterate future, 158–59

power
    electric telegraph, 138–39
    and literacy, 287–89
    processing, increases in, 258–59
    and realism, 291
    of storytelling, 144, 167–68
predictability, human, 273–75
predictions
    of human behavior, 273–75
    about radio, 141–42, 145–46
    by reinforcement learning, systems, 206, 273–75
    about television, 141–42, 146
prehistory, 86
Presley, Elvis, 147–48, 241
primates
    grooming by, 3
    visual signaling by, 52
    vocalization by, 25
printing, xiii, 112–13, 135
printing press, 135, 140, 192
    Gutenberg invention of, 111–12
    Laurens Janszoon Coster myth, 110–11
privacy
    Facebook settings for, 274–75
probability, 203–4, 223
problems
    of choosing, 191–92, 290
    of knowing, 289–91
profit per employee, 278–79
progress
    and counterstories, 144–50, 246–49
    pattern of, 246
    rate of, 139–41
propaganda. *See* MindWar
Protestantism, 133–34
protests, Civil Rights, 144–45
proto-writing, 53–54
Provine, Robert, 143
PSYOP (Psychological Operations), 153
Ptolemy, 114–15

Quakers, 136–39
QAnon conspiracy theory, 243–44

race, 142–50
racism, 242–46
radicals, online creation of, 277
radio
    broadcast, 141–42, 145–50, 251
    fears about, 283–85
    predictions about, 141–42, 145–46
    transistor, 145–50
rapping, 25
ray tracing
    in computer graphics, 259–62
reading
    context in, 165
    critical literacy, 164–68
    debate about teaching, 132–33
    decoding vs., 165
    defined, 157–58, 164–65
    as dialogue, 87
    Dutch teaching of, 133
    and liberation, 166–68
    opposition to teaching poor, 116
    and reasoning, 132, 157–58, 164–65
    self-teaching by, 115
    versus writing, 88
realism
    in computer graphics, 255–62
    and power, 291
    versus reality, 290–91
    in storytelling, 191–93, 255–62
reality
    denial of, 241–42
    and language, 165
    making of, 256, 268–71
    simulation of, 255–62, 267–68, 290–91
    and stories, 11, 218–19, 236
reasoning
    motivated, 241
    and reading, 132, 157–58, 164–65
records, vinyl, 145–47
Reddit, 224–25
Redmond, Michael, 200
Reformation, 134
reinforcement learning
    and attention, 205–9
    collision with MindWar, 207–9
    and conspiracy theories, 242–45
    and COVID-19 misinformation, 232–34
    explanation of, 201–2
    and Facebook, 206–9, 231–34, 242–45
    and homophily, 276–77
    jewel-bugging of, 233, 277
    and meaning, 207, 233, 277
    out of control, 233, 279–80
    predictions by, 206, 273–75
religion
    and conspiracy theories, 237–38
    Dutch literacy and, 133–34
    and vaccination, 228–34

repetition, 3, 23
research, "doing your own," 288–89
resolution, screen, 190, 255–57
revolutions
    counterstory, 246–49
    digital, 278
    and literacy, 134, 287
    scientific, 115
rhyme, xiii, 23, 26
rhythm, 23, 25
Richards, Abbie, 240–43
rights, gay, 246–49
risks
    assessment of, 223
    of conspiracy belief, 241–42
    distraction from real, 286
    of new technology, 282–86
    and probability, 223
robots, in screen manufacturing, 183–87
rock and roll music, 145–50
Royal Society, 116
Russo, Anthony and Joe, 187–89

saltation, of innovation, 112
Salt Hill, England, 136–39
Salvador, Baron Mozes, 109–11
sand, 175–78, 185
Sand Age, 185–87
Saturn (planet), 114–15
science fiction, 240, 262–65
scientific revolution, 115
screens
    economic model of, 185–87
    liquid crystal, 178–82, 184–85
    manufacturing of, 183–87
    resolution of, 190, 255–57
    semiconductor, 179–83, 185
    three-dimensional images on, 255–57
    and Wang's Law, 179–83, 254–56
scribes
    antiquarii, 112
    European output of, 112
    printing press versus, 112
    Sumerian, 57
seals, 53
search engines, and reinforcement learning, 205–9
sediment, 55, 57, 59
segregation, racial
    and homophily, 275–76
    in Memphis, Tennessee, 142–50

self-awareness, need for, 291
self-teaching by reading, 115
semiconductors in screens, 179–83, 185
Senegal, 250–54, 272
sensing, participatory, 271–77
sensors
    arrays of, 267–68
    networks of, 252–54, 266–67
    in smartphones, 252–54
sentience
    artificial, 267–71
    herd, 268–69, 271
    participatory, 271–77
shame, and segregation, 143
Shannon, Claude, 169–75
Silberman, Steve, 249
Silicon Valley, 277–79
Silver, David, 202
Simmel. *See* Heider and Simmel experiment
simulations
    of light, 259–60
    and reality, 255–62, 267–68, 290–91
    by reinforcement learning, systems, 276
singing, 24–29
    versus speaking, 25–26
    transforming audiences into, storytellers, 28
slavery
    American, 135
    branding of, 53
    escaped slaves' autobiographies, 135
    printing's role in ending, 135
smartphone, xiv
    adoption of, 251–54
    for fishing, 250–54
    as identity, 253
    as interface, 253
    and Internet of Things, 252–54, xv
    location data from, 271–72
    participatory sensing via, 271–77
    power of sharing stories, democratized by, xiv
    as sensors, 252–54
    three roles of, 253
    value of, 251–54
Smith, George, 80–82
Snow Crash (Stephenson), 262–65
social bonding
    group singing and, 29
    storytelling and, 3

social media
  addiction to, 273–77
  and conspiracy theories, 242–45
  economic model of, 277–80
  and homophily, 275–77
  out of control, 233, 279–80
  as participatory sensing, network, 271–77
  user-generated content on, 279
Society of Biblical Archaeology, 80–82
Socrates, 84–86, 237
solitary confinement, 109–11
songs, 28–30
Sotheby and Company, 219
sound barrier, 257
sounds
  fundamental frequency of, 26
  socialization using, 1
  writing as pictures of, 59
Space Invaders, 201–2, 259
Spain, King Philip II of, 134
speaking
  brain processing of, 26
  versus singing, 25–26
  singing spectrum with, 25–26
  tone and, 25
special effects, in movies, 189–93, 257–62
speculation
  conspiracy theories as, 240–42
  versus experience, 285–86
  line of, 240–41
Spivey, Victoria, 147
Stadius, Johannes, 115
Staircase Studios AI, 261
standard stories
  America's, 144, 146, 149–50
  business, 179
  changing of, 249
  and counterstories, 144, 149–50, 165, 246–49
  versus counterstories, 116
  defined, 144
  regressive nature of, 116
  resistance to, 246–49
  of television industry, 179–82
stand-up comedy, 4
Star Wars, 224
status quo, 116
Stephenson, Neal, 262–65
stereopsis, 256–57
Stevens, John Paul, 248–49

stock exchanges, 53
stocks (tally sticks), 52–53
stories
  audiences for, xiii–xiv
  conspiracy theories as, 237–42
  death by, 210–49
  industrialization of, 135
  jewel-bugging of, 195
  language given by, 2
  and meaning, 202–4
  power of, 144, 167–68
  and reality, 11, 218–19, 236
  versus reality, 290–91
  story-shaped brains, 11, 224, 273–77, 285
storytelling
  acceleration of change in, 139–41
  communal values and, 3
  conversation and, 5
  digital social, 246–49
  and electricity, 140–41
  evolution of, 13
  fire and, 1–2
  history of, 139–41, 250–54
  industrialization of, 135
  language evolution and, 2
  oral as primary form, 4
  realism in, 191–93, 255–62
  root of language, 2
  seven great revolutions in, xiv
  singing and, 28
  social bonds and, 3
  technologies of, 140–41, 250–54, 272–91
Strasbourg, 111
submersible implosion, 224–25
Sulawesi, Indonesia, 47–48
Sumer, 56–58, 80–82
Sumerians, 56–58
superstimuli, 194–95, 205–6
supremacy, writing as form of, 86
Supreme Court, U.S., 144, 248–49
surveillance, 272, 273–75

tablets, clay, 57, 80
tallying, 52–53, 57
Tawell, John, 136–39
technology
  biological evolution versus, 54
  conversation enabled by, 5
  fears about, 282–86

technology (cont.)
  high-, exports of, 181–83
  myths about, 282–86
  new, response to, 285–86
  storytelling, xiii, 140–41, 250–54, 272–91
  and systemicity, 272–91
telecommunication, 137–41
telegraph, electric, 137–41, 171
telephones
  fundamental frequency, transmission by, 27
  landline, 251
  and Metcalfe's Law, 251
  mobile. *See* smartphones
  switchboards for, 173–74
television
  cathode ray tubes in, 146, 151–52, 178–82
  industry standard story, 179–82
  invention of, 141, 151–52
  Kennedy assassination coverage, on, 234–37
  liquid crystal displays in, 178–82
  and MindWar, 152–57
  predictions about, 141–42, 146
  resolution of, 255–56
testimony, from others, 270, 285
TFT-LCD (liquid crystal display type), 181–82
Tiffany, Kaitlyn, 244–45
Tigris River, 55–56
toasting (Jamaican), 25
tokens, counting, 57–58
Tokyo Telecommunications Engineering Corporation, 145
Tomb Raider (video game), 259
Touba, Senegal, 272
tracking, of mass migrations, 271–72
trade, 52, 56
La Trahison des images, 41–45
transistors, 145–46, 152, 174–75, 179
transliteracy, 160–61
trees, intelligence of, 269–71
trickster archetype, 192–93
Trump, Donald, 243–44
truth
  in conspiracy theories, 238
  and lies, 291
  and MindWar, 153

power and, xiv
  of writing debated, 86
Tukey, John, 172

UFOs, 240–41
uncanny valley phenomenon, 260–61
unemployment, from automation, 277–79
uniqueness bias, 274
United States
  Civil Rights Movement in, 144–45, 149–50
  Civil War, 135
  conversation time data, 4
  COVID-19 deaths in, 213–18
  elderly officials in, 290
  high-technology exports of, 181, 183
  and Iraq wars, 153–57
  newspaper industry in, 278–79
  secret government activities in, 238
  Supreme Court, 144, 248–49
  vaccination rates in, 216–18, 234
Unreal Engine 5, 261–62
unstoried newness, 285–86
Ur, 56
Uruk, 56
Utnapishtim, 81

vaccination
  and conspiracy theories, 228–34
  deaths prevented by, 216–18
  and Facebook, 231–34
  and Terrance Montaine's death, 216–18
  rates of, 216–18, 234
vacuum tubes, 145, 148, 151–52, 178–79
Vallely, Paul, 153, 208
video games, 201–2, 258–62, 285
Vietnam War, 153, 156
vinyl records, 145–47
violence
  and conspiracy theories, 241–42
  online incitement to, 242–46
virtual reality, 262–65
vision barrier, 254–57
visual signaling, 47–52
vocalization
  brain evolution and, 13
  evolution of, 1
  larynx and, 25
  methods of, 1
  primates and, 25
  repurposing for storytelling, 1
voice, human, 26–27

Wang, D. S., 16–20, 178–83, 265–67
Wang's Law, 179–83, 254–56, 265
war
　Iraq, 153–57, 207–8
　and MindWar, 153–57
　of stories, 144, 153–57, 168, 207–9, 291
　Vietnam, 153, 156
WarGames (movie), 286
warning cries 1, 25
warty pig, 47–48
Watkins, Gloria (bell hooks), 161–68
Waze, 271
wealth, xiii, xiv, 132
weather stations, 252
Wells, H. G., 158–59
Weteringschans prison, 109–11
Westworld (movie), 189–93, 258
WHBQ Radio, 148
Whitney, John Jr., 190, 258
Willis, Mikki, 233–34, 239–40
Wilson, David Sloan, 205
wireless technology. *See* radio; smartphones
women, one-person households and, 4–5
wood, 52–53, 134–35
writing, 59–89
　abstractions and, 58
　authority of, 85–86
　clay as material for, 57
　compared to painting, 85
　cultures divided by, 86
　cuneiform, 57
　in Egypt, 64
　by hand versus printing, 112
　as illusion of language, 86
　immutability of, 85–86
　in Iraq, 56
　language versus, 86
　languageless, 53–54
　limitations and powers of, 86
　mass communication and, 87
　as monologue, 87
　numbers and, 58
　oral storytelling versus, 85–86
　pictures of sounds as, 59
　problem of authority, 85
　problem of immutability, 85
　separation of story and, storyteller, 87–88
　signs as, 53–54
　Socrates problem with, 85–86
　Sumerian, 56–58
　supremacy through, 86
　symbols and, 58
　tools for, 54, 57
　unaccountability of, 86
　veneration of, 86

YouTube, 207, 245
yowall (sand), 175–78

Zhang, Sophie, 243–44
Zuckerberg, Mark, , 231–34, 246, 263–66, 273

About the Author

KEVIN ASHTON is a visionary technologist. He coined the term "the Internet of Things," and cofounded the Auto-ID Center at the Massachusetts Institute of Technology. *The Story of Stories: The Million-Year History of a Uniquely Human Art* is his second book; his first book, *How to Fly a Horse: The Secret History of Creation, Invention, and Discovery*, was named 2015's Porchlight Business Book of the Year. Kevin's writing about innovation and technology has appeared in *The New York Times*, *The Atlantic Monthly*, *Politico*, and *Wired*, and he gives talks about storytelling, the future, and innovation to audiences all over the world. He lives in Austin, Texas.